speaking *freely*

Pergamon Title of Related Interest

Spender THE WRITING OR THE SEX? or why you don't have to read women's writing to know it's no good

Related Journals
(Free sample copies available upon request)

ISSUES IN REPRODUCTIVE AND GENETIC
 ENGINEERING: Journal of International Feminist Analysis
WOMEN'S STUDIES INTERNATIONAL FORUM

The ATHENE Series

General Editors   Consulting Editor
Gloria Bowles   **Dale Spender**
Renate Klein
Janice Raymond

The Athene Series assumes that all those who are concerned with formulating explanations of the way the world works need to know and appreciate the significance of basic feminist principles.

The growth of feminist research has challenged almost all aspects of social organization in our culture. The Athene Series focuses on the construction of knowledge and the exclusion of women from the process—both as theorists and subjects of study—and offers innovative studies that challenge established theories and research.

On Athene—When Metis, goddess of wisdom who presided over all knowledge was pregnant with Athene, she was swallowed up by Zeus who then gave birth to Athene from his head. The original Athene is thus the parthenogenetic daughter of a strong mother and as the feminist myth goes, at the "third birth" of Athene she stops being Zeus' obedient mouthpiece and returns to her real source: the science and wisdom of womankind.

speaking *freely*

UNLEARNING THE LIES OF THE FATHERS' TONGUES

julia penelope

PERGAMON PRESS
Member of Maxwell Macmillan Pergamon Publishing Corporation
New York   Oxford   Beijing   Frankfurt   São Paulo   Sydney   Tokyo   Toronto

Pergamon Press Offices:

U.S.A.   Pergamon Press, Inc., Maxwell House, Fairview Park,
                              Elmsford, New York 10523, U.S.A.

U.K.   Pergamon Press plc, Headington Hill Hall,
                              Oxford OX3 0BW, England

PEOPLE'S REPUBLIC   Pergamon Press, 0909 China World Tower, No. 1 Jian Guo
OF CHINA   Men Wai Avenue, Beijing 100004, People's Republic of China

FEDERAL REPUBLIC   Pergamon Press GmbH, Hammerweg 6,
OF GERMANY   D-6242 Kronberg, Federal Republic of Germany

BRAZIL   Pergamon Editora Ltda, Rua Eça de Queiros, 346,
                              CEP 04011, Paraiso, São Paulo, Brazil

AUSTRALIA   Pergamon Press Australia Pty Ltd., P.O. Box 544,
                              Potts Point, NSW 2011, Australia

JAPAN   Pergamon Press, 8th Floor, Matsuoka Central Building,
                              1-7-1 Nishishinjuku, Shinjuku-ku, Tokyo 160, Japan

CANADA   Pergamon Press Canada Ltd., Suite 271, 253 College Street,
                              Toronto, Ontario M5T 1R5, Canada

Copyright © 1990 Julia Penelope

Library of Congress Cataloging in Publication Data

Penelope, Julia, 1941-
    Speaking freely : unlearning the lies of the father's tongues / by
Julia Penelope. -- 1st ed.
        p.   cm. -- (Athene series)
    Includes bibliographical references.
    ISBN 0-08-036556-6 (alk. paper) : -- ISBN 0-08-036555-8
(soft : alk. paper) :
    1. English language--Sex differences. 2. English language--Social
aspects. 3. English language--Gender. 4. Sexism in language.
5. Nonsexist language. 6. Women--Language. 7. Men--Language.
8. Patriarchy. 9. Feminism. I. Title. II. Series.
PE1074.75.P46   1990
306.4'4'082--dc20   89-48169
                                                                      CIP

Printing: 1 2 3 4 5 6 7 8 9   Year: 0 1 2 3 4 5 6 7 8 9
Printed In the United States of America

To my mother, Frances Manston Smith, my first teacher, and Sarah Provost Valentine, who expects my best and accepts my worst

Contents

List of Abbreviations

CUD	=	Cosmetic Universe of Discourse
EP	=	Experiencer Predicate
Gmc.	=	Germanic
Icel.	=	Icelandic
I-E	=	Indo-European
MM	=	*Maleus Maleficarum*
ME	=	Middle English
MSw	=	Middle Swedish
ModE	=	Modern English
NP	=	Noun Phrase
OE	=	Old English
OF	=	Old French
ON	=	Old Norse
OED	=	*Oxford English Dictionary*
PUD	=	Patriarchal Universe of Discourse
RHD	=	*Random House Dictionary*
VP	=	Verb Phrase
WLM	=	Women's Liberation Movement

A Note to Readers

In addition to the abbreviations identified in the preceding list, I use a few typographical conventions with which my readers may not be familiar, and I explain them here in order to facilitate reading this book. In linguistics, the object of study is language. Because we must use language to describe itself, linguists use a variety of typographical conventions to distinguish ordinary language use from *metalanguage*, language that describes language. I have avoided abstract symbols except in those cases when frequent repetition suggested a symbol would be more economical, for example, NP for noun phrase.

In order to distinguish ordinary uses of words and sentences in communication linguists italicize words and phrases being analyzed. I use single quotation marks to identify the meaning, reference, sense, or definition of a word or phrase. Conceptual metaphors, because they are abstract representations, are capitalized to distinguish them from the metaphors that occur in language use. For example, ARGUMENT IS WAR is a metaphorical concept; when we say, "That's an indefensible position," we've used a metaphor based on the metaphorical concept ARGUMENT IS WAR. In this book, I've followed linguistic convention and used the asterisk (*) to represent two different pieces of information: (1) to indicate to readers that, in my judgment, a given word, phrase, or sentence doesn't occur in a language (for example, *career man, *women this walked from up gleefully*; (2) to mark a **proto-**, that is, reconstructed, form for a language (for example, *gwen* 'woman', *sker* 'to cut, separate, sift').

The conventions that govern capitalization weren't always as rigidly codified as we know them today, and I have elected not to capitalize proper names I was taught to capitalize, for example, *u.s., u.n.,* the names of countries, and I capitalize words my readers may not expect to find capitalized, such as *Feminist* and *Lesbian*. I decided whether or not to capitalize specific words on the basis of the importance I attach to the named institutions and objects. Because I consider national boundaries as artifacts of male dominance and control, the first letters in names of countries are lower case; because Feminists and Lesbians are important to me, the first letters of those words are capitalized. Christianity, which I regard as an irredeemable patriarchal institution, is spelled "xtianity."

Introduction

I remember a desperately hopeful incantation from my childhood that I used when other children taunted me:

Sticks and stones
May break my bones,
But words can never hurt me.

That chant, lodged in my childhood memory, asserts one of the primary dogmas of the Patriarchal Universe of Discourse: words (language) aren't important. But the words of cruel children did hurt me, however much I wished that they didn't. However much I denied my pain, their vicious words wounded me and left scars that, even now, throb and smart when I think about them. White men benefit directly when we believe their words are harmless.

Understanding how the structure of English controls the way we think and act is crucial to our welfare. What we say is not an insignificant "issue." Neither are the words we hear. Words do hurt us. *Nigger, fatty, wop, kike, spic, crip, porker, birdlegs, queer* carve emotional wounds that don't heal. The point of those insults is clear: anyone who isn't white, anglo-saxon, thin, and stereotypically attractive is "fair game" for the stupid and vicious. Other words, used by men to insult other men, *motherfucker, son of a bitch, bastard, sissy,* and *cunt,* insult men because they're female words. A "motherfucker" fucks his mother; a "bastard" doesn't know who his father was so his mother is a whore; a "sissy" is a male who "acts like a woman." Because being a woman is the worst thing men can think of, we are most accessible to insult and the basis of men's worst insults.

Words hurt us, but languages are much more than the words in their vocabularies. They are systems of rules, rules which speakers find useful for saying what they want to say. When speakers cease to find rules or words useful, they abandon them and make up new ones. In general, women aren't Speakers in the Patriarchal Universe of Discourse (PUD). We may "speak" English, but men rarely feel that what we say is worth listening to. Certainly, our words are forgotten as quickly as they're uttered or written down, historical ephemera buried under men's debris. Indeed, the language itself is hostile to women's perceptions and thinking; an entire subset of the verbs that describe 'talk' characterizes women's speech as insignificant and worthless: *chatter, prattle, gossip, nag, wheedle, babble, chat, prate, natter, gush, cackle, blather, dither, blab, blabber, gibber, jabber*. Used as nouns, these verbs are often modified by *hare-brained* or *empty-headed*, as though to emphasize the disregard they indicate.

English does more than hinder and hurt women: it proscribes the boundaries of the lives we might imagine and will ourselves to live. The many ways the language obstructs our ability to conceive of ourselves as agents in the world or as capable of rebelling against male tyranny go beyond mere hurt to emotional, intellectual, and physical immobility that keeps us men's easy prey. We find it difficult to think outside of the categorical grooves made by men, and, even as we learn the courage and the necessity of speaking for ourselves, our thoughts still conform to the structures that perpetuate male dominance. Even as we demand the right to live and breathe independent of men and their dependence on us, our ideas slip into the grooves worn by repetition. The record plays: "Mother, slave, housewife, slave, child, slave, woman, slave, whore; slave, slave, slave." What's more, most women remain mostly unconscious of how English forces us to repeat the structures that deny us stature and agency in the world and of the role of language in our oppression. Thinking about how we think is hard.

THE GLAMOUR OF GRAMMAR

I have thought long and hard about the ways English circumscribes women's lives, leaving us to ponder cosmetics while men plan "star wars" and their conquest of the cosmos. One of my purposes in *Speaking Freely* has been to expose how men control the way we think about language in general and English in particular. The first four chapters describe the male tradition of prescriptive grammars and the patriarchal metaphors on which their descriptions of English are based: LANGUAGE IS A CONTAINER, LANGUAGE IS A WOMAN, and LANGUAGE IS A TOOL.

For the title of chapter 1, I have used the title of an essay by Jane Caputi, "The Glamour of Grammar" (1977), to alert my readers to the long-standing philosophical, ideological, and political connections between misogyny (hatred of women) and patriarchal descriptions of English. Although the words *grammar* and *gramarye* found their way into English by different routes, both terms were borrowed from Latin sources.

Grammar was borrowed from Latin *grammatica*, 'the study of letters' (from Greek *grammatike*). At a later date, *gramarye*, meaning 'occult learning' and 'magic,' was borrowed from French *gramaire* (Old French *grimoire* 'book of magic'). The novelist Sir Walter Scott is credited with bringing the Scottish *glamour* ('magic,' 'spell,' with "l" instead of "r") into wide literary use, and etymologists attribute Scott's dialectal variation to a Medieval Latin term, *glomeria*.

The borrowing of two distinct, if related, words to refer to a collection of rules restricting language use, *grammar*, and a book of magic, *gramarye*, may appear to be coincidental. Coincidence or not, the etymological relationship between these two words is but one indication of a pervasive way of thinking in English-speaking patriarchies: men perceive both language and women as property that they have the right to control and restrain and the obligation to protect. Men's grammatical rules prescribe "good" English just as their social rules proscribe the behaviors of "good" women.

During the Burning Time, a period spanning roughly three centuries and known, in patriarchal histories as the "renaissance," hundreds of thousands, even millions of women were tortured, beaten, and burned at the stake because, their accusers said, they were witches with the power to cast "glamours." These glamours, or magic spells, the inquisitors said, caused the genitalia of men to disappear, unmanning them and rendering them impotent, powerless. While women were being tortured and burned alive, male clerics and scholars were writing the earliest grammars of the English language, seeking thereby to fix and standardize its proper usage for all time. Their arrogance is exposed when one realizes that the rules of patriarchal English are glamours: made-up rules said to describe the language that are, in fact, illusions conjured by men's ideas of how the language ought to behave. White men's grammars of English have successfully glamorized the way all speakers of English think and use the language every day of their lives. Like the finery of the fairy-tale emperor's "new clothes," their rules are insubstantial and illusory.

In *Speaking Freely*, I have focused on how English promotes and maintains woman-hating in the u.s., but readers should bear in mind that the development of "standard" English is founded in elitism and anglo ethnocentricity as well. I cannot demonstrate here the structural integrity of the many dialects of English, such as Black English or those of mountain people in southern states, but linguists have done huge quantities of research on regional, social, and ethnic varieties of English, and I hope my readers will use this book as a starting point to pursue these connections for themselves.[1]

Prescriptive grammarians created Standard English, then promoted it as the only "correct," that is, valid, version of English. The story of English is intertwined with misogyny, elitism, and racism. Prescriptive grammar has served white men's purposes for centuries, and its rules have been used to keep economic and social power beyond the reach of the poor and working classes. The English language, accompanied by men's grammars, has also been an instrument of white imperialism, used to destroy the cultures of Native Americans and impose caucasian values and mores on conquered peoples. This linguistic colonization continues. As I write, there is a growing movement in the u.s. whose proponents are introducing state laws to make English the official language in order to restrict the social mobility of immigrants who don't yet speak English and keep them out of the work force. Some states, in fact, have already enacted such laws.

My discussions of the history of English and the prescriptive grammars devoted to maintaining its mythical purity are intended to alert readers to the intellectual corruption of the prescriptive grammatical tradition and the stubborn bigotry of its proponents. The long tradition of this misbegotten ignorance and the errors of fact, logic, and reasoning propagated by it would be laughable if millions of us hadn't been subjected to the dedication of its practitioners for the last two centuries. Like the con-men in "The Emperor's New Clothes," white male grammarians have claimed to fashion rules that garb English in articulate and precise grandeur, and, in spite of our inability to perceive how those rules serve any purpose, like the timid crowd cheering the emperor's good taste, we pay lip service to their existence.

THE EMPEROR'S NEW CLOTHES

Speakers of English continue to pretend that Standard English exists, and praise those who claim to speak it for their linguistic finery, although it doesn't exist. We strain to find meaning in nonsensical utterances, as though the presence of recognizable words promised intelligibility. The author of the following quotation, for example, was elected to two consecutive terms as president of the united states and, in 1989, knighted by Elizabeth II!

> The other day when a major bank in New York, Manufacturers Hanover, reduced interest rates, I thought it was very interesting that the man in charge said that they were reducing them because of a feeling of public obligation that so much of our present problem is psychological. And I think it is. And I think some of what's going on in Congress has held back the psychology change that's needed. And this is why I believe, in addition to the Constitutional amendment being a very practical way of getting us out of a situation that has seen us have deficits in 19 of the last 20 years, would be the psychological effect that would indicate that the Government is really determined to end this kind of runaway spending and have some fiscal integrity and common sense. (Ronald Reagan, transcript of press conference, New York Times, July 29, 1982, 18)

The problems with Reagan's use of English go beyond the obvious: "rambling," "disjointed," "incoherent." What is the connection we're supposed to make between "public obligation" and "psychology change"? What could psychology change mean? That utterance was brought to us by the same man who gave us "Mistakes *were made*," who lied to us as regularly as he took naps, revealed just how much garbage u.s. voters will tolerate, and left behind a legacy of simple-minded solutions ("Just Say 'No' to Drugs"), the trickle-down theory of economics, a budget deficit that future generations will be trying to pay off, and governmental corruption we may never fully know the extent of. This example is not atypical of what passes for meaning in this society; we hear and read language like his all the time. Only our complicity in this pretense made it possible for the media to label Ronald Reagan "The Great Communicator" without derisive murmurs. Why wasn't everyone laughing out loud?

The media subject us daily to similarly garbled utterances of the powerful. What authority supports and perpetuates the linguistic etiquette known as Standard English and convinces us, along the way, to maintain the pretense? There are three identifiable sources that make accepting the statement "That's the way it is" seem easier than trying to expose its falsehood. Two of them are institutionalized supports: (1) the 400-year-old tradition of male-created grammars and the erroneous ideas about English they perpetuate; (2) public school systems, and the grammar books those school systems persist in buying. There is hardly anyone to challenge that grammatical tradition because a third source of complicity resides in the mind of every adult who learned Standard English as a child and believes that somewhere out there is a flawless, pure dialect of English known only to a small, literary elite, a superior dialect that will open the door to wealth, status, and prestige if only they can learn it. We agree and subscribe to the lie because we think we can make it work for us, not against us.

Those of us forced to memorize the rules set out in prescriptive grammars may recall our resistance to what seemed arbitrary and illogical, may remember asking a teacher "Why can't I end a sentence with a preposition?" or "What's wrong with saying *ain't*?" We may even have expected approval or acclaim for these exercises in logical perspicacity, and were rudely surprised when the teacher's response was less than informative: "Because I say so," "That's the way it is," "Because that's what the book says."

As adults we shrink from the word *grammar* as we shrank from exposing our alleged linguistic inadequacies as children. Too often, our own linguistic perceptions about English were ridiculed and labeled "wrong," "incorrect," and "substandard." Our memories of childhood grammar lessons make us uncertain and inarticulate about a behavior that lies at the center of our lives: speech. Added to our childhood list of "don'ts" and "nevers" were a host of grammatical "errors" that might issue from our lips at any time. We never knew, when we spoke, which of these invisible creatures might slip out and sabotage our efforts to communicate. Those grammar lessons put in place a judgmental gatekeeper who determines the worthiness of our speech before we dare to open our mouths. "Correct. Incorrect. Right. Wrong," the gate-keeper intones as we try to organize our ideas. The resulting damage to our self-esteem is inestimable. Language is essential to our lives, in work, in relationships; it is an important factor in how we perceive ourselves. In the private sphere, we feel uncertain about our ability to communicate clearly; that lack of confidence permeates the fabric of our social interactions. In the public sphere, powerful white men use the media to bombard us with lies, distortions, and nonsense, and, with rare exceptions, their uses of English go unchallenged. If we doubt our perceptions about the language we hear and speak every day, who among us has the daring to cry, "The Emperor has no clothes"?

Fiction is more palatable than fact. Year after year, teachers inform another generation of students that the arbitrary rules of Standard English will deter-mine the kind of jobs they'll get and how well they'll live. They tell children that they must learn to "talk right" if they want other people to take them seriously. They force us to abandon the dialects, creoles, and other "sub-" or "nonstandard" varieties of English we speak, substituting Standard English, alleged to be the only correct and acceptable way of speaking (and writing). They drill their hapless charges, week after week, year after year, in the proper forms of the so-called irregular verbs (a misnomer; see fn. 4), the written distinction between the possessive *its* and the contracted *it's*, the difference between the nominative *I* and the objective *me*. "Never say, 'It's **me.**'"[2]

Linguistic deviance is discouraged and condemned by a prescriptive system of grammatical rules created by several generations of educated Englishmen. The name "prescriptive grammar" may be unfamiliar, but the existence of its rules probably isn't. It's what teachers continue to teach as **the** grammar of English, Standard English, a collection of grammatical "dos" and "don'ts," arbitrary rules that dictate the social etiquette of language use. It is a grammar of white English, yet its rules misdescribe the structural properties even of that dialect (e.g., "Never end a sentence with a preposi-tion")[3] ignore the historical development of the language (e.g., rules re-garding the "correct" form of a verb's past participle (*brang* vs. *brought*))[4] warn us away from stylistic infelicities ("dangling" participles, ambiguous readings made possible by structural properties of the language), or forbid dialectal constructions like *ain't*, *y'all*, and *youse* that fill structural gaps.[5] Some of these rules were made up, for example, "Never use double nega-tives. Two negatives make a positive."[6] These aren't rules that describe in-herent properties of the English language. They are *normative* rules[7] of usage that reflect and perpetuate what men have thought the English language *ought* to be, not how it is or has ever been.

English teachers assure us that Standard (white) English is the social sorter that determines who will rise in the social hierarchy and who will not, and they continue to use this claim to justify imposing white English on African-

American speakers and other ethnic groups.[8] But we know they lie. We know from our experience that Standard English is an excuse for denying those of us who aren't white, or men, or both access to wealth and social mobility. We know from our experience that white men, regardless of how they speak, can rise above us, however pitiful their intellectual prowess, however meager their linguistic resources. Lyndon Johnson and Jimmy Carter, for example, both former presidents of the u.s., acquired tremendous political power and social prestige, yet both spoke "sub-standard" Southern dialects stereotypically associated with ignorance and bigotry. Shirley Chisholm, in contrast, an articulate presidential candidate known for her political integrity, was never considered a serious threat to male hegemony because of her sex and race. In spite of her command of Standard English, Chisholm didn't have the credentials to be president. She wasn't white, and she wasn't male.

If so many people know that Standard English is a lie, why haven't we risen up, exposed that linguistic hoax, and refused to go along with it? Because those responsible for our linguistic training have made us feel incompetent and powerless, forcing us to learn their false version of English and abandon our own social, ethnic, and regional dialects, using the promise of upward mobility to herd us into linguistic conformity.

The irony of my preceding discussion has probably not been lost to my readers. It is well-known that women excel in the study of prescriptive grammars. We learn those false rules much faster than our male peers, and we learn them well. In *Language: Its Nature, Development and Origin* (1921), the Danish linguist Otto Jespersen observed: "Woman is linguistically quicker than man: quicker to learn, quicker to hear, and quicker to answer." If we are more articulate than men, **men are linguistically slower than women**. Granting this, however, Jespersen didn't hesitate to turn men's inferiority into a plus for them!

> A man is slower: he hesitates, he chews the cud to make sure of the taste of words, and thereby comes to discover similarities with and differences from other words, both in sound and sense, thus preparing himself for the appropriate use of the fittest noun or adjective. (249)

There's no way we can win the patriarchal grammar game. Women may be fast learners, for example, but men, because they are slow, remain linguistically dominant. The social construction of sex differences supports male dominance, and our well-attested linguistic superiority becomes yet another bit of evidence of our "inferiority."[9]

Men have used our alleged linguistic conservatism against us—in other words, our ability to use the rules of languages they've developed—at least since Cicero, who, describing his mother-in-law's speech, said, "It is more natural for women to keep the old language uncorrupted" (Jespersen 242). Jespersen, less certain that women are more resistant to linguistic change than men, nevertheless claimed that

[w]omen move preferably in the central field of language, avoiding everything
that is out of the way or bizarre, while men will often either coin new words or
expressions or take up old-fashioned ones, if by that means they are enabled, or
think they are enabled, to find a more adequate or precise expression for their
thoughts. Woman as a rule follows the main road of language, where man is
often inclined to turn aside into a narrow footpath or even to strike out a new
path for himself. (248)

By this clever turn, the linguistic abilities of women are made a fault and we
are stripped of our linguistic creativity by the conceptual dipsy-doodles of
male logic. If women speak Standard English, we're unimaginative and
stupid. If we don't, we're sluts as well. Male ineptitude becomes, as usual, a
virtue.

Women are so good at prescriptive grammar that we enter college, major
in English Education, and go out into the public schools to perpetuate "good
English" as male grammarians have formulated it. For learning men's rules
better than they, female English teachers have been caricatured by male
linguists as the stereotype of linguistic evil, "Miss Fidditch."[10] Miss Fidditch,
according to male linguists, is responsible for stifling the linguistic "creativity" of generations of little boys. It's mean Miss Fidditch who coerces and
browbeats them into learning the rules of prescriptive grammar, fails them for
misspelling words, chastises them for saying "ain't," and makes their lives
miserable because she polices their use of English. Not only are we not rich
or powerful because of our control of Standard English, but men ridicule and
make us culpable for our complicity in perpetuating and enforcing the rules
that keep us "in our place"! In what Mary Daly calls a "patriarchal reversal,"
men make women responsible for the "rules" of prescriptive grammar, as
though we made up the rules, viciously ridicule us for practicing and
teaching the rules, and whine about how hard we make their lives!

Trying to follow the twists and turns of male thought is confusing. One
fact, however, stands out from their contradictions: the reality of male power.
That, and their determination to exercise it at any cost, including extermina-
tion of the species.

THE COSMETIC UNIVERSE
OF DISCOURSE (CUD)

The issue, simply stated, is power: who has it and who doesn't. Men do
the things they do to protect their territory. The boundaries are sometimes
shifting and fuzzy, but men will defend to the death every square inch of
what they believe they "own." In this conflict, control of language is the
crucial weapon white men must keep from their enemies because it is the
first and most important method for internalizing oppression in the minds of
those they oppress. Language is an intangible, almost invisible weapon. Its
messages are implanted in our minds when we are babies and left there to

maintain our allegiance to men and their institutions. If the oppressed are convinced that we deserve to be oppressed and can hope for nothing better, the oppressors' work is done with only an occasional show of power.

A Norwegian psycholinguist, Rolv M. Blakar, interested in identifying how language functions as "a means of social power," conducted a variety of tests to analyze the complex relationship between social reality and language (1975). He found that language is not only not a "neutral tool," but that it serves "the interests and perspectives" of those in power, men, at the expense of women (164). Blakar, citing Robin Lakoff's *Language and Woman's Place* (1975), observed that her analysis focused on answers to two different questions: (1) How do women speak English? and (2) How do men talk about women in English? Lakoff herself described her purpose as trying "to see what we can learn about the way women view themselves and everyone's assumptions about the nature and role of women from the use of language in our culture, that is to say, the language used by and about women" (1). Both of Lakoff's questions, and the answers to them, assume a patriarchal frame of reference. That is, Lakoff assumes that all women speak the same self-de-meaning dialect when, in fact, it is only those who want to please men who speak in ways that signal their submission to male dominance. Likewise, it isn't only what men say about women that reveals their hatred of us and their certainty that we are innately inferior to them; men's perceptions of women structure the semantics of the vocabulary itself. Lakoff's way of stating her questions assumed that all women speak differently from men and that the misogyny of English is confined to a small portion of the language. Neither is true.

In *Man Made Language* (1980, 36), Dale Spender observed that many scholars have accepted Jespersen's claims about "women's" language without questioning or challenging them, citing, in particular, Robin Lakoff's book and Mary Ritchie Key's less-cited *Male/Female Language* (1975). Following Jespersen (1921), both Key (1975, 70–77) and R. Lakoff (1975, 53–56) take men's speech as the "neutral" dialect and describe how women's speech deviates from that "norm." These stereotypical features of "women's speech" typify the Cosmetic Universe of Discourse (CUD), a dialect some women use, and only in specific contexts, to signal recognition and acceptance of their subordinate status. I have condensed and arranged those "deviations" here by linguistic level.[11]

Phonological:

1. Women habitually speak at a higher pitch than men;
2. Women use the highest pitch (4) more often than men;
3. Women hesitate or pause more frequently when they talk than men do;
4. Women use the rising intonation that marks questions when they're making statements;

5. Women use emphatic surprise intonation more than men do;
6. Women's speech is more careful (and conservative) than men's, e.g., women say *ing* in verbs like *playing, saying*, men say *n*: [pleyən], [seyən].

Morphology/Word Choice:

1. Women's vocabulary reflects their "interests": fashion, housework, child-rearing, sewing, cooking, and women make finer distinctions and have more words than men do to talk about colors;
2. Women use a lot of "empty" (complimentary) adjectives, such as *divine, charming, adorable, exquisite, precious, sweet*, and *cute*;
3. Women use more modals (*could, might, would*) than men indicating uncertainty and tentativeness;
4. Women's speech contains more hedges than men's, e.g., "well," "sorta," "kinda," and "ya know," which indicate that the speaker isn't sure about what she's asserting;
5. Women use more intensifiers than men, which signal intense feelings, e.g., *so, such, so much*, and *quite*, as in "I had *such* a good time tonight," or "Spending time with you is *so* exciting!"

Syntax:

1. Women use fewer imperatives than men do, substituting "more polite" forms. A woman would say, "Would you mind closing the window?" or "Would you please bring me another beer?", where a man might say, "Shut the window!" or "Bring me a beer!"
2. Robin Lakoff was the first to claim that women use more TAG–QUESTIONS than men. Tag–questions are attached to statements to dilute the force of an assertion and to make it appear that the hearer's approval is being sought. A woman might say, "That was a good dinner, *wasn't it?*" but a man would say, "That was a good dinner," omitting the tag.[12]
3. Women's sentences tend to be longer than men's. Where a man would announce, "I'm going bowling," a woman might say, "If it's OK with you, I think I'll stop by the bowling alley later tonight."

Semantics:

There are no "semantic" traits unique to women's speech.

These characteristics of "women's" speech patterns in English describe the CUD stereotype. Women are said to use intonations, words, and sentence structures that are servile and submissive ("polite"), tentative, uncertain, emotionally exaggerated, and self-demeaning. We are said to avoid aggressive ways of speaking such as imperatives, unqualified assertions, cursing, and brusqueness. More generally, we are accused of talking more than men, talking at great length about "trivial" subjects, and of being more linguistically conservative than men and, therefore, less creative. These alleged traits represent a stereotype of how women talk, **not** the way we do talk. Some women use some of these signals—for example, high pitch, question intonation for statements—only in some contexts, yet the stereotype persists in spite of research that documents its inaccuracy. One might note, for example, that Jespersen's "evidence" that women use more intensifiers than men came from the descriptions of how women talk in novels written by men. Similarly, it's not at all clear that tag–questions necessarily signal a speaker's submission, and R. Lakoff's assertion that women use more tag–questions than men has been challenged on several grounds, among them the fact that male academics often use tag–questions, and parents of both sexes use tag–questions to address observations to children (e.g., "It's raining, isn't it?" "Those are monkeys, aren't they?"). Tag–questions carry with them a patronizing, superior tone, as though the individual so addressed should be grateful to be acknowledged. How English speakers use and interpret tag–questions seems to vary with the relative power among the participants assumed to exist in a speech context.

Any stereotype gains its credibility from those members of the target group who pretend to believe it. There is that minute grain of truth in men's descriptions of our speech that allows them to perpetuate it in spite of all the evidence that contradicts it. Many women do hesitate when they speak; they use "polite" forms; sometimes they qualify and overqualify assertions. CUD is a protective verbal facade, a means of self-defense, however inadequate. Many women still believe that men will treat them kindly if they're "good girls," and "good girls" speak softly, if at all, never raise their voices, carefully couch every assertion with hedges and qualifications, and keep smiling. In like fashion, many women who've been married for many years develop a nonstop way of talking as though to ward off any attempt to interrupt them, loosing swarms of words that crowd the air, sentences that loop and double back on themselves, the end contradicting the beginning. Still, describing only those contexts in which women do fall back on the CUD stereotype and ignoring every other way women use English perpetuates the idea that the stereotype is accurate and fails to expose its partiality and descriptive inaccuracy.

A popular falsehood about women's use of language describes us as "the talkative sex." In fact, men occupy verbal space just as they physically occupy every other kind of space, and women who talk stereotypically do so because their words provide them with a protective cover, a verbal wall, to keep men from interrupting them. Pamela Fishman (1978; 1980) and West and Zimmerman (1975; 1983) identified the linguistic methods men use to dominate and control the topic and direction of mixed-sex conversations among whites. Their research contradicted the popular notion that white women talk "too much" or "all the time," revealing that we not only talk **less** than men but that most of our part in mixed-sex conversations is supportive, encouraging men to talk. Fishman, for example, taped the "at home" conversations of several heterosexual dyads, and found that women kept conversations going, suggesting and abandoning potential topics until they found one that the men were interested in, at which point the men assumed control of the conversations. West and Zimmerman's research concentrated on interruptive patterns in conversation, and they found that men interrupt women an average of three times more than women interrupt men in a variety of relationships, ranging from unacquainted to intimate (1983, 107). Men not only talk more than women, they drown us out.

What emerges from the work summarized here is less than clear. On the one hand, some of the features associated with women's speech reflect the limitations of our experiential domain under patriarchy, "the home." For example, women's use of language avoids much male slang (what linguists call "conservative") because those who still spend most of their lives within dwellings speak to only a few men and so have little need to imitate the linguistic fads of the "man's world." On the other, the evidence for what is put forth as the stereotype of women's dialect remains dubious. Although men typically portray us as talking the way they believe we do, few women actually speak according to the CUD stereotype, as the cheerleaders for the Dallas Cowboys must. The validity of the stereotype itself is more suspect when we realize that studies carried out during the past fifteen years expose the stereotype of "women talk too much" as a *reversal* of what actually occurs in conversation between women and men.

Dale Spender is eloquent on this point. She opens her discussion of "Who Does the Talking?" (1980, 41–50) with a few typical sayings about women's volubility, for example, from Scotland, "Nothing is so unnatural as a talkative men or a quiet woman" (Swacker, 1975, 76), followed by quotations from contemporary etiquette books indicating that, in fact, it's men who talk all the time and enjoy doing so. Spender notes the obvious contradiction: "On the one hand we have a society which believes that women are the talkative sex and on the other hand we have overwhelming evidence that it is men who do the talking" (42). "How," she asks, "do we explain the continued existence of this belief?" Spender's answer begins by examining the phrase "women talk *too much*," paying particular attention to the measurement implied by "too much."

> The concept of women as the talkative sex involves a comparison: they must talk too much against some sort of standard or yardstick and we have erroneously assumed that the measurement of women as talkers is in comparison to men. But this appears not to be the case. The talkativeness of women has been gauged in comparison not with men but with *silence*. Women have not been

judged on the grounds of whether they talk more than men, but of whether they talk more than silent women. When silence is the desired state for women (and I suggest that it is in a patriarchal order, as do numerous other feminists), then any talk in which a woman engages can be too much. (42)

Spender goes on to ask why there is so little research of the kind done by West and Zimmerman, yet so much on "finding the deficiencies in women's words, pronunciation and pitch," an important question too easily ignored. Spender's answer is clear and succinct:

The answer lies . . . in the patriarchal order and the beliefs which are necessary for the maintenance of that order. It is important to substantiate women's linguistic deficiencies and it is necessary to preserve some of the myths upon which those deficiencies depend. . . . That the deficiencies are not found can be explained by the suggestion that researchers have been looking in the wrong place. A new segment is chosen for attention but the assumption persists. This is not the case with studies on amount of talk. The excessive talkativeness of women is readily exposed as a myth with the result that many awkward questions are raised. (43)

True. Exposing the myth of women's talkativeness for what it is **might** raise "many awkward questions," but for whom? The patriarchal notions that women talk "too much" and that the "best" woman is a silent woman continue to be played and replayed in the male-dominated media, while the research that calls those notions into question is persistently ignored. Only the few scholars who read the literature, know that "awkward questions" have been raised and, to date, they have been collectively unable to dislodge such ideas from the minds of those who would probably hold onto them regardless of how much evidence contradicted their cherished beliefs. Regarding the question of how men (and many women) persist in believing that women are the talkative sex, Cheris Kramarae's terse summation supplies the missing standard of measurement implied by "too much": "Perhaps a talkative woman is one who talks as much as a man" (1975, 47).

History will teach us, if nothing else, that facts have a hard time when they contradict belief and prejudice, folk theories of "how the world is." Facts that would endanger the internal coherence of PUD are conveniently ignored or, in those rare instances when they become publicly visible, quickly buried and forgotten. Pamela Fishman (1983) opened her article on the "conversational shitwork" women do with a brief discussion of the social processes at work in the suppression of dangerous information. Citing Berger and Luckmann (1967, 109), she said:

They define power as a question of potentially conflicting definitions of reality; that of the most powerful will be "made to stick." Imposing one's will can be much more than forcing someone else to do something. Power may also involve the ability to impose one's definitions of what is possible, what is right, what is rational, what is real. Power is a product of human activities, just as the activities are themselves products of the power relations in the socioeconomic world. (89)

We are not dealing here with the vague abstraction so often invoked for causal blame: SOCIETY. "Society" does *nothing*. Whatever occurs within a culture is the direct result of "human" actions. In patriarchy, events and situations are caused by those who have the social, economic, and political power to make them happen: **men**. In the u.s., it is white men who have the power "to impose [their] definition of what is . . . real," and, because it serves their purposes to do so, they perpetuate their myths about women and language. Under the circumstances, it makes sense. Why would they want to nurture and propound ideas that would undoubtedly raise "awkward questions" if enough people knew about them?

To my readers who shy away from such generalizations, those who will say, "No, no, no, it's not **all** men," I agree. Women as well as men pay lip service to the preferred dialect of PUD; some women certainly do perpetuate the CUD stereotype of women's speech (but only, I suspect, on television). Indeed, some women speak men's language, by their rules, and excel at it, when men allow them to, for example, Jeanne Kirkpatrick, former u.s. ambassador to the united nations. There are women who are contented with their place in patriarchy, and they are welcome to it. However, those of us who aren't satisfied, who want better lives than we were taught to expect, must stop honoring the rules of PUD. I know some readers will think me "unkind" to men, and I don't want to be misinterpreted. Yes, a few men are as committed as I to halting the proliferation of doublespeak, garble, and lies that has become our standard linguistic fare. Finally, though, men are the only beneficiaries of PUD, and if I am judged unkind for telling the truth about English and how it maintains male dominance, so be it.

THE PATRIARCHAL UNIVERSE OF DISCOURSE (PUD)

Analyzing a language, especially English, and opening up its vocabulary and internal structure to examination, also raises questions about the culture in which that language is a primary means of communicating. Virtually every known society is patriarchal, but each language maintains male dominance in different ways. English has no singular generic pronoun, except for *one*, similar to French *on*, and most u.s. speakers avoid using it because it sounds stiff or formal. (The plural pronoun *they* certainly does serve as a generic, but prescriptive grammarians continue to condemn its use.) Japanese didn't have a passive structure until it was borrowed from English after w.w. ii, but Japanese culture was and is patriarchal.

The interconnectedness of language and culture accounts for the way white men guard English, and their squeamish defensiveness whenever women voice our dissatisfaction with the language or the grammars of it men have prepared. There is no doubt that women have, from time to time, challenged the ways male social dominance has been incorporated into the structure of English, but even prodigious research has managed to recover only a few of their names and less of their work.[13] Men continue to have predictable success at burying and erasing women's words and the process continues.

I say "a few" because, until recently, most women have been unable to say what they thought in the publicly accessible media. Women who do manage to find a publisher may write and write, but little of their work lasts because it is pushed off the shelves and into the remainder bins as quickly as possible (in those cases when the words have appeared as a book; other ways of publishing have an even shorter life). Women's work is buried so quickly that we end up saying the same things over and over, retracing our first conceptual steps out of patriarchy and unable to proceed further. Men drown us out in every medium.

Men have put forth many reasons for our inability to establish ourselves visibly and permanently in the public consciousness: we don't know "how" to write; what we say isn't worth preserving, or doesn't have "broad appeal"; no one is interested in "women's issues"; we're "too"—strident, angry, narrow, man-hating, paranoid, rude, ugly, fat, _____ (fill in your favorite adjective). But all of them boil down to one: men don't want to listen to what we have to say. They don't care what we think when we contradict their pet ideas. No matter how many obstacles we overcome in order to be heard, our words are buried beneath the general male cacophony.

Feminists have developed (again) a thorough analysis of what it means to live under white male patriarchy. What does it mean, though, to say that a language is patriarchal? Patriarchal languages develop to express the concepts, values, and assumptions of cultures ruled by men.[14] The specific linguistic reflexes of male domination differ from language to language, as my discussions in chapters 5, 6, and 7 illustrate, but they share fundamental characteristics:

1. Phonologically:
   Intonation, pitch, stress, and pronunciation distinguish a women's dialect from that of men;
2. Morphologically:
   Women are forbidden to use certain forms of words, to speak words containing the names of male relatives, or may have to add prefixes or suffixes that mean 'female speaker';
3. Syntactically:
   a. women use structures marked as submissive (questions), men use imperatives and assertions;
   b. syntactic structures called "impersonal" are used to describe the world as men perceive it and these descriptions are accepted as "consensus reality";

4. Semantically:
   a. the vocabulary is divided on the basis of sex-specific experiential spheres: women occupy the interior space of dwellings; the rest of the world is [+male];
   b. the male sex is the unmarked, human "norm"; women are marked as Other [−male];
   c. words that are female-specific, including kinship terms, **pejorate**—they develop negative connotations, usually sexual in nature, and become insults; words referring to men are valued positively and there are few, if any, male-specific insults;
   d. most "generic" terms (those said to refer to 'people in general') are [+male]; when women are included in a speaker's reference, they are mentioned explicitly;
   e. women are associated with "evil."

Women are also speakers of language. If most of the world's languages are patriarchal, their grammars written by men, their "standard" dialects controlled by men, and men's perceptions reflected in their structural properties, I must ask: Why have women allowed men to control language so thoroughly for so long? Why have women accepted men's descriptions of the world as true?

What is women's relationship to the patriarchal universe of discourse (PUD) if it describes men's perceptions? Are we to assume, with most of the men who've written on the subject, that what I'm calling the "patriarchal universe of discourse" is the **only** version of reality and that women perceive and think exactly as men do, that is, that man-made languages adequately describe women's perceptions? Or is Susan Grimsdell's analysis of the situation, in her summary of Man Made Language (1980) by Dale Spender, more accurate (1988)? Do women pretend to agree with men's descriptions, "going along" with them in order to survive?

> It could be said that women collude in the perpetuation of sexism in language. True, but we have had little choice. . . . If women are to survive we often feel we have to curry men's favour, make ourselves attractive to them, play the game, act the part, and most definitely avoid antagonising them.
>
> Part of our task in pleasing men is for us to give reality to their definitions of words they associate with us. . . . We modify our faces and our bodies, even in some cases going so far as to have surgery, all to comply with what they have defined as attractive and feminine. What else can we do? We please them in order to get our daily bread. (16)

If Grimsdell's suggestions are accurate, we are in a grim situation. Can it be that women "collude" in perpetuating their oppression, linguistic and otherwise, to get their "daily bread" from men?

Women have had choices, must have, at some now unknowable stage of history. I don't agree with Susan Grimsdell's claim that "we have had little choice," that women have colluded with men "in order to get our daily bread." That description acknowledges male dominance without considering women's role in nurturing and maintaining patriarchy. What's more, I don't think Grimsdell really believed it, either.

> We need more new words, words that express the reality of women's abilities, that convey women's potential strength and autonomy. We must escape from the language trap that has male as norm, woman as deviant. (16)

If we have choices now, women before us have also had them. What did Grimsdell imagine "the reality of women's abilities" to be? She described "strength" and "autonomy" as merely "potential" without explaining how "new words" for our abilities will enable us to "escape . . . the language trap." New ideas generally require new words, but first those ideas must be conceived. Is there a way out of this conundrum? Yes. But like any run for freedom, it will be dangerous, and there will be losses. If women have colluded with men in their own oppression, then we must stop nurturing our oppressors, and recognize that men are our oppressors, that our oppression as women is not an "accident" but systematic and purposeful and will not end until we do what we must do to free ourselves.

These are difficult decisions. Yet, one of the crucial ways of ending our oppression must lie in thinking ourselves free. Yes, new words will help, but only if we perceive ourselves in new ways. New words for the same old shit won't move us toward radical change in our lives. Language is action, not yet another accident that we cannot hope to change. When we speak, we are acting **in** the world. We make choices. Andrea Dworkin knows that our survival depends upon recognizing how words are central to our oppression and to the possibility of freedom:

> Words matter because words significantly determine what we know and what we do. Words change us or keep us the same. Women, deprived of a forum for words, are deprived of the power necessary to ensure both survival and well-being. (1988, 30)

Men know this, which is why they repeatedly assure us that a "good" woman is a silent woman. A woman without words for her experience isn't acting in The World, that is, "Their World." Women who speak and write and think in nonpatriarchal ways will change the world and reclaim it from male domination. Men resist our efforts to change language because they know that language change indicates both social and cognitive changes.

In fact, though, PUD is so flexible that it can absorb and assimilate even radical ideas by turning them to its own purposes, and the media have shown an obstinate talent for recontextualizing and, thereby, distorting various elements of Feminist politics. In the made-for-television movie, *The Billionaire Boys' Club* (1989), one of the rich, white men used the phrase *consciousness-raising* to describe his changed perception of what the club was doing when he saw the body of one of the men his friends had murdered. For all the women who participated in consciousness-raising groups in the 1960s and 1970s, the word referred very specifically (and exclusively) to the resulting process of change in how we perceived ourselves, our situation in the world, and our relationship to men. For us, consciousness-raising was a profound, mind-altering experience that impelled us to change our lives. We couldn't have imagined that that word would be so perverted as to end up describing a yuppie's shocked repulsion when he saw his first dead body!

We must understand that changing language is an act of rebellion that signals the end of our collusion against ourselves with men, and we must ask ourselves how serious we are about ending female submission to male domination. Women have been fighting male control of English for several generations now, and we haven't made much headway against their entrenched resistance. We may fail. They may succeed in gradually distorting, corrupting, and diluting everything we still call *feminism*. Or, we may fail and fail and fail, and eventually succeed. But we won't know unless we're willing to fail and unwilling to give up.

NEW WOMEN, NEW WORLD

I know that readers will find some parts of *Speaking Freely* difficult at first. Unlike psychology, sociology, and history, linguistics isn't general knowledge. When most people hear the world *linguist,* they think of someone who speaks "a lot" of languages. This is the popular misconception. Linguists study the structural properties of language and how language structure reflects conceptual structure. Although linguists often know several languages, both endeavors are more abstract than speaking a language generally suggests.

I'm aware of the lack of familiarity with linguistics and its terminology, and I've tried, wherever I could, to avoid using unfamiliar terms. This wasn't always possible. There are some aspects of English for which there is no conventional vocabulary (e.g., psych-predicates), and others for which linguistics has supplied a more precise characterization (e.g., agent and topic, instead of subject). In every situation, I've weighed both familiarity and precision against my major purpose: to get this information about English to women, to show other women how white men use English to keep our bodies and spirits domesticated and our minds away from "dangerous" questions.

I've endeavored to explain the structural properties of English to an audience I imagine to be resistant to any grammar talk whatsoever and, therefore, unprepared to explore the inner workings of something we can't reach out and touch: our internalized knowledge of the English language. I undertook this project because understanding the structure of English has helped me to unlearn many of the distortions and lies I believed for half my life. I have devoted more than 20 years to studying English and figuring out how it works and why it is as it is. Understanding how speakers can use English to befuddle, manipulate, coerce, or lie is important, and I think my analysis clarifies some of the ways the language works to maintain male domination and its corollary, women's subordination.

I believe that my readers will find the information in *Speaking Freely* not only useful, but important to them in changing their lives, and I have described some of the ways English plays a crucial role in women's socialization to powerlessness. I didn't set out to write a grammar book in any conventional sense, yet I have had to use grammatical terms to describe the structural properties of English in a consistent, comprehensible way. I know that many readers may be put off at first by the terminology, but I ask you to bear with me. My analysis of PUD required both grammatical concepts and their names, and linguistic terminology allowed me to talk about structures that prescriptive grammarians overlooked. Wherever possible, I have tried to avoid relying on jargon, but I also had to have **names** for the characteristics of English I talk about. I've included a Glossary at the end of the book as an aid for readers, and defined there the labels I use in the text.

Our will to change must be founded in a comfortable self-consciousness. In *Language and Women's Place* (1975), R. Lakoff predicted that Feminist attempts to change pronoun usage would be "futile" because the pronoun system is "less open to change" and speakers would resist any changes that make them self-conscious while they speak.

> I think one should force oneself to be realistic: certain aspects of language are available to the native speakers' *conscious analysis*, and others are too common, too thoroughly mixed throughout the language, for the speaker to be aware each time **he** uses them. It is realistic to hope to change only those linguistic uses of which speakers themselves can be made aware, as they use them. One chooses, in speaking and writing, *more or less consciously and purposefully among nouns, adjectives, and verbs; one does not choose among pronouns in the same way*. [My emphases] (45)

Her argument rests on the notion that any changes which require speakers to **think** before we speak will never replace **androcentric** elements of English because no one wants to be SELF-CONSCIOUS about what they say. Rejecting specific changes by assuming that self-consciousness about some linguistic choices (but not others) is too hard or impossible is obtuse as well as vague.

Lakoff readily admitted that her training as a linguist may have "dulled

[her] perception" regarding what she called "neutral *he*," but I suspect that her early training in the rules of prescriptive grammar dulled her linguistic sensibilities, because the pronoun *he* is used pseudo-generically only in contexts where people are **self-conscious** about what they say. In casual conversation, most English speakers use *they*, not *he* when referring to people in general, and I don't know why Lakoff failed to mention this fact. It is well-known among linguists.

In u.s. society, being "made" self-conscious about something is treated as negative, undesirable, to be avoided whenever possible, as though anything that interrupts "the flow" of what we consider "natural," "normal," or "in-herent" hinders our ability to function. English speakers need more, not less, self-consciousness about what we say. Being aware of the cognitive significance and social ramifications of the linguistic choices we make is both necessary and constructive, because it ensures that we won't accept misogynistic language as "normal." Self-consciousness guarantees that we don't remain locked in the biased descriptions of what PUD regards as the norm. Just as whites should be aware of the color of our skin and the able-bodied should be conscious of their mobility, all of us should choose the words and structures we use *consciously*. Pausing and weighing the words we choose to describe what we perceive and feel is essential to unlearning the rules of PUD and discovering people and the world without the male descriptions through which our thoughts have been filtered for years.

Furthermore, R. Lakoff's argument makes language users passive, rather than active. All speakers of English need to develop awareness of our linguistic agency as speakers and as listeners. Listening and reading aren't the passive activities we believe them to be. The sentences speakers use to describe people, objects, and events structure our interpretive processes as much as the words they choose. In the Patriarchal Universe of Discourse, speakers show preferences for some syntactic structures over others just as they prefer specific words to other, equally accurate, ones. Learning to identify such structures and not be taken in by them is a crucial stage in the process of freeing our thinking from PUD descriptions, because the structure of sentences packages information the way speakers want us to understand it.

We learn to think of speaking and writing as active language use and of listening and reading as passive. Linguistic passivity is forced on women. Our earliest lessons as speakers tell us that our "proper" role is to listen to men brag about themselves and to "speak softly," if at all. An important aspect of rethinking English and our use of it is empowering ourselves both as speakers **and** listeners. We will unlearn the insulting, degrading perspective of PUD as soon as we realize that English provides a map of only one version of reality, the male perspective, and omits other, equally viable perspectives.

Women **listen** far more than we speak and, when we do talk, use our conversational skills encouraging men to occupy more discourse space. This learned passivity makes us susceptible to subliminal messages—not what is said so much as **what is not said**: the implicit messages we supply ourselves as we process sentences conceptually. We need to think of ourselves as linguistically powerful, as agents of language acts in our roles as listener and speaker. When we use language, our minds must be constantly engaged, whether we are conscious of it or not. The linguistic processes readers and listeners perform as participants include, but aren't limited to, supplying words and phrases missing from texts as a result of obligatory or optional omissions, making connections between words that affect textual cohesion, and resolving ambiguities when the writer or speaker does not. In chapters 8, 9, and 10, I analyze some of the syntactic processes speakers employ to create the structures we interpret, and my discussion focuses on how syntax functions in patriarchal rhetoric. From that point on, I am as concerned with what speakers leave out as what they actually **say**, and how listeners and readers use structural cues to guess at suppressed information.

The purpose of my analysis is to show readers how to be self-conscious about their linguistic activities. When we are involved as listeners or readers in the creation of a "text," we are conscious of what we're doing only in unusual circumstances, when we have trouble interpreting what we hear or read. I want to provide information so that women can engage in communication more consciously. Whether we are speaking or listening, writing or reading, being conscious of the functions of linguistic structures when we try to communicate or interpret someone else's utterance enables us to identify immediately and **in context** uses of language that are dishonest, misleading, or manipulative. If we are conscious of such linguistic tactics, we are less likely to accept incomplete or distorted descriptions as accurate or to allow speakers and writers to persuade us to think the way they would like us to think. Conscious knowledge is knowledge immediately available during reading or listening, and it gives us the means to change our own linguistic habits and defend ourselves when language is used against us.

If we are to protect ourselves against insidious uses of English, we have to be able to identify such uses and challenge them when someone tries to coerce us linguistically.[15] If we don't understand the structures that serve PUD, we remain the linguistic victims of male rhetoric. Unnamed experience remains unrecognized and inchoate. For those who accept male descriptions of reality, ignorance is, truly, "bliss." But, for those of us who seek a better world and more enlightened ways of living in it, understanding the role of language in perpetuating male dominance is crucial. In chapter 11 I return to the importance of developing linguistic self-consciousness and its role in changing the way we think and our political circumstances.

Women spend our lives as victims of male violence. Some of us realize this. What most are not aware of is the function of language in perpetuating our subordination and victimization. The Patriarchal Universe of Discourse is made up of men's descriptions of what they perceive and what they name as real or unreal, important or insignificant, natural or unnatural, good or bad. Men have succeeded in convincing themselves and a majority of women that their descriptions are true and accurate. PUD is accepted as "consensus reality," those collections of descriptions that most people use to interpret and understand themselves and the world around them.

We are raised to think and live on the basis of how these descriptions present what life is like and what the world is like to our young minds. Gradually, knowing nothing else, having been told nothing else, we believe them. Whatever perceptions we might have had recede into forgetfulness. When our experience contradicts what we have been told to believe the world is like, our identity, our sense of self is endangered. Girls raped by their fathers and other male relatives, women beaten and raped by their husbands, and Lesbians all know what happens in our minds when our experience contradicts the version of reality presented to us. We can decide that "consensus reality" is still true and label our own experience unique, personal, contrary to fact; we can deny that whatever men did to us didn't happen and suppress the information, or we miraculously, against everything we've been taught, accept the validity of our knowledge. If we identify our experience as personal or deny it, we may live out our lives hiding our "secret," certain that its discovery will mean our destruction. If we trust our own perceptions and ability to interpret experience for ourselves, we become intensely protective of our knowledge. Whichever way we choose to deal with our experiences, we believe three things: (1) that we're "the only ones"; (2) that the experience was the result of our own **failure**; (3) that we're alone in the world.

We are either alienated from ourselves or from the society that lies to us. Whichever, our minds strive to reconcile these contradictions between the world described by PUD and our experiences in that world, and try to make sense of them. The psychiatric establishment calls denying and mistrusting ourselves, putting aside or suppressing our contradictory knowledge, "adjusting." Those of us who refuse to "adjust" to the demands of patriarchy are labeled crazy, misfits, malcontents, freaks; those who keep their secret pretend to adjust, believing inside that they're crazy. Some pretend to adjust, others don't. That is the only difference. Each of us believes that "Failure is personal."[16]

When we know that what we're told is lies, we strain the limits of our creativity coming up with theories that will explain, to our satisfaction, the seemingly irreconcilable contradictions between what we've been told (and believed) and what our lives, our bodies, our brains, have **learned**. These explanations, however, are monotonously few and rarely venture beyond the conceptual boundaries of PUD. Because male descriptions are all we know, our theories are grounded on what men tell us life "is like."

The raped daughter believes that her father's violence was her fault; that she "seduced" him, that she was bad, that she deserved to be raped. The beaten wife believes that her husband's violence was her fault; that she wasn't a good wife; that she caused his violence; that she deserved to be beaten. The lesbian believes that loving women is her fault; that there is something terribly wrong with her; that she deserves the mockery, ridicule, and violence men direct at her. PUD demands that women limit our love to men and our inability to find men lovable brands us as outcasts. "Failure is personal."

PUD supplies our imaginations with male perceptions of us: we are carnal, evil, wicked. So strong are male descriptions of the world that we never think to blame them. We believe what they tell us: that we are responsible for what they do to us. Men describe themselves as the victims of *our* treachery, *our* betrayal, and we believe that we are the guilty ones. Our minds do the work of patriarchy. We believe that we are the evil doers in our explanations, and that message etches paths in our minds, paths that are nothing so much as the tracks wild animals wear around the peripheries of their cages, at the boundaries of their lives. "Failure is personal." In order to go on believing men's lies, we blame ourselves, we blame circumstances, we blame their working conditions, the weather, where we live, where we do not live. Women spend their lives making up excuses for men, who they are, and what they do to us. Always, we blame ourselves.

MY ASSUMPTIONS

I've written *Speaking Freely* because I want to change the world. When I talk about structures in the English language as pieces of the patriarchal universe of discourse that coerce us to perceive ourselves as participants in that universe, I'm assuming that the prevailing descriptions of the world are inaccurate and that the world so described is not "the best of all possible worlds." I'm assuming that we want a "better" world to live in, one in which each of us is valued for WHO WE ARE, not devalued because we fail to fit the idea of what someone else thinks we "ought" to be. I'm assuming that we're capable of *unlearning* patriarchal assumptions and values and are equally capable of creating different descriptions of the world, and I'm assuming that understanding the ways English perpetuates patriarchal descriptions initiates these changes.

Yes, the syntax and semantics of languages encode experiences of the world, but my analysis indicates that these experiences aren't *women's* experiences[17] and that the experiences described by English are those of men, who have controlled the development and grammatical explanations of English up to this time. The English language facilitates the expression of patriarchy's preferred and validated perceptions and experiences. Consider, for example, the phrase "to lower standards," as in "If we admit women, African-

Americans, Native Americans, Chicanos, Latinos, and members of other oppressed groups, we'll be forced to *lower our standards*." Now, this description may seem harmless enough. We might shrug it off as yet another example of the white male perspective at work. It is certainly a white male description, but it's far from merely innocuous.

The plural pronoun *our*, in this case, is intended to refer to all the members of a particular college or university or, more generally, to all members of academia. In fact, this statement is always made by a white man. Listed below are the presuppositions of PUD that we accept if we believe *lower* in this description "makes sense":

1. it implies a change in position with respect to an earlier position in time, with respect to an unspecified, but implied, judgment;
2. it implies that the standards were, at an earlier time, higher with respect to the position they might come to occupy if women, African-Americans, and others gain entry;
3. because *low* equals "worse," the projected change in position in standards will, by definition, be worse;
4. therefore: CHANGE IS BAD.

But we don't know what the previous "standards" were; we don't know what the implied measure by which the relative position of the "standards" is or the basis of the unspecified judgment; we have no idea how high the implied *higher* was. Change can be good, bad, or indifferent. Usually, how a specific change is judged depends on whether the individual making the judgment will benefit from it. In addition, the verb *lower* implies human agency to enact what it describes, and that agency must be **voluntary**, which implies that white men could refuse to act. (Why don't they? Because they know their description is a sham?)

What purposes are served when white men talk about "lowering [their] standards"? They're avoiding saying something else that would expose their real reasons for resisting change. The change itself, admitting women and men of various ethnic and racial groups, will alter the nature of the student body, the content of courses, and ways of teaching and grading. The previously white, male student body was more homogeneous. As a result, the criteria for grading were clearer and easier. As long as students were predominantly male and white, the variables that determined grading were simpler. They were variables established and controlled by the admissions process. Teachers could assume their students had a certain level of social and economic privilege; otherwise, they wouldn't have been admitted. Given the assumption of class privilege, a student who performed poorly could be dismissed as a slackard who preferred partying to studying; there were few other acceptable excuses.

Once, however, women and minority men (except for Asian students, who outperform white students so convincingly that a different tactic has to be found, and kept secret) gain entry to academia, the grading process becomes much more complicated because students are no longer homogeneous. The criteria for grading, what is acceptable performance, are broadened because teachers now have to consider additional variables and their previous assumptions must be questioned, examined, and tested. A student body of individuals who come from a wide range of economic, racial, and ethnic backgrounds, introduces ambiguity into teaching (and jokes about women, niggers, and spics that always got a laugh have to be deleted from lecture notes). That one little phrase, "lowering *our* standards," is easier than making explicit everything that it hides and opening up the workings of academia to scrutiny.

If we choose to accept the terms of PUD and the assertions that rationalize white male dominance, it is difficult (but not impossible) to describe the world in heterodox ways. I'm assuming that we must know which aspects of English structure are perceptual and conceptual traps, and that learning to avoid such traps will impel us to dis-cover the descriptions that will enable us to reconceive the world and our Selves as active agents in the world. In the chapters to follow, I describe several of the linguistic ways men perpetuate their dominance: abstraction that refuses to be explicit about events in the world; attribution of agentive status to abstract or inanimate objects; the suppression of human agency and responsibility for events and acts in the world; inaccurate or distorted descriptions that claim to be true statements about the world; an interlocking system of metaphorical concepts that emphasizes only selected aspects of events, objects, and people and hides other, equally significant, features of our experience in the world, even from us.

This is not a book about non-sexist writing.[18] It is a book about how patriarchal thought controls and limits the ways we live in the world, an analysis of how the structure of English developed to perpetuate men's descriptions of what our lives are like and what the world is like. I want to understand and live in another world than the one men have made, and I hope other women will join me in its recreation.

Acknowledgments

This book owes much to the support and research of many people, most of whom I won't be able to mention; I want each of them to know that I remember their contributions to me and to my thinking. Even my expressed thanks here is inadequate. Nevertheless, I must try. I want, first, to thank those who guided and trained me in language analysis: Mary Watts, my high school English teacher, who introduced me to linguistics; Louis G. Heller, who oversaw and supported my early training at The City College of New York; Ruth and Winfred P. Lehmann, who made it financially possible for me to stay in graduate school at The University of Texas–Austin; Arthur Norman, who taught me what he knew about stylistic analysis and how to make mead; Cheris Kramarae, whose friendship and intellectual support I've cherished over the years; and the students in my classes at the University of Georgia and the University of Nebraska–Lincoln who've gone on to better things, especially Sally Stoddard, Kathryn Bellman, Marty Knepper, Christine Lac, C. Colette, Mary Tait, and Morgan Grey, whose quick thinking and astute questions always kept me moving. But James H. Sledd, curmudgeon, directed my dissertation although he disagreed with me and, along the way, taught me the quality of compassion, that academic writing has neither wit nor wisdom, and it's better to be a live jackass than a dead one.

I also want to acknowledge the patience and support of all my friends who've endured my negligence with grace and caring over the years and reconciled themselves to the fact that I may never be a reliable correspondent, but particularly those who took the time to read early drafts of this book, whose perceptive comments helped me by suggesting revisions: Marion Elizabeth, Bett Farber, Morgan Grey, Anne Throop Leighton and Catherine Odette.

I want to thank especially Mary Daly for her Nagging, Janice G. Raymond for her passionate En-couragement for this manuscript and her editorial willingness to guide me through its several versions, Liza Cowan for her support, her suggestions, and a wonderful afternoon wandering the streets of the Village and conceptual byways.

There are two outrageous friends who deserve my profoundest gratitude: Kate Moran and Susan J. Wolfe. Kate read so many drafts, almost uncomplainingly, that we both lost count, and then thrilled me by demonstrating that my analysis does show how we can talk our way out of PUD. Most of all, I want to thank my friend and cohort Susan Wolfe, for her merciless and unrelenting reading of the manuscript and for showing me how I could revise the book to make it shorter and more readable. Susan co-authored several of the articles on which this book is based and generously allowed me to steal her observation that we don't think of avocadoes as agents of verbs like *spank* and *arrest*. Susan isn't always right, just honest.

Finally, I apologize to all those I haven't mentioned, and thank everyone whose mind and spirit contributed to *Speaking Freely*. If this book helps women learn new ways to understand and talk about our experience, it will be due to the help and support of my friends and students. All errors and shortcomings are, however, my own.

Chapter 1

The Glamour of Grammar

In a man's world, language belongs to men. There are two interconnected histories that attest to male control of the development of the English language: the history of the language itself over nearly 2,000 years and the history of **prescriptive grammars** that set forth the "rights" and "wrongs" of English usage. Men have managed changes in the language and legislated its rules, both structural and social. Prescriptive grammarians established, in some cases, made up rules in order to maintain English in a pure, ideal state in which it never existed. The rules men have contrived to preserve the illusory purity of English are set forth in numerous **grammar** books from the seventeenth century to the present. From those early grammars and their Latin sources the distortions and misinformation imposed on the language have been passed on to us as "fact." A brief history of English will expose the hypocrisy of the prescriptivist desire to "purify" the language.

A CONDENSED HISTORY
OF ENGLISH

Language has been, and remains, among the primary methods of subjugating and colonizing other nations. The obliteration of one people's language effectively destroys the ways of thinking and social custom that, together, we call culture. A history of English charts the stages by which men's wars, invasions, and conquests have determined the shape of the language: which words were retained or dropped from the vocabulary and the direction syntactic alterations took. It is a chronicle of whose language or dialect would be accepted and, therefore, spoken or written, and the subjugation and assimilation of women and other men: those who would be acknowledged as acceptable speakers, and those who would not.

At least four **Indo-European** languages contributed to what we call En-

1

glish: (1) several Germanic languages (or dialects), brought to the British Isles by anglo-saxon tribes; (2) Scandinavian, primarily Old Norse, which left its traces on both the vocabulary and structure of English; (3) Norman French, brought to Britain by William the Conqueror; and (4) Latin, which remained the major language of religion and learning until well into the Middle English (ME) period (1100–1500).

The base stock of English is Germanic. Unable to repel attacks by the Picts and Scots from the north, Vortigern, a Celtic chieftain, appealed to the Jutes, then living along the western coast of Europe, for help in 449 A.D. In exchange for driving out his enemies to the north, Vortigern promised to reward the Jutes with the isle of Thanet. This, however, proved an insufficient compensation for the tribe, who began to settle themselves forcibly in what is now Kent. During the remainder of the fifth century and the sixth, other Germanic tribes made the crossing, Saxons, Angles, and Frisians, eventually sorting themselves into seven not very permanent kingdoms known as the Anglo-Saxon Heptarchy (Baugh, 1963, 56). In spite of their fierce resistance, the Celts were gradually pushed westward, into Wales and Cornwall.

Linguists date the Old English period from the beginning of the Germanic invasions in 449 to around 1150. There were four identifiable dialects of Old English (OE): Northumbrian (spoken by those living north of the Humber River), Mercian (spoken in the area between the Humber and Thames Rivers), West Saxon (spoken in the southwest region of England), and Kentish (the dialect of the Jutes in the southeast) (Baugh, 60). It was also during this period that Latin exerted its first significant influence on English. In 597, Augustine set out with a small band of monks to convert the Anglo-Saxons. As xtianity (of the roman catholic sort) gradually supplanted the Old Religion in Britain, over a span of five centuries, Latin words began to find their way into the Old English vocabulary.

The Anglo-Saxons had barely settled in when yet another series of Germanic invasions started that would change OE: the Scandinavian invasions that began, according to the *Anglo-Saxon Chronicle*, in 787 and ended in 1017 when Cnut established his claims to the British throne (Baugh, 107–112). In the process, the Scandinavians burned monasteries to the ground, destroying most of the manuscripts transcribed by monks. (As a result of this destruction, only one charred copy of *Beowulf* remains.) During the next 49 years, there ensued a period of assimilation while the conquerors and the conquered, all Germanic, mixed and mingled their respective languages as much as their genes. Many OE terms did not survive the process, and Modern English (ModE) still shows the results of assimilation in numerous "doublets," for example, *no/nay, whole/hale, rear/raise, eye/egg, from/fro, craft/skill, hide/skin, shirt/skirt, sick/ill* (Baugh, 119; the English word is given first). As a result of these invasions, most of the OE documents remaining are in the West Saxon dialect.

In addition to introducing new words into the English vocabulary, the Scandinavians changed structural properties of the language, most notably the **pronoun** system. In the West Saxon dialect, the one for which we have the most surviving documents, the **nominative** forms of the pronouns were the following:

	Singular	Dual	Plural
1.	iċ	wit	wē
2.	ðū	git	ġē
3.	hē, hēo (hīe), hit		hēo, hīe

The newly arrived Scandinavian speakers changed the OE pronoun system in important ways. By the end of the thirteenth century, the dual pronouns ('we two', 'you two'), for example, had been dropped. In those areas of Britain most affected by Scandinavian influence, the third person plural in Middle English (ME), *hēo, hīe*, had been replaced by Scandinavian *þei*, and by the end of the ME period, *they, their*, and *them* were established as English third person plural pronouns.

Of special interest is the loss of the native OE female third person singular pronoun *hēo* and the acquisition of a maximally distinctive form, *sheo* (*schō, schē, shē*), from a still unidentifiable source. When, because of an otherwise unremarkable linguistic process,[1] speakers began to pronounce *hēo* and *hē* similarly in rapid speech, the two pronouns became indistinguishable. At this stage, speakers of English might have opted for a native generic pronoun, *he*, but they passed up the opportunity for reasons now lost to history, and various pronunciations with /š/ gradually drifted south from Northern Britain to replace the OE *hēo*. Worth noting is that the female third person pronoun forms were apparently homophonous with the third person plural (Cassidy and Ringler 23), both having the interchangeable forms, *hēo* and *hīe*. Yet, the forms diverged. When the /š/ variant of the female singular pronoun made its appearance, the third person plural forms did not follow but, instead, speakers chose the Scandinavian plurals beginning with /th/.

Linguists regard pronominal systems to be "closed," among the properties of language most resistant to replacement or alteration. Otto Jespersen (1964, 212), for example, remarking that loss and change in personal and demonstrative pronouns are infrequent, said that only extraordinary circumstances could be responsible for the changes in the English pronouns:

> They are so definitely woven into the innermost texture of a language that no one would think of giving them up, however much he might like to adorn his speech with words from a foreign source. If, therefore, in one instance we find a language borrowing words of this kind, we are justified thinking that exceptional causes must have been at work, and such really proves to be the case in English . . .

"Exceptional causes" certainly were at work, but, beyond the obvious impact of Old Norse (ON), we may never identify them. In spite of Jespersen's generally accepted observation, linguists have shown themselves to be singularly unimaginative in their explanations of how *she* came to replace OE *hēo* by the ME period. In her history of English, for example, Barbara Strang (1970, 236) echoed Thomas Pyles, using the same poem as an example, when she "explained" the replacement of *hēo* by *schēo*:

> the distinctions between *he, she* . . . were then, as now, fundamental to the working of the language (when, in one of the best-known ME love-poems, the lover says of his lady "He may me blisse bringe," the danger of misunderstanding is evident).

"Misunderstanding"? Did English speakers adopt *she* because they were afraid others might think them "queer"? Pyles himself, writing earlier, was explicit about the "distinctions" (1964; 1971, 171) that Strang described as "fundamental to the language":

> The feminine pronoun had a variety of subject forms, one of them identical with the corresponding masculine form—certainly a well-nigh intolerable state of affairs, forcing the lovesick author of the lyric "Alysoun" to refer to his sweetheart as *he*, the same form she would have used in referring to him.

How the poem "Alysoun" has come to exemplify "a well-nigh intolerable state of affairs" for contemporary linguists is as inexplicable as the linguistic change it purports to explain. Had *hēo* merged phonologically with *he* in ME, as it undoubtedly would have, ModE would have a generic third person singular pronoun.[2] But it didn't and we don't.

The third language that influenced the development of English was Norman French. While the Danes were settling in Britain, other Northmen occupied the district of France called Normandy, quickly adapting themselves to French culture and its language. In 1066, around the beginning of the Middle English period, the king of England, Edward the Confessor, died without a successor, and Harold, the son of the West Saxon earl Godwin, was elected king. Harold, it seems, had previously promised William, the Duke of Normandy and a second cousin to Edward, not to seek the kingship or oppose William's election, but was disinclined to honor his pledge when the time came. As a result of Harold's duplicity, William of Orange, the Duke of Normandy, invaded Britain, defeated Harold, and Norman French became the language of commerce, government, and religion in Britain; the three terms themselves, *commerce, religion, government*, were borrowed into English during the period of French occupation.

Historians and linguists alike agree that the Norman Conquest profoundly altered the primarily Germanic culture of Britain. Among the continental fads the Norman French transported to Britain were medieval romances, the rules of courtly love, and the ideal of chivalry. While the nobility were conversing in Norman French, the peasants were eating and swearing in English, which the French perceived as "an uncultivated tongue, the language of a socially inferior class" (Baugh, 138). The monetary value of one's table determined the food one was likely to eat on it and what the food was called. While the Norman French dined on venison, mutton, beef, pork, and veal, the peasants ate deer, sheep, oxen, swine, and calf. Just as our social and economic class affects the kind of food we eat, connections between our class, the way we talk, and social valuations of our dialects have been with us for a long time. Contrary to the often-repeated assertion that changes in English have "always" been initiated by the upper classes (sometimes disguised as the "best authors"), the lower classes controlled the development of English from its beginnings, and for several centuries, without the benefit of linguistic paternalism, if only because they continued to use their Germanic language to discuss their daily needs and preoccupations.

After the Norman Conquest, the status of women, in particular, degenerated. Both Cecily Clark and Elizabeth Williams, in their respective contributions to Christine Fell's *Women in Anglo-Saxon England* (1984, chapters 8 and 9), have argued that it was the Norman Conquest that relegated women to the marginal position we know today and defined our limited social role.

Historical linguists use the Norman Conquest of 1066 to separate the Old and Middle English periods. As is true of every language, ME differed from county to county. Early in the thirteenth century, however, the London dialect of English (East Mercian) began to replace Norman French as the elite language, at least partly due to the rise of the middle class (Baugh, 169–71) and nationalistic fervor (Baugh, 157–58). Of this period, Geoffrey Chaucer (1340–1400), the author of *The Canterbury Tales*, is probably the most familiar literary figure, and his work, written in the London dialect, contributed to the new respectability of English. By the end of the fourteenth century, English was the language generally used in the schools (Baugh, 179), although Latin continued to be the accepted language of scholarship. Up until the end of the renaissance, it was the rules of Latin grammar that schoolboys memorized, as set forth in W. Lily's Latin grammar (prescribed for use in the schools in 1540 by Henry VIII) (Robins, 110), and Cicero and Virgil who were copied for their classical styles.

Cursory as it is, this historical sketch of the history of English and the invasions and influences that shaped the language reveals the intellectual depravity of linguistic purism. What we know as Modern English is a mixture of several different languages (and their dialects), not a linguistic monolith that developed uninterruptedly. When we consider what is involved when we talk about the "assimilation" of two (or more) distinct cultures, the conqueror and the conquered, in combination with the distinctions marked by social class, it becomes clear that there has never been a "pure" dialect of English at any stage in its development. Although English is demonstrably Germanic in its origins and the influence of Scandinavian introduced addi-

tional Germanic elements, both Latin and Norman French contributed vocabulary and sentence structures typical of Romance languages. English is a
mongrel language.

GRAMMAR, STANDARDIZATION,
AND LINGUISTIC PURITY

The preceding sketch of the development of the English language showed
the effects of wars and invasions, typically male preoccupations. From my
discussion, readers may also have realized that, during the Old and Middle
English periods, many speakers of "English" were **bilingual** from birth, using
OE at home and Scandinavian or Norman French for business and trade.[3]

When we consider the activities of reading and writing, the situation must
have been different. Those activities, which remain the defining characteristics of literacy, were privileges reserved to royalty and the religious and
political aristocracies, and, within those groups, we have only some evidence
that a few women managed to learn either. Until the Norman Invasion in
1066, Latin was the most important language, the language in which affairs
of state were conducted; since, with only exceptional instances, men controlled the institutions that governed people's lives, most of the women who
did learn Latin were nuns.

Because Latin was the language of intellectual privilege for so long, the
only grammars that existed were Latin grammars. Grammars, understood as
textbooks in which some uses of language are held up as correct and others
condemned as wrong, ignorant, or illiterate, come into existence only when
some powerful group of speakers decides to screen those who would acquire
privilege. In the seventh and eighth centuries, both Bede and Alcuin produced Latin grammars, and, around 1000, Aelfric wrote one of the first
grammars of Latin directed at English-speaking students. R. H. Robins, in fact,
suggests that, because Aelfric thought his grammar "would be equally suitable as an introduction to (Old) English, . . . it may be taken as setting the
seal on several centuries of Latin-inspired English grammar" (70–71). Monks
(church clerics) devoted their lives and eyesight to painstakingly transcribing
scriptures, word by word, and a few selected (and edited) secular texts such
as the OE epic *Beowulf*. Reading and writing were simply not available to
common folk who had neither the time nor the need for either. They spoke
the language of the poor, Old English. As a result, no grammarians felt
compelled to record the language or to make up rules governing its use. For
several centuries, English (or anglo-saxon) was the language of the peasants,
who chatted and carried on the activities of their lives uninterrupted by
grammatical "dos" and "don'ts" and never had to take spelling tests.

Histories of writing generally attribute the movement to standardize languages, **prescriptivism**, to the European invention of printing[4] from movable

type by Johann Gutenberg (1400?–1468?) (Baugh, 240–41; Robins, 112–13), postulating that the widespread availability of numerous printed materials *required* standardized spellings and grammars, lest dialectal differences interfere with the intelligibility and interpretation of the printed language. In 1476, William Caxton introduced the printing process into England (Baugh, 240–41). Printed materials, ranging from pamphlets to huge folios, were now within the reach of many men, and those new readers increasingly demanded a standard, uniform language. The spellings that represented dialectal pronunciations must have made identifying some words difficult and tedious. As R. H. Robins observed, "The invention of printing made standardized spellings more important, and, in turning attention to the relation between writing and pronunciation, aroused interest, since then perennial, in the problem of spelling reform" (1967, 112–13).

The relationship between the spelling of an English word and its pronunciation has always been problematic and, at times, downright fanciful. In the fourteenth century, for example, *femelle*, from Latin *femella* ('little woman'), borrowed into English from Norman French, had been "standardized" to *female*, by analogy to the word *male*. This "standardization" simultaneously fixed the spelling of *female* **and** made the word look as though it were derived from *male*. (In fact, the two words are not etymologically related.) Here, as in other areas, men's certainty of their innate superiority to women elevated the ridiculous to the status of "fact," and misogyny, masquerading as standardization and "correctness," fabricated an etymology to justify a whimsical spelling.

The demand for identifying the "correct" spelling of words opened the way for the first "grammars" of English, which began to appear during the seventeenth century. At first, they were hardly more than lists of "difficult" latinate words (Baugh, 279–80), but the errors and distortions still taught in public schools were gradually introduced by self-styled grammarians for whom the analysis of English was a diverting avocation. Baugh, always a restrained scholar, said of those early grammarians: "Most of these books were the work of men with no special qualifications for the thing they attempted to do" (331).

Grammarians, like other writers, need an audience and a market. The audience in this case consisted of those who had the leisure and the money that literacy requires: upper-class, aristocratic men. The illiterate, most women and poor men, incapable of reading or writing, had no use for the rules of linguistic etiquette. Prior to this, dialect differences apparently hadn't impeded communication; only some men, and fewer women, were allowed the luxury of education and with it, reading and writing. There wasn't much to read, after all, aside from the bible, and reading that required a knowledge of Hebrew and Greek, as well as Latin. As Chaucer's dialect (East Mercian) grew in importance, men felt that it had to be made "respectable," particularly in its written representation. The accessibility of printed materials, combined with other social changes—the recently acquired respectability of the English language, the rise of the middle class, and nationalism—created a market for the Latin-based grammars written in the early modern period and the standardizations they advocated. International rivalries and nationalism determined that the language had to be protected from "bastardization," so several generations of self-elected "experts" set themselves the task of establishing the rules that would perpetuate their ideas about linguistic purity. From the beginning, grammars of English were written **by** men for a predominantly male audience.

The tradition of English grammar began with descriptions that were inherently inaccurate and distorting (they could not be otherwise), and its confused development has left a legacy that school boards and publishers are unwilling to discard. They have too much money invested in error. That prescriptive grammar has managed to sustain its credibility for so long testifies to the efficacy of persistence and repetition. The modern "back to the basics" movement is only the most recent voice of this pernicious legacy from the past.

The reverence for things classical typical of the renaissance[5] permanently distorted our ideas of what English is or might have been like. As Robins observed: "Men started with the framework handed down from the late Latin grammarians and suggested by Aelfric as suitable for Old English as well as for Latin" (119). That the Early ModE Latin-based grammars purported to describe and elucidate had changed significantly during the eight centuries separating it from OE failed to deter most of those early English grammarians. As a result, in spite of occasional protests, Latin-based grammars and their inadequacies became the standard texts for describing English by the nineteenth century, and their influence has continued, without disruption, through this century.

With notable exceptions such as the *Grammatica Linguae Anglicanae* (1653) by John Wallis and William Loughton's *Practical Grammar of the English Tongue* (1734), early grammars of English generally began with the eight "parts of speech." The idea of dividing the vocabulary of a language into "parts" of speech originated with Greek grammarians, Dionysius Thrax (c. 100 B.C.) and Apollonius Dyscolus (Alexandria, second century A.D.; Robins, 30), and were applied by the Roman grammarian Priscian (c. 500 A.D.) to Latin (Robins, 54). In his sixteenth-century Latin grammar, W. Lily took those "parts of speech" from classical Latin grammars and imposed them on English structures without the benefit of critical thought (Robins, 110).

There was a struggle, though, and some challenged the imposition of Latin and Greek categories onto the structure of English. Loughton, for example, decried those who "attempted to force our Language (contrary to its Nature) to the Method and Rules of the Latin Grammar," and refused to use terms borrowed from Latin grammars, such as *noun, verb, adjective* (Baugh, 330).[6] Unfortunately, the voices of dissenters like Loughton and Wallis were submerged by the appeal of English grammars based on Latin, and classical imitators like Lily triumphed.

The grammatical tradition derived from Latin and Greek generated much confusion and introduced numerous idiocies to the study of English. Those early grammars imposed upon the language and its speakers "rules" that had little to do with the structure of English, borrowed, often without qualification or modification, from grammars of the classical languages.[7] English was forced to "fit" into the categories established first for Greek and then Latin, according to the individual grammarian's notions of linguistic "logic." Some grammarians couldn't figure out what to call the English class of articles (or determiners), *a(n)* and *the*, because they weren't in Priscian's Latin grammar (Latin didn't have articles). When Bullokar (*Bref grammar for English*, 1586) classified English words according to the Latin system of categories, he mentioned the articles only as "identifying adjuncts" of nouns. Others, like Ben Jonson's *The English grammar* (1640), did assign them to a distinct class (Robins, 119–20). The rule forbidding us to "split" our infinitives, *to* + verb (*to eat, to dream*), was introduced because one cannot "split" infinitives in Greek or Latin. It's an impossibility. In English, it's not only possible, but often necessary to neatly split one's infinitives. We "split" infinitives in English because we can.

Rather than list and describe every one of the linguistic inaccuracies perpetrated by the imposition of Latin rules onto the English language, a discussion that concentrates on one area of grammar will better demonstrate the lack of fit between language and grammar fostered by linguistic prescriptivism. Of the subjects that suggest themselves, the description of tense in English—how many there are, and how the tense of a verb specifies the time of an act in the "real world"—specifically with reference to the function of the English **modal** verbs, exemplifies how far removed from linguistic reality the prescriptive grammars of patriarchy are.

If we examine the rules for tense formulated by prescriptive grammarians and compare them to what we know intuitively about English (reflected in our usage), the more puzzling the longevity of those rules becomes. Consider, for example, the claim that English has three tenses: present, past, and future. A glance at the ways tense is marked in English suggests that this assertion, borrowed from Latin grammars, is suspect. First, we add to or change verbs in identifiable ways only for the present and past tenses in English. We indicate the present with the suffix *-s*, but only in the third person singular (*sits, eats, drinks*), so that it is more accurate to say that no ending is added to the verb for the present tense (except in the third person singular), while the past is marked by the suffix *-ed* and various vowel changes in the so-called irregular verbs (*drink > drank, sing > sang*). The "future" tense, however, is said to be marked by two model verbs, *shall* in the first persons singular and plural (*I shall, we shall*) and *will* in the second and third persons (*you will, they will*). The future "tense" of the prescriptive grammarians is signalled by two modals that are separate words from the main verb, which suggests that what is traditionally called the "future" in English is something other than tense, a more complicated feature of the language altogether.

If we stop to think about it, we realize that **every** modal (the so-called helping verbs) refers to some future, hypothetical action, not just *shall* and *will*, and the discrepancy between what we know and what we've been taught about tense in English becomes clearer. You may recall being told that *shall* is the "correct" form of the future "tense" for first person subjects and that *will* is to be used only with the second and third persons. According to this rule, saying "I will" is "ungrammatical," even though we say it all the time. In fact, we aren't violating English structure; it is the prescriptive rule that is in violation. Prior to 1622, **no** English grammar mentioned a distinction between *shall* and *will*, because there wasn't one. It wasn't until 1653 that Wallis stated the "rule" still taught in schools in his *Grammatica Angli-canae* (Baugh, 337). This particular prescription was given its final formulation, the one still included in contemporary textbooks, by William Ward in his *Grammar of the English Language* (1765), although Ward's rules didn't gain currency until Lindley Murray copied them in his 1795 grammar.

In order to grasp the inaccuracy of prescriptive descriptions of tense, consider the "past" forms of *will* and *shall*. (I'll return to the problems of describing the so-called future shortly.) Used in either a declarative sentence or a question, both *would* and *should* stipulate that the action of the verb occurs in some hypothetical future beyond the present context of the utterance in which they appear.

1.1 a. I *would* go to a movie.
    b. *Would* I go to a movie?
1.2 a. I *should* go to a movie.
    b. *Should* I go to a movie?

In the statements, 1.1.a. and 1.2.a., *would* and *should* both indicate that the act of going to a movie isn't likely to happen, but they differ in the degree of control the speaker implies with respect to the event. *Would* indicates that external factors will affect the speaker's decision; *should* suggests that internal or external pressure is compelling a decision one way or the other. In questions, however, these modals are contrastive: *would* repeats a previously asked question as if to clarify or confirm the speaker's understanding of it; *should* requests that someone other than the speaker offer pros and cons about a possible decision.

In spite of differences in meaning, other modal verbs have the same temporal range as *will/would* and *shall/should*, placing the verb's action in a time to come after the utterance in which they occur. *Can/could, may/might, must*, and the semi-modals, *ought to* (in ME the past form of *owe*), *want to, have to, got to*, and *need to*, indicate that the action of the verb with which they are used is cast in the future, as the following examples illustrate.

1.3 a. I *will*
 b. I *would*
 c. I *shall*
 d. I *should*
 e. I *can*
 f. I *could*   eat pizza for supper.
 g. I *may*
 h. I *might*
 i. I *must*
 j. I *ought to*

The modal and semi-modal verbs all point to an unspecified future time beyond the time of the utterance in which they occur. (From this point on, the semi-modals will be spelled *oughta, hafta, wanta, gotta*, and *needta* to represent the way speakers pronounce them in rapid speech.)[8]

The meaning differences observable among the modals in 1.3 have nothing to do with "tense" or "time," and do not affect the use of these verbs to indicate futurity. Note that I have limited the "subject" of all the example sentences to "I" to show that *will, shall, can, may* (so-called present tense forms), and *would, might*, and *could* (the "past" forms) all indicate that the first person speaker has control (volition) over the action designated by the verb (in [1.1] and [1.2] *go*, in [1.3] *eat*). *Should, must*, and *oughta* are ambiguous with respect to control. The four modals differ in the way they signal the probability that the event will occur. *Will, shall*, and *must* tell us that there is a 99% likelihood (barring unforeseen circumstances) that the speaker is going to eat pizza, whereas *can, may, would, should, could, might*, and *oughta* indicate probability determined by factors known only to the speaker. Adding explanatory clauses will illustrate this conditionality in *can, may*, and *could*:

1.4 a. I *can* eat pizza
     { when I leave work / if I want to / till the cows come home } .

     b. I *may* eat pizza
     { when I leave work / if I want to / till the cows come home } .

     c. I *could* eat pizza
     { when I leave work / if I want to / till the cows come home } .

Each modal specifies the strength either of the speaker's volition or the external pressure to act, and a range of probability that the action described by a verb will occur. In English, modals like *must, should, oughta*, and *hafta* are ambiguous with respect to whether the impulse to act originates with the agent of the verb or external factors. When someone says, "I *must/hafta* eat pizza tonight," only additional information tells us whether the modal of obligation is used because of the speaker's desire or some external pressure. With *must* and *hafta*, perhaps the speaker's craving for pizza is so intense that nothing else will satisfy her at the time, or pizza could be the only thing available to her on that particular evening. Likewise, *should* and *oughta* are moot regarding the source of the articulated necessity to eat pizza. If someone says "I *should/oughta* eat pizza tonight," the determining factor might be that the speaker knows that pizza is the best thing for her to eat (internal) or that a friend she's having dinner with expects to eat pizza (external) and will be angry if her expectations aren't met.

Two of the semi-modals excluded from prescriptive grammars of English exemplify the semantic contrast of internal volition versus external pressure to act: *wanta* and *needta*. *Wanta* signifies the speaker's **desire** to do something, and is not ambiguous; whatever the specific action is, the speaker indicates that she wishes to do it. *Needta*, in contrast, is ambiguous with respect to whether the speaker is indicating internal will or external pressure to act. Unless she makes clear to us that the origins of the hypothetical act are internally or externally motivated, we have no way of identifying the impulse's source for ourselves. We may *wanta* win a trip to New Orleans, but there is no internal or external necessity that we *must, should*, or *oughta* do so. We may *needta* buy groceries, but the source of our expressed urgency can be internal or external. Whether we say we **want** or **need** to perform some act, the modals indicate only the **likelihood** that we will act.

Wanta and *needta* represent the semantic tension between individual control and external pressure to act. Each of the English modals can be imagined as occupying some semantic location along two axes: AGENT ABILITY (the degree of control the individual has over whether an act will or won't occur) versus FORCE OF CONTINGENCY (the extent of control held by external events or individuals) and DEGREE OF PROBABILITY. The perceived relationship between the speaker's will to act and the extent to which contingencies will affect the probability that an act will occur determine which modal verb we choose. I've diagrammed the positions of the modals with respect to these two axes in Figure 1.1: DEGREE OF PROBABILITY (0% to 100%) is the horizontal axis; AGENT ABILITY (internal) versus FORCE OF CONTINGENCY (external control) is the vertical axis.

My diagram represents the underlying semantic parameters that determine our choice of a modal verb as speakers, and how, as listeners, we interpret their use. The modals provide us with ways of hedging our bets. If

DEGREE OF PROBABILITY

0%	50%	100%
oughta		must
should		hafta
would	needta	gotta
may/might		
could		gonna
wanta	can	will/shall

(vertical axis label: AGENT ABILITY ~ FORCE OF CONTINGENCY)

FIGURE 1.1[10]

we look at the four modals at the extremes of Figure 1.1, *oughta, must, wanta,* and *will/shall,* and their placement with respect to the horizontal and vertical axes, AGENT ABILITY (Internal)~FORCE OF CONTINGENCY (External) and DEGREE OF PROBABILITY, our reasons for choosing one rather than another is clearly a function of the degree of commitment or obligation combined with other variables—explicit or implicit—when we speak.

Oughta and *must* are at the top of the diagram because both indicate that external factors weigh greatly in determining whether an action will or will not occur. They differ in meaning because *must* means that the action will probably occur because it's obligatory, whereas *oughta* implies that the speaker acknowledges the pressure to perform the action but may, in fact, not do it. *Oughta* and *must* contrast in meaning with *wanta* and *will/shall,* respectively, in terms of the speaker's control or desire to act. *Wanta* indicates that the speaker would like to carry out the act but may not, while *oughta* suggests that the speaker isn't personally committed to acting but feels obliged to. *Must* and *will/shall* contrast in the same way, but differ in the probability they describe. If I were betting on the likelihood that a speaker would act, I'd bet on someone who said *will, shall,* or *must. Oughta, wanta,* and *may/might, could, would, needta,* and *should* as well, are deliberate **hedges** that speakers use to give themselves latitude with respect to acting.

The modal *can* is different from the other modals. It is the most "neutral" verb within the parameters represented in Figure 1.1. Speakers use *can* when they have the ability to act in some conceivable future, but won't specify the likelihood of acting. Being able to do something, saying, "I *can* do that," doesn't mean that one will, yet the assertion of capability can be interpreted as placing the probability somewhere above 0% but far below 100%.

Other speakers may find that their own interpretations differ from my own. Other factors determine how we interpret English modals, especially our intonation and whether we use a modal in its full form or contracted, for example, *will/'ll, could, would/'d*. *Would* and *could* become indistinguishable in their contracted forms, for example, "I'd've" is ambiguous as to whether it was the speaker's ability or desire to do something. (Note that *must* cannot be contracted.) Certainly, our interpretations are affected by whether the modal occurs in a statement or a question, and the person (first, second, third) who appears as the **agent**. For a speaker to say to another individual, "You *wanta* diet," as a direct assertion clearly violates the boundaries of the addressee's volition, and constitutes verbal aggression, unless the accompanying intonation pattern indicates that the utterance is intended as a question, in which case it can be interpreted as a statement of disbelief or a request for confirmation.[11] Using *will* or *must* in a statement with a second or third person agent constitutes a claim of authority, either as having the power to control someone else's behavior or certainty based on prior knowledge or information outside of the immediate context. If I say, "You will eat pizza tonight" or "You'll eat pizza tonight," I'm either informing my hearer that she has no choice in the matter or I'm making a prediction. "She *will* eat pizza tonight" implies that the speaker has the power to make her eat pizza, whereas "She'll eat pizza tonight" sounds more like a prediction. The contracted form of the modal may imply less power on the part of the speaker, but again, intonation indicates the extent to which the speaker is asserting control over a third party.

The preceding discussion illustrates the complexities of the modal system in English and the inadequacies of patriarchal descriptions of how we signal "future" time. The prescriptive grammarians thought that English "ought to" have a "future tense" only because Latin and Greek did. Since English specifies future time semantically, no grammar that imitates classical models is adequate. Isolating *shall* and *will* as the "future tense" doesn't begin to describe the subtleties of modal verbs, and this discussion suggests that the alleged one-to-one correlation between the tense (present, past, future) of a verb and time (in the world) will not withstand scrutiny. None of the "past tense" forms of the modals has anything to do with time prior to an utterance; each one refers to some time to come after the utterance in question.[12]

Yet, English teachers persist in telling us that the "present" tense is used to describe "present time," and we memorize the rules they force on us even though we **know** that what is called the "present tense" is actually used in a continuative sense to describe behaviors that are habitual and engaged in consistently over time, for example, "I **eat** cereal," "She **looks** for trouble." We consent to perpetuating this lie, but we actually use what is called the "progressive **aspect**" (*be* + Verb-*ing*) when we describe an activity occurring in the present, for example, "I **am eating** cereal," "She **is looking** for trouble."

The progressive aspect, not the present tense, marks an action as taking place **at this moment**. The present tense, in fact, is rarely used, with the exceptions of stage directions ("Crowd **exits** right") and the examples contrived for grammar books.

My brief histories of the English language and the Latin-based grammars written to fix its usage illustrate how thoroughly men have controlled not only specific elements of the development of English structure but the way we understand its structure as well. Patriarchal grammars justify descriptions of language as men would have it. Male ideas about English (and language in general), passed from generation to generation as "The Rules," when examined critically, turn out to be as dubious as the "received wisdom" about women we hear every day. The longevity of both false descriptions (of English, of women) is no accident, of course, because men perceive language and women as unruly objects they must tame and control.

Chapter 2

Language Is a Woman

Historically, men have controlled the English language and its use in much the same way they have dictated the rules and roles they expect women to live by. Upper-class, white men decreed that English, like women, must be "pure," unsullied by the speech of other men, those they keep illiterate, and they endeavored to protect English against the violations of those "out to do her wrong." Like the cars and boats that men possess, English is referred to as if it were female—the "mother tongue." Men will tolerate only **proper women** and **proper English**. Linguistic deviance, like social deviance, must be suppressed or forced into conformity. What men deem unspeakable must also be unthinkable. In PUD, LANGUAGE IS A WOMAN.

We must understand that the connection between **proper women** and **proper English** isn't a historical "accident." It's one of the crucial connections inherent in the logic of patriarchal thinking. Just as men have asserted that their descriptions and idealizations of women are accurate, so they have made their descriptions of English seem plausible, even valid. If a language isn't pure, it is described as "bastardized," one that has been "debased" or "corrupted." Just as men claim that women need protection from their predation,[1] so they claim to "protect" English from the predations of their "inferiors"—the poor, non-native speakers of English, and women.

In our efforts to gain some measure of control over our lives, women have gone along with perpetuating men's absurd descriptions of English and the rules that keep everyone but white men powerless and invisible. But we can choose, as a class; we can refuse to cooperate with men in the project of maintaining their economic and political dominance. We can stop pretending that we see the nonexistent finery of prescriptive grammars and say "no" to the doctrine of "correctness." Why do we help to sustain this farce, nodding and waving, cheering the emperor's nonexistent clothes, when we

16

know they don't exist? We must challenge the myths that control our lives and break the linguistic habits that signal our compliance.

One starting place is to free our tongues, our minds, and our thinking from bondage to the idea of linguistic "purity." Women, especially white women, must forego the strokes we receive for "talking right" and let go of our prowess with men's rules of linguistic etiqette. Being good at following grammatical rules formulated by men has gotten us nowhere.

The construction of grammars and grammatical speculations in the west have been male-only enterprises from the beginning, studies dominated by philosophers concerned with rhetoric, on the one hand, and ethics, on the other. Although ethics and rhetoric have clearly parted company, a phenomenon particularly evident in the proliferation of distorted and dishonest communications in the u.s., the writing of English grammars has remained a male domain, in particular upper-class men. If women refuse to go along with the patriarchal linguistic agenda and expose how white men benefit from prescriptivism, we will destroy a crucial support of patriarchal culture: the lie of linguistic purity.

THE PROTECTION RACKET:
PURE IN WORD

The English have habitually taken their cultural cues from their European neighbors, particularly France and Italy, and the movement to purify and standardize the language was no different. Both countries had already established academies charged with keeping their languages pure and the learned men of England weren't going to sit by while rival nations purged their languages of foreign influence and decided rules of correctness that would forever protect their linguistic identities from the corruption of the dialects of the poor and lower classes. Italy, for example, established several academies, but the best-known was the Accademia della Crusca, founded in 1582, which published a controversial dictionary of the Italian language in 1612. The fourth edition of that dictionary (1729–1738) filled six folio volumes (Baugh, 316).

In 1635, Cardinal Richelieu founded the Académie Française. The statutes which defined its purpose were explicit: "The principal function of the Academy shall be to labor with all possible care and diligence to give definite rules to our language, and to render it pure, eloquent, and capable of treating the arts and sciences" (Baugh, 317). As part of its effort to cleanse French, the Academy was charged with the preparation of a dictionary, which finally appeared in 1694.

The English were slow to follow suit, but not to be outdone, and literary men, among them John Dryden and Daniel Defoe, clamored for an English Academy. The Royal Society, founded in 1662 to encourage scientific interest, resolved in 1664 to establish a committee to "improve" the English language, but its 22 members apparently met only three or four times (Baugh, 318–19). In 1712, the Irish satirist Jonathan Swift (who also said, "I never knew a tolerable woman to be fond of her own sex")[2] was the first to announce "the ideal of grammatical correctness" in a letter written to the Earl of Oxford (Baugh, 320–21).

While I don't know what kinds of women Swift might have found "tolerable," his commitment to misogyny (woman-hating) and linguistic purity wasn't coincidental. For 400 years male grammarians have dedicated themselves to maintaining his prejudices. As an American grammarian, Henry Froude, declared in 1906, concerning feminists' protests against *he* as a "generic" pronoun, "[W]e [men] shall probably persist in refusing women their due here as stubbornly as Englishmen continue to offend the Scots by saying *England* instead of *Britain*. . . . " (*The King's English*, 2nd ed., 67).

In spite of the support of figures like Dryden and Defoe, resistance to an academy of English grew, and Swift's dream languished unfulfilled. One of the prominent resisters was Dr. Samuel Johnson, whose *Dictionary*, when it finally appeared, stood as the English substitute for an academy. About the French and Italian Academies, Johnson had this to say in the Preface to his *Dictionary* (1755):

> With this hope, however, academies have been instituted, to guard the avenues of their languages, to retain fugitives, and repulse intruders; but their vigilance and activity have hitherto been vain; sounds are too volatile and subtle for legal restraints; to enchain syllables, and to lash the wind, are equally the undertakings of pride, unwilling to measure its desires by its strength. The French language has visibly changed under the inspection of the academy . . . and no Italian will maintain, that the diction of any modern writer is not perceptibly different from that of Boccace, Machiavel, or Caro. (239)

Unfortunately, such wisdom is too easily ignored. Ignorance rules the man-made world. In spite of Johnson's eloquently phrased observations on the nature of language and the wind, his less-intelligent compatriots persisted in their efforts to purify English, perpetuating the myth of Standard English, and hope for the establishment of a watchdog academy has never died. What we are taught as Standard English is a dialect created and developed to keep English "pure."

Johnson's insight was accurate: grammarians and meteorologists have a lot in common. The first group makes up rules to coerce Standard English from our lips (and writing implements); the second seeds clouds to force rain to fall from them. Their efforts accomplish nothing beneficial. The idea of "linguistic purity" requires us to believe at least two impossible things:

1. that a language exists, at some point in its history, in a genetically untainted form, some version in which no hint of "foreign" influence has intruded;

2. that a language can be stopped from changing, that its "purity" can resist internal and external pressures to change.

Linguistic purists are opposed to a process which is inevitable in language change. Baugh, a thorough chronicler of the history of English, attributed the mistakes of the early grammarians to "their ignorance of the processes of linguistic change," noting that "[t]he historical study of English was still in its infancy" (1957, 344) when men wrote their first grammars, but their latter-day emulators have no such justification. Those who espouse linguistic elitism can obstruct and slow down the process, but **languages change**. The question, removed from the focus of male grammarians, should be "Whose changes will prevail?"

Linguistic "purity" is the intellectual colleague of class and racial "purity." This is apparently true regardless of the specific western language under consideration. L. R. Palmer, commenting on the history of Latin, observed:

> Finally we shall be faced with another phenomenon of constant occurrence: the centralization of government in organized states, the domination of a certain class, the prestige enjoyed by its social habits, of which not the least important is its mode of speech, result in the growth and imposition of a standard language. (1954, 119)

Although Palmer didn't challenge the underlying political processes by which governments are "centralized" and "a certain class" comes to "dominate," he stated the power relationship between social classes and why the literate classes enforce a standardized language. Most telling is his failure to recognize that "growth" and "imposition" don't necessarily follow one from the other, even as he draws the distinction for us. "Growth" implies a "natural" process, uninterrupted and unmediated by social factors, but "imposition" makes explicit the fact that dominant classes use their power to force just those changes that serve their political goals. Just as the members of ruling classes bar the socially "undesirable" from their ranks, and racists strive to prevent their blood from mixing with that of groups they perceive themselves as being "superior" to, so the ideal of linguistic purity is said to protect a language from polluting elements acquired from a variety of sources.

English, however, is not immune to the social and political forces that set changes in motion, regardless of how strenuously the elite oppose those changes. Still, white men persist in their efforts to promote Standard English as a "pure" dialect, prestigious because its "correctness" maintains its purity against the constant onslaught of the barbaric, illiterate, unwashed masses—the rest of us. They never stop. Douglas Bush, for example, took up the defense of purity in the Phi Beta Kappa journal, *The American Scholar* (1972, 41). Conceding that linguists are correct in their assertions that languages change continually, he stubbornly persisted in maintaining linguistic elitism:

"[A]ccceptance of the perpetual process [of language change] does not or should not mean blind [sic] surrender to the momentum or inertia of slovenly and tasteless ignorance and insensitivity." "Insensitivity" to what? "[T]asteless ignorance?" Does this mean, as Bush's phrase implies, that ignorance is supportable just as long as it's **tasteful**? Apparently so, for he proceeds to assert that linguistic changes "should be inaugurated from above, by the masters of language (as they [changes] often have been), not from below" (244). The "masters of language," of course, are "masters of all they survey," and their power over language is maintained in exactly the same way they retain power in every other social sphere: omission, mystification, distortion, and deception. The ridiculous idea of linguistic "purity" justifies the perpetuation of a prescriptive system of grammatical nonsense, and that accomplished tradition of illogical fabrication points to the linguistic frippery of Standard English as though it existed.

The idea of "gender" is only one among many such fabrications, but it is an essential element of the heterosexualization of grammar. I will return to the topic in greater detail in a separate chapter, but here I will illustrate how gender has been forced on English nouns to justify male domination in the language. The misnomer "gender," as a label for systems of noun classification, is among the most contorted constructions in which misogyny and prescriptivism cooperate to befuddle and mislead us. Significantly, whatever rules men come up with to justify their ungainly creation never work, yet they will go to inordinate lengths trying to explain away every one of the many "exceptions" that betray the lack of correspondence between what they want us to believe about English (and other languages) and the structural properties "gender" purports to explain. As is usually their habit, the men who imposed the rules of Latin onto English were most eloquent when it came to rationalizing the distinction of gender and explaining its perfection.

Lindley Murray, perhaps as responsible as a single grammarian can be for the rules still being taught to children in the schools, formulated the description of gender and English nouns that remains a staple in grammar books:

> Figuratively, in the English tongue, we commonly give the masculine gender to nouns which are conspicuous for the attributes of imparting or communicating, and which are by nature strong and efficacious. Those, again, are made feminine which are conspicuous for the attributes of containing or bringing forth, or which are peculiarly beautiful or amiable. Upon these principles the sun is always masculine, and the moon, because the receptacle of the sun's light, is feminine. The earth is generally feminine. A ship, a country, a city, &c. are likewise made feminine, being receivers or containers. (1795, 24)

Murray, however, was neither creative nor innovative in his formulation. Although his is the version still echoed by purists today, he was merely elaborating the ideas of his predecessors. The writing of grammars and the making of dictionaries, both, are histories of plagiarism and its rewards. It was

James Beattie, in 1788, who placed the classification of English nouns in the religious context in which it was to be understood, thereby imposing xtian values on a system considerably older than the xtian religion and the language he claimed to describe.

> Beings superiour to man, although we conceive them to be of no sex, are spoken of as masculine in most of the modern tongues of Europe, on account of their dignity; the male being, according to our ideas, the nobler sex. But idolatrous nations acknowledge both male and female deities; and some of them have given even to the Supreme Being a name of the feminine gender. (*The Theory of Language*, 137)

English, we are to understand, is as "god" would have it, and **he** is the ultimate patriarchal authority. At this stage in the construction of grammars, the patriarchal view of women, in language as well as in society, could be stated without apparent embarrassment, as though it were self-evident: Because men believe they are the "nobler sex," the "god" they created must be male; because "god" made women to be receptacles or containers for male ejaculations, the nouns men conceive to be receptacle-like must belong to the "feminine gender." Oddly, a majority of contemporary speakers seem to experience little or no discomfort with the spiritual elevation of maleness and show no awareness that such selectivity requires justification. More credulous future generations remain satisfied with the standard assertion, "That's how it's always been."

To some, my explanation of how patriarchal grammarians have imposed their lies about English and their distortions of its structure on native speakers during past centuries may seem a strident attack on the innocuous claims of well-intentioned "scholars." After all, one might say, "No harm is done." One might think that being forced to learn arbitrary rules that contradict one's intuitions about English (or French or Italian) is harmless enough, or argue that the discipline involved in memorizing falsehoods is "good for the soul" and "builds character." We have a plethora of clichés for expressing such opinions, and there's a reason: for millions of European women, their paths to the stake were laid out and justified with righteous platitudes. What one man said, generations have repeated.

In citing Jonathan Swift earlier, I indicated that his desire for an English Academy and his misogyny weren't simply an idiosyncratic, intellectual kink. It is no accident that, during the centuries when xtianity was strengthening its political hegemony in England and Europe, men were establishing their control of the then-prominent European languages, English, Italian, French, Spanish. Separating the male urge to dominate women from their persistence in trying to freeze language, as their histories do, would obscure the "logic" of their compulsion to "purify" and "tame" both. The chronological overlap of the "renaissance" and the Inquisition are too close.

THE PROTECTION RACKET:
PURE IN DEED

Patriarchal historians commonly discuss the renaissance (from the French, 'rebirth') and the witch hunts in Europe as distinct and unrelated processes. One, they say, marked a significant stage in the development of western civilization, the other they dismiss as an unfortunate aberration.

The renaissance period lasted from the middle of the fourteenth century, 1350, to the end of the sixteenth. It is usually represented as a "good thing," a "rebirth" of classical art, literature, and learning, and contrasted with the alleged backwardness of the Middle Ages. Male scholars describe the characteristics they attribute to that era with enthusiasm:

> [These include] . . . the growth of individualism in private as well as public life, the expansion of scientific and philosophical horizons, the creation of new social, political, and economic institutions, and the arrival of a new view of man and his world [sic!]. (Benét, 1965, 849)

What isn't obvious is the identity of those who benefitted from the metaphorical rebirth celebrated in the above passage. For it was, of course, white male individualism that waxed and flourished; it was the "horizons" of white male philosophers and scientists that expanded, and it was surely white men who "created" the social, political, and economic institutions that elaborated and justified the limited place allotted to women in that "new [read: "old"] view" of (white) man's world. Before they could "expand" their horizons and create "new" institutions though, they had to subdue and control those who opposed them. While scientists sought ways of controlling nature, the xtian brotherhood sought to tame women. In *The Death of Nature* (1980), Carolyn Merchant connected the "new science" of the renaissance with the witch burnings:

> The images of both nature and woman were two-sided. The virgin nymph offered peace and serenity, the earth mother nurture and fertility, but nature also brought plagues, famines, and tempests. Similarly, woman was both virgin and witch: the Renaissance courtly lover placed her on a pedestal; the inquisitor burned her at the stake. The witch, symbol of the violence of nature, raised storms, caused illness, destroyed crops, obstructed generation, and killed infants. Disorderly woman, like chaotic nature, needed to be controlled. (127)

Men were determined to control women. They would subdue or obliterate us. Still unknown numbers of women were tortured, raped, and burned at the stake. Because they were female; because they were, according to the "wise men," wild, impure, carnal, and defiant of male authority. Male scholars did debate whether or not a language could be pure, but there was no doubt about the impurity and inherent baseness of women. Unlike linguistic purity, the innate "impurity" men attributed to women wasn't debatable; it was a non-question.

Only 100 years into the renaissance, the European witch hunts intensified in their scope and brutality; the burning of women for "witchcraft" accelerated during the fifteenth century, and continued through the reformation in the sixteenth century (when protestant sects separated from the roman catholic church), and lasted well into the age of "reason," c. 1450–1750. For 300 years, no woman was safe. Every woman was at the mercy of anyone who hated, envied, or distrusted her. Yet, if it is mentioned at all, the Burning Time is treated by patriarchal historians as an aberration, an infamous event for which apologies and explanations may be in order, but an aberration nonetheless.

An accident of converging historical processes? No. The "new view of man and **his** world" was founded in the bone-strewn ashes that had been living women. The struggle between the Old Religion of the Indo-Europeans and xtianity began when roman catholics undertook to impose their religion on the known world, erupting into one of the bloodiest and most brutal periods of spiritual and intellectual colonization. To eliminate the female threat to their domination, the secular and religious "humanists" formed a malicious alliance. Until the religious and political organzations in which women were powerful were subdued and controlled, the "new view," in which white men extended their domination of the planet, could not proceed without challenge. What men still call western "civilization" could no longer tolerate even the remnants of a gynecentric past.

What men call "rebirth" women know as the Burning Time; both are part of the same movement to establish patriarchal culture as the only viable civilization in the west, to enshrine, once and for all, male perceptions as "reality," to suppress or erase any other ideology that contradicts or challenges the descriptions of the world fashioned by the male mentality. For 300 years, the towns and villages of Europe were the battleground on which women fought the imposition of the patriarchal version of "ultimate" reality and died to uphold the integrity of our perceptions and knowledge.

There can be no doubt that the Burning Time was the scandalous evidence of the xtian patriarchy's determination to conquer the world and erase every individual who would not bow to its authority. Just as men were establishing themselves as "experts" on language and making themselves guardians of its "purity," so the churchmen set about consolidating their secular power. In order to accomplish their aims, they had to exorcise the power of women, the "witchcraft" to which the peasants of Europe clung tenaciously. The Inquisition began.

The *Malleus Maleficarum* (*Hammer of Witches* [literally 'evil ones']; hereafter *MM*), written by Heinrich Kramer and James Sprenger, two German Dominicans delegated as inquisitors in the 1484 bull of Pope Innocent VIII, was the single most important text of the Inquisition, for it established and circulated the view of women as inherently evil that still predominates in xtian patriarchies. In the 1928 Introduction to his translation of the *MM*, Montague Summers boasted that the work of Kramer and Sprenger "was continually quoted and appealed to in the witch-trials of Germany, France, Italy, and England. . . . " (xxxviii–xxxix). 1486 is the likeliest year of its first publication; between 1487 and 1520, there were 14 editions of the book, and at least another 16 editions between 1574 and 1669 (1948 Introduction, vii–viii).

In his unqualified praise for the Inquisition, its methods, and the millions of deaths it rationalized, Summers admitted that what Kramer and Sprenger identified as "witchcraft" was "inextricably mixed with politics" (1948 Introduction, iv), and the witches themselves "a vast political movement, an organized society which was anti-social and anarchical, a world-wide plot against civilization" (xviii).

Summers' list of the witches' goals confirms that at least some of those unfortunate women died for what they believed in and were committed to accomplishing: overthrowing the patriarchal order, erasing the inheritance laws that mandated first sons as entitled to inherit goods and property, abolishing the institution of marriage that enslaved women and made them the property of men, and defeating the xtian religion that had stolen first their rituals and observances and converted them to its own uses, then had taken their lands, and, finally, had destroyed their cultures. "It was against this that the Inquisition had to fight," Summers solemnly counseled his readers. Lest any of them remember the gory details, he was ready with a disingenuous response:

> [W]ho can be surprised if, when faced with so vast a conspiracy, the methods employed by the Holy Office may not seem—if the terrible conditions are conveniently forgotten—a little drastic, a little severe? (1928 Introduction, xviii)

For their "heresy," those who refused to acknowledge xtian authority were beaten, raped, tortured, publicly humiliated, dismembered, and burned at the stake. "A little drastic"? "A little severe"?

That the Burning Time was a class struggle is beyond doubt. As Summers admits, most of the "Masters" of witchcraft may have been men, but those burned at the stake were the most vulnerable, the powerless, the majority probably women (xviii). Nine million women, according to some accounts. Men, as well as women were murdered, for among the "most vulnerable" were certainly the poor and the illiterate—those who were stigmatized because of their dialects. Even so, there is no question that women were the primary targets of the Inquisition's bloodthirsty campaign. Women in general were the objects of Kramer and Sprenger's analysis; old women, unmarried women, midwives, and herbalists in particular bore the brunt of their misogyny. Summers not only admitted the misogyny of the Inquisition and the book that rationalized it, but in his 1928 Introduction cited woman-hatred as one of the valuable aspects of it.

Possibly what may seem even more amazing to modern readers is the misogynic trend of various passages, and these not the briefest nor least pointed.
However, exaggerated as these may be, I am not altogether certain that they will
not prove a wholesome and needful antidote in this feministic age, when the
sexes seem confounded, and it appears to be the chief object of many females
to ape the man, an indecorum by which they not only divest themselves of such
charm as they might boast, but lay themselves open to the sternest reprobation
in the name of sanity and common sense. (xxxix)

The timing of both editions of Summers' translation of *MM* reveals an
ancient connection between the power of women who live independently of
men and the craft of wicca: it first appeared in 1928, a few years after u.s.
women won the right to vote; the 1948 edition was published following ww
ii, when masculist propaganda urged women to surrender their jobs and
return to "kinder, kirche, küche." Was the razing of entire villages in Germany sanity or common sense? What manner of intellect can thus parade
itself as learned, even wise? In the patriarchal world view, "sanity" and
"common sense" translate into: men **must** rule women, women **must** be
oppressed.

The *MM* is a treatise on the inherent evil and carnality of women, an
encyclopedia of every vicious idea about women that men had uttered up to
that point, and a handbook of woman-hatred. Kramer and Sprenger quoted at
great length, as their "credible witnesses," every man who had written down
what he thought of women, as though sheer verbosity and tedium might
disguise the malignance of their ideological hatred; then they proceeded to
detail how women's evil is evident in every part and movement of our bodies,
but especially the "mouth of the womb."

All witchcraft comes from carnal lust, which is in women insatiable. See *Proverbs* xxx: There are three things that are never satisfied, yea, a fourth thing
which says not, It is enough; that is, the mouth of the womb. (47)

This was the "misogynic trend" Montague Summers thought was a "wholesome . . . antidote" to the feminism of his time!

In England, which chose Dr. Johnson instead of establishing an academy
to foster the purity of English, the murderous craze known as the Inquisition
didn't attain the ferocity it achieved in Europe. Merely thousands were killed
in Britain, millions in Europe. As a result of approximately 5,000 witch trials
in England, half of those tried for witchcraft were executed. With the dawn of
the eighteenth century, the Inquisition began to wane, more slowly in Europe
than England. In 1722, the last witch was executed in England, and the Act of
1736 did away with penal laws against witches. In 1775, the last witch was
killed in Germany. (But as late as 1785 in England, Sarah Bradshaw, accused
of witchcraft, agreed to be "swum" at Mears Ashby. When she sank to the
bottom like a stone, everyone present was convinced of her innocence.)

Dividing western societies into two factions was the aim and consequence
of the Burning Time. The message of *MM* is as arrogant as it is simplistic:

Women are inherently evil and must be purified, whether we like it or not. Apparently, it was a popular text among men. The white men of Europe escalated the war they have waged against women for millenia: the inquisitors burned women while the male members of the academies debated how to purify "their" languages. During that 300-year siege, men standardized "spelling," killing women accused of **spells**; men began to write grammars of the western languages, established academies to protect some of them, and burned women for casting **glamours** that made men's penises disappear.³ Since that period, **proper women** have depicted as obsessed with "glamour" and cosmetics, leaving to men the writing of grammars and the naming of the cosmos. Language is easily contaminated and must be kept pure. A language without an academy is, alas, like a woman without a man: wild, out of control. If no one takes it upon **him**self to subdue both, almost anything might happen: political anarchy, social chaos, the destruction of "civilization."

We may not hear about it much, but male domination of English and the assumption of male superiority in its grammars have not gone unchallenged by women over the centuries. In the twelfth century, St. Hildegarde of Bingen constructed a women's language consisting of 900 words and 23 letters.⁴ In 1715, Elizabeth Elstob dedicated the first grammar of Anglo-Saxon to the Princess of Wales (Kramarae, Treichler, and Russo, 9). In 1776, Abigail Adams warned her husband about the consequences of excluding the rights of women from the u.s. constitution, a subject reactivated during the first wave of u.s. feminism, and addressed by feminists like Charlotte Stopes in *The Sphere of 'Man' in Relation to That of 'Woman' in the Constitution* (1908). Nineteenth-century writers like Susan Ferrier and Miss Mulock so outraged some male grammarians that their names, if not their words, have been preserved for us in those grammarians' responses to them. In 1913 Elsie Clews Parsons published a feminist analysis of language and sex (Kramarae, Treichler, and Russo, 61). In 1948 Ruth Herschberger's *Adam's Rib* provided numerous examples of the ways women are linguistically subordinated.

The masculist tradition persists in ignoring, denying, and ridiculing women's work, despite these and other women's protests identifying and explaining how and why established English usage is offensive to and oppressive of women. Male linguistic domination, bolstered and financed by male economic dominance, has most recently declared itself alive and well in *The Story of English* by Robert McCrum, William Cran, and Robert MacNeil (1986). Robert Burchfield, editor of the *Oxford English Dictionary*, has said of this book, "The study of the language will never be the same again," but the contents and organization of the book indicate that this "new" study of English is really the "same old thing," rephrased and served up yet again as a definitive treatise. *The Story of English* (there is only one version!) contains no reference to Feminist research on English, and not a whisper about the fact that Middle English speakers rejected the possibility of a sex-neutral pronoun in English. Only one page (15) of *The Story of English* hints that women have protected male dominance and female invisibility in English, and that is the appearance of the word *sexist* in a patronizing reference to the Feminist spelling *wimmin* (now, ironically, legitimized by the *OED* itself). If we are to believe this "story" about English, we must also believe that women have, at no time, ever, in the past or the present, had anything worthwhile to say about the structure and development of English that challenged or contradicted the male version, a belief that is clearly false. *The Story of English* is only another attempt to assert and maintain male control of English.

LANGUAGE IS A WOMAN

Men have waxed eloquent with "their" languages, played with syntax and words, punned, experimented with style and rhetorical forms, debated this or that relationship among languages, added words they felt they needed, sworn the vilest oaths, and blocked attempts by powerless groups to become significant, visible speakers. According to the evidence men have recorded, women never had a chance. Early on, the Hebrews claimed that god bestowed on Adam the task of naming everything he perceived, but the Greek philosopher Plato is generally acknowledged as the "father" of the western grammatical tradition, a tradition in which men have conceived language to be an **Object** for **their** inquiry, **their** analysis, **their** description, **their** amusement.

> Plato was called by a later Greek writer "the first to discover the potentialities of grammar," and his conception of speech (*logos*) as being basically composed of the logically determined categories of noun and verb (the thing predicated and its predicator) produced a dichotomous sentence-analysis which has fathered most grammatical analyses since, whether the parentage has been acknowledged openly or not. (David Crystal, *Linguistics*, 51)

It wasn't until the beginning of the seventeenth century, though, that male grammarians began to incorporate what their priests and ministers told them about women into their descriptions of English. The consequences of this long patriarchal tradition remain with us, and have, till now, circumscribed not only how we think and talk about English but the process of communication as well. The Conduit Metaphor is a good example of the results of their diligence.

Metaphor and Thought, an anthology edited by Andrew Ortony (1979), included an article by Michael Reddy entitled "The Conduit Metaphor—A Case of Frame Conflict in Our Language about Language," in which he argued that the prevalant metaphor in western descriptions of language, including attempts to improve and understand communication, is the Conduit Metaphor. Using Schön's work (Ortony, 254–83) on how descriptions of problems determine the possible solutions proposed, Reddy observed "that merely by opening our mouths and speaking English we can be drawn into a very real and serious frame conflict" (285).[5] He underlined the seriousness of this problem by reminding us that communication isn't improving, and suggested that the failure is due to our reliance on the Conduit Metaphor. In spite of technology and the advertising promotions that praise the sophistication and efficiency of "mass communication," public and private communications are deteriorating steadily. Following Schön's analysis, Reddy proposed that examining how people talk about failures to communicate would expose the underlying frame they use to ask "what is wrong and what needs fixing?"

Using the Conduit Metaphor to talk about communication forces us to think of words as having "insides" and "outsides," as **containers** into which we insert ideas and feelings. When one woman accuses another of using "empty rhetoric," she's saying that the other woman's language is a container that she hasn't put anything into, as though words and sentences are objects we fill, like gas tanks. The framework of the Conduit Metaphor forces us to conceive of all varieties of language as containers, and thoughts and feelings as objects we insert into them, successfully or unsuccessfully.

To illustrate his argument, Reddy collected more than 140 examples of people describing failed communication. He estimated, on the basis of his evidence, that "at least seventy per cent" of our descriptions of communication in English are "directly, visibly, and graphically based on the conduit metaphor" (298). From his data, he identified four categories of description that make up the "major" frame of the Conduit Metaphor:

> (1) language functions like a conduit, transferring thoughts bodily from one person to another:
> "Try to get your thoughts across better"; "Her feelings didn't come through to me clearly."
> (2) in writing and speaking, people insert their thoughts or feelings in the words:
> "You load your sentences with more thoughts than they can hold"; "You have to capture your good ideas in words."
> (3) words accomplish the transfer by containing the thoughts or feelings and conveying them to others:
> "Your words are empty of meaning"; "Her sentences are filled with emotion."
> (4) in listening or reading, people extract the thoughts and feelings once again from the words:
> "I don't get any anger out of her words"; "Did you actually extract meaning from that prose?" (290)

Reddy also identified three categories of what he calls the "minor framework" of the Conduit Metaphor:

> (1) thoughts and feelings are ejected by speaking or writing into an external 'idea space';
> (2) thoughts and feelings are reified in this external space, so that they exist independently of human beings who think or feel them;
> (3) these reified thoughts and feelings may, or may not, find their way into the heads of living humans. (291)

As Reddy's analysis suggests, the inherent danger of the Conduit Metaphor is that it makes us think of communication as a simple process, like a drive-in bank's pneumatic tube, one that "guarantees success without effort" (295). We are taught to think that, in order to communicate, all we have to do is pluck ideas and feelings out of our minds, place them in language containers, send them off through the air, and they will always land, perfectly reproduced, perfectly intelligible, and impervious to misinterpretation, in the receptive mind of our listener.

Should we fail at such an easy task, we can be assured that someone will tell us it's our own fault. Because the Conduit Metaphor structures the way we think of communication, we are surprised, too, when our attempts at communication fail, as they often do, and English teachers have convinced us that our failed attempts make us "stupid" or "bad." Reddy conceded that abandoning the Conduit Metaphor and creating new models for communication will be "a serious alteration of consciousness" (286), but an endeavor we must make if we are to understand communication and learn how to say what we mean.

Reddy's hypothesis has been influential among some linguists, in particular George Lakoff, who adapted it for his collaboration with Mark Johnson, *Metaphors We Live By* (1980). They described the Conduit Metaphor as a complex metaphor that "is so much the conventional way of thinking about language that it is sometimes hard to imagine that it might not fit reality" (11). According to Lakoff and Johnson, a complex metaphor has three parts: two simple metaphors produce a third that follows from them. They represented the Conduit Metaphor as a three-part sequence:

IDEAS (OR MEANINGS) ARE OBJECTS.
LINGUISTIC EXPRESSIONS ARE CONTAINERS.
COMMUNICATION IS SENDING. (10)

Arguing that coherence across metaphorical concepts is the case rather than the exception (105), Lakoff and Johnson pointed out that English speakers use the Container Metaphor, of which the Conduit Metaphor is one example, to describe various events and perceptions and to structure their comprehension of numerous aspects of their experience: the visual field ("The ship is *coming into* view"), events, actions, activities, and states ("Are you *in* the race on Monday?", "She's *immersed in* her work right now," "She's *in* love this week") (29–32).

The more general Container Metaphor is extremely important in the conceptual organization of English, but Lakoff and Johnson missed what seems to me an obvious anatomical source for that metaphor. According to those scholars, speakers conceptualize language as a container because that metaphor is readily available to them, not because they like it, or because it makes sense, or because it's accurate. What Reddy and Lakoff and Johnson do not ask is **why** some metaphorical concepts are more popular than others in patriarchal culture. What does "readily available" explain, after all? Although Lakoff and Johnson were quite explicit about the fact that metaphorical concepts "structure (at least in part) what we do and how we understand what we are doing" (5), and discussed how different metaphors would restructure our understanding and, as a consequence, our behaviors (10–11), they didn't explore why certain metaphors proliferate while equally useful possibilities are never explored. Why, in patriarchal society, are so many ideas, like language, understood in terms of the CONTAINER metaphorical concept?

Because men are obsessed with their penises, in particular, the act of inserting their penises and penetrating spaces they perceive as objects whose sole reason for existing is to serve as containers, receptacles for their occupation. Like women. Men perceive women to be the primary objects for insertion of, penetration by their penises. If this sounds like a *reductio ad absurdum*, it is not of my making. The "great thinkers" of every generation have evolved complex philosophies that boil down to, "I see hole. Me fuck. Ergo: me powerful." Peggy Holland, in her excellent essay, "Jean-Paul Sartre as a NO to Women" (1978), culled numerous examples of the concept WOMAN IS A HOLE from Sartre's *Being and Nothingness* (1975). That existentialist philosopher's language reveals that his thinking was directly descended from that of his "forefathers," Kramer and Sprenger. Contrasting the "being" of men with the "nothingness" of woman, he made explicit the way men perceive women:

> It is only from this standpoint that we can pass on to sexuality. The obscenity of the feminine [sic] sex is that of everything which "gapes open." It is an *appeal to being* as all holes are. In herself woman appeals to a strange flesh which is to transform her into a fullness of being by *penetration* and *dissolution*. Conversely woman senses her condition as an appeal precisely because she is "in the form of a hole." . . . Beyond any doubt her sex is a mouth which devours the penis—a fact which can easily lead to the idea of castration . . . the hole . . . is an obscene expectation . . . (Holland, 1978, 74)

Sartre obviously had a "problem," but, as usual, he described it as women's "fault." WOMEN ARE CONTAINERS/RECEPTACLES, into which men ejaculate their sperm. This idea is at least as old as Aristotle, undoubtedly the authoritative source for male grammarians, Kramer and Sprenger, and Sartre as well. The Conduit Metaphor might just as well be called the PENILE THEORY OF LANGUAGE (PTL). It's not only that the metaphor is "readily available" but that it represents how men perceive the world and their relationship to it.

Reddy's list of examples contains phrases that men use to describe their experience of coitus; the congruity shows the intimate connection men perceive between women and language as "vessels":

> *Insert* that thought elsewhere in the sentence.
> . . . try to *stuff* the essay with all your best ideas.
> He *crammed* the speech with subversive ideas.

Unload your feelings in words— . . .
Don't *force* your meanings *into* the wrong words.
The poem is meant to be *impenetrable*. (312–15)

While not every one of Reddy's examples has words like *cram, stuff, force, unload, insert* or *impenetrable*, some, like "I can't seem to *get these ideas into* words," frequently occur in sexual statements: "I'd like to *get into* your pants."

Men talk about being "into" many things. Virtually any container, pipe, conduit, what-have-you, can be perceived as a hole. In fact, the connection between the four "major" and three "minor" categories of Reddy's analysis of the Conduit Metaphor, especially the first minor category, "thoughts and feelings are ejected by speaking or writing into an external 'idea space,'" is to be found in the merger of two complex metaphors, LANGUAGE IS A CONTAINER and WOMAN IS A CONTAINER: LANGUAGE IS A WOMAN. This complex metaphor combines two essential patriarchal premises. The parallelism, represented in the following diagram, is unmistakable. The observable overlap in these complex metaphors results from men thinking of the world in terms of what they can insert their penises into, literally as well as figuratively. Men must keep both "containers" "pure" if they are to be "worthy receptacles" of their ejaculations; otherwise, they are "unfit vessels" for male progeny. Reddy's "idea space" is, then, not external, but **internal**.

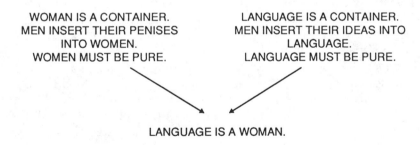

WOMAN IS A CONTAINER.   LANGUAGE IS A CONTAINER.
MEN INSERT THEIR PENISES   MEN INSERT THEIR IDEAS INTO
INTO WOMEN.   LANGUAGE.
WOMEN MUST BE PURE.   LANGUAGE MUST BE PURE.

LANGUAGE IS A WOMAN.

I know my readers will be recalling utterances in which the LANGUAGE IS A WOMAN metaphor occurs, but perhaps a few examples of the way the metaphorical concept surfaces will make its uses easily recognizable.

2.1 a. For the first time in his life he was reading for pleasure. And **like a boy who has just been initiated into the pleasures of sex by an older woman, he was wallowing in it**.
(Stephen King, *The Dead Zone* [New York: Viking Press, 1979] 308)

  b. From this point of view the *Malleus Maleficarum* is one of the most **pregnant** books I know. . . .
(Montague Summers, Introduction to the 1928 edition of the *Malleus Maleficarum* [New York: Dover Publications, 1971] xl)

c. The act of writing itself is done in secret, like **masturbation**. . . . For
me, it always wants to be sex and always falls short—it's always that
adolescent handjob in the bathroom with the door locked. . . .

Nowadays writing is my work and the pleasure has diminished a
little, and more and more often that **guilty**, **masturbatory** pleasure has
become associated in my head with the coldly clinical images of
artificial insemination: I **come** according to the rules and regs laid
down in my publishing contract. . . . I **get it off as hard as I can every
fucking time**. Doing less would, in an odd way, be like going faggot—
or what that meant to us back then.
(Stephen King, "Fall from Innocence: The Body," 375–77)

The metaphors that reflect the underlying concept LANGUAGE IS A
WOMAN are all too familiar—the "penetrating style," the "sentences pregnant with meaning," "the seminal idea," and on and on. A style that isn't
"strong," "forceful," "masculine," is "weak," "limp," "effeminate." The fore-
going examples illustrate a few of the ways the metaphorical concept LAN-
GUAGE IS A WOMAN is used by men to describe their participation in
communicative acts. To men, any language act is construed as sexual. Men
fuck language, just as they fuck women, impregnating words with meaning,
stuffing it with their ideas.

None of this is new, either. The relationship between both language and
women and grammar and sex has a long tradition among male scholars. As
J. N. Adams commented in *The Latin Sexual Vocabulary* (1982), "Since any
aspect of everyday life may generate sexual metaphors, it is not surprising that
those with grammatical or scholastic tastes should have found sexual symbols among the objects of their interests" (38). The grammarian Eunus, according to Adams, was "a *cunnilingus*" who saw "in certain objects of his
professional interest (letters) a resemblance to the object of his sexual interest
(the *cunnus*)" (39). Adams also claimed that "[i]t was above all in the Medieval period that grammatical and scholastic sexual metaphors came into
vogue" (39).

But Adams' assertion that the equation between grammar and sex "came
into vogue" in the Middle Ages may be an error. In *Alan of Lille's Grammar of
Sex* (1985), Jan Ziolkowski had this to say concerning Latin equations of
grammar with male sexuality:

> Not all the classical Latin erotic metaphors would have been interpreted in the
> Middle Ages as alluding specifically to grammar. . . . not many of the classical
> metaphors came up in works which circulated widely in the Middle Ages. For
> these reasons, the classical metaphors may be labeled parallels more securely
> than sources for the sexual metaphors of Alan. (56)

Elsewhere, describing the use of grammatical terms as metaphors for sex in
De Planctu Naturae, Ziolkowski observed that "[t]he similarity of such metaphors obviously cannot be explained on the basis of shared sources or

mutual influence; rather, it is due to the similarity of the cultures in which they were cultivated" (52). Patriarchal cultures, in which men are the only ones who write, cultivate the metaphor GRAMMAR IS SEX, and the one that gives it meaning, LANGUAGE IS A WOMAN.

Alan of Lille's *De Planctu Naturae*, probably written sometime after the middle of the twelfth century (Ziolkowski, 10), is a boring poetic treatise on patriarchal ethics and morals, in which grammar functions as an extended metaphor for sex. If Ziolkowski's analysis is accurate, Alan was particularly concerned with eradicating homosexuality and establishing heterosexuality as the "natural order."

> According to Alan's ideal, a man should modify, through sexual intercourse, a woman, just as a predicate modifies a subject. . . . He charges that, in the decadence of the times, men attempt to act both roles by themselves and hence assume the grammatical endings of both the first (feminine) and second (masculine) declensions. In this way sodomy upsets the correct state of verbs, predicates, and noun declensions; the whole world of grammar is thrown upside down through the black magic of Venus. (15)

Ziolkowski also pointed to Alan's prescription for the "repeated practice conjugation of 'amo, amas, amat'" ('I love,' 'you love,' 'he, she, it loves') (74). Perhaps *amar* ('to love') is one of the first verbs Latin students must learn to conjugate because of the long-standing equation of sex and grammar. The use of specific grammatical terms, such as *conjugate* and *copulative verb*, borrowed from Latin and Greek grammarians, can finally be understood as part of the patriarchal linguistic tradition, GRAMMAR IS SEX And LANGUAGE IS A WOMAN. Whether Alan's use of grammatical metaphors to describe patriarchal concepts of sexuality was borrowed or not, there is clearly a tradition of using grammatical terms to describe patriarchal valuations of heterosexual and homosexual sex in Europe, including England. In the patriarchal world view, if men haven't fucked something, it's insignificant, and they believe that they confer significance on something or someone when they fuck it.

Some of these fuckers fancy themselves as "knights in shining armor," and many eager crusaders have thrust themselves forward to rescue our "Mother Tongue," which they think of as a "damsel in distress." Among the more visible "knights" anxious to rescue English from the dragons of error and misuse are Edwin Newman, The Underground Grammarian, and John Simon. Simon, more so than others, has been explicit in his use of the LANGUAGE IS A WOMAN and GRAMMAR IS SEX conceptual metaphors.[6] Following the xtian tradition of blaming Eve for the fall and invoking the idea of an ancient utopian age of English now lost, Simon invoked Milton's *Paradise Lost* by entitling his essay collection *Paradigms Lost* (1980). In his introduction, "An Education in Love," Simon cast himself as a "heartsick lover," and English as the coy, chaste maiden he would protect from those who wish to corrupt her. For example, he discovered poetry at roughly the same time he encountered romance, when he wrote a poem to an older woman at the age of six (xi). That poem, he said, was "unfaithful to the beloved" because it was **enamored of its language, of the words that intoxicate anyone who gets close enough to them to experience their sensuousness and aroma"** (xi).

Born in Yugoslavia, he later took a "crash course" in English, and chose Edgar Rice Burroughs' Martian novels because of "their shocking-pink heroine, Princess Dejah Thoris." According to his account, this reading material caused "English [to become] eroticized for" him (xi–xii). Simon explained how one of his male teachers at his first American school was writing a novel about a "chastitute" (*chastity* + *prostitute*), and this **neologism** taught him that "language could grow new shoots." (Such is the nature of male linguistic creativity.) Contemplating this neologism made him "again confound poetics with erotics" (xii). He littered the remainder of his Introduction with other examples of the metaphor, LANGUAGE IS A WOMAN, in which he described "the seductive power of style" and his "love affair with words" (xii–xiii). For a man quick to ridicule clichés in the writing of others, Simon comfortably tolerates them in his own writing, just as he praised creations like *chastitute*, but ridiculed and trivialized feminist attempts to neutralize areas of the English language such as the pseudo-generic *he* and *man*. "It is hard," said he, "to resist the conclusion that feminists either hate their feminity or smart under their lack of feminine comeliness—unhealthy situations both" (31). Feminist attempts to dethrone male dominance in English are not due, then, to valid anger at male control of English or a political commitment to make English a more adequate language for women. Any woman who would dare challenge male dominance in language (or anywhere else) either hates being a woman (Simon's "feminity") or is "ugly" (in male terms). Simon perceives the likes of *chastitute* as just fine, but women had better "stay in our place" and leave English alone.

Simon, a less intelligent latter-day Swift, is committed to keeping women and English firmly under male control. The prescriptive grammars of English that Simon defends proscribe linguistic appropriateness, just as dozens of etiquette books dictate appropriate social behaviors to women. Those who challenge masculist definitions of patriarchal social and linguistic behaviors are "evil," "corrupt," "ugly" daughters of Eve intent on destroying the patriarchal version of reality. Well, yes. Simon, the seduced Adam of *Paradigms Lost*, seeks to reenter the linguistic Eden of his fantasies, and will protect the purity of English against all who threaten to defile it.

What, then, can the relationship of women be to the English language, a language whose structure and grammatical tradition are thoroughly patriarchal? Should we try to change the language? Can we re-form the language to make it ours? Or, should we, as Dale Spender (1980) and Deborah Cameron (1985) have suggested, set about creating a new context? This is the singular strategy of Mary Daly in cahoots with Jane Caputi's *Websters' First New Intergalactic Wickedary of the English Language* (1987), a way of hearing and speaking English words in a **Background** context.

Linguistic reform and the creation of a new context, a new understanding of the world and how women might be, and act, and move in that new conceptualization, are not mutually exclusive. One creates the other. But before we can begin creating both a new context and a new way of speaking in the world, we have to understand how the patriarchal world view has determined the structure of English. Otherwise, that view will turn us against our Selves, undermining and eroding us when we imagine we're at our "best." Once we have identified the ways English serves patriarchal modes of perceiving and categorizing the world, we can avoid, and think around and outside of patriarchal conceptual structures. As we unlearn the ways of thinking we internalized as children, we will also create woman-centered ways of thinking and acting in the world.

Chapter 3

The Patriarchal Universe
of Discourse

One morning, a man knocked at my door, asking if I knew where a client with whom he had an appointment lived. I suggested he ask the people next door. Before he left, he asked if I had a few minutes for him to tell me about an auto club he represents. I said, "No, I don't have a few minutes." He laughed good-naturedly, and said, "Most housewives say they don't have a few minutes." When I told him I wasn't a "housewife," he left. That evening my phone rang, and when I answered it a woman's voice cheerily asked me if I was "the lady of the house." I told her no ladies lived in this house, and hung up.

I've offered only two examples from a single day, but I often have such exchanges in my life because I live, like everyone else in the u.s., in a thoroughly (hetero)partriarchal society. I am perceived, described, related to, and judged according to the ideas, assumptions and values of a world view that I don't fit. The context isn't of my choosing, and I avoid contact with it as much as possible. Perhaps some readers will perceive my behavior as what they'd call "rude"; after all, those individuals were only trying to be friendly! Well, maybe they were trying to be what they consider "friendly," but they were primarily interested in selling me something I didn't want, and the approach that may work most often for them didn't work with me.

What is obscured by words like *friendly* and *rude* is the friction created when two different universes of discourse come in contact with each other. What I'm calling a "universe of discourse" is a cultural model of reality that people use daily to decide how to act and what to say in specific contexts. The model provides descriptions of what the culture believes to be important categorizations of those objects, events, ideas, and beings which give them their "place" in the world, and assigns certain values to behaviors. These models determine what is meaningful ("makes sense") to members of a culture. A **universe of discourse** is the same thing as "consensus reality," and those who accept its terms assume that it is an accurate description of reality, that the model gives them all the information they need to move and act in the world, and that its assumptions can accurately predict behaviors even in novel situations. In fact, people can be so attached to "consensus reality" that its assumptions and predictions override contradictory evidence. When speakers encounter a situation in which people or events do not fit the categories provided by their model of reality, they are more likely to describe those people or events to make them "fit" the model rather than change or revise the model itself.

A universe of discourse isn't a completely closed system; some aspects of the system, however, are harder to change than others. It has to be open-ended in some respects in order to accommodate things previously regarded as unknowns. Also, individuals organize their lives according to some aspects of a culture's model of reality and reject others, choosing, instead, to trust their own perceptions when the model isn't accurate for their experience. If a significant number of individuals reject the descriptions and values of important conceptual areas of a consensus reality, the model restructures itself to assimilate the dissidents or reinforce the dominant perspective.

In the u.s., the preferred descriptions of the world make up a Patriarchal Universe of Discourse (PUD). The descriptions of PUD provide the conceptual framework that imposes meanings and interpretations on what we perceive. For example, when the salesman called me a housewife, he did so on the basis of two observations: I was female and I was at home during the day. The way he interpreted these observations revealed his assumptions about the world and who I am. In the u.s., any white female at home during the day is, *ipso facto*, a housewife. When I corrected his assumption, his only perceptible acknowledgment was to avert his eyes (look at the ground) and display a knowing smile (smirk).

The woman who dialed my number made a similar mistake, applying the rules and predictions of patriarchal reality to me. She assumed that a household consists of at least two adults, a woman and a man. (She may also assume that they are married to each other.) When she heard my voice, she leapt to the conclusion that I must be "the lady of the house." In PUD, *lady* is said to be a "term of respect." In my universe of discourse, however, it is an insult, because *lady*, in addition to its upperclass overtones, signals assumptions about how women should act—assumptions I find offensive and presumptuous. "Ladies" behave in feminine ways: they sit with their legs crossed at the knees, they wear make-up and high heels, they tease, perm, and curl their hair, and they eat daintily. I live in a different universe of discourse, one with different assumptions, different values, and different ways of talking about the world.

PUD divides the world into two, unequal, stereotypical spheres: one female, the other male; it describes these two spheres in well-defined, discrete areas of the English vocabulary that name people, their behaviors, attitudes, and activities in the world. This split reflects the patriarchal idea that specific behaviors and activities are "properly" female, while others, those men choose to perceive as "important," are "properly" male. In English, this division is represented by pairs of words in various parts of the vocabulary, ranging from the anatomical, *vagina/penis*, to occupations, *waitress/waiter*, to types of equipment, *utensil/tool*, *appliance/machine*. The pairs of etymologically related terms mentioned in chapter 2, for example, *text/textile*, *spelling/spell*, *cosmos/cosmetic*, and *grammar/glamour* (cf. Daly, 1978, 1984), belong to sex-specific spheres of discourse as well as areas of social influence. What men deem important discourse topics they have named and reserved to themselves; what men perceive as significant in this universe, and the way they talk about such topics, is the only meaningful mode of public discourse. Among the topics categorized as belonging to the male sphere are war, penises, money, sex, cars, sports (hockey, baseball, and football), and politics (as men define it), not necessarily in that order. Women, in contrast, talk cosmetics, food prices, babies, penises, fashion, recipes—all "trivial" topics in PUD and so "OK" for women to have and express opinions about (with the exception of penises).

Intersecting metaphorical concepts connect the topics reserved for male confabulation: men use the same metaphors for talking about apparently dissimilar objects. Politics and sex borrow metaphorical expressions from sports and war, both of which are metaphorically interchangeable, WAR IS A GAME∿A GAME IS WAR, and men draw on all of their metaphorical resources when they describe women and their relations with women, for example, the "battle of the sexes," "getting to first (or second) base," "scoring." These metaphors are the verbal expressions of what George Lakoff (1987, 282–83) described as the "image schemas" that structure conceptual frameworks.

In chapter 2, I showed how the two complex metaphors, LANGUAGE IS A CONTAINER and WOMAN IS A CONTAINER, merged to produce LANGUAGE IS A WOMAN. According to G. Lakoff, such conceptual mergers are to be expected; the CONTAINER image schema is a primary element of "general conceptual structure" (282). In PUD, another popular metaphorical concept for talking about language, LANGUAGE IS A TOOL, illustrates how male conceptualizations are interrelated, drawing on a limited perceptual reservoir.

LANGUAGE IS A TOOL

Male metaphorical concepts connect their obsessions. When Michael Reddy identified the Conduit Metaphor and explained how it forces speakers to think of communication as an easy process, he didn't have to look far for a contrasting metaphor to illustrate the implications of his observation: the Toolmaker Paradigm (1979, 292–96). TOOLS, all kinds of tools, are productive terms in patriarchal analogies. After the Conduit Metaphor, LANGUAGE IS A TOOL is the next most frequently used analogy for talking about language, among linguists and laypeople alike.

Introductory textbooks on the subject of linguistics, somewhere early in the first chapter, invariably explain that language is a tool or instrument. "[W]e are learning about this rather remarkable and purely human *instrument* of communication" (R. W. Langacker, 1968, 3). "[A]s a human rather than a mechanical *implement*, one subject to the cultural, psychological and historical vagaries of mankind [sic], language is a complex and complicated *instrument*" (Larson and Logan, 1980, 1). A telling example of the metaphor LANGUAGE IS A TOOL occurred explicitly in a chapter entitled, "What Is Language?"

> *Language is a tool*. It is *the tool* for talking and for writing and for thinking. It is *the all-purpose tool* for people, *the tool* that makes us human, that gives us "dominion over the fish of the sea, and over the fowl of the air, and over every living thing that moveth upon the earth." [Emphases mine] (Nilsen and Nilsen, 1978, 1).

Because the LANGUAGE IS A TOOL metaphorical concept maintains the description's coherence, language sounds like a slice 'em, chop 'em, dice 'em gadget advertised on late-night television. Notice that the authors' promise to their readers is not fulfilled: a list of the "purposes of language" doesn't answer the chapter's title question, "What Is Language?"

LANGUAGE IS A TOOL betrays a functional definition of language (and its study) which assumes that people (read: 'mankind') "fabricate language" (as "toolmakers"). This utilitarian concept of language further assumes that language exists **because** of its presumed purpose: communication. Indeed, most theories regarding the origins of language assume that a specific purpose impelled people to make arbitrary sounds serve as signals, for example, the "pooh-pooh" and "yo-he-ho" theories derided by Jespersen (1921, 412–16) and, in the 1960s, the theory put forth by Hockett in *Scientific American* and elaborated by Hockett and Ascher in *Current Anthropology*.[1]

It may be that language is a "useful" method of communication, but it's by no means the **only** way people communicate. Consider, for example, how frequently language is used in this society to cover up messes, euphemize violence and murder, and lie. Accepting the equation, LANGUAGE IS A

TOOL, hides aspects of language from our observation, and focuses our attention on language **use** as its defining characteristic. *Use* implies three related terms that find their way into talk about language: the noun *abuse* (sometimes *misuse*), as an antonym of *use*, and two adjectives, *useful/useless*.

If we concentrate on the idea of **use**, we're not likely to go much beyond the limits that it suggests, perhaps getting only as far as "useful." It's common practice in explanations of why some words become obsolete or archaic and new words enter the English vocabulary, for example, to appeal to usefulness. Words become obsolete because speakers no longer find them useful; new words enter a language when speakers need them to talk about something. Functionalism is an important PUD explanation of "how things are in the world." The implications of the LANGUAGE IS A TOOL metaphor and the USE/TOOL analogy lead us, again, to the LANGUAGE IS A WOMAN conceptual metaphor.

In American English, PUD divides the inanimate and animate worlds into objects and beings that men perceive to be USEFUL and those things/people for which they haven't yet found a use. Things and beings that are "useless" are candidates for "control," a euphemism for their annihilation. Plants designated *weeds*, for example, are plants that men haven't found a way to use, so "weed control" is thought of as a "good" thing. *Pests* are "useless" insects whose existence depends upon eating things that men regard as **their** possessions, for example, houses, cotton fields. Termites and boll weevils consume wood and cotton bolls, respectively, as their food, but men call these insects *destructive*, thereby legitimizing their destruction, called "pest control."

What men find useful to them they try to tame and domesticate. What is wild must be conquered and dominated, made to serve men's purposes. Moreover, creatures and objects that men label useless are usually beings and things that have either resisted or escaped male attempts to domesticate and dominate them. Such creatures may remain wild and free for a time, but eventually even they must be conquered, tamed, or annihilated. The size and weight of the great whales may have made them unattractive for domestication, but men persist in hunting them to the brink of extinction because they are useful. Concern about the imminent extinction of the snail darter in Tennessee streams was ridiculed as sentimental and obstructionist, and the fear generated by the movie *Jaws* was enough to justify shooting sharks from the safety of hovering helicopters. Those sharks, after all, were "hurting" the tourist industries of coastal resorts, and they're not "useful." We have trout and catfish farms, but no shark farms.

Underlying the *useful/useless* distinction is the male desire to control everything on this planet. It is no accident that yet another primary metaphorical concept in the patriarchal universe of discourse is NATURE IS A WOMAN.[2] Women and natural events both defy the male sense of "order," and so "must" be controlled. Under patriarchy, control and power are synonymous with domination and conquest. What men cannot indirectly control with their rules, laws, bribes, and intimidation, they subdue or annihilate by physical or mechanical means. What is wild is annoying or dangerous, and so must be neutralized (killed). This attitude is explicitly advertised in a bumper sticker:

> If you love something, set it free.
> If it doesn't come back, hunt it down and kill it.

What men believe they have the right to control and dominate—the fish in the sea, the beasts of the field, the weather, the courses of rivers, the insect population, language, and women—must be tamed, predicted, dammed, exterminated, purified, or married, all in order to serve men's purposes. These subjugations are called "problem solving," and PUD metaphorical concepts connect each to the other. Solving the problem of bankrupt savings and loan banks, for example, was characterized as MARRIAGE in a 1988 issue of *U.S. News & World Report*: "Washington likes to get rid of sick savings and loans by **marrying them off to strong mates**. But some cases are so hopeless that **no suitor can be found**" [My emphasis] (June 20, 1988, 13). Savings and loans, like daughters under patriarchy, should be "married off" when they become financial burdens (useless) to "daddy," the federal government.

One other antonym of *use* central to the LANGUAGE IS A TOOL metaphorical concept must be mentioned here: *abuse*. (The *use/abuse* dichotomy is similar to other pairs, e.g., *normal/abnormal*.)[3] We hear too frequently about "abuses of power," "abused children," and "abuses of language." To speak of "abusing" an individual, an object, or an abstraction as though there are "wrong" **uses** of them is to assert implicitly that there are "right" uses of objects and people, and the concept of abuse thus serves to buttress the claim that men have the "right" to the "proper uses" of power.

We live in a country in which "abusers" of power are elevated to the status of heroes, as in the case of Oliver North, and the principle of "selective enforcement" operates in the linguistic sphere as conspicuously as it does in politics. Changes in English supported and promoted by white men they perceive as "natural" or "inspired." Linguistic changes promoted by women or African-American men, in contrast, are quickly labeled "abuse" or "misuse" and the upstarts thoroughly ridiculed. In a recent issue of *The Recorder* (Greenfield, Massachusetts), for example, Paul Seamans characterized various contemporary changes in English as the result of the efforts of those he called "the social levelers" and "language bashers." Both phrases referred to the same people—the miscreants who would destroy the marvelous "masculinity" of English.

> Social levelers, wherever the medium is the word, have diligently and persistently adulterated our [sic!] language, gradually effecting here an uninspired linguistic *sexlessness* that is flat and ordinary. What ought to be a *virile, vig-*

orous, native American speech is turning into a form of *neutered* expression, lacking *muscle* and color. [My emphases] (February 5, 1988, 8)

Of course, one of the primary groups of "language bashers" identified by Seamans are people who want to eliminate English expressions that purport to include women but are, in fact, male-specific in their reference, for example, *brother, man*, and *mankind*. English, here described by Seamans as male, is the victim of "battering," a primarily female experience. The implied contradiction of a "masculine" language being desexed, "neutered," by feminist "violence" clashes with the metaphorical concept, LANGUAGE IS A WOMAN. This conceptual conflict caused Seamans to trap himself in a mixed metaphor when he shifted to the female-specific "Mother Tongue" in what he must have believed was a "clever" turn.

> Adding words and phrases to our [sic] Mother Tongue in the natural progression of language growth is one thing, but *spaying* the Old Lady for the sake of change is another matter. Let the liberal social-levelers keep hands off.

Predictably, behind the label "social-levelers" is linguistic elitism. Typically, this kind of statement comes from those who believe that they are "above" the alleged improprieties of those they chastise. But Mr. Seamans couldn't untangle his metaphors, and seemed unable to decide whether to think of English as female or male. Whichever, he was determined to protect its genitals from those "bashing" (castrating?) women who won't "stay in their place"! How nobly men rush to defend their language from "battering"; how slow they have been to admit to their violence against women and children!

This metaphorical dilemma isn't solely Seaman's problem. Using [+female] terms to describe language, as in "Mother Tongue," is "traditional usage," and so is the idea that English, more so than other languages, is uniquely "masculine" in its structural properties. Otto Jespersen, for example, devoted some 16 pages to praising English for its "business-like, *virile* qualities" (1958, 10; my emphasis).

> [t]here is one expression that continually comes to my mind whenever I think of the English language and compare it with others: it seems to me positively and expressly *masculine*, [his emphasis] it is the language of a grown-up man and has very little *childish* or *feminine* about it . . . the language is more *manly* than any other language I know. (2)

To justify his perception, Jespersen began with the English sound system. He contrasted English phonology, which permits one or more consonants to end words (*feasts, months*), with Hawaiian, in which words typically end in vowels and never with two or more consonants. English words contain consonant clusters, Hawaiian has vowels; consonants sounded "masculine" to Jespersen, vowels "feminine." On the basis of his perceptions, Jespersen asked his readers: "Can any one be in doubt that even if such a language sound pleasantly and be full of music and harmony the total impression is *childlike* and *effeminate*?" (3; my emphases).

The alleged "masculinity" of English must be preserved. "Abuses" of English, according to Mr. Seamans and his brethren, Douglas Bush and John Simon (discussed in chapter 2), are just those changes in the language that threaten white male domination of its terms and rules. An "abuse" becomes, of necessity, not the infraction of a structural property, but any attempt to introduce **neutral** wording in male-specific clichés, expressions more properly characterized as uninspired and trite. I want to remind my readers of a sense of the word *abuse* that may have occurred to many anyway: its reference to masturbation in the term *self-abuse*. Many religions forbid masturbation because the resulting ejaculation has no reproductive purpose. The penis, a **tool**, is thought of as not being *used* for its "natural purpose," impregnation of a female. "Jerking off" is an "abuse" because sperm isn't deposited in its "appropriate" receptacle, a womb. Language "abuse," then, is a metaphor based on the concept LANGUAGE IS A WOMAN.

Seamans' choice of the pronoun "our" typifies male discourse about language; it excludes women and becomes a men-only pronoun announcing the *droit de seigneur*. It is ultimately male linguistic proprietariness that LANGUAGE IS A TOOL signifies, for tools belong to the male sphere, along with related terms like *instrument, implement, equipment,* and *machine.* The English words related to *tool* follow the patriarchal dichotomy of sex-based task assignment: the inside of a house, the female realm, and the outside, male sphere of activity. *Housework,* tasks performed inside a house, are "women's work," while tasks performed outside are "men's work." This division of labor is meaningful to English speakers even though they may not be conscious of its existence. Men use tools, instruments (with the exception of a few musical instruments), implements, machines, and gizmos outside. Women use utensils, appliances, and gadgets inside. In English, we speak of kitchen utensils, kitchen appliances, and kitchen gadgets—used by women, they are not considered tools. A search of the tools listed in *Roget's International Thesaurus* (1977) reveals only a few items stereotypically used by women (tweezers, nail file, bread knife, scissors), but numerous names for equipment reserved to the male sphere specifying types of drill, clutch, saw, plane, hammer, and wrench. Recently, though, KitchenAid has begun to advertise one of its mixers as a POWER TOOL, a tactic that blurs the boundary between the two experiential domains. Its actual effect, however, reenforces the barrier. Because women are leaving their interior domain for the male domain of "real" work, the ad imports the [+male] phrase, *power tool,* and applies it to the equipment women use in a kitchen.[4] Nothing has to change but the label applied to the objects women use; our "domain" remains the kitchen.

Man, the anthropologists tell us, distinguishes himself from other animals by his use of tools. Any object restricted to male use and ownership is a "tool," whether it's language, a hammer, or a penis. Men speak of their penises as *tools*, and describe their activity in heterosexual intercourse as "screwing," "nailing," "banging," "reaming," "drilling," and "hammering." So intense is the male obsession with their "tools" and females as containers or holes they penetrate that any two objects suggestive of that description, for example, electrical outlets and plugs, nuts and bolts, will have the metaphor imposed upon them. The essential distinction of PUD is the one which identifies the FUCKER and the FUCKEE.

The LANGUAGE IS A TOOL metaphorical concept leads us back to the complex metaphor analyzed in chapter 2, LANGUAGE IS A WOMAN. LANGUAGE IS A TOOL translates as LANGUAGE IS A PENIS, just as LANGUAGE IS A CONTAINER becomes LANGUAGE IS A WOMAN. The two metaphors are linked by the USE/ABUSE and USEFUL/USELESS conceptual axes, although each borrows its apparent coherence from a different element of the FEMALE/MALE dichotomy. The sex-specific metaphors which seemed to be contradictory in Paul Seamans' essay can apparently be ignored at the abstract level if it suits the writer's purposes. In an article published in *Esquire*, Jack McClintock ascribed the feature [+male] to knives, but later described them as [+female].

> A knife is an extension of the brain and eye, a tool, a weapon, a friendly and intimate presence, a romantic symbol, an object of repellant fascination, *an atavistic expression of the aggressor and penetrator in man.* [My emphasis] (July, 1975, 138)

> It [the perfect knife] would be stainless and rustproof. It would be *like a woman*, as one maker puts it, and have "warmth, character, and a good shape." [My emphasis] (140)

Like a penis or tool, language can be *useful* as a hammer or knife is useful, and *used* to intimidate, coerce, dominate, penetrate, punish, or conquer. It can also be described as *abused* or *misused*, whether it's conceived of as [+female] or [+male].

Shortly, I'll describe how the dichotomy of [+female]/[+male] has framed western discourse about language since the Greeks. First, however, I must explain one of my own assumptions that has been implicit up to this point. What we say, the words we choose, and the sentence structures with which we organize our words reveal how we perceive the world. The "what" and the "how" of our speech are inseparable. We believe that what we perceive is "real," what is "out there." But what we perceive is a combination of physical stimuli, extrapolation based on previous experience, and what we've been taught to perceive. When we look at a tree, for example, we assume that it is roughly circular, and has another "side" even though we can't actually confirm this assumption unless we walk around the tree. Even then, we only see the portion of the tree we're looking at at the moment, and **assume** that it has a roundish trunk.

In *Understanding Grammar* (1979), Talmy Givón discussed the relationship between our descriptions of events and where we conceive ourselves to "stand" in the world, using an example reminiscent of the descriptions of a glass containing liquid as half full or half empty. Imagine, he said, that you and a friend are walking together and both of you perceive a roundish object that, at one moment, is attached to the branch of a tree and, the next moment, is resting on the ground. Although both individuals have, presumably, seen exactly the same object and the same event, their descriptions can differ. Speaker A might say, "The apple fell from the tree," focusing on the apple's initial state, while B could say, "The apple fell to the ground," describing the apple's resulting state. Other descriptions are possible, and might posit causality: "The wind must be blowing hard. It knocked an apple off that tree," or "Looks like apples are ripe now."

Givón's observation explains a variety of semantic facts about the English vocabulary, things most speakers "know," but don't know consciously. (Linguists call this "intuitive knowledge.") We choose among specific pairs of adjectives in English according to how we perceive/conceive of an object with respect to the horizon of our vision, for example, *long* and *tall*, *deep* and *tall*. If we describe a flagpole as "tall," our audience assumes that it stands vertical with respect to the horizon; if we say that it's "long," they imagine that it's lying on the ground, parallel to the horizon. (*Short* is the antonym of both *long* and *tall* and so doesn't imply contrast to the horizon but to some abstract notion of relative height or length.) The examples in 3.1 illustrate how the choice of one adjective or the other informs us about the speaker's perspective which we then use to interpret statements.

3.1 a. We're right back where we started from: standing in a **tall hole**.
       (*Dragnet*, December 21, 1977)
    b. The largest [Kodiak bear] on record was a male about **nine feet long**. . . .
       ("Ask the Globe," *Boston Globe*, October 12, 1987, 70)

The choice of *tall* rather than *deep* in 3.1.a. may, at first, sound strange to the hearer. Although *tall* is an unusual adjective for describing depth, the speaker succeeded in emphasizing his imagined perspective from a position standing at the bottom of the hole. Describing a hole as "deep" may be fine for someone standing outside and looking down into it, but "tall" makes us visualize how a hole twice our height in depth would look to us if we were at its bottom. When the size of a Kodiak bear is described in terms of length, rather than height in 3.1.b., however, we know that the writer is talking about a **dead**, not a live, bear, because *long* describes something lying parallel to the speaker's visual horizon. Perhaps only dead bears can be measured, or those who managed to ascertain a Kodiak's correct height didn't live to tell about it.

THE SEMANTIC GAME

The culture we live in determines, to a large extent, how we categorize the world and understand the things we perceive because it is culture that provides the vocabulary from which we choose our words, including the information about which vocabulary choices are the preferred terms for talking about certain situations and events. The semantic structure of a language can be thought of as a grid, a conceptual frame, that its culture imposes on the experience and perceptions of its speakers. I'm aware that lots of dysfunctional communication in this patriarchy is swept under the rug with comments like "It's **just** a semantic problem," "It's only a question of semantics," or "Don't play semantic games with me," as though semantics were irrelevant, or a way to muddy the waters that someone else thinks are "clear." Semantics **is** important. We cannot adopt as valid the patriarchal assertion that semantics is trivial.

There are, for example, conversational rules governing who can say certain kinds of words. Only men are permitted to use the slang of sexual slurs, and they generally observe one restraint on their use of that vocabulary: they rarely exhibit the full range of it in the company of women. Women, in contrast, are generally forbidden the use of that vocabulary, are chastised should they experiment with its terms as children, and usually don't learn most of its words. Women's liberation hasn't significantly weakened this taboo, and it's not clear that we should want to.[5]

In other areas of the vocabulary, the relative quantity of terms may be a significant indication of the value placed on abstract concepts. Individual words rarely exist in a social or semantic vacuum. They are related to other words by an abstract, conceptual system of **semantic** features, and such a group of words is a **semantic** set. Semantic sets contain related words speakers use to refer to objects, events, actions, or people, and the features represent how the words within a set make culturally determined distinctions among the objects, people, whatever, and reveal how cultural perspectives structure languages.

The words available to speakers of a language segment the world in ways that maintain the social structure, and the relative size of those sets indicates the importance societies accord some aspects of their experience. Eskimos, for example, distinguish more than 40 types of snow; Malaysians need more than 90 terms for talking about varieties of rice. Berlin and Kay's *Color Terms* (1969) demonstrated the close connection between a culture and the semantic sets in its language by correlating the quantity of terms to distinguish colors with the level of industrialization. Swahili, for example, has only three

specific color terms, 'white', 'black', and 'red', while English has an indefi-
nitely expanding set.[6] The reference of the word *lesbian* was expanded by
German sexologists in the late nineteenth century to name women who
refused to marry men and chose, instead, to make their primary emotional
commitments to other women. This doesn't mean that there weren't any
lesbians until the late nineteenth century. The creation of the word indicates
an apparent need to name (finally) relationships that men perceived as threatening to their institutions.

In English, some semantic sets appear to be symmetrical while others are
asymmetrical. We have many words and phrases to describe dishonesty or
degrees of lying, and to distinguish the relative significance of lies, but only a
few words for honesty, for example, *candid, frank*. The asymmetry between
these related sets correlates with the cultural value placed on "going along,
getting along." Conformity to socially acceptable behavior is highly prized,
even though a majority recognize it for the hypocrisy that it is, while
"whistle-blowers" and "wave-makers" are punished. (Remember "The Emperor's New Clothes"?) English has more than 1,200 words meaning 'fuck',
as Eric Partridge boasted,[7] but only a few for 'love' and related feelings, for
example, *like, affection*. In the popular music of our time, even the word *love*
is used synonymously to mean 'fuck', as in "I'm gonna give you every inch of
my **love**."

A culture's vocabulary reveals how its speakers learn to perceive and think
about objects and events in the world; semantic sets (such as color terms) are
conceptually organized on the basis of distinctions, that is, semantic features.

"JUST TWO KINDS OF PEOPLE
IN THE WORLD"[8]

As resistant as some readers may be to the idea that our perceptions and
descriptions of the world are specifically MALE perceptions and descriptions,
consider what we know of history and which sex has been the most vocal
and visible when it comes to *naming the world*. Patriarchal religions routinely claim that god gave *men* the "right" to name the world they perceived
around them. Like Suzette Haden Elgin,[9] I think the perceptions and descriptions of the world made possible by English would be vastly different if, in
fact, women controlled the naming process. The world, too, would look
quite different to us.

Men control naming, an important aspect of any language. What men
notice and, therefore, name, is "real." First, men name whatever it is that they
think needs labeling. The names, once chosen, set the boundaries on what
will make sense to members of a culture. Once they've established the limits
of what counts as legitimate commentary and what doesn't, various distinctions must follow as they protect the internal coherence of their discourse

against evidence that contradicts their descriptions. Once men have brought
something under their control by naming it, recategorizing it or renaming it
becomes a difficult task, since most people seem willing to accede to the
"what is" (and "is not") of patriarchal reality.

Sitting in a Denny's restaurant, I chanced to overhear the following exchange:

> First waitress: "'Cream and sugar.' Why do we say that? Why not 'sugar and
> cream?'"
> Second waitress (to a third): "We say it because that's the way **they** named it!"

What caught my attention was the second waitress's absolute conviction that
what the first waitress had asked was a NON-question; she clearly thought
the first was stupid to question something so patently "obvious." Her voice
was full of disdain as she affirmed the linguistic *status quo*, even though she
might have realized, after a moment's reflection, that we **do** say "sugar and
cream." Daring to question what "they" accept as "established" exposes the
questioner to ridicule.

Nevertheless, we must challenge the descriptions of men's naming. The
vocabulary of a culture, in this case anglo-american society, reflects just those
ideas that the speakers believe are "real" and those distinctions that a majority consider to be "meaningful." In order for an utterance to make sense,
to be heard as "English," the words and the relations among them must
follow the PUD map of the world which most speakers believe to be true.
One of the most crucial dichotomies that makes "sense" in English is that
between "female" and "male." This allegedly biological (therefore valid)
distinction is the defining feature that structures the semantics of English
nouns that refer to human beings, and extends into the class of adjectives
with several antonymous pairs, *womanly/manly, feminine/masculine, wom-
anish/mannish*. This dichotomy makes sense to most speakers of English, and
without it familiar portions of PUD would be exposed as meaningless.

Some adjectives seem to exist only because this society believes that
biological sex is a conceptually "useful," that is, "meaningful," way to talk
about human beings. Terms like *feminine/masculine, womanish/mannish*,
are semantically symmetrical (paired), but conceptually asymmetrical. Socially, being "feminine" means something very different from being "masculine," and dictionary definitions of such terms reflect this asymmetry. To be
"feminine" is to behave in "womanly" ways, while being "masculine" is to
be a paragon of "manly" virtue (brave, honest, courageous). These paired
terms exist only to define the limits of how women may act, while specific
adjectives and their derivative adverbs further delimit "acceptable" female
behaviors, for example, *appropriate, fitting, proper*. Whenever we hear or
read one of these words, it warns us that the judgment it modifies derives its
validity from heteropatriarchal values.

Adjectives like *femininity* and *masculinity* set limits on what is "permissible" appearance and behavior for women and men. Their **meaning** main-

tains male dominance. Patriarchal semantics equates femininity with female-ness and masculinity with maleness, assuming that biological sex determines behaviors and personality traits. On the basis of that equation, PUD stipu-lates that only feminine women and masculine men are "valuable." This is not, however, a "separate but equal" dichotomy. It serves an idealized hier-archy in which anything conceived to be male, and, therefore, masculine, is more highly valued than whatever is assigned to femininity/femaleness. The most abstract, highest level in this hierarchy is called *humanness*, but its qualities aren't generic; the qualities attributed to maleness, and described as *masculinity*, are also understood to be the standard by which one's "human-ness" is judged.

These two cultural spheres determine how individuals and our behaviors are valued. What is labeled "masculinity" is the ideal of what it means to be **human**; the female who embraces the femininity forced on her by the patriar-chal construct is, by definition, **sub-human**. Femininity is made to seem attractive to women because the only other known alternative is to act "like a man," which is to place oneself in the category deviant, and, therefore, "bad." The patriarchal feature hierarchy, with its resulting valuations, places women in a classic "double bind"[10]: women who act "like women," who display "feminine" behaviors, are devalued and trivialized; women who refuse to learn such behaviors are perceived as "like men," and ridiculed because they aren't "real women." Women who try to live out PUD values don't qualify for "personhood," and those who behave as they wish are non-women. Either way, men stigmatize us.

The misogyny that stipulates femininity as inherent in being female simul-taneously devalues it as a "human" attribute; masculinity is the human norm, but, because femininity is normal for women, we're "abnormal" if we show behaviors attributed to maleness. If we act human, we're deviant. Positively valuing attributes explicitly devalued and described as inferior keeps women bouncing back and forth within the extremes of the dichotomy. There's no way for a female to live by the patriarchal rules and be considered "good." The words *masculine* and *feminine* exist because they provide de-scriptions essential to the maintenance of patriarchal reality. But the exist-ence and continual use of these words doesn't mean that they denote real or actual things. In order to understand how such terms function, we need to examine the semantic relations among the terms that make them seem "meaningful."

Diagram 3.1 presents the basic semantic dichotomy of the patriarchal world of English and its logical structure. It represents an important piece of the semantic system called "consensus reality," a way of visualizing how this portion of semantic space functions in our long-term memory, a picture of the grid patriarchy imposes on our experiences. (Note: I use words rather than abstract semantic features at each level.)

Diagram 3.1 reflects what being born a woman or man means in PUD.

LEVEL	CATEGORY	FEATURE	
		+ MALE	- MALE
I	BIOLOGICAL	MALE	FEMALE
II	FUNCTIONAL (Breeders)	MAN FATHER	WOMAN MOTHER
III	BEHAVIORAL	REAL MAN MASCULINE MANLY	REAL WOMAN FEMININE WOMANLY
		WOMANISH	MANNISH

DIAGRAM 3.1. Patriarchal Semantics

These terms are the cultural filter through which we learn to perceive ourselves and others as we move and act in the world. The essential dichotomy that gives this grid its meaning is the much-touted sexual dimorphism of *homo sapiens* [sic!]. That is, the species is described as having two sexes, which differ from each other in primary and secondary sexual characteristics.

Sexual dimorphism is the foundation of patriarchal semantics, politics, and personality. Biological sex dictates personality, according to this universe of discourse. Biology determines behavior, mannerisms, appearance, emotional style, what one wears, and how one thinks. This is a monocausal ideology. Sexual dimorphism is the reproductive strategy for numerous species, but it's neither necessary, inevitable, nor biologically superior to other reproductive methods, as many believe. Species in addition to our own reproduce parthenogenetically (lizards, fish, seagulls, and some plants). Only men seem to be obsessed with their reproductive capacity, as though they'd invented and perfected it. Contrary to popular thinking, it's not at all obvious that biological sex or reproductive potential is the basis of personality. One might just as well posit the position of constellations with respect to the earth at the time of one's birth as the source of personality, as patriarchal astrology does.

Heterosexuality doesn't appear in Diagram 3.1 because it's assumed in PUD. An individual is assumed to be heterosexual unless proven otherwise; the assumption of heterosexuality is so strong that it overrides all contradictory evidence, no matter how vehemently asserted. The logic of patriarchy assumes that heterosexuality **necessarily** follows from sexual dimorphism. The possession of genitalia of a specific kind is believed to necessitate its use in a specific way. In common terms, this assumption is expressed as the "Stick-in-the-Hole Theory of Behavior," or "Function Follows Form": (1) Men have penises, women have vaginas; (2) penises exist to be stuck in vaginas. This primitive explanation, that form dictates function, and its corollary, that use follows from potential, are essential to the illusion of coherence in PUD. That which is assumed, primary, and implicit is difficult to contradict. Heterosexuality and its "naturalness" aren't supposed to be questioned. If you doubt this, put a bumper sticker on your car, bike, or skateboard that says, "If Abortion is a Crime, Fucking Should be a Felony." A female's right to terminate a pregnancy is open to question; the necessity of heterosexual coitus (fucking) isn't.

The leftmost, vertical portion of Diagram 3.1 divides patriarchal semantic space into three discrete levels: BIOLOGICAL, FUNCTIONAL, and BEHAVIORAL. The internal logic of PUD posits an **entailment** relation between each level: Given that one is born either MALE or FEMALE, it follows that one is either MAN or WOMAN in FUNCTION (*father* or *mother*). From this functional description, it follows that one's BEHAVIOR will necessarily be "appropriate" to one's FUNCTION and BIOLOGY, *masculine* or *feminine*. If one happens to be born female, as a majority are, then one is also necessarily a woman and, being a woman in this patriarchal culture, one is also **necessarily** "feminine" and "womanly." This entailment relation makes *female* and *feminine* synonymous in English; "being feminine" is used as though it meant "being a woman." The meaning of being a female in the u.s. **is** being *feminine*. A female who is not feminine is an unacceptable contradiction in male terms.

At the BEHAVIORAL Level (III), I've placed the most commonly used adjectives that describe the behaviors attributed to each sex. The significance of the +male/−male dichotomy and the rigidity with which PUD maintains it is explicit in two ways. First, I've included "real men" and "real women," which both presuppose the existence of "unreal men" and "unreal women," that is, "queers." In usage, these phrases assume the accuracy of the entailments among Levels I, II, and III. If one is female, then one must be a heterosexual and a breeder, and behave in appropriate, "feminine" ways. If she doesn't, if she fails to symbolically enact (and validate) the entailments of Level II or III in some way, she isn't a "real woman." She's "something else" because she contradicts the logic of the patriarchal semantic system.

Second, the importance attached to these semantic features is exposed by the final pair of adjectives, *womanish/mannish*. In PUD, both words signal a feature negation (or "violation") within the system. A man described as "womanish" is behaving in some way thought to be *like a woman*, "unmanly." He may cry when he's angry, frustrated, confused, or grieving; he may cross his legs at the knee; he may bend from the waist to pick something up off the ground. Whatever he's done, he has acted inappropriately according to the patriarchal semantics. Likewise, a woman described as "mannish" has negated the feature dichotomy by "crossing the line." She may be aggressive or withdrawn; she may wear her hair "too" short; she may be "too" tall, or weigh "too much"; she may take large steps instead of small ones; she may not smile at men. Whatever the specific behavior interpreted as a violation of her category, the attribute of *mannish* is intended to be both an insult and a warning: Don't go "too far," or you're "out." Semantic violation becomes semantic exclusion; semantic exclusion becomes social exclusion.

Patriarchal semantic space is so well maintained that the attempts of some Feminists to introduce "androgyny" or "gynandry" were bound to fail. First, both terms validate the MASCULINE/FEMININE dichotomy they're intended to replace. If two distinct kinds of behavior didn't exist, one reserved for men, the other for women, there would be nothing to combine. Without the pre-existing distinction, no fusion would seem possible. Second, gynandry (or androgyny), as proposed by such Feminists, operates only at Level III, the BEHAVIORAL. They were concentrating on personality traits, habits of behavior, as described by patriarchal conceptual structure. But substituting a combined idea, 'androgyny', did not disturb or challenge the entailment conditions between the levels, and it certainly didn't affect the perceptual foundation, sexual dimorphism. Finally, promoting change within the system would work only if one started at Level I, and infiltrated Level III by establishing different entailment conditions between the levels. But this strategy, too, is blocked by the adjective pair, *womanish/mannish*. The derogation of those terms interrupts attempts to blur the distinction carried by *feminine/masculine*.

Words exist and are created because they serve the values and attitudes central to a culture. Dictionaries record cultural meanings. Definitions of *womanly, mannish,* and *manly, feminine* and *masculine* from the *Random House Dictionary*[11] reveal the cultural values modifiers denote and perpetuate. As long as women use these words as though they describe something real or explain observable phenomena, we lend credence to the idea that people can and should be characterized by the dichotomy they represent. As one could predict, the "real meaning" of each word is revealed in the definition of its opposite.

> **womanly**—like or befitting a woman; feminine; not masculine or girlish. *Womanly* implies resemblance in appropriate, fitting ways; *womanly decorum, modesty.*

> **manly**—having the qualities usually considered desirable in a man; strong, brave; honorable; resolute; virile. *Manly* implies possession of the most valuable or desirable qualities a man can have, as dignity, honesty, directness, etc., in opposition to servility, insincerity, underhandedness, etc. It also connotes strength, courage, and fortitude.

> **feminine**—pertaining to a woman or girl: *feminine beauty, feminine dress.* Like a woman; weak; gentle.

masculine—having the qualities or characteristics of a man; manly; virile; strong; bold; a deep, *masculine voice*. Pertaining to or characteristic of a man or men: *masculine attire*.

mannish—applies to that which resembles man: . . . Applied to a woman, the term is derogatory, suggesting the **aberrant possession of masculine characteristics**. [My emphasis]

The qualities listed under *manly* and *masculine* are the "good" things an individual might wish to be: strong, brave, determined, honest, and dignified. Not a single one of the negative qualities commonly attributed to maleness are listed here: aggressive, violent, narrow-minded, self-centered, defensive, easily threatened, domineering, penis-obsessed, intrusive, predatory, immature, dependent, energy-sucking, or territorial, egotistical, and warmongering. In contrast, the adjectives *womanly* and *feminine* are not really defined. Look closely at the long list of characteristics in the definition for *manly* compared to the circularity of the pseudo-definition for *womanly*, "like or befitting a woman." That's not a definition; it assumes that we already know the behaviors that "befit" a woman. The real definitions for *womanly* are **implied** as "oppositions" to "manly qualities": "servility, insincerity, and underhandedness." Under *feminine*, we find two more adjectives, *weak* and *gentle*, but that's it. Positive attributes commonly associated with females, nurturing, kind, and loving, have been omitted, exactly the "feminine" traits that some women want to "reclaim." But those didn't make it into the *RHD* descriptions.

Most speakers of English accept as "fact" the descriptions forced by this semantic structure. They assume that the descriptive limits of English are, in fact, the limits of reality. One is or is not a man. This assumption was expressed in a television advertisement for a magazine, **Savvy**, aimed at a female audience: "You don't have to be *like a man* to succeed in business. You can allow yourself *to be a woman*." The opposition of *woman* and *man* in the ad accepts the idea that members of both sexes are utterly different, assumes as givens the descriptive adjectives for both sexes omitted from the *RHD* definitions, and implies that being "like a man" is an undesirable thing for a woman, even if she wants to "succeed in business" (a "man's world").

But PUD dictates that "being a woman" cannot be a "good thing." What isn't apparent in Diagram 3.1 is the equation of "feminine" and "childish" behaviors described by Otto Jespersen. This equation turns up in other places where it isn't as obvious. Consider, for example, paired phrases like "jock itch"/"feminine itch," "adult supporter" (jock strap)/"feminine apparel" (underwear), or the euphemistic "adult movies," "adult bookstore," both of which refer to **male** pornography. Such examples reflect the equation of [+male] with 'adulthood', and the corollary notion that women, because [−male], are non-adult ("childish").

When we consider the definition for *mannish*, "the aberrant possession of masculine characteristics," the idea of a woman who is honest, strong, dignified, forthright, and brave is revealed as negative. Men have reserved the positive attributes for themselves. Women are implicitly defined as "appropriately" weak, gentle, insincere, servile, and underhanded, and any woman who is honest, forthright, dignified, brave, or resolute is "aberrant," that is, *mannish*. PUD dictates that those born female who reject the dichotomy, who refuse to behave in feminine, "appropriate" ways, will be labeled "masculine" by semantic default. This semantic trick makes it seem as though the adjectives describe behavior accurately, but their existence maintains patriarchal consensus reality at the cost of the individual's integrity. These words will become obsolete just as soon as speakers, especially women, realize such words name culturally valued behaviors, not inherent, biological attributes, and stop using them. Our continued use validates these descriptions.

Chapter 4

Gender: The Sex of Nouns

Semantic structure creates meaning. Without semantic structure, meaning does not exist. In chapter 3, I described the underlying semantic structure of sexual dimorphism in English and how specific words wouldn't exist without its assumptions. What happens, then, when that language of acculturated behaviors is superimposed on linguistic categories as their descriptors? In other words, what are the consequences for grammatical analysis when the words associated with a sex-based dichotomy are elevated to usage as **metalinguistic** terms, and put forth as grammatical explanations of a language? As one might expect, when those terms become defining categories in a grammatical description, sexual dimorphism and heterosexuality are imposed on linguistic phenomena and become the filter through which those phenomena are perceived and interpreted.

This is what has happened with the description of noun classification systems in grammars of all the Indo-European (I-E) languages.[1] Some readers may recall having to learn what was presented to them as "grammatical gender" when they studied Greek, Latin, or one of the modern languages, and being told **not** to interpret it as referring to sex. They may also remember having difficulty understanding the idea of "grammatical gender," and being confused about its function in the description of the different kinds of nouns in the language they were learning. If my readers have had this experience, the following discussion of how "gender" has distorted descriptions of I-E languages will explain its sources.

MYTH AS THEORY

"Gender," as a grammatical description, is one of the many inaccuracies perpetrated by the imposition of Latin (and Greek) rules onto many contemporary languages, English among them, by the patriarchal grammatical tradition. That the term *gender* has recently found widespread currency as a euphemistic substitute for the word *sex*, especially among academic scholars in the social sciences, makes it timely as well as significant, because *gender* seems now to be understood as a synonym for **sex**, both in biological and social contexts, largely as a result of the narrowing of the term in traditional grammars. What follows illustrates how generations of men have controlled one small segment of linguistic discourse: gender. From its beginnings in classical grammars, the label *gender* was misconstrued, misapplied, and misinterpreted, primarily because Protagoras, the fifth century b.c. Sophist credited by Aristotle with its description (Robins, 25), chose the Greek equivalents of the English adjectives *masculine* and *feminine* (the category *neuter* seems to have been added later) when he identified the noun-classes of Greek. The consequences have been unfortunate, to say the least.

The English grammatical term *gender* is derived from Latin *genus*, from Greek, which meant 'race', 'class', or 'kind'. It did not mean 'sex', biological or grammatical, as Dennis Baron (1986) has observed.

> This association of grammatical gender with human generation was introduced as early as Priscian's sixth-century Latin grammar, and it was developed by medieval grammarians and accepted by their successors. Richard Johnson ([1706] 1969, 13) derives the word *gender* [whose original meaning 'kind, or sort,' had nothing to do with sex] from Latin *genus*, 'birth, species,' and from *gigno*, 'to beget', a direct reference to the physical act of engendering. (91)

Protagoras's choice of *feminine* and *masculine* to label noun classifications seems to have had a hypnotic effect on virtually every grammarian since. Within the patriarchal philosophical framework, however, the conflation of gender with sex and their development as virtually synonymous terms was probably inevitable. Had Protagoras adopted terms that weren't sex-linked, for example, cowrie, acorn, obsidian, countless pseudo-problems would have been avoided in the western grammatical tradition. Male grammarians have been certain that linguistic relationships mirror heterosexual behaviors, and, in the grip of their fervor, false etymologies that strengthened that perception became fixed items in the vocabulary of grammatical analysis. Protagoras himself was reportedly so convinced that biological sex was inherent in the names of things that he lamented the fact that Greek *menis*, 'anger,' and *peleks*, 'helmet', belonged to the feminine gender, and urged that they be switched to the masculine gender (Robins [1967] 1979, 15–16).

I do not know what motivated Protagoras to choose the adjectives *feminine* and *masculine* to describe noun classifications in Greek, and I haven't read a historian of grammars who has asked. R. H. Robins, whose *Short History of Linguistics* is widely respected, described the continuing influence of the classical grammarians on grammars of modern languages, and seemed to think it beneficial.

It was in the field of grammar that the Greek (and the Roman) world did its best work. In this we not only see the purposeful and fruitful building of later generations on their predecessors' results, but we know of authoritative books written on Greek and Latin grammmars, several of which are extant, and the grammatical descriptions provided in them were maintained by a continuous tradition through the Middle Ages and the modern world to become the basis of the standard grammars of these languages today. Moreover the theories, categories, and terminology evolved by ancient scholars in relation to the grammars of their own languages have become part of the general grammatical equipment of descriptive linguists of our own day. (24–25)

Without a doubt, Robins was correct in his assertion that generations of grammarians have built on the linguistic descriptions first recorded by the Greeks, but I would argue with his characterization of that tradition as "fruitful," even though the adjective is consistent with the reproductive metaphor. A likely answer to my question is that Protagoras was among the first to introduce the metaphor GRAMMAR IS SEX into grammatical discourse, an equation adopted by the Latin grammarian Priscian, and already discussed with respect to the work of Alan of Lille.

Until recently, the sex-linked adjectives *feminine* and *masculine* were analytically opaque even to linguists, who have questioned so many of the assumptions and descriptions of prescriptive grammarians. As Robins observed, those category labels are "part of the . . . grammatical equipment of descriptive linguists of our own day." They are in place, everyone uses them as though they are meaningful, and no one has said there might be a serious problem even though numerous grammarians have commented on "anomalies" created by the sex-based description of nouns. Yet linguists continue to use *feminine* and *masculine* even when they acknowledge the problems. Anne E. Mills, for example, in her cross-linguistic study of gender acquisition in German and English (1986), introduced the concept of gender as follows:

Most Indo-European languages base their system [of noun classification] on the **natural** sex distinction, hence the term 'gender'. (6)

She knew better. In a footnote to that statement, she acknowledged that the term *gender* is derived from Latin *genus* and "originally meant category in general," but then unintentionally (I think) revealed the cognitive reversal at work: "the term [*gender*] now refers to sexual categories and will be used in this sense" (6). She accepted, apparently without question, the idea that sex distinctions are "natural," even though she alluded to languages that base their noun classification on other criteria (e.g., "Some North American Indian languages classify according to the shape and size of the referent"). If she had not assumed that sex distinctions are "natural," the *caveat* of her footnote might have given her pause.

It's no secret that the equation of gender with biological sex has forced grammatical confusion on speakers and circular reasoning on those who've tried to justify it. John Lyons' discussion of grammatical and "natural" gender in *Introduction to Theoretical Linguistics* (1969) described the problem that speakers of French experience when an adjective, which must agree in number **and** gender with the noun it modifies, occurs with a noun (such as *le professeur*) categorized as "masculine," when it is being used to describe a woman. This situation makes it impossible to say, "The new professor is beautiful," if the professor is a woman, without violating a prescriptive rule.

> Neither the masculine form of the adjective (e.g., *beau*) nor its feminine form (*belle*) can be used appropriately in these circumstances without resolving, as it were, the "conflict" between "grammatical" and "natural" gender. Neither *Le nouveau professeur est beau* (which necessarily refers to a man) nor **Le nouveau professeur est belle* (which is ungrammatical) is possible. (287–88)

Lyons concluded his discussion of gender by reasserting the importance of "gender-agreement" in communication, without once wondering if the terms *feminine* and *masculine*, and the resulting equation of gender with sex, might be a large, and unexamined source of the "conflict."

Instead, as I. Fodor's survey of the significant contributions to the literature on gender shows, some of the most distinguished historical linguists succumbed to the appeal of Protagoras's labels and based their theories on the origin of "gender" on the assumption that nouns were classified according to some semantic-psychological notion of 'femaleness' or 'maleness'.

> Permeated by the idea of anthropomorphism it was thought reasonable and consequently superb that natural gender was reflected in language through such subtle grammatical devices and further, that through the neuter gender even those concepts could be set apart that were indifferent in point of sex. Following in the footsteps of Adelung and Herder, even Bopp and Grimm looked upon gender as the reflection of sex. (1959, 3)

I would add to anthropomorphism the tendency of men to regard themselves as the "crowning glory" of the human species. Only that arrogance can explain the thorough-going patriarchal (and paternal) character of linguistic analyses, and the fact that so much intellect has been wasted trying to unravel the snarled mess created by Protagoras's misnaming.

Not until the twentieth century did linguists have another look at the accepted, sex-linked analysis of noun classifications in the I-E languages. In the 1920s, Antoine Meillet, refusing to begin his analysis of gender with the more usual morphological and semantic motives, started by searching for an explanation in syntactic relations (Fodor, 1959, 19–21). The hypothesis that results from his investigation is interesting not only for this discussion but in connection with the rhetorical differences between active and passive sentences (chapter 9).

Meillet suggested that at an early stage, I-E nouns weren't differentiated at all except according to their functions in specific utterances, and that differentiation occurred in stages. I-E did have a case system (**nominative, dative, genitive, accusative**),[2] but nouns didn't have distinctive endings for the nominative and accusative cases. Meillet hypothesized that, in certain syntactic situations, where it was necessary to know which noun was functioning as the **agent** (nominative) and which one was the **object** of the verb (accusative), the Indo-Europeans developed a suffix for nouns in the accusative case which they used when the agent and object in a sentence might be confused. Ordinarily, persons, living beings, or personified concepts occurred as agents (nominatives) in sentences, and other, non-animate things were talked about as objects (accusatives) and were less frequently agents. So distinguishing inanimates in the nominative and accusative cases wasn't always necessary.

The group of non-animate nouns, Meillet suggested, developed into the inanimate (neuter) gender. The result, in Indo-European, was a noun classification system based on the semantic feature [± animate]. That is, at some stage of I-E, two genders developed, in the true sense of the word, the non-neuter (animate) and the neuter (inanimate) genders, not, as many have supposed, a three-gender system based on biological sex. Had Protagoras's labeling not seemed so "natural" to succeeding generations of patriarchal grammarians, the I-E noun-class system might have been accurately ascertained sooner as one based on a syntactic distinction between animate and inanimate things originating in the kinds of things one said about them. Protagoras could have spared himself anguish and students wouldn't have to puzzle over the alleged "grammatical gender" which characterizes German *Mädchen* as "neuter" and *Weib* as "masculine."

When men get an idea into their heads and resolve that it's a "fact," it becomes an unshakable, fixed star in their conceptual firmament. Once *feminine* and *masculine* were chosen to designate noun classes, gender and sex became synonymous and the necessity of distinguishing between "grammatical" and "natural" gender followed, a distinction which purports to explain the pseudo-problem created by Protagoras's choice of labels for noun classification. What shouldn't exist at all continues to plague otherwise astute linguists because it's there. (Why they have neglected to question these labels in the course of their presentations on the subject is a mystery.)

Since neither linguists nor grammarians have challenged or replaced the terms *feminine*, *masculine*, and *neuter*, however, some discussion of the resulting distinction between grammatical and "natural" gender must precede an examination of how male grammarians imposed the equation of gender and sex on English. Aristotle seems to have been the first man to recognize that the labels *feminine* and *masculine* required some further distinction, namely that between "grammatical gender" and "natural gender."

In language, "grammatical" gender is said to be an internal requirement that specific grammatical elements must agree with each other in gender, in addition to number (and sometimes case). This rule is known as "concord" or "agreement." Grammatical gender is said to require agreement between nouns, the adjectives and determiners (articles) used with them, and the pronouns that replace them in subsequent discourse. In Lyons' example from French, the noun phrase *le professeur* would have to be replaced by the male pronoun *il* even if it referred to a woman. The grammatical gender of a noun is generally held to be independent of the biological sex of its referent; obviously, sex is characteristic only of animate nouns (but recall Protagoras's musings about the Greek words for 'helmet' and 'anger' because these seemed to him to "partake" of male characteristics). Fire, chairs, planets, houses, and other inanimate objects do not, as far as I know, possess sex-linked traits, and so should not cause concern in discussions of grammatical gender (but they do).

In German, which is said to have "grammatical" gender, every noun must be classified as feminine, neuter, or masculine, and the **definite determiners** reflect the grammatical gender of their singular nouns in the nominative: *die* = feminine, *das* = neuter, and *der* = masculine. **Indefinite** articles and possessive pronouns show gender agreement only for feminine nouns, *eine*, *meine*; the neuter and masculine nouns are the same (*ein, mein*), with the exception of the accusative (object) case (*mein, meinen*). (This evidence seems to support Meillet's hypothesis.)

Mills (1986), discussing some of the semantic, phonological, and morphological rules that determine the grammatical gender of a noun in German, used the research of Zubin and Köpcke (1982; 1983). A representative sampling of the semantic groupings indicated that the notion of some underlying "natural sex distinction" failed to account for grammatical gender assignment in German. (The same can be said of other contemporary I-E languages.) Generic (superordinate) nouns (*das Obst*, 'fruit'), colors (*das Grün*, 'green'), chemical elements (*das Silber*, 'silver'), abstract units of measure (*das Watt*, 'watt'), and games (*das Poker*, 'poker') are categorized as neuter. Nouns associated with speech acts (*die Rede*, 'speech'), power/strength (*die Gewalt*, 'force'), hunting (*die Jagd*, 'hunt'), musical instruments (*die Orgel*, 'organ'), knowledge (*die Kunst*, 'art'), seafaring signs (*die Boje*, 'buoy'), numbers (*die Nummer*, 'number'), and temperature (*die Glut*, 'burning heat') belong to the feminine gender, while nouns referring to waste (*der Dreck*, 'muck'), cloth (*der Taft*, 'taffeta'), stone/sand (*der Quarz*, 'quartz'), birds (*der Habicht*, 'hawk'), plants (*der Pilz*, 'mushroom'), precipitation (*der Reif*, 'frost') and wind (*der Passat*, 'tradewind') are assigned to the masculine gender. The prefix *ge-*, which means 'collective', determines that a noun belongs to the neuter gender, as do the diminutive suffixes *-lein* and *-chen*

(Mills, 1986, 26–30). One would have to stretch a bit to explain why temperature is feminine, while wind and precipitation are masculine.

As Mills' discussion indicates, grammatical gender in German is a complicated system of categorization, made more opaque by the assumed development from a classification system based on sex. German illustrates what is meant by "grammatical gender" in the I-E languages, in contrast to the situation in ModE, which is said to have "natural" gender. Added to the confusion of gender with sex, then, we also have to contend with the resulting confusion of "grammatical" and "natural" genders, which are presented as though they actually described something.

Old English had a system of noun classification much like that of Modern German, based on the distinction between animate and inanimate, inherited from earlier I-E. Gradually, (through phonological processes not germane to this discussion), the suffixes that matched nouns to their grammatical categories disappeared from English, which is said to classify nouns on the basis of "natural gender" now. "Natural gender" refers to a noun classification system supposedly based on the biological sex of the person to whom a noun refers. According to this description, all nouns that refer to females carry the semantic feature [+female]; likewise, all those referring to men are categorized semantically as [+male]. This analysis appears to work well for certain human nouns. Thus, words like *mother, aunt, niece, widow, wife, girl, woman,* and *daughter* all belong to the [+female] (or [−male]) category and the pronoun *she* can be substituted for them in subsequent discourse. Nouns such as *father, uncle, nephew, widower, husband, boy, man,* and *son* carry the feature [+male] and are replaced by the pronoun *he* where necessary.

The description of English as possessing a noun classification system based on "natural gender" will occupy much of chapter 7. At this point, I'll mention only a few of the idiosyncrasies that make this analysis suspect. Readers will have noticed, for example, that virtually all the nouns I listed in the preceding paragraph are **kinship** terms; that is, they belong to a set of words that name familial relationships, along with others, for example, *sister/ brother.* Once we leave such terms behind, the noun classification system in English reflects anything but "natural gender." Idiosyncrasies that come to mind include an apparent reluctance to use the pronoun *it* for inanimate objects or beings of indeterminate sex (such as unknown babies), and the use of the pronoun *she* to refer to countries, ships, cars, and cats,[3] *he* for specific animals, such as lions, bears, and dogs, and what Mills called a "general tendency to 'masculinize'" (24). (She explains this "tendency" as "traditional usage.")

What Mills called "traditional usage" is, of course, nothing other than the rule mongering of the prescriptivists discussed in chapter 1, the largely male grammatical descriptions of English that established usage still held up to us as "correct." As one might expect, English grammarians from the seventeenth century on have waxed long and eloquently on the subject of "gender," accepting the classical idea that nouns were categorized according to the distinction of biological sex. Because English had already lost the suffixes that marked grammatical gender in OE, a number of adjectives have been used to describe "gender," such as "natural, notional, referential, or semantic."[4] Whichever term grammarians settled on, they were determined to force English nouns into conformity with the "superior" classical languages they revered. Although, as Elizabeth Sklar (1983) has pointed out, these men recognized that the English system of classifying nouns differed from other I-E languages, Latin and Greek included, that knowledge didn't stop them from imposing the classical model, with its assumptions, on English.

By the seventeenth century, when grammarians set themselves the task of "standardizing" and "purifying" English, their explanations of how nouns were categorized as *feminine* or *masculine* were also fairly standardized. Although the English vocabulary contains many nouns that can't be classified by sex, those for which the sex distinction can be made to seem plausible were the focus of grammatical discussions. Inanimate nouns (e.g., *table, chair, step, poison*) received little attention. Where inanimate nouns were discussed, they were treated as though "neuter" were a catch-all category for nouns that couldn't be categorized by sex, as, indeed, it seems to be.[5] R. Harrison, for example, in his *Institutes of English Grammar* (1777), perceived the sex-based distinction to be primary.

> Nouns have properly two GENDERS; the *Masculine*, to denote the male kind; and the *Feminine*, to denote the female.
> When there is no distinction of sex, a Noun is said to be of the NEUTER Gender. (4)

In *The Theory of Language*, first published in 1788, James Beattie, too, posited the distinction of sex as the primary basis of noun classification for English, but went a step further by making explicit the patriarchal religious significance of sexual dimorphism.

> Another thing essential to nouns is gender. For language would be very imperfect if it had no expression for the sex of animals. Now all things whatever are Male, or Female, or Both, or Neither.
> The existence of hermaphrodites being uncommon, and even doubtful, and language being framed to answer the ordinary occasions of life, no provision is made . . . for expressing . . . Duplicity of sex. . . .
> Beings superiour to man, although we conceive them to be of no sex, are spoken of as masculine in most of the modern tongues of Europe, on account of their dignity; the male being, according to our ideas, the nobler sex. But idolatrous nations acknowledge both male and female deities; and some of them have given even to the Supreme Being a name of the feminine gender. (134–37)

The plurality of Beattie's pronoun in "our ideas" can only refer to men, unless one attributes his choice to a presumption that those ideas also belonged to women. The "idea" of male superiority, in grammar as in all other things, was often elaborated in grammatical treatises. Some of these men were succinct, others were not. Poole's statement of the relative values associated with sex in his grammar of 1646, *The English Accidence*, is terse: "The Masculine gender is more worthy than the Feminine, and the Feminine is more worthy than the Neuter" (21). A longer excerpt from John Fell's *An Essay Towards an English Grammar* (1784) links the assignment of sex to nouns to what PUD calls "nature": the entailment relation described previously (in Diagram 3.1) between biological sex (Level I) and behavior (Level II).

> In poetical or theoretical expression of this kind, moral qualities, such as *wisdom, truth, justice, reason, virtue,* and *religion,* are of the feminine gender. The passions must be determined according to their different natures: the fiercer and more disagreeable are masculine—the softer and more amiable are feminine. *Mind* is masculine, *soul* feminine; for the latter term more of the affections are frequently implied than in the former. The *sun* is masculine, the *moon* feminine, the *Heaven* neuter—the *earth* is feminine; mountains and rivers are commonly masculine; countries and cities are feminine—and nature, as comprehending all, is feminine. (5–6)

If Fell's explanation for the way English nouns are personified as male or female were accurate, women would be running world governments. But Lindley Murray's account, in *English Grammar* (1795), made explicit the patriarchal metaphors that frame the male perception of "sense": men *impart,* women *receive.* Such ideas persist, not because they're "true" or accurate, but because men **like** them. The idea that the sun is male and the moon female has a long tradition in the west that continues today. Shakespeare's *Romeo and Juliet* contains a sonnet in which the basic metaphors are ROMEO IS THE SUN and JULIET IS THE MOON, and Mario Cuomo paraphrased Shakespeare during the 1984 Democratic convention: "She [Geraldine Ferraro] will be *the moon to Mondale's sun.*" I doubt that Cuomo would have characterized Mondale's running mate in this way if it had been a man.

The entrenchment of these ideas as grammatical "fundamentals" was assured by the middle of the nineteenth century. In 1850 the British Parliament passed an Act declaring that the pronoun *he* would henceforth be interpreted as including reference to women as well as men (discussed in chapter 7), and, in 1851, Goold Brown produced his reference grammar for the English language, *Grammar of English Grammars.* His "Observations on Gender" is lengthy, but two excerpts from sections one and six are relevant here: the first because Brown based the English gender system in "the order of nature," the second because he explained why *he* should be the "common gender" (generic) pronoun.

> 1.—The different genders in grammar are founded on the natural distinction of sex in animals, and on the absence of sex in other things. In English, they belong only to nouns and pronouns; and to these they are usually applied, **not**

arbitrarily, as in some other languages, but agreeably to the order of nature. [My emphasis] From this we derive a very striking advantage over those who use the gender differently, or without such rule; which is, that our pronouns are easy of application, and have a fine effect when objects are personified. Pronouns are of the same gender as the nouns for which they stand. . . .

6.—The gender of words, in many instances, is to be determined by the following principle of universal grammar. Those terms which are equally applicable to both sexes (if they are not expressly applied to females), and those plurals which are known to include both sexes, should be called masculine in parsing; for, in all languages, the masculine gender is considered the most worthy,* and is generally employed when both sexes are included under one common term. Thus *parents* is always masculine. . . .

"Natural" gender in English, according to the patriarchal grammatical tradition, assigns the feature [+male] to every human noun in the vocabulary unless it is conceptualized as female.

The preceding discussion illustrates how male control of naming in one area, noun classification, has falsely described Indo-European (and later languages derived from it), obscured whatever the original system might have been, and distorted all subsequent discourse on the subject. Since *gender* was equated with biological sex and the labels *feminine, masculine,* and *neuter* became established for noun categories, no analysis of how nouns are classified has been possible without using those labels. The ensuing confusion has been caused by a nomenclature that inaccurately names the objects it refers to, and we may never extricate ourselves from that framework, even if linguists exert considerable effort to replace the names. (To date, virtually no linguistic terminology has found its way into everyday conversation about language.) Once named, objects and events are forced to conform to the boundaries of PUD, whether or not the names are accurate descriptions and no matter how much counter-evidence accumulates. Once the sex-specific adjectives that proscribe socially acceptable behaviors for women and men were attached as descriptors of noun categories, the entailment relation between Levels I and II (of Figure 3.1), the assumption that *masculine*=male and *feminine*=female became an explanatory fixture of prescriptive grammars.

Regardless of how inadequate such descriptions prove to be, patriarchal labels continue to control and limit even the best analyses (as Mills' study illustrates), perpetuating the idea that the labels *feminine* and *masculine* have, from the beginning, described linguistic structure when, in fact, the false descriptions initiated this centuries-long error. Trapped by perceptual and cognitive distortions, the evidence that can't be accounted for multiplies, and is dismissed as "irrelevant," shoved aside as an "anomaly," or imaginatively "explained."

---

*"The Supreme Being (*God* . . .) is, in all languages, masculine; in as much as the masculine sex is the superior and more excellent; and as He is the Creator of all, the Father of gods and men."—*Harris's Hermes*, p. 54. (Brown, 254–255)

THE WORLD ACCORDING TO PUD

Our point of view, our perceptions, our consciousness determine and limit how we describe events, objects, and people. PUD constructs the world as men perceive it; it is a *male* "idealized" conceptual framework that defines the boundaries of "sense" for us: which statements about the world "make sense" to us and which statements we describe as "non-sense." Patriarchal assumptions structure the language we speak, the primary mediator of our experience. The linguistic choices we make reveal much about our assumptions. Sometimes it's specific words or phrases that signal our conceptual framework, as illustrated in my discussions of the apparent "clash" between the LANGUAGE IS A WOMAN and LANGUAGE IS A TOOL metaphorical concepts and traditional explanations of how nouns are categorized in English. But the universe of discourse within which we conceive ourselves as speakers governs our choices over much larger linguistic spans as well. This is true of everything from sentences to paragraphs to entire novels. Sometimes our assumptions are made explicit by our linguistic choices. Other times what we don't say, what we decide to leave out, can be just as significant to our intended audience.

Describing languages as though speaking were a sexual act and noun categories as though they are determined by sex-specific characteristics aren't the only ways men control how we understand what language is. Every day of our lives we hear and read language intended to stick in our minds. Patriarchal descriptions of "how the world is" surround us like the air we breathe, and, whether we want to admit it or not, we have only limited control over what our brains take in and preserve at the subconscious level—like the commercial jingle that I sometimes wake up to find caught in my mind, the one that replays itself no matter what I do to try and dislodge it. Or, sometimes, I'll find myself humming the catchy tune of a popular song that has misogynist lyrics, and nothing I do will drive it out of my mind. Such examples may suggest that the LANGUAGE IS A TOOL metaphor is an accurate way of talking about language because we're certainly dealing with uses of language. It feels, at least, as though English is being *used* in intentionally harmful ways. The choices we make when we select words and the sentence structures that order those words reflect the way we categorize events and objects in the world inside our minds.

Evidence of how PUD manipulates our perceptions and behaviors surrounds us. There are four identifying features that make PUD unmistakable.

1. the systematic misinterpretation of actions and statements, and a stubborn insistence on what are **acknowledged** to be misinterpretations;
2. the patriarchal method of imposing its descriptions and then maintaining them in spite of evidence to the contrary;
3. substituting an inanimate object or event as the agent that "causes" the

speaker to commit some act, or making an abstract entity responsible for the feelings of the speaker;

4. Separating individuals from the consequences of their perceptions and actions by means of either personification or reification, thus creating a gap between actual cause and effect.

It's way past time for women to say aloud that the language to which PUD subjects us daily doesn't make any sense, that there is little or no correspondence between what we hear being said and what we know or perceive. No woman has to remain trapped within the masculist perspective. Learning to recognize the sentence patterns, phrases, and words that effect PUD discourse strategies is relatively simple. Women don't have to remain the silent co-conspirators in maintaining masculist pretense. We can learn to think and speak differently.

Chapter 5

Woman's Place Is
in the Home

Two well-known clichés state the situation accurately: "A man's home is **his** castle"; "A woman's place is in the home." We hear both assertions, all too often, mouthed by women and men alike as though they stated some essential truth. There is the male domain, called "The World," which men describe for themselves, and the female domain, of "the world" but not The World. When men talk about The World, they describe **their** experiential domain, making it seem to be all there is. In one sense, this is true, but only because women's allotted sphere lies confined within the domain of men. "Women's world" is our place in "man's world." They treat other worldly aspects, especially women's experiential domain, as incidental marginalia, at best, lacunae, at worst. Yet, men appear to be steadfastly unaware that women's daily labor supports their privilege, and deny that they have privilege when we say we're dissatisfied or comment on our exclusion from "Man's World."

Languages serve the purposes of their speakers. There are no exceptions. If women are to change the ways we perceive ourselves as well as the context of our lives, we must first understand what our situation is and how patriarchal languages perpetuate our state of oppression. To the best of my knowledge, there are no languages in existence based on women's perceptions of or experiences in the world.[1] Some people talk about "women's languages," but these aren't **languages** at all. Rather, they are social **dialects** women are taught to speak, and the features characteristic of these women's dialects mark us as subordinate to men in the world, as "weak," "passive," "stupid" because we talk "like women." The women's dialects of many languages signal our inferiority to men. Should a woman be bold or fed up enough to speak the male dialect of her culture, she is marginalized and labeled outcast, at least, for her daring.

Up to this point, I have discussed how men have controlled English through their grammars of the language and the conceptual metaphors they use to describe how language "works," and sketched the internal structure of the Patriarchal Universe of Discourse, the two experiential spheres within PUD that mirror the distinction of biological sex. I'll turn now to a more detailed consideration of the ways patriarchal languages subordinate women and maintain the myth of male superiority as "consensus" reality (PUD). There are at least four ways women figure in PUD; the first two are already familiar:

1. DELIMITING: as objects, women's being and behaviors are named by men;
2. RESTRICTIVE: as speakers, women are forbidden to use specific areas of male-dominated languages, and/or taught to speak with a distinctive (read: "feminine") intonation pattern, with the result that what men call a "women's language" develops;
3. GRAMMATICAL: in patriarchal languages, biological sex must be marked with distinctive affixes or particles;
4. ADVERSARIAL: women sometimes rebel against male linguistic domination, and their rebellion takes several forms.

In the course of this chapter, I'll describe languages that demonstrate one or more of these possibilities. In none of them, however, are women speakers of significance. Men reserve that distinction to themselves.

THE FATHERS' TONGUES

Historically, most linguists have been, and are, men. A majority of those who have worked in the field collecting, transcribing, analyzing, and writing grammars of languages have been men. In many cultures, men speak only to men about "the world," so male linguists have gathered their linguistic information from male subjects, ignoring the female members of societies. Until women began going out into the field to collect information about languages, women were excluded as linguistic subjects, with the result that most descriptive grammars of languages were written by men on the basis of what male speakers told them.[2] Male dominance is so taken for granted, even among linguists, that it seems not to have occurred to many that women's linguistic knowledge should be sought out and recorded with the same attention paid to men's.

In Male/Female Language (1975), Mary Ritchie Key described the first time she realized that languages have sex-based differences. Studying the languages spoken among Indians in Bolivia, she visited a village inhabited by the Ignacianos. Working from a male linguist's field notes, Key was supposed to check the linguistic evidence he had gathered. Her Ignaciano informant was a bilingual woman who spoke Spanish as well her native language. When Key read a certain word aloud, the woman began to laugh; the informant laughed so hard that Key thought she might topple from her stool. Key quickly discovered that she had read a word only men could say, a word never spoken by Ignaciano women and that had caused the woman's hilarity (13). Key didn't explain whether her informant's amusement was caused by her uninformed assumption, based on the male linguist's data, that the word was commonly used by both sexes or the fact that a female was uttering the word.

The incident, however, piqued Key's interest. Once she concentrated on identifying sex-based linguistic differences in language, she realized that "linguistic sex distinctions undoubtedly occur in every language of the world" (13). Since white men invaded the Americas, there have been numerous accounts of separate female and male languages among the Indians, some more accurate than others.[3] In those cases where male linguists have mentioned the possibility of sex-based linguistic differences, they have been reluctant to treat them as credible. "Interestingly enough," she continued, "they have not been reported upon widely. Of the four to five thousand languages of the world, I can find linguistic statements about sex distinctions in fewer than a hundred."

Otto Jespersen's chapter, "The Woman," in *Language: Its Nature, Development and Origin* (1921), is probably the most frequently quoted by scholars concerned with sex-specific linguistic distinctions. Of almost 450 pages of text, that chapter (XIII) is only 17 pages long. (Its title suggests that the remaining 30 chapters of the book are about **men's** languages.) Jespersen, a relatively careful linguist, observed that what are usually characterized as "totally different languages" are "distinct dialects" (an important qualification I'll return to shortly). In order to support his observation, Jespersen discussed languages from several different language groups, beginning with an account by Rochefort of the sex-distinct languages spoken by the Caribs of the Small Antilles, among whom Rochefort lived in the mid-seventeenth century.

Noting that the sex-differences of the Carib language are to be found in the vocabulary, among the kinship terms, Jespersen attributed the existence of distinct kinship vocabularies to "tabu"; linguistic distinctions based on sex mark the separation of the two experiential spheres.

> Rochefort himself (p. 497) very briefly says that "the women do not eat till their husbands have finished their meal," and Lafitau (1724) says that women never eat in the company of their husbands and never mention them by name, but must wait upon them as their slaves; with this Labat agrees. (238)

Extrapolating from this social observation to language, Jespersen concluded that

> we have here simply [sic!] an instance of a custom found in various forms and in varying degrees throughout the world—what is called verbal tabu: under certain circumstances, at certain times, in certain places, the use of one or more definite words is interdicted, because it is superstitiously believed to entail certain evil consequences . . . (239)

He neglected to identify these verbal taboos as male interdictions forbidding women to use specific words, and his repetition of *certain* de-emphasized that what he called "customs" are patriarchal social restrictions on women's freedom to speak and act (sometimes, also, children's and young men's).

Jespersen did connect the Carib women's restricted speech with other verbal taboos. Note that his use of "old Caribs" and "tribe" in this quotation excludes women.

> Now as a matter of fact we find that verbal tabu was a common practice with the old Caribs: when they were on the war-path they had a great number of mysterious words which women were never allowed to learn and which even the young men might not pronounce before passing certain tests of bravery and patriotism; . . . It is easy to see that once a tribe [sic] has acquired the habit of using a whole set of terms under frequently recurring circumstances, while others [sic] are at the same time strictly interdicted, this may naturally [sic] lead to so many words being reserved exclusively for one of the sexes that an observer may be tempted to speak of separate "languages" for the two sexes. There is thus no occasion to believe in the story of a wholesale extermination of all male inhabitants by another tribe, though on the other hand it is easy to understand how such a myth may arise as an explanation of the linguistic difference between men and women, *when it has become strong enough to attract attention and therefore has to be accounted for.* [My emphasis] (239)

In addition to Carib, Jespersen included other languages in his survey of sex-based dialects: Bantu (Zulu, specifically), the Chiquitos of Bolivia, the Yana language of California, Swahili, and the bilingualism of German and Scandinavian immigrants in the u.s. Forgetting his earlier distinction between language and dialect, Jespersen said that "the connexion between a separate women's language and tabu is indubitable" (239). Among the Zulus,

> a wife is not allowed to mention the name of her father-in-law and of his brothers, and if a similar word or even a similar syllable occurs in the ordinary language, she must substitute something else of a similar meaning. In the royal family the difficulty of understanding the women's language is further increased by the woman's being forbidden to mention the names of her husband, his father and grandfather as well as his brothers.

This isn't "women's language" but "non-men's language." It's less a matter of what women *can* say than what they *cannot* say. The women's "language" of the Zulus consists of nothing more than a series of substitution rules governing the names men forbid women to utter.

The penalties for women who break men's rules are often extreme and fatal. Yet, when Jespersen described the consequences for women who won't observe men's linguistic rules, he achieved the distanced tone men prize.

> If one of these names [of the male relatives] means something like 'the son of the bull,' each of these words has to be avoided, and all kinds of paraphrases have to be used . . . the interdiction holds good not only for meaning elements

of the name, but even for certain sounds entering into them; thus, if the name contains the sound z, *amanzi* 'water' has to be altered into *amandabi*. If a woman were to contravene this rule she would be indicted for sorcery and put to death. (239–40)

Sounds "objective," doesn't it? He accomplished that effect with four passive verb phrases, *has to be avoided*, *have to be used*, *has to be altered*, and *would be indicted*, without mentioning the "understood" logical agents.

In the language of the Chiquitos of Bolivia, the dialects of women and men differ both phonologically and morphologically; it is the male dialect, however, that is marked, not the women's, and the men's speech that specifies sex. For example, men attach a suffix, *-tii* to nouns and verbs indicating the male agent of a sentence. Yet, Jespersen treated the women's speech as "deviant" when he illustrated how the distinction appears in men's utterances:

5.1 a. He went to his house: *yebo**tii** ti n-ipoos**tii***.
   b. He went to her house: *yebo**tii** ti n-ipoos*.
   c. She went to his house: *yebo ti n-ipoos**tii***.

Women, in contrast, would say, *yebo ni n-ipoos*, to express all three of the men's sentences; in men's speech it could only mean 'she went to her house'. In addition, Chiquito men prefix vowels to nouns, which women don't do. Women say *petas* 'turtle', *tamokos* 'dog', and *pis* 'wood', but men say *o-petas*, *u-tamokos*, and *i-pis*. As with the Caribs, there are also sex-based distinctions in the kinship terms: for 'father', 'mother', and 'brother', women say *isupu*, *ipapa*, and *icibausi*, respectively, whereas men say *iyai*, *ipaki*, and *tsaruki* to name the same relationships (Jespersen, 240).

Jespersen, following Dixon and Kroeber's analysis in *American Anthropologist* (1903), described the California language Yana as the only one of the Native American languages in that state in which women and men differ in their use of vocabulary items other than kinship terms, although many of the languages mark the sex of the speaker morphologically. According to Jespersen, Yana women's words are "shorter than those of the men, which appear as extensions" (240). Mary Ritchie Key, however, supplied contrasting lists of women's and men's terms (based on Edward Sapir's examples), and it isn't clear that the length, *per se*, is the only distinctive feature, as the following words indicate.

	Yana Male	Yana Female
'to eat':	mó'i	mó$^{'i}$
'deer liver':	imamba	imamp$^{'a}$
'crow':	gāgi	gāk$^{'i}$
'dog, horse':	cūcu	cūc^{u}
'inside':	īwūlu	īwūl^{u}
'woman':	mari'mi	mari$^{'m}$

Key's presentation of Yana suggests that women's speech differs from men's not in the length of words but in other phonological ways, which include **devoicing** and accompanying **aspiration** of the consonant in the final syllable, as in *gāk'ⁱ/gāgi* and *imamp'ᵃ/imamba*, and higher pitch or tone on the final vowel.

In her book, Key provided numerous examples from additional languages showing differences in female and male ways of speaking, including the Cham language of Vietnam, Gros Ventre, spoken by Native American tribes in Montana, and Koasati, a Muskogean language. As she said, "In some languages, in some words, males and females pronounce some sounds with distinct patterns" (68).[4] As Yana and the Chiquitos' language show, these aren't women's "languages" at all, but sex-specific dialects of a single language controlled by men.

Both Jespersen and Key observed that speech differences among women and men often reflect distinctions of *class* as well as sex. Linguistic variations within a language may reflect social as well as geographical differences. Social dialects originate in social distinctions, and the different ways women and men speak a given language are "social dialects." I want to emphasize this connection between sex and class and how the intersection of the two socially determined factors affects what we say as well as how we say it. Key, for example, quoted S. K. Chatterji's description (1921) of social dialect in Bengali: "In the speech of women and children and of the uneducated classes there is a tendency . . . to pronounce an 'n' for an 'l', in initial positions [when /n/ begins a word]" (Key, 1975, 70).

When Key discussed sex-determined differences in English, she commented: "The variations between the pronunciations [of *ing/in* among children], however, were not solely sex-differentiated, but were intricately involved with status, personality, mood, formality, and specific verbs." The differences in pronunciation appear to be associated with verbs, the use of which seems to be sex-linked: the *-ing* pronunciation of the girls occurred with verbs such as *criticizing, correcting, interesting,* and *visiting,* whereas the *-in* characteristic of the boys' speech turned up in *punchin, flubbin, chewin,* and *hittin.* As she observed, "The semantic categories are obvious; one can further extrapolate on the interest domains permitted boys and girls" (71).

Turning his attention to western languages of the Indo-European group, Jespersen believed that I-E languages (which he called "Aryan")[5] showed "few traces of real sex dialects," and described as "curious" the fact that in old Indian drama, "women talk Prakrit (*prakrta,* the natural or vulgar language) while men have the privilege of talking Sanskrit (*samskrta,* the adorned language)" (241–42). But he accurately attributed the difference not to sex, but to social class (caste):

for Sanskrit is the language of gods, kings, princes, brahmans, ministers, chamberlains, dancing-masters and **other men in superior positions and of a very few women of special religious importance**, while Prakrit is spoken by **men of an inferior class, like shopkeepers, law officers, aldermen, bathmen, fishermen and policemen, and by nearly all women**. The difference between the two 'languages' is one of degree only: they are two strata of the same language, one higher, more solemn, stiff and archaic, another lower, more natural and familiar, and this easy, or perhaps we should say slipshod, style is the only one recognized for ordinary women . . . and if all women, even those we should call the 'heroines' of the plays, use only the lower stratum of speech, the reason certainly is **that the social position of women was so inferior that they ranked only with men of the lower orders and had no share in the higher culture which, with the refined language, was the privilege of a small class of selected men**. [My emphases] (242)

Although I don't know which distinction came first, class or sex, the history and use of sex as a determinant of one's social and economic status in I-E cultures, such as those of Greece and Rome, suggest that women were probably the first subordinate class, and that men of the ruling class did exactly what they do to this day: they treated other men they had subjugated or regarded as inferior to them as women. Class status for men in patriarchal cultures other than India, with its caste system, seems to have been less a matter of birth than of circumstance. In both Greece and Rome, for example, men who had been members of the ruling elite in societies conquered in warfare became slaves, "like women," if they weren't killed. It may have been difficult or virtually impossible for a man to move up from a lower to higher class, but moving down from a higher to lower status, from king to slave, often occurred. Men's shifts in status were recognized in the goddesses Tyche of the Greeks and Fortuna of the Romans, both of whom represented fortune or chance. The same idea was symbolized in the Wheel of Fortune, a popular medieval symbol used by Chaucer in *The Monk's Tale* (in *The Canterbury Tales*).

A patriarchal culture is a society ruled by men, for men. In most of what is called "history," the events and deeds recorded have been those significant to men, including stories of how men overcame the matriarchal or matrilineal societies that preceded patriarchy. If we're curious about what women were doing in a particular era, we have to extrapolate from what men say they were doing and guess at how their activities affected women's lives. History is largely a chronology of the lives of "a small class of selected men," as Jespersen noted. He failed to say **who** might have "selected" them, but history suggests it was a process of violent *self-selection*. The social and economic class of a woman, then as now, was largely determined by her father's position, which, in turn, decided the class of her husband. Regardless of her father's or husband's economic class, she belonged, by definition, to the subordinate class of women, and, with very few exceptions, could not hope to gain and exercise political or social power in her own right. Women who could not or would not attach themselves to men had no social status. Given what we know of women's lives under several thousand years of male rule, it is more likely that "men of the lower orders" were "ranked" with women than the reverse, as Jespersen described it. That men can easily be demoted from the ruling class and treated "like women" is something apparent even in recent history, whereas the elevation of a woman from her political and social "inferiority" is a rare occurrence.

Jespersen was doubtless correct in his assertion that what many call "women's languages" are, in fact, *social dialects*, patterns of speech that mark us as belonging to a politically subordinated group. Men reserve to themselves just those linguistic patterns they label "standard," and men of lesser status adopt the dialect associated with women's status as representative of their "inferior" class. The same may be said of male children; they use the women's dialect until they are initiated into the ruling class, at which time they cease to speak as subordinates and use the standard, male dialect of their native language.

Social dialects, then, not only distinguish the experiential spheres determined by sex within PUD, but also maintain the political and economic inequality of all women and any men defined as "inferior." The ways sex differences affect language use can be subtle and extensive. The "inside" (of a house) is women's domain, while the "outside" (the rest of the world) belongs to men. Since men think of a house as their "castle," which women maintain for them, women have no space at all. In English, the two spheres determine the use of terms for kinds of equipment; *appliances* and *utensils* are used **inside** by women, *machines* and *tools* **outside** by men.

The dichotomy between what lies inside or outside of a dwelling, and its linguistic effects, appear clearly in Jespersen's discussion of language "conflict," a situation in which speakers are bilingual. What he said about German and Scandinavian immigrants in the u.s. and the Basques of the Pyrenées is interesting for its description as well as its substance.

> A difference between the language spoken by men and that spoken by women is seen in many countries where two languages are struggling for supremacy in a peaceful way—thus without any question of one nation exterminating the other **or the male part of it**. Among German and Scandinavian immigrants in America the men mix much more with the English-speaking population, and therefore have better opportunities, and also more occasion, to learn English than their wives, **who remain more within doors**. It is exactly the same among the Basques, where the school, the military service and daily business relations contribute to the extinction of Basque in favour of French, and where these factors operate much more strongly on the male than on the female population: there are families in which the wife talks Basque, while the husband does not even understand Basque and **does not allow his children to learn it**. [My emphases] (241)

What is being "exterminated" in such situations is whatever belongs to the women's domain; whatever is locked inside, what is not taken outside—in this case native language and culture—dies, unless extraordinary measures are taken, as in the case of the modern Basque Separatists fighting assimilation. The men who control access to the "outside world" of business and money impose their linguistic supremacy. The imposition of Norman French on the conquered English is a typical example. Within English dwellings—the women's domain—native Germanic words such as *ox*, *sheep*, *lamb*, and *eat* were used, but Norman French replaced English as the language of "worldly" (read: male) affairs.

How the two experiential domains determine the language or dialect one speaks answers at least one question posed by contemporary psycholinguistic research. On the one hand, some scholars give priority to the mother's language, which children learn and speak during their formative years. This alleged priority then seems to contradict the findings of other researchers, who point to the well-documented fact of male control of standard languages and grammars. If women are the earliest teachers of native speech, and if it is their linguistic patterns that children learn, how can one talk about "male linguistic control"? The answer should be obvious now. As long as male children remain inside, within their mother's sphere of influence, they imitate her speech. As soon as they step outside of the dwelling, however, into the world of the fathers, they must either abandon their "mother tongue" or find themselves consigned to a limited, impoverished existence beyond the home. The "question," then, isn't a question at all, but a consequence of the separate experiential spheres constructed by PUD. Aspects of the woman's sphere are restricted and contained within the world named by men. The function of language in maintaining and perpetuating patriarchal social structures and assumptions is more complex than it may at first appear, but it is also consistent across cultures.

ON WOMEN, FIRE, AND DANGEROUS THINGS

In chapter 3 I pointed out that sexual dimorphism is perceived and described by cultures other than Anglo-American and the resulting manifestations of sex distinction affect the structures of those languages in a variety of ways. In English, sexual dimorphism is coded in the third person singular pronouns and in the nouns referring to people and other animals, for example, *woman/man*, *daughter/son*, and *cow/bull*, *goose/gander*, *hen/rooster*. These sex-specific nouns form a large, if asymmetrical, set in the vocabulary. English exemplifies how PUD construes the world: it identifies the FUCKERS, men, and the rest of the world, including women, the FUCKEES. Before I discuss the semantic structure of common, human nouns in the English vocabulary (chapter 7), however, I want to illustrate how the two experiential spheres of women and men are coded in the structures and vocabularies of other non-Indo-European languages: Japanese, Chinese, and Dyirbal.

Of the world's approximately 4,000 languages,[6] most reflect the effects of male domination and describe the world as men perceive it. The male sphere encompasses what is to be perceived as the "official" reality, which includes defining the "place" men expect women to occupy in that reality. The male sphere becomes, by naming itself, the "superordinate"[7] sphere, making the female sphere, by naming it Other, the "subordinate" domain. The internal structure of some languages, like Japanese (Cherry, 1987, 10) and various I-E languages, may retain vestiges of an earlier matriarchal or matrilineal culture, but the contemporary languages reflect a patriarchal conceptual structure. The classification system of Dyirbal, an aboriginal language of Australia, illustrates how beings and objects are categorized from the male perspective.

G. Lakoff, using R. M. W. Dixon's description of the Dyirbal classification system (1982), elucidated what he called "the domain-of-experience principle": "[c]onceptual categories marked by the grammars of languages are important in understanding the nature of cognitive categories *in general*" (91; my emphasis). In the Dyirbal universe of discourse, all things belong to one of four categories, and this class membership is grammatically marked by *bayi*, *balan*, *balam*, or *bala* every time a noun occurs. Lakoff, following Dixon, identified membership in the four categories as follows:

  I. *Bayi*: men, kangaroos, possums, bats, most snakes, most fishes, some birds, most insects, the moon, storms, rainbows, boomerangs, some spears, etc.
 II. *Balan*: women, bandicoots, dogs, platypus, echidna, some snakes, some fishes, most birds, fireflies, scorpions, crickets, the hairy mary grub, anything connected with water or fire, sun and stars, shields, some spears, some trees, etc.
III. *Balam*: all edible fruit and the plants that bear them, tubers, ferns, honey, cigarettes, wine, cake
 IV. *Bala*: parts of the body, meat, bees, wind, yamsticks, some spears, most trees, grass, mud, stones, noises and language, etc. (92–93)

There are several ways Dixon's analysis may be flawed, and I don't know how contaminated his interpretation of his data was. In his discussion (1982), he didn't mention the sex of his informants, and the way he classified the nouns may have been influenced in a number of ways by his own western conceptual framework. If all his informants were men, then all his data reflected how Dyirbal men classify nouns, and he might have misinterpreted the information. For example, maybe "female" nouns should be Class I, rather than Class II, but I don't have the information that would contradict his analysis.

On the basis of his classification, Dixon proposed the following general categories for Dyirbal nouns:

I. *Bayi*: (human) males; animals
II. *Balan*: (human) females; water; fire; fighting
III. *Balam*: nonflesh food
IV. *Bala*: everything not in the other classes (Lakoff, 93)

The first two categories, marked by *bayi* and *balan*, contain words belonging to the sex-determined experiential spheres, the female and the male. Lakoff, of course, was interested in discovering the "general principles" according to which "human" cognition operates. The "most general principle," which, he said, Dixon "takes for granted," was "the domain-of-experience principle": "If there is a basic domain of experience associated with *A*, then it is natural for entities in that domain to be in the same category as *A*" (93). For Dyirbal, this principle predicts that we will find what we find. "The domain-of-experience principle says that there are certain domains of experience that are significant **for Dyirbal categorization**" (99; my emphasis).

Throughout his discussion Lakoff assumed that women and men share a single domain of experience, but his own description of "Dyirbal categorization" cannot be generic. If "danger is an important domain of experience" (99) and some chain of association links women with "other dangerous things," that domain of experience must be specifically **male**, not female, because the conceptual links are male. If nouns were classified on the basis of a Dyirbal female domain-of-experience, would women categorize themselves as dangerous-to-themselves?

Lakoff's domain-of-experience principle predicted that Dyirbal words are classified as *bayi* or *balan* on the basis of "category chains" linked by associations that "may be culture-specific," branching out from the central terms of the category. For example, "women are linked to the sun, which is linked to sunburn, which is linked to the hairy mary grub" (95).

> The links are: women (via myth) to the sun (via relevant domain of experience) to fire. By the same means, we can link danger and water. Fire is dangerous, and thus dangerous things are in the same category as fire. Water, which extinguishes fire, is in the same domain of experience as fire, and hence in the same category. (100)

Interestingly enough, Lakoff described the conceptual links of the members of Class II, but didn't analyze the nouns in Class I. Apparently, the relationship among the Class I nouns seemed "obvious" to him and less in need of explanation, so he didn't think that the conceptual links among the Class I nouns required elaborate analysis or explanation. (Note, too, that he named his book after members of Class II, not Class I.)

Having concentrated on Class II, Lakoff carefully asked several questions before proceeding to his "Tentative Conclusions" (102), but the questions that he didn't ask as he proceeded multiply quickly. Positing a system of two "human" categories (I and II) versus "edible plants" (III) versus "inanimates" (IV: everything else in the world), he asked why most animals belong to the male class, *bayi*. His reasoning is illustrative.

> It seems to be a reasonable guess that if animals are going to go anywhere in a system like this, it will be with the humans rather than with the edible plants. And it would make sense that if the animals are unmarked for gender, they would be categorized with the *unmarked human category*, if there is one. In most languages that have classification by gender, *the male category is unmarked* [assumed to be the "norm"]. **On the basis of such universal tendencies, it is not a surprise to find the animals categorized with the human males**. [My emphases] (102)

Typically, Lakoff conflated "gender" classification with distinctions based on sex, but the connection between grammatical sex-based distinctions and male nouns as the default category remains implicit. At no point did he say that the Dyirbal classification system is, like most known languages, based on that version of reality, including myths and other aspects of the belief system, that comprise the **male** perspective. He took this for granted. He may have found it "reasonable" to classify other animals with human males, but asserted, without further speculation or analysis, that the "male category" requires no explicit marking in most of the languages that use sex as their basis for noun classification. Certainly, I was struck by the parallel: **If** the noun categories of a language are based on the distinction of female from male, **then** the category in which the male is the central member need not be grammatically signified! The corollary to this must be that in such languages the female category **must** be grammatically marked in some way.

What this means, in terms of conceptualization, is that whatever is "human" must be *male*, unless otherwise indicated. The "general principle" identified by Lakoff, the "domain-of-experience" principle, is the **male** domain of experience. What's more, this equation of "things male" with "things human" apparently eluded him. The universe of discourse mapped by the Dyirbal categories, as reported by Dixon, is one in which men stand at the center. Class II, nouns marked with *balan*, contains those beings and objects that men *perceive* to be "dangerous" to them!

There is no other way of explaining that women, along with fire and other dangerous things (e.g., two stinging trees, a stinging nettle vine), **have been placed** in a category separate from that men reserved for themselves and their preoccupations. Nor is there any explanation of the conceptual "links" that (somehow) relate objects like fire, echidna, and some snakes to the central term of Class II, *woman*. It is not sufficient to say, for example, that women are cognitively associated with the sun by *myth* without also asking *whose* belief system created and maintains that myth. Clearly, Lakoff wasn't describing the Dyirbal woman's domain-of-experience **or** her belief system; maybe Dyirbal women have a mythic system distinct from that of the men.

Like Lakoff, I am speculating, since neither he nor his source, R. M. W. Dixon, commented upon the sex of the Dyirbal informants. The reluctance of male linguists to take such distinctions seriously, combined with the masculist bias of most grammars, makes it impossible to be certain whether it is women's linguistic habits being described or male perceptions of how women think and talk in various cultures. Linguistic evidence from other cultures suggests the latter possibility.

CHEERFUL SLAVES

Japanese illustrates the complex interaction between male social/political dominance and control of language use. It manifests not only the three ways patriarchal language infiltrates our minds and the ways we talk (or are *permitted* to talk) or are talked about by men, but also provides instances of women's defiance of PUD rules. When men name the world of their perceptions, they also name the place of women in that world; these names lexicalize men's concepts and form semantic sets within a culture's vocabulary. When men control the social and grammatical rules of a language and have mandated their dialect as the standard, they define what women are allowed to say and the way in which they must say it. The "place" of a woman in a man's world isn't only reflected in certain sets of words in the language's vocabulary but is also marked in her speech by specific suffixes. Japanese women aren't utterly silent, however, and have words for describing their own experiences, including derogatory terms for men.

In a 1988 Weekend Edition, National Public Radio (NPR) did a segment called "Japanese Women's Language." A man's voice introduced the segment as "a story about sexism, although most people in the country we're about to visit wouldn't call it that." Patronizingly acknowledging that, "of course, the United States has its share of sexism," he went on with his ethnocentric description of "sexism" in Japan:

> now imagine a culture that forbids women most of the time to speak the same language as men, a society where women actually have to use different words than men do to say the same thing, or else they'll be shunned.

Men's subjugation of women in Japan goes back at least 1,000 years, to a time when women were forbidden to speak to men. In the 1930s, the Japanese government issued edicts warning women not to use words reserved to men, and the resulting differentiations remain in force, if not the edicts themselves (NPR). The significant adjectives that distinguish *onna kotaba*, 'women's words', from the male dialect are 'soft' and 'harsh', the equivalents of English 'weak' and 'forceful'. One example of the pressure on women to speak softly and submissively, if they speak at all, is the custom of hiring elevator "girls" in Japanese department stores.

According to the NPR report, women hired as elevator "girls" must be "pretty, young, and very, very feminine." One of the behaviors that conveys *onna-rashisa* (the stereotype of femininity) is the ability to speak women's "language" correctly, and this aspect of the elevator operator's job performance is closely monitored. They are expected to talk in "perfect women's language," and "never slip and use a masculine word." Their fluency in the linguistic display of submissiveness is insured by one-half hour of mandatory daily practice, during which any "unfeminine" pronunciations are corrected. In order for a woman, any woman, to be perceived as "nice," she must speak "correct women's language" (NPR). Women who don't speak the submissive dialect men assign to them don't get jobs.

R. Lakoff (1975) and Mary Ritchie Key (1975) both noted that the sentences of English-speaking women are likely to be longer and wordier than those of men, and the same apparently holds true for Japanese. A man might be able to say, "Open the window!" but a Japanese woman, in order to get the same thing done, would have to say, "Please open the window a little bit, if you don't mind." The result is that a woman's sentence has only one or two words in common with a comparable male utterance (NPR) and is much longer. Not surprisingly, Japanese women's dialect is perceived as more subservient and tentative than men's, because the women must use submissive, self-effacing phrases equivalent to the tag–questions that Robin Lakoff (1975) associated with women's speech in English. These phrases translate into English as "do you think," "I can't be sure," and "will it be," and their use in commonplace statements means that Japanese women say an average of 20% more words than men to describe the same thing. In Japanese, it is impossible for a woman to speak informally and assertively at the same time (NPR).

Japanese also has numerous ways of marking the forms designated as women's dialect. In 1921, Jespersen noted that Japanese women made "more frequent use than men of the prefixes of politeness *o-*, *go-* and *mi-*," in addition to other linguistic traits shared with French and English women, "namely, the excessive use of intensive words and the exaggeration of stress and tone-accent to mark emphasis" (243). There are, in fact, specific particles in Japanese that distinguish women's speech from men's: *no ní/kusé ni* (both convey some sense of deceit and are said to be common in the speech of women and children); *né/ná* (particles that "soften" a statement and invite confirmation from the hearer); *wá* (a particle used almost exclusively by women at the end of informal sentences). And, where men would use *suru yó*, 'indeed', which asserts a claim and is said to have "a masculine sound," a woman would have to use either *suru no yó* or *suru wa yó*.

The grammatical reflexes of the sex-distinct dialects of Japanese are also evident in the pronominal system. According to Kittredge Cherry (1987), the choice of a word for the first person singular, 'I,' identifies the speaker not only by sex, but also by age and status relative to the listener. Men and boys use *boku* ('manservant'), *ore*, or *washi*, while women use *atashi*, *atakushi*, or *atai*. In formal situations, giving speeches, answering the telephone, or talking to strangers or superiors, women and men use *watakushi*, and both sexes can use the informal abbreviation, *watashi*. Cherry noted that "a minority of Japanese females between the ages of twelve and twenty-five" defy the rules of the Japanese version of PUD by using the male pronoun *boku*, and claimed that these "*boku* girls" illustrate how the rigid system of sex-distinct dialects is "breaking down" (38). But changes in usage of the second-person singular pronoun, *kimi*, show a different tendency. Bodine (1975b, 141), citing Obayashi (1974), pointed out that the use of *kimi* has been reversed. In the eleventh century, speakers of both sexes could use *kimi* when they spoke to a man of higher rank. Now, only men of higher or equal social status use *kimi* to address individuals of either sex who are of equal or lower rank; women can no longer use it.

Male subordination of women in Japan bears an uncanny resemblance to the forms and underlying assumptions of the anglo-american patriarchy. How Japanese men think and talk about women isn't much different from what we hear in English. "Beauty," for example, whatever its transient manifestations, is strictly a female attribute. *Bijin*, literally 'beauty-person', refers only to women in spite of its seeming generality in translation, and men attach it to various job titles when the individual so employed is female, for example, *bijin anaunsa*, 'beauty-announcer', *bijin hosutesu*, 'beauty-hostess,' and *bijin henshusha*, 'beauty-editor' (surely an occupation in which one would not expect "beauty," present or not, to be worthy of comment). Where the physical attributes of women are the crucial, if not only, measure of their worth, being perceived as "ugly" means a corresponding devaluation of one's worth. Japanese men have a particularly nasty word for women who don't meet their standards of beauty, *busu*, which "means a woman with a hideous face," but has the emotional impact of "Fuck you!" in English (Cherry, 22). According to Cherry, *busu* is among the worst words a Japanese man can say to a woman.

The physical beauty of women is so important to Japanese men that the expression *yoshi tanrei*, 'graceful figure,' appears frequently as a job qualification in help wanted ads for women (Cherry, 19–20). The emphasis on female beauty and its connection with femininity, *onna-rashisa*, is part of "doing business" in the department stores of Japan. *Onna-rashisa* is defined in terms identical to English descriptions of *femininity*: "kind," "gentle," "polite," "submissive," and "graceful." Cherry noted that "weak" is added sometimes, and that "[m]any people would also add cheerfulness to the list of what gives a woman *onna-rashisa*" (32).

The stereotype of Japanese women is partially constructed by the way women talk, but it is also emphasized by how men talk **about** them. Again, the appearance of **submission** is the significant factor. Japanese men have several insulting terms descriptive of women who venture beyond the limited role allotted to them, for example, *hinoeuma no onna*, 'fiery-horse woman,' *otoko masari*, 'male surpasser', and *sukeban*, 'boss girl'. *Otoko masari*, for example, is not something Japanese women aspire to, in spite of its positive sound to some western ears. According to Cherry, "[t]he word implies not only extra ability, but also lack of femininity" (33). As in the u.s., women who refuse to hide their competence and intelligence are labeled "unfeminine"; that is, they have refused to meet the male standard for being a "woman," which requires that they pretend to be both stupid and incompetent (q.v., the *RHD* definitions discussed in chapter 4).

In Japanese, the sex-specific experiential domains are overtly expressed in the vocabulary. Like all women born into patriarchal cultures, Japanese women's submission to men entails severe restriction of their spatial mobility. What must be teased out of the semantic structure of the English vocabulary is explicitly named in Japanese. The woman's designated experiential sphere is the **inside** of a dwelling. A number of words and usages reflect this spatial limitation, but the most striking one is *okusan*: 'Mrs. Interior'. Cherry described its meaning:

> Whether they are at home, at work, or outdoors, married women in Japan are addressed as 'Mrs. Interior' (*okusan* or, more formally, *okusama*). *Okusan* is the most common word for talking to or about other men's spouses—one of many situations with its own specialized wife vocabulary in Japanese. *Oku* means not just interior, but the depths far within a building. . . . [o]*kusan* can never be used to denote a Mr. Interior, no matter how much time he spends in the deepest recesses of his home. As the language makes clear, that is traditionally considered the woman's place.

She pointed out that the origins of *okusama* lie in the feudal system of pre-industrial Japan, and related it to other household terms of address.

> Like the English word 'lady,' *okusama* has been vulgarized into an all-purpose term for women. For conversing with or about other people's husbands, the current male equivalent of *okusan* is 'honorable master' (*goshujin* or *danna-san*). These terms for husbands are used even now in discussions of slavery as well. (66–67)

Japanese men call their wives *kanai*, 'house-insider', when talking about them, while women must speak of their husbands as *shujin* or *danna*, or use the more informal *teishu*, a term which refers to the master of an inn or teahouse (Cherry, 67).

Other [+female] words that describe the circumscribed lives of women in Japan are *shojo*, 'home girl', and *hako-iri musume*, 'daughter-in-a-box'. Even though Japanese has a word for male virginity, (*dotei*, *do*, 'child' +*tei*, 'chastity' or 'fidelity'), the double standard nevertheless exists. Both *shojo*, literally 'female in the home', and *hako-iri musume* are among what Cherry called "a large harem [sic] of synonyms" used to describe premarital chastity (67), and both specify the **interior** (non-public) nature of a Japanese woman's place. (The restriction of women to **non-public**, personal domains adds layers of

meaning to the WLM slogan, "The *personal* is the political.") *Hako-iri musume* is a metaphorical expression which means 'sheltered maiden', and
likens a daughter to the prized possessions the Japanese store in wooden
boxes. There is no male equivalent for this expression (Cherry, 41–42). The
ideal of chastity is associated with females so strongly in Japan that a woman
who engages in heterosexual relations before marrying is called 'damaged
goods', *kizumono*, but a quick operation, *shojomaku saisei* ('maidenhead
regeneration'), will "repair the damage" by sewing the hymen back together
or reconstructing the membrane with plastic (Cherry, 119).

The Japanese version of patriarchy, like its Anglo-American brother, assumes heterosexuality and defines women in terms of male perceptions, with
the result that most insults and compliments specifically addressed to women
focus on their success or failure as caretakers of men and breeders. Thus, a
woman should feel complimented if she is called *anegohada*, 'big-sister
type', or *ryosai kenbo*, 'a good wife and wise mother', or *hobo to kangofu*,
'sustaining mom and watchful protectoress'. Likewise, men expect a woman
to be wounded if they refer to her as *umazume*, a barren woman, (literally,
'stone woman'), or *urenokori*, 'unsold goods', that is, unmarried. And although Japanese pornography has always used the idea of lesbianism for
male titillation, the actual existence of Lesbians in Japan "has long been
discounted." The language itself was noticeably silent on the subject until
after ww ii, when *lesbian* was borrowed into the vocabulary as *rezubian*.
Resu, an abbreviated form, is derogatory (Cherry, 115), as *lezzie* is in English.

In Japanese, there is an unbridgeable gulf between thought and language,
if not for men, certainly for women. Like any patriarchal language, Japanese
proscribes and describes the experiential boundaries of women's lives, and,
thereby, shapes them according to male desire. What Japanese men say about
women and the way women are supposed to speak show us the lives of
women defined and limited by male domination, an experiential sphere that
is socially subordinate to and smaller than the unlimited space occupied by
men and, as a result, economically and politically powerless. The experiential reality described in the language is that of women oppressed, enslaved,
and exploited.

In the reports of National Public Radio and Kittredge Cherry, we do hear
that Japanese Feminists protest the linguistic expressions of male social and
economic dominance (Cherry, 32) and that teenaged women are, "at least
some of the time," talking "like boys" (NPR). What is the prognosis for
positive changes in the lives of Japanese women, however? Not very good if
we are to believe the linguist, described as "a modern, liberated woman,"
whose statement ends the NPR story:

> We need two languages. Because if we talk in the same way, how can I show my
> femininity to my husband, to my lover . . . ? If I speak like man, nobody will

listen to me. . . . It's a very clever way to make people do what I want them to do.

Unwilling to acknowledge that she does have choices, she seems content with manipulation, "a clever way to make people [i.e., men] do" what she wants them to, and doesn't challenge the destructive Japanese ideal of femininity, *onna-rashisa*. For the rulers ("those who rule the rules") of PUD, a cheerful, willing slave is the best kind.

WICKED WOMEN, FAWNING SLAVES

The Chinese language betrays the misogyny and male dominance of the culture in a way familiar to members of european societies: according to Geoffrey Wade (1987) and Chan Wing Cheung, who transliterated the characters for me (1987), Chinese has a female-specific radical (i.e., root), nu^3,[8] that marks **ideographs** (the written language) associated with women in much the same way that diminutive endings like -*ess* and -*ette* mark words in English as [+female]. As long as the terms containing the radical nu^3 denote female individuals, one is unlikely to be disturbed by its meaning. For example, all of the characters that denote female relatives contain nu^3.

In addition to terms for female relatives, however, nu^3 appears in four other vocabulary sets in Chinese:

1. words that refer to an occupation, position, or state of women in society;
2. words that include actions or activities that include women;
3. words which describe attributes men believe to be "desirable" in women;
4. words which refer to evil or evil characteristics of people in general.

I will quote Wade's descriptions of the last two groups of words (5.5 and 5.6) at the appropriate points so that readers can perceive for themselves how a man apparently sympathetic to women's social status chose to describe the words and their cultural significance. His language is telling.

The written representation of Chinese words for female relatives, transliterated into roman characters representing the Mandarin dialect,[9] all contain the female-specific radical. In Chinese script, the character is 女. (Chinese speakers also indicate the age of individuals relative to the speaker, e.g., *elder, younger*.)

5.2 ma^1 — 'mother'
          jie^3 — 'elder sister'
           zi^3 — 'elder sister'
          gu^1 — 'father's or husband's sister'
        mei^4 — 'younger sister'
           xi^2 — 'daughter-in-law'
           yi^2 — 'mother's or wife's sister'
          po^2 — 'mother-in-law'

jin⁴ —'wife of mother's brother *or* wife of the brother of one's wife'
shen³ — 'wife of father's younger brother'
zhou² — 'wife of the brother of one's husband'
  sao³ — 'elder brother's wife'
    bi³ — 'deceased mother'
     gi¹ — 'wife'
      li³ — 'wife of the brother of one's husband'

The second set of words in Chinese that contain the female-specific radical are those which refer to an occupation or position occupied by women or denote a state or condition experienced by women, such as pregnancy.

5.3   mei² — 'matchmaker'
     niang² — 'form of address for an elderly, married woman'
         ni¹ — 'girl'
         bi⁴ — 'maid; slave girl'
        niu¹ — 'girl'
          ji¹ — in ancient Chinese:
                a. a complimentary term for women
                b. 'a concubine'
                c. 'a professional female singer'
         fei¹ —   a. 'emperor's concubine'
                  b. 'wife of a prince'
        ren⁴ — 'be pregnant'
    shuang¹ — 'widow'
         mu³ — 'children's nurse'
        biao³ — 'prostitute'
      chang¹ — 'prostitute'
          ji⁴ — 'prostitute'

Of course, Chinese isn't the only language that has a large vocabulary for referring to women who sell their bodies to men for money. (In English, the set of such terms appears to be one capable of infinite expansion.)

The third area of the Chinese vocabulary marked by the radical nu³ contains words for activities or actions performed by women or done by men to women, such as marriage. Some of these terms, it should be clear, are only used by men.

5.4   hun¹ — 'marriage'
       gu³ — 'marry a woman; take to wife'
      yin¹ — a. 'marriage'; b. 'relation by marriage'
     gou⁴ — a. 'to wed'; b. 'sexual intercourse'
      pin¹ — 'cohabit'
       jia⁴ — 'marry a man'
     piao² — 'to visit prostitutes'

By and large, these terms reflect a specifically **male** perspective of the uses to which men put women. This perspective is evident in gou^4, which denotes 'sexual intercourse' as well as the act of marrying a woman, and no distinction between the two actions is indicated: the word means 'fucking', with or without social sanctions.

As we move from one set of words to the next, a perceptible pattern emerges: the focus of the male perspective evident in the terms becomes clearer, less the result of attempts to name, as in 5.2, or address, as in 5.3, and more specifically concentrated on how men perceive women, positively or negatively. Between the word groups in 5.2 and 5.6, the illusion that the words describe "reality" gradually fades, until we realize that words marked by the nu^3 radical exist, not to describe what is "real," but to call forth a reality satisfactory to men's ideas. The female-specific terms listed in 5.5 reflect what Wade described as the attributes that "Chinese society" finds "desirable in women," but let's not fool ourselves. Using "society" in this context explains no more than it does when someone attributes agency to "American society." "Society" disguises male agency, and, as the words in 5.5 reveal, the attributes of this group, mostly adjectives, name male perceptions and criteria.

5.5 yu^2 — 'to amuse, to please'
        wan^3 — 'complaisant'
        yao^2 — 'elegant'
        kua^1 — 'pretty'
        yan^2 — 'elegant'
        $luan^2$ — 'attractive'
        wu^3 — 'seductive'
        e^1 — 'graceful'
        $ting^2$ — 'graceful'
        $yuan^4$ — 'a beautiful woman'
        $niao^3$ — 'delicate'
        yi^4 — 'compliant'
        nen^4 — 'tender'
        yan^1 — 'captivating'
        rao^2 — 'fascinating'
        $xian^2$ — 'elegant'

If we remember that men of the Chinese patriarchy were "fascinated" and "captivated" by the putrid stumps produced by foot-binding, and that the women's feet so mutilated and ruined were perceived as "elegant," "delicate," and "graceful," the cruelty of how men use women becomes more obvious. Surely a woman unable to walk and constantly in pain will appear "complaisant," "compliant," and eager to "please," whether she intends to or not. When we imagine what it would be like to live most of one's life with bloody, rotting stumps instead of feet, the adjective meaning 'tender' is ambiguous, euphemistic if it is construed as an attribute of the women's feet. I have no evidence for terms of Chinese that name and describe the women's perceptions and feelings about foot-binding.

Chinese men, unsurprisingly, want women to be beautiful, elegant, and complaisant, but, as Wade described the contrast between the attitudes of the words listed in 5.5 and those of 5.6, the male desiderata of 5.5 are "fairly mild compared with what is to come." Indeed. The language of his introduction to this set of terms merits quotation here.

> [W]e come to the most interesting set of characters. The Chinese people [sic], or at least those who developed Chinese characters, obviously saw women **as the most evil aspect of humanity**. [My emphasis.] You will see that virtually every evil characteristic of mankind [sic], when depicted in the written Chinese language, is preceded by 'nu(3)', or has the radical 'nu(3)' somewhere in its composition.

As in English, women are equated with the idea of 'evil' in Chinese. The words in 5.6 would have worked well in the *Malleus Maleficarum*:

5.6 nu^2 — 'slave'
    $wang^4$ — 'reckless, foolish'
    $jian^1$ — 'wicked'
    yao^1 — a. 'evil spirit'; b. 'strange, weird'; c. 'bewitching, coquettish'
    du^4 — 'jealousy'
    $fang^2$ — 'hinder, obstacle'
    $shan^1$ — 'ridicule'
    $jian^1$ — 'debauched, licentious'
    lan^2 — 'greedy, covetous'
    mei^4 — 'to fawn, to toady'
    $xian^2$ — 'suspicion, dislike'
    ji^2 — 'jealousy, hate'
    man^4 — 'insult, despise'
    lan^3 — 'lazy'

If English were like Chinese, there would be an equivalent for the radical nu^3. Certainly, the associations of evil, greed, and the ability to "bewitch" with the female sex are familiar to speakers of English. Wade's inclusion in this particular list of the generic term for 'slave', nu^2, may seem strange because it is so unlike the word for 'female slave', bi^4 (in 5.2), but it differs only in tone from the [+female] radical itself. Perhaps, though, its presence explains the inclusion of lan^3, 'lazy', an attribute men commonly associate with those they've enslaved.

Wade's closing description of the words listed in 5.6 is worth quoting in its entirety:

> Freud would have had a field day if he had been able to read Chinese. But, as it is, every new generation of Chinese youth grows up learning these charac-

ters and healthily [sic] associating the radical 'nu(3)' with suspicion, greed and laziness.

Being female, I suspect that Freud would have interpreted these words as accurate descriptions of women's "character" and attributed them to unresolved Electra complexes or "penis envy."

HOMELY TRUTHS

The languages discussed in this chapter illustrate three methods of excluding women as speakers in PUD, and each one affects grammatical structure as well as vocabulary. First, each language divides the sexes in the conceptual categories that form the semantic structure of its vocabulary, a division that establishes men as the standard of what it "means" to be human and classifies women as **less than human**. In Dyirbal and Chinese women are conceptually categorized as inherently evil and dangerous. Second, women are the objects of male discourse, and the male distinction between "good" and "bad" women is amply provided for in the vocabulary, as in Japanese. And, because a "good" woman is one who lives to "please her man," Japanese has an elaborate system of sex-specific particles women must use to mark their subordinate status and acknowledge men's dominance. This class distinction determines the third linguistic difference, creating a women's dialect that reinforces men's perception of us as weak, stupid, and insignificant. Generally, the second-class women's dialect is marked phonologically, by differences in intonation and pitch, as in Japanese (and English), or by the addition or lack of syllables, as in Yana. In most cases, the cultural penalty for women who transgress the linguistic dictates of PUD is ostracism and social exclusion. In Zulu, however, in which women are forbidden to utter the names of men or to say words that contain sounds in a man's name, the penalty is death.

However dire the cultural penalties are for women who defy PUD rules, the result is the same: the languages mark women as socially inferior to men and as conceptually Other. What this tells us about cognitive categories in general is that men seem incapable of perceiving women as human beings like themselves and, on the basis of their cognitive limitations, create linguistic ways of marking and maintaining women's powerlessness. In general, men deny women their rights as actors and speakers in male cultures, limiting women's domain-of-experience to domestic, interior tasks that serve men's desires, while their domain encompasses "the world," understood to include women as well. In general, we have little or no linguistic evidence about how women perceive ourselves in the world.

Chapter 6

The Place of Women in English: History

Before I discuss the historical development of the human nouns in English, I want my readers to have an idea of how the vocabulary of a language reflects the culture's version of reality and how its overall shape, what is named, what is not named, corresponds to "received reality." There are two ways of approaching the vocabulary of a language. On the one hand, we can look at existing words and draw conclusions about which aspects of the world members of the culture think are worth talking about. Or, we can examine the vocabulary for lexical gaps, holes in a vocabulary where the language doesn't provide words to describe people and events. An analogy may help my readers visualize how vocabularies represent culturally preferred ways of organizing our perceptions of the world.

Let's say that a vocabulary is like a topographical map, which represents the geological features of the earth's crust—its mountains, hills, valleys, lowlands, and rivers. Maps are only as accurate as the perceptions of those who describe the features they represent; some aspects are missed altogether, some are exaggerated or distorted, others are represented as being where they aren't. Comparing older maps to newer ones emphasizes the inaccuracies and misrepresentations of earlier map makers. Land masses were too big or too small and their shapes were misconceived and out of proportion. On very early maps, some continents were missing because no one knew they existed. Lakes, rivers, and streams didn't appear on maps until someone "discovered" them. Recent maps more accurately represent the earth's features because technology has increased the perceptual information available to cartographers and we've reduced the number and size of the uncharted areas that remain.

The sets of words in a vocabulary describe some of the features of the world, but exaggerate, distort, and misrepresent the perceived landscape of reality. We have no words for aspects of the world we don't recognize, and a few for those features considered insignificant. Gaps in the vocabulary of a language reveal spheres of reality we don't perceive. The mutually reenforcing relationship between what we perceive and what we can talk about is a cognitive loop: we perceive what we have words for and vice versa. What we can't talk about we often fail to perceive. Every once in a while, someone notices a previously ignored feature of the world and then we need a new word. As cultural values, customs, and behaviors change, some words cease to be useful and others change their meaning. Using both approaches to a vocabulary, what we can describe within its framework and what we cannot, we can draw inferences about what is or is not considered "consensus reality" by speakers.

The vocabulary of a language consists of words for those people, objects, and events that its speakers consider important enough to warrant a unique term for. Topographically, large sets represent the mountain ranges and oceans of reality; small sets are insignificant features of the terrain. These have "low visibility." English has a huge vocabulary based on sexual dimorphism for talking about women and men and what heterosexuals do to each other. Until 1897, the word *lesbian*, in contrast, referred only to an inhabitant of Lesbos or a particiular kind of measurement. During the nineteenth-century wave of Feminism, when women threatened men by refusing to marry for appearances and loving one another more openly, Havelock Ellis identified the phenomenon as "sickness" and extended the word's definition to name what the heteropatriarchy wanted to destroy and he claimed to be able to "cure." (Interestingly, the word *heterosexual* postdates *lesbian*, because the culture assumed that everyone was innately heterosexual. Naming the deviance from that assumption brought it into conceptual contrast; if it was going to be talked about, it had to have a label, too.)

Phrasal constructions often supply expressions that fill lexical gaps. In Swahili, for example, only three words exist that name colors, 'black', 'white', and 'red'. In order to talk about colors like yellow, green, or blue, Swahili speakers use a phrase, 'color of _____ ', filling the blank portion of the phrase with the name of something familiar; for 'blue', they say "color of sky," for green, "color of grass," and for yellow, "color of saffron." The Swahili vocabulary lacks lexical items for the numerous colors named in English, and speakers of Swahili may or may not perceive the same fine distinctions we make in hue or intensity—for example, between what we call "aqua" and "turquoise."[1]

The semantics of human nouns in English is based on sexual dimorphism and its corollary assumption, heterosexuality. These are the features of the experiential landscape identified as significant. They are the foundations of

PUD, and the English vocabulary provides a map of patriarchal culture's world view. Dividing a species into male and female is only the most explicit step, however. Patriarchal ideology defines men as inherently superior to women, born to rule **over** us, and women as inherently inferior to men, born to **serve** them. There is no "logic" involved here. Conceptual distinctions based on observable differences needn't result in the linguistic distortions that exist in modern languages. The CAUSE-EFFECT relationship between biological difference and male dominance stipulated by patriarchal science does not inhere in "nature." It is a construct imposed on the landscape that could be described in numerous other ways. Nevertheless, the development of English shows how the language incorporates men's perceptions of women as their "inferiors."

How did the OE vocabulary map the topography of human relationships? Historical evidence suggests that the social status of women hasn't always been conceived as we know it. Christine Fell (1984) attributed women's social decline to the combined effects of the Norman Invasion and the Gregorian Reform. She described the result succinctly: "Practically, the status of women deteriorates. In literature it becomes stereotyped" (14). Prior to the Scandinavian invasions of the eighth to eleventh centuries (chapter 1), the anglo-saxon vocabulary for talking about human beings, female and male, was structurally different from the way those nouns are semantically organized in ModE. The Scandinavians had barely begun to settle in amid the anglo-saxons, their germanic relatives, when the Norman Conquest imposed Norman French as the official language of Britain. Both invasions caused widespread changes between Old and Middle English (OE and ME), including the substitution of Old Norse (ON) pronouns for those of Anglo-Saxon (AS), the appearance of *scheo* as the maximally distinctive female third person singular pronoun, and other significant losses and additions in the vocabulary.

But drawing conclusions from the existing evidence isn't simple. The written documents of OE pose several problems. Most of the surviving evidence for OE is written in the West Saxon dialect, because most of the documents written in other OE dialects were destroyed when the Scandinavians burned monasteries to the ground. Other problems, especially of interpretation, were introduced in the surviving manuscripts by the xtian clerics who wrote them down. For example, reconstructing the culture of the Anglo-Saxons is tricky because it's hard to determine which aspects originated before the xtianization of Britain and Ireland. Nevertheless, the OE vocabulary must have been as systematic as any language for which we have more accurate records of its developmental stages (e.g., Latin). What my readers may not know is how profoundly the two European invasions altered both the daily lives of the Anglo-Saxons and the semantic structure of the OE human nouns. Understanding the impact of the changes in this segment of the vocabulary and their origins in the social and cultural upheavals caused by the succeeding invasions of Scandinavians and Norman French demonstrates that English has changed in the past, and will change again. If we understand how the shape of our vocabulary has changed previously, we can better determine how we want to change it in the future.

Between OE and ME (c. 450–1150), the vocabulary of English changed radically: some native Germanic (Gmc.) words were abandoned, replaced, in some instances, by Norman French; the referential scope of others narrowed. Some far-reaching shifts between OE and ME are well documented, and must have been set in motion by changes in the social roles and behaviors of women and men. Those changes involved the generic *man(n)*, cognate with Modern German (ModG) *Mann*, *wīf*, cognate with ModG *Weib*, and *wer*, derived, through borrowing from Old French (OF), from Gmc. *werre*. The consequences for women were predictable: as men claimed most of the semantic space as their territory, women had less and less space to occupy, linguistically and socially.

In some ways, the OE vocabulary for people of both sexes seems to have been more extensive and, perhaps, more flexible in its reference than ModE. I must, however, briefly caution my readers against confusing the grammatical **gender** of OE with what is called "natural gender" in ModE (chapter 4). We can be misled by contemporary stereotypes and preconceptions that govern contemporary use of human nouns. OE had several **generics**, words that referred to 'all people' or 'people in general'. Each generic had grammatical "gender," as did all nouns in OE, either neuter (n.), feminine (f.), or masculine (m.). The words considered together suggest a distinction between local and national "peoples" and global "humanity."

lēode (f.pl.)	— 'people'
folc (n.)	— 'people, folk'
þēod (f.)	— 'people, nation'
man(n) (m.)	— 'person'
menniscnes (f.) —	'humanity'
cyn(n) (n.)	— 'race, family, kindred'

Cyn(n), *lēode*, *folc*, and *þēod* indicate a distinction typical of tribal cultures: a word that denotes 'people', its reference restricted to members of the clan or tribe; those who aren't members of the group are 'not-people', "foreigners." *Cyn(n)* served as the basis of compounds that referred to each sex as a group, *wīfa cyn(n)*, *manna cyn(n)*, 'womankind' and 'mankind', respectively. Both were neuter in gender, as were *ĉild* and *bearn*, 'child'. *Geogoð*, *-uð*, which referred collectively to 'young people', was feminine.

The OE vocabulary had numerous sex-specific terms, most of which were dropped from usage by the end of the eleventh century. Their numbers alone suggest distinctions, shades of meaning, that we can't even guess at from the context in which they were used. Three pairs of features, however, are clear enough: sex, [+female] and [+male], class, [±free-born], and age, [±adult]. Before proceeding, I will explain my choice of features for these three semantic distinctions.

SEX

Mary Ritchie Key (1975, 80–81) described three of the methods linguists have used to represent the distinction of sex in vocabularies. The most common method assigns to male-specific words either the feature [+male] or, borrowing the terminology of gender, [+masculine]. Female-specific words are then marked as either [−male] or [−masculine].[3] Of this symbolism, Key wryly commented, "One might conclude that the plus/minus analysis is good Freud, but not necessarily adequate description" (80). The second method, which I adopt for OE, treats features as positive attributes of nouns, either [+female] or [+male], following Katz and Fodor (1964).[4] About this method of assigning features, Key cited the comments of Jeffrey Gruber (1967), who described what seems to be the case for the OE class of human nouns:

> [F]eminine (in the semantic sense) is not the absence of masculine or even the necessary complement of masculine. It is not a linguistic principle that there be two sexes, nor does the existence of one of the sexes necessitate (as a linguistic principle) the existence of the other.

In spite of our inclination to think of words for women and men as **opposites** of each other (antonyms), and so representing a dichotomy, as is the case with some adjectives (e.g., *hot/cold, high/low, natural/unnatural*), where the use of one implies its opposite, we should not think of the OE words as contrasting pairs, but as independent sub-classes. As Gruber put it: "The existence of one feature does not necessitate the existence of some other feature contrastive to it" (81).

Key's third way of representing sex-specific words came from the field of embryology. Because fetuses begin as female and maleness is the result of the later appearance of androgen, she suggested that [+female] be the basic (**unmarked**) feature, and that male-specific nouns be **marked** contrastively as [−female]. As she observed, "This analysis has never been suggested in any grammar book or linguistic discussion, but . . . has more basis in fact than either of the previous models of analysis" (81). Much as I would like to pioneer a radical semantic description (that isn't my task here), I will use Gruber's semantic features for OE, and binary features (plus/minus) for ModE.

The differences in the two vocabularies require different representations of their semantic structure. The OE vocabulary of sex-specific words for both sexes, e.g., wīf/wer, and words or compounds that referred to the social functions and divisions of labor between the sexes—for example, for women, ides, fǣmne, mēowle, wīfman(n), hlǣfdiġe, for men, beorn, guma, ċeorl, rinc, wǣpman, hlāfweard—were inherited from I-E (Indo-European). In the case of these sets, grammatical and "natural" gender coincide, with the exception of wīf and wer, the first belonging to the neuter class of nouns, the latter to the feminine **declension**. Remember, though, that grammatical gender didn't make a noun sex-specific, and many OE human nouns referred to persons of both sexes. Hūsbonde, for example, which meant 'peasant who owns both house and land', could refer to a woman or a man. I will mention other examples as they arise in the following discussion.

The semantic parameters of the two sets of words reflect the social structure of the time, and then, as now, designated the experiential domains of the sexes. Fell suggests that the most common term for 'woman', wīf, whose origin is obscure, is related to words for 'weaving' (OE wefan), because "the duties of cloth-making seem to be the ones most consistently linked" with the social role of women (1984, 39). Similarly, many of the male-specific words were connected with war. Beorn, guma, and mago, for instance, are often translated as 'warrior' as well as 'man'. Fell's suggestion explains the frequent linking of wīfmann and wǣpman in documents, wīfmann (which developed into our word woman) meaning 'person who weaves' and wǣpman, 'person who bears weapons'. Similarly, the compounds hlǣfdiġe and hlāfweard, from which our modern lady and lord derive, meant, literally, 'loaf-kneader' and 'loaf-guardian'. That sex-specific words originated in social occupations is plausible, and suggests that the word wer, as obscure in its origins as wīf, was related to the occupations of war,[5] as in werian, 'to defend', and werod, -ud, 'force, troop, band, company, army'. But however "typical" this division of labor may appear—women bake bread and weave, men protect women and make war—the landscape described by the OE vocabulary isn't that different from the map most of us were taught to "read" as we grew up. The distinctions based on biological sex were reflected in the vocabulary. Maybe they weren't as rigidly recognized in daily life and women did have more social and economic room in which to move, but the vocabulary represented cultural expectations and values.

AGE

The other two semantic distinctions I suggest, child/adult and free-born/slave, require some explanation. The vocabulary and what we know of the society indicate that OE speakers thought very differently about adulthood, which seems to have been identified with the age at which one married. The line between adulthood and childhood was a social determination: people became adults on the day they married, regardless of their chronological age, and they married much younger than most do in contemporary societies, often between the ages of 10 and 11. (Betrothals occurred even earlier, sometimes as soon as children were born, especially among the upper classes.) *Cild* and *bearn* referred to fetuses and children of both sexes. Compounds were used when the speaker wanted to be specific about sex, for example, *wīfcild* ('womanchild'), *wāepnedcild*, *hysecild* ('manchild'). The period between childhood and adulthood was 'youth'. (Words like *adolescent* and *teenager* weren't yet part of the English vocabulary.) The word for a 'young person' was *wencel*.

CLASS

Social class wasn't the invention of the Norman French. The Anglo-Saxons had a class hierarchy in which the most significant distinction was that between those who were "free-born" and those who were not: those who served others and those who were served. Again, my interpretations are guesses, but the words themselves call for such a distinction. There were, of course, words for royalty (*cwēn*, 'queen', *cyning*, 'king', *hēafod-mon(n)*, 'head-person', *heah-gerefa*, 'chief official', *frēo-mǣg*, 'noble kin', *frum-gār*, 'leader, chief') and landholders (*eorl* or *ealdormann*, *hlāfweard*, *ceorl*, 'freeman of lowest rank', *hūsbond*, 'head of household'). Those who served might be called *gingre* or *þeowen* if they were women, *secg* or *esne* if they were men. A group of retainers might be referred to as *heorð-genēat*, 'hearth-sharers', or *heorð-werod*, 'hearth-band'. Those without property were *feoh-lēas*; those in bondage were *haeft-nīed*.

Using the sixth century as a timeline roughly midway between the arrivals of the Anglo-Saxons and the Scandinavians, Diagram 6.1 represents some of the common human nouns of OE and their relative positions within the three semantic parameters I've described: sex, class, and age.

Diagram 6.1 points up the numerous changes in the vocabulary between the Norman Conquest and our own time, and reveals significant gaps in the OE vocabulary and differences in the number of words. Most of these words disappeared after 1066: some narrowed in their range of reference (*wīf*, in particular), while others derogated (became insults), for example, *ceorl*, modern *churl*, and *cnafa*, modern *knave*. The distinction of class appears to have been more important for women than for men, and irrelevant until one was considered an adult. There are, for example, more words for 'man' and 'warrior' than there are for 'woman'. Age, too, seems to have been more socially important for women. Among the words for 'young female', several are usually translated as meaning 'virgin', such as *fǣmne*, *mǣgden*, *maegeð*, and *ides*, although both *fǣmne* and *mǣgden* could also refer to

Speaking Freely

FEMALE		MALE	
+ADULT	-ADULT	+ADULT	-ADULT
cwēn		cyning	
hlāefdige		hlāfweard	
			cniht
wīf		wer	hyse
wīfman (n)		waepman (n)	mago
			cnapa
	mǣgden	beorn	
	mǣg (ð)	ceorl	
	fǣmne	guma	
	ides	manna	
	meowle	rinc	scealc
cwene	gingre	secq	cnafa
	þēowen		esne
	þinen		

DIAGRAM 6.1. Common Human Nouns of Old English.

chaste men. Another fuzziness in the semantic boundaries of OE, not apparent in Diagram 6.1, is that words for a young female, especially fǣmne, mēowle, and maegeð, frequently referred to adult women, and vice versa. According to Hildng Bäck (1934), "the limits were not sharp" (243).[6]

Contrary to Christine Fell's hypothesis that the Norman Conquest and Gregorian Reform combined to cause the deterioration of women's status in the British Isles, the OE vocabulary reflected already well-entrenched ideas of the "proper" social roles for women and men. That **some** women waged war, owned or managed their own land, and occupied positions of power (as Fell demonstrated) doesn't contradict the sex-based allocations of roles and power, anymore than it does in the twentieth century. It isn't unusual for the word denoting 'female human' to be used also to refer to females attached to men in the I-E languages,[7] and OE wīf must have been used with both meanings until the original sense gradually disappeared from usage. By the end of the OE period, the concepts 'woman' and 'wife' had, to all intents and purposes, merged. A female human being was some man's wife; she had no other identity, and the stages of her life were described only in terms of her marital status. Before a woman married, she was supposed to remain a virgin (a heterosexual one), hence the use of words meaning 'girl' (i.e., **unmarried** female) to refer to adult females as well. In the event that a woman's husband died before her, she was, and still is, called a *widow*, a word that marks a woman as having been attached to a man.

Whether the preoccupation with female virginity can be attributed solely to xtian interference isn't clear. The existence of the OE verb, wīfian 'to take a wife', and the lack of a parallel 'to take a husband', argue against such a facile assertion. (ModG has a proper noun, Weibertreu, which means 'the faithfulness of wives'.) The social effects of the Norman and xtian invasions doubtless worsened the social status of women and enforced the roles more rigidly, but the pattern was already in place in OE.

A language is systematic, and so are its alterations. Languages don't "just" change unless social and cultural changes motivate the linguistic changes. Before the Normans invaded England in 1066, several changes in the OE vocabulary were already underway. Consider, for example, the narrowing of man(n) and wīf and the loss of wer. Why did wer become obsolete? Toward the end of the OE period, man(n) was no longer used as a generic; its referential scope had narrowed and it had become a male-specific noun. Once men had taken over the generic, wer could quietly disappear from usage, leaving as its only contemporary reminder the compound wer(e)wolf. Since the socially significant indication of adulthood was marriage, the noun wīf must have been, at some point, synonymous with 'adult female', in which case its contemporary, narrowed meaning, 'woman legally attached to a man', was socially motivated. Once the meaning of wīf was so restricted, wīfmann apparently moved in to fill the gap, 'adult female', left by wīf.

The female-specific compound wīfmann is a strange concoction however one looks at it. How should we translate it? 'Wife-person'? 'Woman-person' (assuming that -man(n) retained vestiges of its earlier, generic sense and that, because its reference had narrowed, the word wīf by itself seemed insufficient or imprecise)? Is 'person' the best translation in this case? I suspect not. Other compounds in which -man(n) occurs are occupational or functional terms, such as brim-man(n) 'sailor', gedwol-man(n) 'heretic', ealdor-man(n) (alderman) 'chief noble', hēafod-mon(n) 'leader'. Without knowing the sex of those the words referred to, I must suppose that in each case -man(n) (or -mon(n)) is male-specific. In the case of wīfman(n), likewise, attaching -man(n) to wīf was probably not intended to be generic but to underscore what men considered to be every woman's primary function or occupation, to be the possession of a man she was supposed to perform for.

The historical development of this semantic set in other Gmc. languages demonstrates that words ModE speakers regard as "natural" and "appropriate" are the result of social and cultural choices. The word for 'female human being' in ModG. is Frau, while the words in both Norwegian and Danish, kvinne and qvinde, respectively, are cognate with the OE [+female] term for royalty, cwēn. Hūsbond, which had meant 'freeholder' without reference to sex, also narrowed in its meaning to become the male-specific word it is today, 'male legally attached to a woman'. These changes didn't occur overnight; they took centuries. The English vocabulary lost many near-synonyms, also losing, as a result, much of its flexibility.

Loss and narrowing of the reference of existing human nouns isn't all the story. Between OE and ME, there were additions to the vocabulary of such nouns, words that indicate new distinctions in the social/conceptual structure of English speakers. Conspicuously absent from Diagram 6.1 are four sex-specific words in common usage in ModE, *girl, boy, spinster,* and *bachelor.* With the exception of *boy,* they aren't attested (in written documents) until two or three centuries after the Norman Conquest. *Girle,* whose etymology is obscure, doesn't appear until the ME period, and then as a generic in 1290 that referred to children in general, becoming a [+female] term between 1290 and 1530. By 1530 *girle* referred only to female children and was commonly applied to all young, **unmarried** women. Its addition indicates increased specificity with respect to the chronological age of individuals, especially females, during the intervening 240 years. The origins of the [+male] noun, *boi,* are equally obscure, although it has been likened to a similar term in E. Frisian that meant 'young gentleman'. It appeared in writing in Middle English (ME) around 1300, but its original sense remains uncertain. In the entry for *boy,* the *Oxford English Dictionary* (OED) notes that its Germanic standing is "doubtful," perhaps because we have no earlier evidence of its use. The now archaic word *lad* is also attested around 1300; it, too, is of uncertain etymology.

The word *lass,* often paired with *lad,* has a more complex, if less obscure etymology, appearing in writing around 1300. The *OED* suggests that *lass* was derived from the ON adjective **lasqa,* 'unmarried', attested in Middle Swedish *lösk kona,* 'unmarried woman'. The editors of the *OED* explain the semantic development as follows:

> The adj[ective] means primarily 'free from ties': hence the above sense and those of 'unoccupied', 'having no fixed abode', which are also recorded in MSw. The Icel[andic] *losk·r* occurs only in the sense 'idle, weak'.

The additions of *girl, boy, lass,* and *lad* suggest firmer distinctions with respect to chronological age. Similarly, the appearance of two sex-specific words that refer to one's marital status indicate a need to distinguish those who were married from those who declined to participate in the institution. Of *spinster* and *bachelor,* we have the earliest evidence for the use of *bachelor* in the eighth century when it apparently referred generally to "rustics" of either sex. The *OED,* noting that its original meaning is uncertain and, therefore, the chronology of its various senses doubtful, records the following uses for *bachelor:* 1297, 'a young knight'; 1390, 'yeoman of tradeguild'; 1362, 'one who has taken the lowest university degree'; 1386, 'unmarried man'; 1632, 'a maid, single woman'. The latter use the *OED* editors label "rare." When *bachelor* is used to refer to a woman in ModE, it modifies a sex-specific noun, for example, "bachelor girl," when a woman wishes to avoid the negative connotations of *spinster.* A 35-year-old woman, for example, writing for advice to "Dear Abby" because she had lied to her boyfriend about her age, started her letter with "I am a *bachelor girl* and in love for the first time in my life." The origin of the word is usually attributed to borrowing from OF, but this derivation is also dubious.

Spinster, in contrast, belongs to a group of words that share the Gmc. [+ female] agentive ending *-ster*, most of which are related to cloth-making or cooking, such as *brewster, baxter (<bacestre), webster, folster (<fullestre), dyster, lister, seamster*, activities still associated with women's experiential domain. One might expect that because of its Gmc. origins *spinster* would have appeared in written documents before *bachelor*, but this is apparently not the case. Its earliest attested use, according to the *OED*, is 1362, well into the ME period. Fell, commenting on the puzzling lateness of its written appearance, observed: "The word 'spinster', in the sense of 'one who spins' is first found in ME but **presumably** derives from a non-recorded Old English form" (1984, 41; my emphasis). Whatever the case, *spinster*, too, could be used of either of sex in its original occupational sense, until the seventeenth century, when it became the legal designation for an 'unmarried woman'. That the word could still refer to an individual of either sex in the seventeenth century is indicated by Howell's coinage *spinstress* in 1643, adding the diminutive *-ess*. By 1719, however, it had become a female-specific noun with its ModE meaning, 'a still unmarried woman, one beyond the usual age for marriage, an old maid'. The abstract noun *spinsterhood*, referring to the **state** of being a spinster (i.e., "old maid"), didn't appear until 1823, a harbinger of things to come.

During the Middle Ages, as Norman French words gradually supplemented the Germanic vocabulary of OE, we come full circle to find three Anglo-French (AF) additions replacing the now obsolete generics: in 1292, *people* (AF *poeple* < Lat. *populus*) replaced *þēod*; *person* (OF *personne*) entered the vocabulary in 1225 and *human* (OF *humaine*) appeared in 1398, both replacing the lost generic senses of *man(n)*. By 1290, the noun *hūsbond* from Old Norse had become male-specific, shifting to its now-accepted meaning, 'a man joined to a woman by marriage', and, in 1297, a new word appeared, *bastard*, also from OF *bast*, 'linden bark' + *ard*, a pejorative suffix, literally 'pack-saddle child'.

That the losses from the vocabulary were anglo-saxon and the additions were from Scandinavian and Norman French indicates that the cultural attitudes of the invaders reenforced the misogyny of the xtian church, already present in the british isles, giving new impetus to the elevation of men to social superiority and resulting in subordination of women. If one social group raises itself, it does so at the expense of and by standing on the backs of other groups it must convince of their inferiority. I have already mentioned (chapter 1) that English speakers rejected the potential development of a generic pronoun, borrowing, from unknown origins, the distinctive *schēo*. Similarly, males took over the formerly generic semantic space of *man*, which gradually narrowed its scope to refer only to males, setting in motion the semantic changes in the vocabulary of human nouns still characteristic of ModE. Between the fifth and eleventh centuries, as men squeezed them out of the generic *man(n)*, women lost their most stable general term, *wīf*, and, as a class, occupied less semantic space than they had previously.

Chapter 7

The Place of Women in English: Today

If one accepts the idea that biological sex is a significant feature, one might suppose that that distinction would result in semantic features like [+male] and [+female], as is the case in Old English. For centuries, however, men have used the distinction of sex to construct language structures that perpetuate their dominance and to force women to speak a dialect of submission. Semantically, sexual dimorphism is coded in ModE as [+male] and [−male].

MARKED FOR LIFE

By the end of the middle ages and the beginning of the ModE period in britain, the semantic shape of the English vocabulary for human nouns had become essentially the one we still struggle with today, represented in Diagram 7.1.

At this stage in the development of English, sex-marking is so thoroughly and rigidly established that binary features (+, −) suffice to represent the dichotomies. Before I discuss Diagram 7.1 specifically, however, I must briefly explain the linguistic concept of **marked** versus **unmarked** forms. The binary features that distinguish semantic "opposites" also figure in the linguistic process called **markedness**, a concept central to my analysis and discussion of the examples to come, in which the difference between marked and unmarked terms figures prominently.

Markedness was a corollary concept to the use of binary features introduced by the Linguistic Circle of Prague. The term refers to "the amount of information that is coded in a form."[1] In phonology, for example, /d/ and /t/ are contrasting phonemes; /d/ is said to be **marked** because it has one more

101

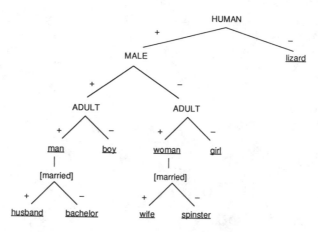

DIAGRAM 7.1. Semantic Features of ModE Human Nouns.[2]

plus feature—**voicing**—than /t/ which is **unvoiced** and **unmarked**. It is the phonological feature [±voice] that distinguishes numerous pairs of words that we might otherwise confuse: *fat/fad, dot/tot, petal/pedal*. (In syntax, to which I will turn in the next chapter, the active **voice** is described as **unmarked**, while the passive is regarded as **marked**.) In semantics, words are **marked** by adding a feature, such as [±male].

G. Leech, in *Towards a Semantic Description of English* (1969), explained the use of binary features: "[S]emantic features are the factors, or contrastive elements, which it is necessary to posit in order to account for all significant meaning relations" (20). Interestingly enough, he used four sex-specific words, *girl/boy* and *woman/man*, to illustrate how binary features account for "meaning relations." To describe the contrastive element in such words, Leech used [±male]. Obviously, *boy* and *man* are [+male]. Not so obviously, *girl* and *woman* are [−male]; that is females are **non**-men. We are, in English, 'those without penises', because the penis is the basis of the semantic contrast. Terms that are so marked indicate the speaker's sense that without an explicit feature the word might otherwise be misinterpreted as referring to the default, unmarked category, that is, [+male].

What all this means is that, if linguists actually did a semantic analysis of English, virtually all of the so-called human nouns would be understood to refer to men. Instead of carrying the feature [+male], they would be [+human] (to distinguish them from lizards, gnats, and rattlesnakes). Just those few words categorized as female would be marked [−male]. In the semantics of English, the male sex is the unmarked norm, the standard; the female sex must be marked as that which is non-male (other).

Words for occupations offer familiar examples of how maleness is assumed unless a label is explicitly modified by a female term. In English, most prestige references are understood to belong to the default category [+male] unless they are preceded by a female-specific word or carry a [−male] suffix such as -ess or -ette. Persons addressed as doctor, lawyer, artist, author, engineer, surgeon, sculptor, mayor, or jockey are assumed to be male unless a special form is used, such as *majorette, woman* doctor, *lady* lawyer, au*thoress*, or sculp*tress*. This is true of all prestige occupations. The suffix -*ette* signals the social barriers between a majorette and a major: economics, political power, age, sex, and significance. The occupational labels assumed to be inherently female, which require overt modification if the person is male, refer to low prestige, low pay occupations: secretary, prostitute, nurse. When a man holds one of these occupations, he is called a *male* secretary, *male* prostitute, or *male* nurse. Assuming that the male sex is normal and the female sex deviant also underlies the use of pseudo-generic *man*, and the use of *he* as though it encompassed women in its reference. In English, all persons are assumed to be male unless otherwise specified.

There are obvious differences between the semantic representations of 6.1 and 7.1. What had been a three-dimensional semantic space in OE is now two-dimensional. CLASS is no longer an overtly marked semantic parameter. *Lady*, although often used (and overused), has become a euphemism for *woman*,[3] a way of avoiding the sexual connotations men attach to the word. *Lord*, in the u.s. especially, is archaic and appears mostly in xtian hymns. Other terms for royalty, *princess, princeling, prince,* were borrowed from Norman French. Words for working-class occupations, for example, tend to be [+male], unless they are performed **inside** and then they are female-specific. Thus, women may be included when someone of the moneyed class talks about "servants," but *maid* refers only to women. *Servant*, however, may cognitively be [−male], as the compound *manservant* suggests. (There is no corresponding term *womanservant.) That tending a house is a specifically [−male] occupation is explicitly marked in *charwoman, cleaning woman, housemother*, but implicit in *housekeeper*. There are no *charmen or *housefathers, and a "cleaning man" is a *janitor* or *sanitation engineer*.

In ModE the feature [+female] no longer exists. Instead, words are now either male [+male] or **non**-male [−male]. Women are beings characterized as not-men, therefore not-**persons**, and defined only in terms of their relationships to men. Use of the adjective *single* as an antonym for *married* marks the conceptual dichotomy. But the stigma of "single" applies only to women, a fact apparent in the asymmetry of *mrs.* and *mr.* While the title *mr.* lacks the feature [±married], *miss* and *mrs.* make the distinction explicit for women. Feminists attempted to erase the female-specific distinction by urging adoption of the title *ms.*, with some success. Now, however, PUD speakers use and interpret *ms.* as a title that refers only to "single women" who are "trying to hide" the fact that they aren't married. Married women in particular bear responsibility for this construal because they enjoy marking their [+male] institutional status explicitly. So the PUD distinction remains in force; only the form of address has changed.

In Diagram 7.1, the redundancy of the features [±adult] and [±married] is unavoidable because English contains sex-specific pairs with both features, which represent sub-classes of [±male]. One might argue that [±married] takes precedence over [±adult], but rearranging the diagram in this way would further obscure at least one fact of usage not immediately obvious: both *girl* and *boy* often refer to adults of both sexes, whether or not they're married. Wives talk about their activities with "the girls" and men demand their "nights out with the boys." Of course there's the cliché, "Boys will be boys," accompanied by elbowing and a leer suggesting tolerant complicity. (Its companion expression, "Girls will be girls," seldom appears; when it does, it draws its force from the male version, and is delivered in a condescending manner.)

Nevertheless, *girl* occurs frequently in contexts in which speakers, both female and male, use it in contrast to the [+male, +adult] noun *man*. This usage appears often in novels and is a staple of commercial advertising and rock lyrics.

7.1 a. If a *man* has any regard for a *girl's* feelings, there is one thing he cannot refuse: a return bout [i.e., sexual encounter] if she wants one. (Robert Heinlein, *Glory Road*, 276)
  b. In less time than it takes you to shave, Bullworker can start building you the kind of 'he-man' body other *men* envy and *girls* adore. (Margrace Corp. brochure)
  c. *Girls* and *men*, Photographic summer work. (Help Wanted Ads, *Village Voice*, July 7, 1975, 56)

The contrastive force of pairing *girl* with *man*, which equates women with children and casts men as adults, indicates that the apparent redundancy in Diagram 7.1 is not an error of my analysis but rather a discrepancy inherent in the conceptual scope of these English human nouns. One's initial inclination to explain the scope of *girl* and *boy* as encompassing [+adult] nouns as a consequence of ageism, a desire to feel, appear, or be younger than one is, will miss the fact that PUD conceptualizes age very differently with respect to women and men.

That *girl* is not parallel semantically to *boy* is evidenced in the many pejorative uses of the female term in all-male contexts, such as locker rooms and military camps.

7.2 a. Q: "How did you manage to take the horseshoe championship away from your brother?"
    A: "He broke his finger."
    Q: "How did he break his finger?"

A: "He hit me."
Q: "Why did he hit you?"
A: "I called him a *girl*."
("On the Road," television documentary, June 16, 1975)

Calling any male, regardless of age, "a girl," is a standard insult in PUD. Among men, *girl* is a "fighting word."

Additional evidence that the feature [±adult] takes precedence over [±married] is the fact that *girl* is often used as a euphemism to refer to Lesbians. Two examples of this use occurred in Michael Crichton's novel, *The Terminal Man*.

7.3 a. There were a lot of men here—and a lot of tough-looking *girls* with short hair. (165)
    b. These *girls* liked *girls*, she realized. (462)

Thus, although both *spinster* and *old maid* are often used as euphemisms, both to emphasize the cultural assumption that a woman's only social identity is defined in terms of men and to avoid saying *Lesbian*, Crichton's use of *girl* also tells us that the assumptions of the OE semantic structure remain in force: a female isn't an adult until and unless she marries a man. The conceptual structure of PUD also considers the act of fucking to confer adult status on women, as 7.4 illustrates.

7.4 The author attaches little importance to Edward's partially concurrent affair with Lady Furness, except to emphasize that all three were *married women*, the Prince being incapable of falling for *unmarried girls*. (Elizabeth Langford, "The Rebellious Monarch," *Saturday Review*, May 3, 1975, 20)

A woman who hasn't fucked men, who doesn't limit her life to the boundaries of the interior world, is, by definition, [−adult].

But the idea that women **are** children is so strong in the English version of PUD that even women who are married and have children of their own are frequently described as though they aren't adults. In advertising, where women are regularly featured as mothers, verbal messages combine women and children as a category, syntactically contrasting them with men. A typical example of how this syntactic contrast is managed occurred in a Jell-O ad in the June, 1919 issue of the *Pictorial Review*:

7.5 All these [varieties of Jell-O] can be made into cool and sparkling 'plain' desserts or the more substantial Bavarian creams that *women and children are so partial to* and *men find so satisfactory that they always want more*. [My emphasis]

In this example, there seem to be other implications attached to the syntactic contrast. Notice that "women and children" are described as being "partial" to Bavarian creams, while men are said to "find [them] so satisfactory." The adjectives used here are very different: *partial to* suggests an emotional bias contrasted with the rational connotations of *satisfactory*. In addition to the pseudo-objective tone of "find . . . satisfactory," the adjective *satisfactory* also suggested an appetite that needs to be satisfied, while *partial to* implied something less than a need—a liking, or a desire for, something less important or crucial than a need. Furthermore, being "partial" to something doesn't mean that one will necessarily get it, and I interpret the juxtaposition of these two different descriptions as implying that, **because** men "want more" of the desserts, women and children may get less than they'd like to have.

In fact, the PUD concept of women as [−male, −adult] and socially marginal if [−married] is now well entrenched in ModE usage. A *Time* article by Richard Stengel, "The Underclass: Breaking the Cycle" (October 10, 1988, 41–42), pairs sex-specific words illustrating how the semantic formula is worked out in usage. Stengel's stated purpose was to document "America's Underclass," people "caught in a vicious cycle of poverty and despair," to demonstrate that "American Democracy" has failed to mete "out liberty and justice for all" (41). But how we define a problem determines the solutions we seek, and Stengel described the underclass's cycle of poverty as though the sex-specific domains aren't part of the problem. His sex-specific references indicate that, however "liberty and justice" are eventually meted out (by someone), sexism, as well as race and class distinctions, are operating.

Writing of people who "live lives *without*," Stengel characterized them as "*mothers* without *husbands, men* without *work*." Women can be mothers without having husbands, and this feature, in and of itself, isn't a class- or race-linked characteristic. Stengel simply assumed that mothers in the underclass "should" have husbands. The men, in contrast, belong to the underclass because they don't have "work." The plight of the women was defined in terms of the interior experiential domain, while that of the men was placed in the external domain. That the women ought to have work, not husbands, apparently didn't occur to Stengel. Having jobs that pay a fair wage for both sexes wasn't a conceivable solution for him: the men should have "work," the women "must" have men.

"The Underclass," Stengel wrote, "is defined less by income than by behavior." They are the "prisoners of a ghetto pathology . . . marked by *teenage pregnancy* [and] *fatherless households*" (41). The behavioral features that define the "pathology" of the underclass, we are to understand, are pregnancy and households, both [−male]. (He didn't explain why this configuration is "pathological.") Stengel here implied that the real problem is women who lack men, without explaining why a man is necessary to any household; he couldn't imagine that a woman might constitute a household independently. His pairing revealed the corollary PUD assumption, that men govern the interior experiential domain, while they restrict women to it.

Stengel's arrangement of the statistics demonstrates that only men are considered adults in PUD. In what he called the "Seven Ages of Underclass Man and Woman," of the six he described, only two are generic; four are sex-specific.

Birth. More than half of all black infants are born *out of wedlock*—and in the inner cities, that figure can reach 90%.

Childhood. Two in five black children are dependent on public assistance—and at least 100,000 are homeless.

Adolescence. Nearly half of *black females* are pregnant by the age of 20.

School days. The high school dropout rate in many inner cities is well over 50%.

Adulthood. Only about half of all *black men* in the ghetto have jobs.

Death. The leading cause of death for *young black men* is murder by another young black man. (41)

These aren't the "seven ages of underclass man **and** woman" as Stengel labeled them; they are selective descriptions that represent an "age" in terms of one sex or the other. Black women disappear from his statistics after adolescence, and the young (i.e., adolescent) black men weren't mentioned until Stengel described Death. Adulthood was defined strictly in terms of work. Since "work" belongs to the [+male] experiential domain, black women apparently skip adulthood in Stengel's formulation (although they work long and hard, frequently at the most menial, lowest paying jobs), and he was utterly silent about their deaths from poverty, malnutrition, and male violence. If we accept Stengel's description of the underclass as accurate, we also accept his conceptualizations.

Of course, Stengel isn't the culprit—his analysis merely reflects and bene-fits from the PUD dichotomy by which men occupy all available space and relegate women to interior nooks. The semantics of common, human nouns in English incorporates the assumptions explicit in the Japanese address, 'Mrs. Interior' (discussed in chapter 5), and implicit in Stengel's descriptions of the underclass. The conceptual boundaries of this PUD dichotomy reveal themselves in a variety of other ways. References to home ownership, for example, commonly assume that men own homes as shown in 7.6, directly in a simile, indirectly by contrasting paired nouns.

7.6 a. According to a recent *New York Times* article, real estate marketing specialists say the Age-of-Aquarius generation leans toward formal dining rooms and foyers, much like those in *the house owned by dear old Dad*. (*Twenty One*, July, 1988, 6)

b. "I'd rather see *homeowners and housewives* use a stun-gun." (*P. M. Magazine*, September 22, 1980)

Men own the homes in which they expect us to work, but even the labor women perform in that space must be marked as *housework*, to distinguish it from **"real" work**, which only men do. Familiar phrases reflect the dichotomy between "woman's work" **inside** dwellings and the "real work" men do **outside** in the "real world." We mark occupational deviations to foreground facts which contradict cultural assumptions, using phrases like *career woman* or *working mother*, which in turn ignore the labor women do in houses. A "working mother" is one who earns money outside the home. The telling distinction is that of **earning money** because the labor women perform inside a dwelling for males to whom they are related is unpaid. In the background, and unmarked, is the assumption that only men are wage-earners.

What is assumed need not be made explicit, so English has no phrases, such as *career man, *working father, to pair with the female-specific ones. A woman inside a house is ordinary; a woman outside a house is noteworthy. The word *husband*, for example, now indisputably a [+male] noun, referred to a woman in the made-for-tv movie *This Wife for Hire*: a woman starts a "wife-for-hire" business, supplying unmarried men with surrogate wives to clean for them and cook their meals. Viewers assumed that all of her customers would be men, as did the entrepreneur herself. When a businesswoman walked into her office asking to hire a "wife," the owner exclaimed, "Congratulations! You're our first *woman husband*."

The boundaries between the social roles defined as appropriate for women and men are well understood. A comic used the following "illocutionary mistake"[4] to elicit laughter from her audience in a joke about her inability to balance her checkbook: "I promised my banker that *I wouldn't cash checks and he wouldn't cook meals*." Stereotypically, money matters are beyond the intellectual abilities of women and cheerfully left to men. Cooking, an interior task, is "women's work" unless it is performed for money, a distinction coded in the nouns *cook* and *chef*. Women are cooks, men are chefs. Being a chef is a [+male] occupation and so more prestigious.

Any occupation or social position occupied by men is assumed to be more prestigious as the examples in 7.7 illustrate.

7.7 a. Every new field of study, *like a dog marking its territory*, seeks to assert its claim to its area by sticking new labels on the phenomena it is interested in. (Morton Hunt, *The Universe Within*, 23)
b. Before the revolution, Markiewicz spent her time *as a woman*. (Student essay)

Research is a prestige occupation. In 7.7a, Hunt was thinking of fields of study as [+male] domains, an assumption made explicit when he compared the creation of jargons to the male canine habit of marking territory by urinating along its boundaries. Being a revolutionary may not be generally regarded as a prestige occupation, but political activity is assumed to be within the male experiential domain. The contrast between Markiewicz's revolutionary activities with her earlier life "as a woman" signalled that she had crossed the boundary between the female and male spheres in the student's mind. Once she entered the male domain of politics, she was no longer a "woman" according to its social reference.

The generic human nouns in ModE[5] illustrate the use of the conceptual structures represented by semantic markedness. The Women's Liberation Movement (WLM) focused public attention on the nouns *man* and *mankind*, which prescriptive grammarians described as generics that refer to both women and men (in spite of the fact that the *OED* labels such usage obsolete). Feminists asserted that these terms were pseudo-generics that referred only to men and excluded women, conceptually as well as verbally.[6] A number of linguistic tactics for developing ways of speaking generically have been suggested:

1. avoiding the word *man* and its derivatives altogether, substituting *people* or *persons*;
2. using *woman* and *man* together when we think we're talking about "people in general";
3. devising ways of neutralizing the [+male] feature of *man* so that it acquires the sense [–male], too.

Of the three tactics listed, avoiding *man* is the easiest. Regularly saying "women and men" requires effort and the breath of two additional words.

The third tactic is the most dubious, in spite of its appeal. Can we use *man* as a generic; can it somehow lose its [+male] feature so that it refers to all people? Common use suggests that the answer is "no." There is a variety of ways to demonstrate that *man* and *mankind* aren't generics. In 7.1, I provided examples in which *man* had male-specific reference and contrasted semantically with *girl*. As 7.8 illustrates, there are numerous contexts in which *man* might at first be interpreted generically, but is later revealed to refer only to men by the use of a [–male] word, a cue that forces reinterpretation.

7.8 a. "*Man* was not meant to fly."
     "Who said that?"
     "Some *woman.*"
     (*Hagar*, February 17, 1982)
   b. The license to wed, which was designed by *man* as a means of protecting children, the home, and *his wife*, was followed by the license to

bear children. (David Levy, *The Gods of Foxcroft*, New York: Pocket Books, 1971, 121)

c. *Man* is himself a problem in search of a solution, and his prejudices against minority groups—and *women* constitute a social minority group if not a numerical one—are groping expressions of his confused attempts to solve his problems. (Ashley Montague, *The Natural Superiority of Women*, New York: Macmillan, 1974, 57)

d. *Mankind* has, ever since he began to think, worshipped that which he cannot understand. . . . Yet *man* is now in the position of facing the ultimate unknowable, which can never be penetrated as long as he remains in his present physical form. . . .

When he has grown safely to adulthood he can wake up in the morning in his heated or air-conditioned house, use the latest techniques to prepare food for himself, drive off in his heated or air-conditioned car, and spend the day in a glass and plastic office. . . . And to cap it all he may, if he really so desires, *stay at home and change into a she!* [My emphases] (John G. Taylor, *Black Holes: The End of the Universe?* New York: Random House, Inc., 1974, 11–12)

7.8.d. is particularly telling. One might, in spite of the use of the verb *penetrate*, initially assume that Taylor's use of *mankind* is generic. Women do, after all, grow to adulthood, drive cars and work in offices. Some men have been known to cook for themselves. But Taylor's final sentence, intended to "cap" his description of the comforts technology provides, betrayed him: *stay at home and change into a she!* brings us up short if we have been interpreting *mankind, man* and *he* as generics that include women and forces us to reanalyze every previous us of those words. Taylor's use of *man* and *mankind* followed the boundaries of PUD's experiential domains: when he wrote about outside activities, he used male-specific terms; when he shifted to a [–male] reference, he signaled it by specifying the interior domain, "stay at home."

Other words, such as *people, person,* and *human,* which we might believe have generic reference, turn out, in actual use, to be [+male] in their reference as well.

7.9 a. He had been under stress, and *people* under stress often do strange things—*cup their testicles through the pockets of their pants*, click their teeth together . . . (Stephen King, "Summer of Corruption: Apt Pupil," *Different Seasons*, 145)

b. "They have come to see that this is not a detriment to them as a *human being* or as a *woman*." (Staff volunteer for Rape Crisis Center, Channel 13, *Rape, Crime of Passion or Violence?*, August 24, 1979)

c. Probably the next prejudice was toward *women*. Early *humans* learned that *women* were not as physically strong as *men* and therefore couldn't possibly be the equals of *men*. . . . Therefore *they* started treating *women* like any other possession. (Student essay)

d. "You see, being *human* does have advantages, like being able to appreciate a flower or *a woman*." (*Star Trek*, "By Any Other Name")

In each case, we have to reinterpret what initially seemed to be a generic when a [– male] noun follows. In a., King's use of *people* can be interpreted as generic—women as well as men do "strange things" under stress, but cupping our testicles through the pockets of our pants isn't one of them. The rape crisis volunteer in b. clearly felt that being a woman had to be distinguished from one's status as a *human being*, and the student author of c. betrayed the nongeneric reference of *humans* with the final sentence, "*they* started treating women like any other possession." Up to that point, readers of the essay might have granted that women, too, realized that they weren't as strong as men, but when *women* is used as the object of *treating*, a generic reading of *humans* becomes impossible.

Turning from generic terms to occupational labels referring to "real work," understood to be labor performed **outside** the home and for which one is paid money, men predictably dominate. In fact, examining how occupational terms are marked or unmarked in English reveals how usage reenforces semantic structures, buttressing PUD's consensus reality. The examples of 7.10 illustrate how thoroughly English speakers associate paid labor with men.

7.10 a. The *poet* writes under one restriction only, namely, that of necessity of giving immediate pleasure to a *human being* possessed of that information which may be expected of *him*, not as a *lawyer*, a *physician*, a *mariner*, an *astronomer*, or a *natural philosopher*, but as a *man*. (William Wordsworth, Preface to *The Lyrical Ballads*, 1802)

b. If a *boss* makes a pass at an *employee*, and if *he* threatens to fire *her* . . . the best thing to do is to marry *him*. (WOW radio announcer, Omaha, Nebraska, November 19, 1976)

c. Q: I read in the papers that Joy Baker—wife of Sen. Howard Baker (R., Tenn.), who wants to be President—is a recovered alcoholic, the same as Betty Ford. Do *politicians drive their wives* to drink?—Didi Mason, Hilo, Hawaii

A: No more than do *writers, actors, physicians* or *engineers*. (*Parade Magazine*, n.d.)

d. Even though *policemen's* attitudes toward *women co-workers* have been slow to change, *their wives'* fears of marital disruption are largely groundless. (*Parade Magazine*, July 27, 1980, 5)

e. When I was going to school I spent most of my time talking to *teachers* and *their wives*. (Edward Albee in an interview, *New Yorker*, June 3, 1974, 29)

f. We find that *holders of the M.A. and M.S.* who enter this department do well in graduate work here. *Their* applications, like those of *women*, and of members of minority groups, are welcome. (Flyer, Department of Psychology, University of Tennessee, Knoxville, 1975)

g. Happy hour for *fishermen and their wives.* (Poster displayed in a Provincetown store window)

h. Even in the most serious of roles, such as that of *surgeon*, we yet find that there will be times when the full-fledged *performer* must unbend and behave simply as a *male.* (Erving Goffman, *Encounters*, 140)

i. *Sociologists qua sociologists* are allowed to have the profane part; *sociologists qua persons*, along with other *persons*, retain the sacred for their friends, *their wives*, and themselves. (Erving Goffman, *Encounters*, 152)

Regardless of the year in which a specific use occurred, it's obvious that nothing much has changed between 1802, when Wordsworth's Preface was published, and today. Whatever the occupation, whether it's poet, lawyer, sociologist, surgeon, politician, or police*man*, speakers of English assume, unless informed to the contrary, that the individual who performs the work, holds whatever degrees are necessary, is male. The writer of f. revealed, in the subordinate afterthought, that he assumed the "holders of the M.A. and M.S." of whom he wrote to be not only men, but white, too.

The assumption that only men perform "real" work is thoroughly embedded in PUD descriptions, and the economic rewards attached to specific occupations determine not only the social class to which individual men belong but the sex best equipped to perform the labor involved. As the salary paid for the work of occupations increases, so does the prestige value assigned to them. Prestige occupations, usually those with high monetary value—the "professions"—are assumed to be the province of men. This assumption is revealed in the very different interpretations English speakers give to the word *professional* when it is used of women and men. Robin Lakoff (1975) briefly discussed this phenomenon using a pair of sentences that differed only in the pronoun:

7.11 a. *He's* a professional.
    b. *She's* a professional.

Theoretically, these sentences should be semantically parallel. If one knew no more about the subjects of the discourse than what is stated in these sentences, one might assume that the first sentence referred to a doctor, lawyer, dentist, college professor, or some other occupation distinguished as a profession. As Lakoff observed, however, it is unlikely "that one would draw a similar conclusion" when interpreting b. Instead, a majority of English speakers would assume that "she" earns a living in the "oldest profession," prostitution.

> [A] man is defined . . . by what he does, a woman by her sexuality, that is, in terms of one particular aspect of her relationship to men. (30)

Even In contexts in which a woman belongs to a profession, the semantic incongruity of the word *professional* used of women rather than men reverberates.

7.12 "That's really very *professional*," Gallagher said. "I am a *professional*, you fool," she told him. He grinned amiably. "Jesus, girl, I bet you look great in that nurse's uniform." (Jack Higgins, *Night of the Fox*, New York: Pocket Books, 1987, 301)

Here, in a passage in which *professional* was at first presented as a surprised commendation for a woman's competence, the male character speedily turned the intended compliment into a sexual leer when the woman asserted her right to the label as a "serious" worker. Note the author's use of *amiably* to describe the man's grin, his attempt to persuade readers that his character was being friendly, not condescending. (Men often smile when they want to deflect women's objections to being trivialized and patronized.)

That men conceive themselves as the exclusive proprietors of the professions is glaringly clear in those contexts in which writers, in a fit of liberal expansiveness, attempt to demonstrate that women, too, can be "professionals" in the "serious" (i.e., male) sense of the word. An article on veterinarians, published in a 1987 issue of *Pets 'n' People*, illustrated the patriarchal assumption at work when the author pointed with pride to the "inclusion" of women in the field of veterinary medicine. The excerpt of 7.13 illustrates how context betrays the assumptions of "liberal" men. (I've omitted portions of the article not immediately relevant to the purpose of this example.)

7.13 The reality is that a veterinarian is a highly educated *person*, skilled in preventing, diagnosing, and treating animal health problems. In his book *A Doctor in the House*, Henry Pleasants, Jr., M.D. compared human and animal medicine:

> In order to get into the world at all, a *person* must have the services of an obstetrician. In order to grow up a pediatrician must direct *his* diet. To teeth [sic] properly, an exo- or orthodontist must be consulted. If *his* glands misbehave, an endocrinologist is required. If *he* be plain sick, an internist must be called, whose duty it is to state what the trouble is, and to whom the sufferer must be sent for treatment. If *he* breaks a leg an orthopedist is essential. If *he* develops an actively inflamed appendix, a surgeon may be called. Should *he* become mentally unbalanced, a psychiatrist may be needed to get *him* back on the intellectual beam. **If *he* loves unwisely and too well in the wrong company, *he* may need attention from a competent urologist. When *he* marries, *his***

mate should depend upon the opinion of a gynecologist. Should **she** crack his skull open with a rolling pin, the services of a neurologist will be needed to tell the neurosurgeon what has happened and what should be done. *His* dreams must be interpreted by a psychoanalyst. If *he* gets too fat or too thin, a metabolist must estimate the activity of *his* various organs. If *he* should get peculiar sensations around *his* heart a cardiologist must interpret the electrocardiograph as well as the x-ray films taken by the roentgenologist. As *he* begins to totter down life's pathway, a geriatrist will be needed to give *him* assistance. When *he* finally dies, the pathologist will be required to take him apart to see what was wrong.

Here are 21 *men*, each specializing in a different field of medicine, to take a *person* from prenatal days to postmortem. And yet, there is ONE *man* who must be all of these to take a dog through *his* span of life.

He is, of course, your *veterinarian*. . . .

Growth of Women Professionals

The face of the profession is changing as more and more *women* enter the field, a trend that is expected to continue. . . . [W]hen you visit your veterinarian, you can appreciate the investment *this doctor* has made. [My emphases] (1)

This passage depends on several assumptions to make its point—that veterinarians perform services for animals that 21 specialists perform for humans—and the writer tests our credulity as he expounds his thesis. It is not true, for example, that babies "must have the services of an obstetrician" to "get into the world." Likewise, many of us manage to grow up without pediatricians directing our diets, and we teethe satisfactorily without the expensive attentions of either exo- or orthodontists. Thankfully, our hypothetical "person" finally dies in line 32, but not before the writer has revealed to us that he thinks of the word *person* as [+male]. I'm assuming that, as generous readers, we cooperated up to that point by accepting the idea that *he* referred to women as well as men and gave him the benefit of the doubt. If we were reading *he* as a generic, we're in for a surprise. The slip that betrayed the sex of this otherwise anonymous individual occurred when the author wrote that, having loved "unwisely and too well in the wrong company, *he* may need attention from a competent urologist." In this description, "the wrong company" referred euphemistically to prostitutes, and "he" will need to pay a urologist to treat his venereal disease.

If, however, we missed this cue because the language is indirect, the next sentence, in which the pretense to sex-neutral conceptualization dissolved, confirms the male-specific reference of *person*. Even here, though, we must go through an inferential process to identify the object of *marries* and determine that the "mate" who "should depend upon the opinion of a gynecologist" has to be a female. (Exactly *why* she should do so is never addressed by the author.) This [−male] interpretation of *mate* is validated when we encounter the only female pronoun in the article, when the writer proposed that the services of a neurologist might be in order if she cracked open "*his* skull" with a rolling pin (one of those tools identified with the female experiential domain).

Had we nurtured any doubts about the sex of all those medical experts, the writer proceeded to assure us that none of them are women. Glibly, he wrote, "here are 21 *men*," then informed us that the veterinarian, too, is a man. We aren't told that women as well as men are veterinarians until the last, brief section of the article, which is ambiguously entitled "Growth of Women Professionals." (This is doubtless the work of those pediatricians!) Even here, however, only one sentence mentioned those "women professionals," and it asserted that they are changing "[t]he face of the profession" without bothering to explain exactly *how*. Indeed, women in any of the medical professions reading this article would have difficulty believing that they have changed anything in their professions because men repeatedly erase them.

NO MAN'S LAND

The occurrences of *man, he,* and *his,* as well as *person* in 7.13 have an exclusively [+male] reference. In the one instance when women were in the mind of the writer, the hypothetical "mate" hits the author's hypothetical "educated person" over the head with a rolling pin. At that point, *she* replaced *mate*. Unless one concedes that *he* and *his* are generic and that Dr. Pleasants could have been writing about a Lesbian household, the interpretation of every occurrence of a [+male] pronoun forces us to read the nouns they replaced (e.g., *obstetrician, pediatrician, orthodontist, endocrinologist, veterinarian*) as male-specific.

The issue of pseudo-generic *he* is the most visible part of male dominance in English, and I will discuss it here briefly. Early prescriptive grammarians didn't state explicitly that *man* and *he* were generic in their reference, but in practice they consistently replaced *man* and *mankind* and other nouns, such as *child, student, youth,* and *writer,* with *he*. In fact, men used three devices to establish *he* as a pseudo-generic. The first two were "grammatical" arguments; the third was legislation, an 1850 Act of Parliament.[7]

Those grammatical arguments relied on the classical statement that pronouns must agree with their antecedent nouns in number, person, and gender. Of course, in order to make this rule seem to fit English, the prescriptivists had to maintain that almost all the singular human nouns were understood as inherently [+male], and that the only nouns that could refer to women had a special "feminine marker." Without such assertions and an audience willing to agree with them, the argument collapses.

The second contributing factor was the indefinite pronouns, for example, *anyone, everyone, someone,* which the prescriptive grammarians decided were inherently singular in reference, not plural, in spite of the fact that

English speakers have always used *they* as plural. Lindley Murray, in 1795, was the first grammarian to combine those assertions and claim that *he* was the correct singular pronoun. But he didn't actually state a rule saying that *he* was the correct pronoun to replace antecedent nouns. Instead, he slipped the assertions in under *Rule V—Rules and Antecedents*, where he used a quotation as an example of violation of pronominal agreement. Although his preceding definition of agreement didn't apply to the example, it seems, as a result, purely gratuitous: "Can *any one*, on *their* entrance into the world, be fully aware that *they* shall not be deceived?" (Murray, 96). Without further comment or explanation, Murray corrected the alleged error, replacing the *their* and *they* with *his* and *he*, respectively. In this way, he condemned the popular use of *they* to replace nouns of general reference,[8] a practice most of us continue today, and established *he* as the "correct" usage.

There was no explicit rule proclaiming *he* as a generic until the nineteenth century. As late as the middle of that century, one could still find grammarians describing *she* and *they* as pronouns of general reference, as well as *he* (Bullions, 1856; Kerl, 1859 [see Alston]). Ann Bodine (1975), analyzing pronominal usage in English, pointed out that the use of *they* to replace singular nouns has a long and honorable history in English going back to Chaucer, a history that prescriptivists since Murray have consistently chosen to ignore.

It was also Bodine, citing Evans and Evans (1957), who brought attention to the 1850 Act of Parliament that made into law the grammarians' fanciful assertions under the guise of making parliamentary acts shorter.

> An Act for shortening the language used in acts of Parliament . . . in all acts words importing the masculine gender shall be deemed and taken to include females, and the singular to include the plural, and the plural the singular, unless the contrary as to gender and number is expressly provided. (Evans and Evans as cited in Bodine, 1975a, 136)

By the beginning of the twentieth century, pseudo-generic *he* was thoroughly entrenched as the only "correct" singular pronoun. As my own high school teacher explained when I questioned the logic: "Always use *he* to replace an antecedent noun, even if you're talking about a group you believe to be all-female, if there's a possibility that one male might be in the group." This ridiculous sort of logic, if one can call it that, continues to predominate, and we hear and read *he, he, he* replacing nouns such as *child, adolescent, employee, employer, homeowner,* and *attorney* all the time. Of course, we continue to use *they* in our everyday conversations, in spite of the grammarians' prescriptions and acts of parliament, but we hear *she* only when the sex of the person is known to be female.

In English, the pronoun *she* has its own "special" uses: (1) it regularly replaces just those nouns men believe to be inherently female: *secretary, nurse, prostitute*; (2) *she* refers to any object men conceive of as "theirs": cars, boats, guns ("Isn't *she* a beaut?"); (3) *she* refers to men's nations, some abstract nouns (such as justice and virtue), and oceans (which men eroticize as their "mistress"). In short, we hear the pronoun *she* only when men are talking about something they perceive as female. The examples in 7.14 illustrate some familiar uses of *she*.

7.14 a. This *spider* always carries *her* own supply of air about with *her*. (von Frisch 34)
   b. Our *America* is singing!
      In *her* schools and colleges
      on *her* streets and in *her* camps,
      . . .
      (Mckeesport High School Yearbook, 1944, 91)
   c. On the pasture lands each *stock beast* was accompanied by *her* young . . . (Ursula LeGuin, *The Dispossessed*, 166)
   d. If your *secretary* questions you about when that memo was written, yell at *her*, blame *her*, stomp away. (Donald M. Murray, "A memo to myself," *Boston Globe*, October 13, 1987, 67)
   e. [T]he *world*'s power requirements are far outstripping *her* capacity . . . (Taylor, *Black Holes*, 20)
   f. *She* runs the office for men who run the world . . . *She*'s a *secretary* . . . (Valentine, *American Essays*, 21)

The ways *she* and *he* replace antecedent nouns in my examples in this chapter indicate that gender, however one construes it, simply doesn't apply to English. John Lyons (1969), discussing gender from a linguistic point of view, described how "natural gender" guides our pronoun selection.

> Gender plays a relatively minor part in the grammar of English. . . . There is no gender-concord; and the reference of the pronouns *he, she,* and *it* is very largely determined by what is sometimes referred to as 'natural' gender—for English, this depends upon the classification of persons and objects as male, female, or inanimate. (283–84)

According to Lyons' description of how "natural" gender functions in English, speakers choose their pronouns on the basis of whether they think a given noun is classified as "male, female, or inanimate." Put another way, every noun for which speakers substitute *he* is classified (somewhere) as [+male], and every noun for which *she* is substituted is classified as [−male], while inanimate nouns aren't classified on the basis of sex. What we have here is a marvelous circularity: English nouns have "natural gender"; nouns are classified as male, female, and inanimate; pronouns are chosen on the basis of this "natural" classification. And this "natural" classification, if it can be said to exist anywhere, exists only in the minds of English speakers!

By now, the assertion that English has "natural gender" should be suspect. Certainly, the uses of both *he* and *she* daily fail to show any such thing. In fact, something that one might call natural gender (seriously) is functional in the grammar of English only with respect to a limited, I would say closed, set of human nouns called **kinship** terms. This set includes words such as *mother, father, aunt, uncle, sister,* and *brother,* among others. Even here, however, some terms appear to carry more weight than others in specific kinds of reference. Consider how often we hear talk about "brotherhood" (as in "the brotherhood of man") and "brotherly love" (Philadelphia is called the City of Brotherly Love). Why should the sibling relationship named by *brother* be preferred to, say, **sisterly** love? We do use kinship terms in other expressions to characterize love: *motherly love* and *fatherly love.* When the idea of love is qualified by a kinship term, the implication seems to be that sexual intimacy is being excluded, and we're supposed to conjure for ourselves the familial ideal that PUD presents to us: nurturing, safety, shelter, warmth (even coziness!), and unconditional love.

But as the wraps come off the frequency of male rape of female family members, the phrase "fatherly love" is, perhaps, a bit much. To imagine that the love of a father should mean safety and unconditional love to the 25 million plus women in the u.s. raped by a male relative is asking a lot of forgiveness. And the PUD description of "motherly love," while generally accepted as synonymous with warmth, tenderness, and caring, provides a tacit background to attract consumer dollars to brand-name products.

The kinship term *mother,* on the other hand, does seem to have its own privileged conceptual niche in PUD, which is why, perhaps, so many women feel compelled to pay lipservice to the stereotype. But the way the relationship and its cultural associations are used in advertising suggests that motherhood is less privilege and more drudgery. DelMonte, for example, has a child say, "Nothin's too good for daddy and me, mom brings DelMonte home," and I imagine daddy and the children lounging at home while good ole mom trudges up and down the aisles of a grocery store buying canned goods. I grew up with "Father Knows Best," but Hellman's knew fathers wouldn't sell mayonnaise when their advertising firm came up with "Mother knows best, mother knows Hellman's." Car dealers, anxious to attract women's money to their showrooms, wracked their brains for a sales pitch, and came up with: "And the hatchback model holds 16 bags of groceries—something that'll make mom happy!" Of course! Why else would a woman need a car except to carry groceries? One woman, at least, knows her place: on the back of her car is a bumper sticker that says, "If a woman's place is in the home, why am I always in the car?" And there's the television commercial in which Robert Guillaume cozies up to the camera and coos about how M.O.M. always takes care of us when we're sick. But M.O.M., of course, is an acronym for Milk of Magnesia.

In spite of all the movies and television sitcoms showing how wonderful "dads" are, "fatherly love" won't work on the emotions of a large segment of the u.s. population; "motherly love" means, essentially, slavery. "Moms" wash dirty clothes and worry about which detergent to use, do the grocery shopping, cooking, and, in their spare time, bake chocolate chip cookies. "Sisterly love" isn't "catchy" enough—it's female-specific, and we all know that female nouns can't become "generic" in PUD. Elimination leaves us with "brotherly love," a male-specific brand of love. *Brother* functions to exclude the *idea* of sexual activity, specifically among men. That is, talking about "a brotherhood of men" draws a line that men aren't supposed to cross in a heteropatriarchy. Men can love each other as long as they don't express their love sexually, so "brotherly love" doesn't threaten their heterosexual pose.

My earlier discussion of human nouns, such as *poet, lawyer, fisherman, boss, politician, engineer,* and *physician,* demonstrated that occupations outside the home are conceptually classified by English speakers as male-specific, and so commonly replaced by the pronoun *he.* The kinship terms are the only nouns in English that demonstrate "natural gender" in the pronouns that replace them. Other examples, such as the one from *Pets 'n' People* and those in 7.14 show that *she* is used to refer to a noun only when a speaker thinks of that noun as [+female]. That is, women are explicitly mentioned in discourse only if some activity is thought of as *womanly* or *feminine.*

The relative distribution of *she* and *he* as replacements for nouns in ModE indicates that the noun classification system set forth by the prescriptive grammarians (chapter 4), in which the nouns of power and domination are [+male] and those of inferiority and subjection are [−male], is now established. A galactic linguist, having collected data on the ways English-speakers in the u.s. categorize objects, people, and other animate beings, would probably arrive at a classification very much like R. M. W. Dixon's description of noun categories in Dyirbal. Restricting my attention only to what he presented as Class I and Class II nouns, [+male] and [+female] nouns, respectively, the evidence from pronoun usage indicates that English nouns are conceptually organized into two groups according to the sex-specific experiential domains characteristic of PUD. Whereas Dyirbal speakers use *bayi* (male) and *balan* (female) to identify their classes, *he* and *she* serve that function in English.

CLASS I: man, father, son, uncle, brother, grandfather, nephew, husband, dog, doctor, lawyer, artist, author, poet, sculptor, writer, professor, scientist, engineer, radical, president, general, veterinarian, boss, employer, official, beast, animal, wizard, mister, major, steward, elder, lord, lion, bull, rooster, sun, trees, stallion, wrestler, some knives, some planets (Mars, Saturn, Jupiter, Neptune, Mercury, Pluto, Uranus), courage, honor, duty, and so on.

CLASS II: woman, mother, daughter, aunt, sister, grandmother, niece, wife, bitch, nurse, receptionist, secretary, prostitute, nymphomaniac, teacher (in pre-college schools), employee, witch, mistress, majorette, stewardess, lady, cat, cow, chicken, spiders, moon, flowers, mare, languages, nations, cities, all vehicles (cars, boats, tanks, motorcycles), some knives, guns and rifles, bodies of water, nature, volcanoes, the planet Venus, justice, virtue, chastity, purity, obedience, patience, fidelity, and so on.

The English system of noun classification, if organized on the basis of pronominal evidence by a galactic linguist, is surprisingly similar to that of Dyirbal. Whether this similarity is attributable to Dixon's interpretation of his data or to the way men think, I don't know. There are, of course, differences in specific words, but those are cultural and social. Neither Dixon nor Lakoff listed abstractions or the names of planets for Dyirbal. Dyirbal classifies the sun as female, the moon as male; English classifies them in reverse. In Dyirbal, dogs are thought of as female, in English, male; storms are male in Dyirbal, but hurricanes, once given only female names in English, are now either female or male.

PARADIGMATIC WOMAN

There is more yet to be said about those nouns in English conceptualized as uniquely [−male]. One particular class of nouns shows two linguistic phenomena that don't occur with the [+male] class. First, it contains what some might call a sub-class, a group of terms of which the most neutral is *prostitute*. Second, as Muriel Schulz (1975) demonstrated, any word that is [−male] gradually pejorates, developing increasingly negative connotations and implications.

Again and again in the history of the language, one finds that a perfectly innocent term designating a girl or woman may begin with totally neutral or even positive connotations, but that gradually it acquires negative implications, at first perhaps only slightly disparaging, but after a period of time becoming abusive and ending as a sexual slur. (65)

The semantic subset of words related to *prostitute* exists because every word refers to women as **sexual objects**, as though the only way men are capable of thinking and talking about women is as **holes, receptacles, containers**—things they can or want to fuck. There is no equivalent sub-class of [+male] nouns in terms either of quantity or lewdness. Nor do [+male] nouns in English develop pejorative connotations as the [−male] ones do, with, perhaps, the exception of *prick*. Both linguistic phenomena not only typify nouns that refer exlusively to women and are restricted to them, but share an important distinction: they happen only to words men use to describe women. Women may know and even, on occasion, use some of them (such as *slut* and *whore*), but they belong to the male vocabulary.

The Prostitute

In "Paradigmatic Woman: The Prostitute" (1977), I collected words belonging to the male vocabulary that describe women's availability to them as sexual objects and extrapolated the semantic parameters that structure the subclass. Because these [−male] words belong primarily to male slang, the set itself is in constant flux, with some terms being discarded as new terms are added. I began with the most commonly known words men use for women they believe are sexually available to them, *hooker, whore, slut, pussy, gash,* and *slit*. With the aid of colleagues, students, and friends, I added terms and phrases found in slang dictionaries and novels and heard on television,[9] until I was sure that whatever terms I'd missed wouldn't affect my analysis. I ended up with more than 200 such expressions, and Schulz (1975) found another 100 (74, en. 7). The magnitude of this semantic set and the fact that new terms are constantly being added suggests that it can expand infinitely.

I began this research thinking that I was looking for synonyms for *prostitute*, but quickly realized that men use them to refer to any woman: to call a woman *whore* or a *piece of ass*, for example, the man needn't know her or have had any personal contact with her. What I was actually collecting turned out to be *part* of the vocabulary of insult with which men express their perceptions of and thinking about *who women are*.

What I found in my analysis was the paradigm (or model) of the PUD concept, 'woman'. The paradigm itself is defined by at least three parameters, or semantic axes: COST, METHOD OF PAYMENT, and LENGTH OF CONTACT. Of these, COST and LENGTH OF CONTACT are continua rather than simple binary features. COST ranges from free to cheap to expensive, but, as the feature METHOD OF PAYMENT suggests, no man perceives consenting sex with a woman as "free"; the only question in his mind is how much it will cost him to get a woman into bed with him. A disc jockey, for example, having just played "Treat Her Like a Lady (and she'll be good to you)," said: "Yeah, treat her like a lady and maybe she'll give you a money-back guarantee." *Lady,* one of the more positive [+female] words, means only that sex is expensive for the man. A woman who frequently engages in sex with different men without charging them is perceived as utterly stupid and worthless. Mothers warn their daughters, "Don't *cheapen* yourself," hoping to protect them from such harsh judgments. Sex and its cost are so thoroughly related in PUD that women and men both use the words *slut, mattress,* and sometimes *whore* as the worst insults that can be hurled at women. A woman who thinks so little of herself as to not get something in exchange for sex is perceived as pitiful, the lowest of the low.

LENGTH OF CONTACT is, like COST, a range of possibilities from "Actual Contact Irrelevant" to "Brief Sexual Contact" to "Extended" and "Extensive" sexual contact. These degrees of contact indicate whether the man has any contact at all with a woman and, if he does, how long that contact lasts. The names men call women who pass by them on the street, such as *cunt, broad, bitch, nooky*, require absolutely no contact whatsoever for their use. A man can call *any* woman one of these names. I defined "Brief Sexual Contact" as a "trick" or "one-night stand," and representative terms and phrases include *tart, flapgap, tail, hooker*, and *painted lady*. Only three words fell within the space labeled "Extended Contact": *professional, prostitute*, and *entertainer*. "Extensive Contact," in contrast to "Extended Contact," implies some sort of long-standing relationship, for example, *concubine, courtesan, mistress, wife*. The difference between a mistress and a wife is that the latter relationship is legally sanctioned. Palimony suits, however, which came into existence after I'd done my analysis, have made the line between *wife* and *mistress* fuzzy.

METHOD OF PAYMENT, the only binary feature for this semantic set, can be either "direct" (cash) or "indirect" (dinner, movies, jewelry, a concert, clothes, whatever the man thinks will achieve the results he wants). How much he spends, directly or indirectly, determines whether the word he uses comes from the "free/cheap" or "expensive" group.

Men define female human beings as "things" whose only reason for existing is to be fucked by them. In this PUD paradigm, three features are conceptually relevant: how much will he have to pay, what form will the payment take, and how much time (or, perhaps, accessibility) will his money buy? There is a fourth possible parameter, ACCESSIBILITY, but its boundaries aren't clear. Men assume that all women are accessible to them, that all women want men to fuck them. Men call women who declare themselves inaccessible to them *dykes* or *lezzies*, because no "real woman" would pass up a "good fuck." (And "all lesbians need anyway is a good fuck," which, in the world according to PUD, brings them back within the "accessible" range.) So most of the 200 terms I analyzed would carry the feature "accessible." Exceptions to this might be *ballbuster, bitch*, and *hag*, depending on the context in which they were used.)

In addition to establishing the place of each term in the semantic space, I cross-classified each one in four other ways:

1. according to their **connotations,** negative (NEG), neutral (NEU) or positive (POS);
2. as **euphemistic** (EU) or **dysphemistic** (DYS); that is, whether a word or phrase showed disdain for women or concealed it;
3. as **metonymic**, 'part for whole' (P/W), if the word or phrase referred to women as a part of their bodies;
4. as **metaphoric** (MET), if the term or phrase named women as another animal or object.

In this way, each word or phrase occupied some point within the semantic space defined by COST, METHOD OF PAYMENT, and LENGTH OF CON-

TACT, and was labeled to indicate its connotation, whether it was euphemistic or dysphemistic, and whether it was a metonym or metaphor.

To give you some idea of how these words for women are interrelated, imagine a visual representation of the semantic space that defines these [−male] nouns, with LENGTH OF CONTACT (irrelevant, brief, extended, extensive) as its upper, horizontal boundary and COST (free, cheap, expensive) as its lefthand, vertical boundary. METHOD OF PAYMENT (direct/indirect) is within the COST boundary. (This feature applies only to irrelevant and brief contact; it becomes fuzzy under Extended Contact; under Extensive Contact most payments are understood to be Indirect.) Starting at the leftmost boundary, under CONTACT IRRELEVANT, all the words for women are marked as FREE/CHEAP and Direct/Indirect (METHOD/PAYMENT). At the center of this portion of the semantic space are the words *broad* and *girl*. These are the "core" (central) terms for this area. To the left of these two words are *fox, honey pot, cunt, bitch,* and (*piece of*) *ass; cunt* and *ass* are metonyms (P/W) while *fox, bitch* and *honey pot* are metaphors (MET). To the right of the core terms are *nooky, baggage, mattress,* and *lightheels/roundheels. Baggage* and *mattress* are marked (MET), both *lightheels* and *roundheels* are metonymic euphemisms, and Partridge (1967) suggested in his entry for *nooky* that it might be baby-talk and is an "almost polite" word (1266). Placed below the core words are *nympho, ballbuster, minx,* and *hotpot,* because men use them to talk about women who participate actively in heterosex. Only *ballbuster* and *hotpot* are (MET); all have very negative connotations. (Men also describe such women as "oversexed.")

With only a few exceptions, the words and phrases found under Brief Contact require Direct Payment. The core terms for this area are *hooker* and *tart. Two-bit whore* is a representative phrase. Among the dysphemistic, metaphoric terms are *bat, meatcooker, bullseye, posthole,* and *bedpan;* euphemisms include *painted lady, corner girl,* and *lady of the night.* Typical metonyms found in this area are *poxbox* and *fastfanny.* The METHOD OF PAYMENT is either Direct or Indirect only for *corn-hole, bedpan, tart, mama, bedbug,* and *doxy.*

Only a thin line separates Extended Contact from Extensive Contact; the words here differ primarily according to whether payment is Direct, for Extended Contact, or Indirect, for Extensive Contact. Both groups are small compared to the others in this semantic set. Under Extended Contact are *prostitute, professional,* and *entertainer* (both euphemisms), and *call girl,* which, because the contact may be lengthy, can shade into *mistress,* becoming a more permanent relationship. COST can be either Cheap or Expensive, depending on LENGTH OF CONTACT.

The words found under Extensive Contact are used to describe some sort of living arrangement. The woman may have her own apartment (*call girl, kept woman, concubine, mistress*) which the man visits when he wants to, or she may live with the man (*common-law wife, wife*). What??? **Wife**??? I was astounded, too, when my male informants told me that they included *wife* among these terms. Then they explained their logic to me: "When we marry a woman, we pay, and pay, and pay, sometimes for life, for her accessibility. It's the highest price we can pay."

As we move from the left side of this semantic space—where the terms and phrases are general and can be used by any man to describe any woman—toward the right, the expressions become more and more specific in their reference. *Wife* and *mistress* are both very specific. In the semantic space occupied by terms like *courtesan, common-law wife,* and *wife,* we arrive at the point where the church and the state institutionalize men's use of women as sexual objects, breeders, and all-purpose caretakers. The more time and money that a man is willing to invest for the use of a woman, the more legitimacy he confers on her existence in PUD. With the exception of a few tokens, it's the "best" a heterosexual women can do for herself.

The Semantic Derogation of Woman

Muriel Schulz's work (1975) identified yet another 100 derogatory sexual words for women, but the results of her analysis encompassed more of the [–male] semantic space because she showed that terms for women are more prone to pejoration (disparagement) than "equivalent" terms for men. She began by comparing pairs of words such as *spinster/bachelor* and *witch/warlock,* in which the [+male] term is either innocuous or, like *bachelor,* almost always positive in its connotations, while the [–male] word is always negative. Such pairs can't really be said to be equivalent. The same, she observed, is true for sex-marked words referring to elderly people. For old men, English speakers use *geezer* and *codger;* for old women, however, the set of terms is not only much larger but more negative: *trot, hen, heifer, warhorse, crone, hag, beldam* and *frump* (65).

Other sex-specific pairs show the same pattern: the male term is positive, often denoting a powerful social or political position; the female term minimally trivializes the social position it denotes, is often negative, and is always open to pejoration:

lady	lord
governess	governor
courtesan	courtier
mistress	master
majorette	major

In fact, all of the female kinship terms can be used as pejoratives, and many have been used euphemistically to mean 'prostitute': Schulz gives as examples *niece, daughter, mother, wife, cousin, aunt,* and *sister* (66). Words for women who work as domestic servants, *needlewoman, spinster, nurse, laundress,* have been especially popular as euphemisms meaning 'mistress' or 'prostitute'. Of this group, the word *housewife* has an interesting history. As its use in rapid speech gradually reduced the compound's pronunciation, its meaning was gradually degraded. Finally, *housewife* became *hussy,* synonymous with *tramp* and *slut* (66–67). Once this had happened, of course, men simply re-created the compound *housewife* to make it seem as if the two words have unrelated senses in PUD.

All female-specific terms, including *nun, aunt, mother, madam,* eventually become pejoratives in English. While any female-specific term can be used as an insult, male-specific terms that might be taken as pejorative, (*prick, gigolo*), eventually become compliments. Female-specific terms pejorate over time, male-specific words become "honorifics." The political and economic imbalance that subjugates women is encoded and perpetuated by linguistic asymmetry in the structure and usage of English.

Looking back through the data for English in this chapter, the semantic relationship between the female and male experiential domains in English becomes clear: asymmetries in power and significance create semantic asymmetry between "pairs" of sex-specific terms—the difference in power signaled by the frequent use of *girl* and *man* together; any word that refers to women eventually pejorates and becomes an insult or explicit sexual slur; the sheer quantity and apparent endlessness of men's "creativity" when it comes to thinking up new ways of insulting women, and the fact that every "generic" or prestige occupational term is assumed in PUD to be [+male]. From the OE period to the present, men have gradually occupied virtually all of the semantic territory covered by the human nouns until they now control all of the PUD foreground. Women, in contrast, have constantly been squeezed into smaller and more negative semantic spaces until the territory we can call our own is trivial and pitiful, guarded on all sides by the language of men's perceptions.

Now you have some idea of the shape and size of the problems women confront in the English language. We move and breathe and spend every day of our lives in negative semantic space, kept deep within the nooks and crannies of the world men inhabit. The PUD vocabulary of human nouns names us, restricts our movements, limits our aspirations, and, should we somehow manage to emerge from the "interiors" men have consigned us to, we trail our femaleness behind us in *-ettes* and *-esses* and other trivializing signs. Without words to describe our perceptions, a vocabulary that speaks of and to our experiences, ways to name ourselves as willful, conscious, active agents in the world, we are forced to find nonverbal ways to become the women we are. Without a visionary vocabulary, we uncertainly navigate the conceptual distance between victim and survivor.

Chapter 8

"That's How *It* Is!"

In this chapter, I move from the semantic properties of the English vocabulary to the more difficult level of syntax. I say "more difficult" because, in my experience, most people can readily analyze individual words, but have trouble discussing the more abstract rules English speakers know and use to produce the structures we recognize as English sentences. The syntactic rules of English, like those of all human languages, are highly economical: using a few syntactic rules we can produce an infinite number of sentences that we have never said or heard before (for example, the sentences you've just read and understood, although they are "new" sentences).

SUBJECTS, AGENTS, TOPICS, AND EXPERIENCERS

I'll use several labels for the syntactic roles of noun phrases (NPs) in the chapters to come that many readers may not know. Before I explain how the structures created by English syntax serve PUD rhetorical strategies, I want to clarify why I use some terms, but not others, to describe how NPs function in sentences. The traditional label for one of those roles, *object*, I have no quibble with. (Some linguists prefer the term *patient* for the NP that a verb's agent acts upon, but it's too medical for my taste.) The names of other roles are more problematic.

There are three terms for the first NP in a sentence: *subject, agent,* and *topic.* Of these words, *subject* is probably more familiar than *agent* or *topic,* because we learned that term in school. In prescriptive grammars, subjects are identified as nouns, a word that names the person, place, thing, or idea about which something is being said. When we learned this rule, we also learned to look for subjects at the beginning of sentences. In general, the strategy worked for us, even with passive sentences, and we casually identified NPs, such as *the juice* in *The juice was consumed by the thirsty chimpanzees,* as subjects even though, somehow, the identification didn't make sense to us. In specific types of sentences, however, the strategy failed. In sentences beginning with *it* (e.g., *It's tax time again.)* or *there* (e.g., *There were six players on the field.),* we were told that *it* and *there* functioned as place holders for the NPs "tax time" and "six players," respectively. Because teachers could be sure that most of us were thoroughly confused by the circularity of prescriptive definitions and grammarians' attempts to make logical what was essentially illogical, those sentences turned up as trick questions on tests. In prescriptive grammars, the vague term *subject* is used without making the distinction implied by the terms *agent* and *topic.* Confusion is the result.

When I talk about the *topic* of discourse, I use the word as it is commonly understood. A **topic** is what we're talking about in a discussion or conversation. But the word also has a more restricted sense among linguists, referring to the first NP in a sentence, one not preceded by a preposition. Among linguists, *topic* refers to a syntactic position (or slot) that several of the NPs in a given sentence can fill. When I talk about the topics of sentences, I'm referring to a syntactic position and how that position functions in discourse. What traditional grammarians call the **subject** of a sentence, linguists call the *topic;* in this chapter and those that follow, I'll use the linguistic term to refer to the first NP in a sentence.

In active sentences, agents are simultaneously *topics. Agents* have a semantic connection to the main verb regardless of where they occur in a sentence; they name the individual or group who performs whatever action the verb describes. They are said to be necessarily animate, but bureaucratic prose abounds with counter-examples in which *inanimate* agents hide the human agency purposely suppressed by the authors. In the u.s., people don't **do** anything: guns kill; the White House speaks; "services" impound our belongings without a trial. As a topic, the first NP of a sentence has a specific discourse function: it is the foregrounded subject of the statement. As agents, these NPs name the individual(s) who performs the action of the verb. I've italicized the agents/topics in the following sentences so you can identify these dual functions for yourself.

8.1 a. *The police officer* handcuffed the burglar.
   b. *The flight attendants* served breakfast.
   c. *Men and their governments* fight wars for economic reasons.
   d. *She* reluctantly opened her eyes.

Whether the initial NP is singular (a), plural (b), compound (c), or a pronoun replacing an antecedent NP (d), it is both the agent of the verb (e.g., *handcuffed, served, fight, opened)* and the topic of the sentence.

But agent and topic don't always coincide. In the passive voice semantic objects are topics, and agents occupy the object position. These changes in position alter how we interpret assertions because the structure foregrounds the object of the verb and backgrounds (or suppresses altogether) the agent responsible. In a passive sentence, such as *Grenada was invaded by the u.s.*, *Grenada*, the object of *invaded*, is foregrounded by its topic position and *the u.s.*, the agent, has been backgrounded because it is in the object position, where it can now be suppressed (*Grenada was invaded*).

By now, readers may have already identified how the prescriptive labels, **subject** and **object**, have led us to misconstrue the relationship between the syntactic functions of NPs and how women are described in PUD. To say that men treat us as the "objects" who "receive" the actions they perform is accurate enough. But to proceed to say that we want to be the "subjects," not the "objects" of discourse won't alter the conceptual structure of PUD because, of course, women are often the subjects of male discourse. If we want to change our lives, we have to change our descriptions, and reject the false polarity of the labels subject/object. What we want is to be the **agents** who initiate and carry through our own actions in our own universe of discourse, neither the subjects nor objects of PUD. By understanding ourselves as *agents*, we reposition ourselves with respect to male conceptual frameworks and radically restructure how we think about ourselves and who we are.

One other unfamiliar term requires some explanation before I proceed—*experiencer*. **Experiencers** occur with *seem* and *appear* (so-called impersonal verbs), with verbs and adjectives that describe sensations and report psychological experiences, including *strike, occur, clear, obvious, apparent*, and the class of **psych-predicates** (which I'll discuss in chapter 10). The term *experiencer* applies to animate nouns, beings thought to be sentient (*woman, sister, cat*); linguists use it, rather than *agent*, for such nouns because, although a being who experiences a sensation might logically be said to be the agent, in fact, the semantics of sensation predicates in English (hereafter EPs, "experiencer predicates") requires experiencers as **objects** of the verb. As a consequence, whoever is said to experience a sensation (or perception) can never function as the topic of a sentence. (Only with psych-predicates can experiencers also be topics.)

We have, then, three terms to describe the roles (or functions) of NPs in syntactic structures: topic, agent, and experiencer. Any NP that occupies the initial position in a sentence is the topic; in active sentences, it is also the agent. *Agent* and *experiencer* refer to an NP's semantic relationship to its predicate, which doesn't change. *Topic* refers to a syntactic position NPs occupy in specific sentences. The ways these semantic and syntactic functions interact in discourse determines meaning.

To introduce syntactic structure and how it organizes the patriarchal descriptions typical of PUD, I will focus on a rule that replaces NPs with one of several pronouns, for example, *it, this* or *that, these* or *those*,[1] depending on the speaker's point of view. We say, for example, "Mary was surprised when *she* opened *her* door," instead of the cumbersome and repetitive "Mary was surprised when *Mary* opened *Mary's* door," and "I went over to *the chair* and sat down on *it*," not "I went over to the chair and sat down on the chair." If we didn't have ways of substituting pronouns for repetitious elements, sentences would seem unnecessarily wordy.

Linguists say that pronouns replace NPs only when there are identifiable antecedents in the immediate context[2] and make discourse "cohesive,"[3] but our use of pronouns doesn't always result in textual cohesion; they have many uses, not all of them cohesive. Maybe we assume that, when something is replaced in a sentence, we can find an antecedent in order to arrive at an accurate interpretation. But our assumption is often frustrated. Speakers use certain structures because they serve their purposes, suppressing information whether their audience can recover what is missing or not.

DEIXIS

Deixis may be an unfamiliar word, but it's a good way to label the way certain words, especially pronouns and determiners (*the, that*), can function in English. *Deixis*, from the Greek word meaning 'to show directly' and related to the Latin *digitus*, 'finger', means 'to point to'. Words that serve a pointing function in language are called *deictics*. Lawyers know how important one of these little words can be. Suppose, for example, that you're on the witness stand testifying about an automobile accident, being cross-examined by an attorney who asks, "Did you see *the* broken headlight?" Her use of the definite determiner *the* is important in that question because it presupposes that there was a broken headlight for you to see. Whether you answer "yes" or "no" to that question, you've granted the **presupposition** that there was a broken headlight. The same question with the indefinite determiner, *a*, "Did you see *a* broken headlight?" doesn't presuppose that there was a broken headlight at all.

Deictics serve to identify, to point out, in different ways. Determiners like *a* and *the*, for example, can be definite or indefinite. It makes a difference if I say, "Bring me *a* book" or "Bring me *the* book." In the first request, you can bring me any book at all, because I haven't identified a specific book. The second request, however, indicates that I want a specific book and, further, presupposes that you know which book I'm talking about.

In speech and writing, deictics not only identify specific objects, people, and events, but they can serve a cohesive function across spans of discourse. In the preceding sentence, I substituted the pronoun *they* for the noun *deictics*, and you interpreted *they* as referring to its antecedent noun (I hope). *They* functions to connect statements about the same object or entity from one clause or sentence to another. *It* is used in the same way.

Two other words function deictically in discourse, *this* and *that* and their plurals, *these* and *those*. In the singular or plural, *this* and *that* provide another kind of information: they indicate how close or distant a specific thing is from the speaker's location. These words describe relative spatial relationships from the speaker's perspective. I could, for example, say, "Bring me *this* book" or "Bring me *that* book." If I use *this*, you know that I'm talking about a book that's close to me; if I say *that*, you know that I want a book that's relatively distant from me.

Deictics replace noun phrases, clauses, and entire sentences. We use pronouns, including *it* and *they*, and the **demonstratives**, *this/these* and *that/those*, to indicate things that we assume have already been identified, as with the pronouns, or that can be readily identified, as with the demonstratives. My use of the word "assume" in the preceding sentence is intended to be cautionary. When we use *it*, *this*, or *that*, we assume, often erroneously, that our listeners or readers can identify the element that those words have replaced.

FALSE DEIXIS

Because deictics require the reader/listener to identify their reference, both *it* and *this* are "flag words." When a deictic has no identifiable referent in the context, it is a **false deictic**. It points to nothing. False deixis occurs as a result of linguistic ineptness or to implement a rhetorical strategy. Any deictic used nonreferentially is a false deictic. False deictics make false linguistic claims; they say to readers and hearers, "My use of this deictic word tells you that it points to something in the immediate context of this utterance, and you can easily identify its reference."

In fact, speakers and writers use deictics to trick us into supplying information from our own assumptions, beliefs, and misinformation.[4] "Dummy *it*"[5] illustrates that listening is an active linguistic act. We are often forced to do the work of speakers/writers when we must supply implied or nonexistent antecedents for pronouns like *it*, which can cover a lot of contextual territory. Dummy *it* can refer to a conceptually null set (while appearing to carry semantic information), or substitute for emotions and perceptions we refuse to mention. From bumper stickers, "Roofers do *it* higher," popular songs, "Ain't *It* a Shame?," to emotional declarations, "I've had *it*!," dummy *it* serves a variety of functions: titillation by euphemism, false reference, and refusal to make explicit one's feelings and assumptions. Failure to identify such uses when they occur makes us the victims of our own descriptions as well as those of others.

Before proceeding to examine false deixis as a rhetorical strategy, I want to emphasize that we use it often without being aware that we are doing so. We say and hear deictic words used without antecedents all the time. Dummy *it*, for example, occurs frequently in conversational clichés and advertising slogans:

8.2 *It*'s what's happenin'.
    You can't escape *it*.
    It's up for grabs.
    It's in the bag.
    Come off *it*.
    Let's get on with *it*.
    She's out of *it*.
    Go for *it*!
    That's *it*!
    Don't throw *it* all away.

Why don't we stop speakers when we hear them using dummy *it* and ask them exactly what they're talking about? Because I think we prefer to go along with the speaker and pretend that we know what *it* refers to in each instance. If we look closer at the above examples, *it* is being used with global reference, reference so broad that we can't identify an antecedent. In such phrases, *it* refers vaguely to something both speaker and hearer believe they already understand. If they do understand such implied references, then they don't want to say out loud whatever *it* has replaced.

We hear and use *it* without specific reference so often that we have become, I think, utterly numb, as though we've accepted the notion that it's OK for language to be detached from its contextual moorings. Advertisers know we aren't inclined to listen to language closely and they use our linguistic laziness to sell products. A familiar example is "Coke is *it*!" **What**, exactly, **is** Coke being asserted to be? The be-all and end-all? The ultimate something? The "real thing"? Michelob entices us to drink their beer by assuring us, "Oh yes. You can have *it* all," as though beer will enhance our way of living, make us "successful," rich and/or popular. Mountain Dew urges us to "DEW *it* to *it*!"

From childhood on, our lives are filled with a plethora of *its*. The nondeictic pronoun *it* turns out to be a nasty, if common, source of weak-witted attempts at humor, and, as a false deictic, it is used to degrade or wound when it means 'you are so despicable that I can't categorize you.' Children learn quickly that *it* has the potential to signal a lowered status when they joyfully cry out "You're It!" or that it carries the force of insult, to mark another child as an outsider, when they point derisively at the nonconformist and say, "You're an It." At the age when children use *it* as an insult, to exclude another child from their circle, they have already learned the social value of sex-marking (*she* or *he*), that nonconformity is a "bad" thing, and that calling another child an "it" will cause that child pain.

In many cases, *it* acquires a not-quite-ambiguous quality of innuendo. I say "not-quite-ambiguous" because superficially the word has no reference at all. But, at a level we understand perfectly well, *it* refers to heterosexual coitus (fucking). In a large city, a billboard advertises a brand of vodka. Most of the billboard space is occupied by a sultry, reclining woman in a long, black gown. Above her, the billboard urges, "Make *it* with Dark Eyes" (the name of the vodka). "Make *it*" could mean "be successful," but the reclining woman clearly invites men reading the billboard to fuck her, to equate drinking vodka with fucking her.

In "I'm Your Man," Wham! sang, "If you're gonna do *it*, do *it* right. Do *it* with me." Tina Turner revived her career singing, "What's Love Got to Do with *It*?" The sexual innuendo of *it* turns up in numerous bumper stickers proclaiming drivers' occupations and the sexual expertise to be associated with them. These proliferating bumper stickers assert a pathetic obsession with "getting *it* on" and "doing *it*."

8.3 Roofers do *it* hotter
  Lefthanders do *it* backwards
  Nurses do *it* with great care
  Iron workers do *it* higher
  Telephone workers do *it* till your bell rings
  Muzzleloaders do *it* up front
  Auto workers do *it* the American way! (UAW Local 11)
  Publishers do *it* between covers
  Do *it* on a scaffold [on a scaffolding truck]
  Do *it* in a pickup
  Bow hunters do *it* naturally
  Atomic Bombs only Do *It* Once

The people who decorate their vehicles with such sayings apparently think they're cute and clever, as though the sexual innuendo of *it* advertised their wit. Readers, however, may have detected an ominous implication in some of the examples, for example, "Bow hunters do *it* naturally" and "Atomic Bombs only Do *It* Once." In the bow hunters example, *it* can mean killing animals or fucking. The ambiguity links both activities in our minds. Atomic bombs do nasty things to people, but what has *it* been substituted for? The pronoun suggests that a noun has been replaced, but when I think of what atomic bombs do, I mentally substitute verbs like *explode* or an entire verb phrase, like *blow you to smithereens*, for *it*.

The link between male violence and heterosexuality is made explicit when the reference of *it* shifts from the act of fucking to the penis. Recently, I saw a woman wearing a T-shirt that said, "Get *it* up, Keep *it* up." The threat, "Sit on *it*," is familiar to most readers. On television, the implied references of *it* have been used to slip innuendoes past the censors. In one episode of *The Hogan Family*, for example, the following exchange occurs:

8.4 M$_1$: "I don't get *it.*"

    M$_2$: "You'll probably never get *it*, but Hogan did last night."

This dialogue demonstrates the psychological reality of verbal elements that have been omitted from what is actually said, and how a syntactic rule that removes a repeated phrase can be turned to other purposes. In this case, *did* replaced the second mention of *get it*.

The statements in 8.4 were uttered during a session of male gloating, M$_2$ and Hogan participating, because Hogan had fucked a woman the night before. Enter the nerd, M$_1$ for whom fucking didn't seem to be a priority and who may not be sure what the word *sex* refers to. "Get it," in the nerd's vocabulary, can only mean "I don't understand what you're talking about"; there's no temptation to read in a sexual innuendo when he speaks. When we hear M$_2$ tell the nerd, "You'll probably never get *it*," we interpret "get it" as the nerd used it. But when M$_2$ reintroduces the heterosexual context by adding, "Hogan did [get it] last night," the omitted "get it" forces us to go back to M$_2$'s use of "get it" and revise our initial interpretation of **it** as identical in meaning to the nerd's. In the already established conversation about fucking we have to "go back" mentally and reinterpret M$_2$'s use of "get *it*" as having two different references simultaneously. But if the deleted "get it" were not psychologically available to us, we'd feel no impulse to revise our first interpretation.

We use deictics euphemistically for sex-related references because their dependence on contextual signals makes them ideal carriers of information we don't want to name explicitly. ("Down there," for example, is often used to refer to our genitals.) In the following exchange, a female speaker (W) used *that* in what seemed to be an innocuous reference to having more children, but the male host (H) of the gameshow, "Play the Percentages," used the nonspecific reference of *that* as an excuse to impose a sexual interpretation on what she said. The audience thought this was very funny.

8.5 H: "Are you going to have any more children?"

    W: "No. We're not going to do *that* anymore."

    H: "That sounds like a hasty decision! (laughter) We'll find out later what *that* means!"

Up to this point, the examples of *it* I've discussed have been ambiguous, but the pronoun has had some kind of reference we could guess at. In other uses, however, *it* has no reference at all, or its referential scope is so extended that its reference is lost. False deixis occurs when *it*, *this*, or *that* have no identifiable reference (or no antecedents) in the context in which they occur. In 8.6, the examples illustrate how false deixis makes us strain to come up with an interpretation that makes sense in the context we're given.

8.6 a. The way *it* felt. Turn *it* on today, at OLDIES 103 FM. (Ad for a radio station in the *Boston Globe*, Oct. 13, 1987, 23)

b. I gained the knowledge that all women are bunnies, but *it* doesn't have to be *that* way. (Last line of the movie based on Gloria Steinem's infiltration of a Playboy club, *A Bunny's Tale*)

In (a), there is no antecedent for either use of *it* anywhere else in the ad, so the lack of reference is purposeful. *It* is used twice, but the two *its* don't refer to the same things at all. In fact, when we attempt to figure out exactly what each *it* might mean, we find that we have one nonspecific reference conceptually embedded within another. The first *it*, in "The way it felt," we might interpret to mean "life as a teenager (in the '50s, '60s, and '70s)," "adolescent experience," or "my first fuck." The *it* in the second sentence has a wider referential scope that envelops all of the first sentence, including the nonreferential *it*. The second sentence can be interpreted as "Turn on the way your experience felt to you when you were a teenager today." But none of us has exactly the same experience, and the nonspecific use of *it* invites us to supply memories of our individual experience. What we read into the ad then becomes what we expect to re-experience when we listen to the radio station.

The all-encompassing use of *it* in 8.6.b., recorded for me by Kate Moran, occurs frequently in the prose of inexperienced writers, who tend to use *it* or *this* to refer to several preceding sentences or an entire paragraph. In order to interpret the use of *it* in this example, the audience has to refer to the entire text of the movie **and** share the narrator's interpretation of the plot. If we fill in all the information that *it* stands for, plus adding some of the author's assumptions, we arrive at the following cumbersome paraphrase: "I gained the knowledge that all women are bunnies [to men], but *the world in which men perceive all women as bunnies* doesn't have to be that way." "That way" is reflexive, and refers to all of the inserted information.

False deixis serves a variety of rhetorical strategies for English speakers. False deictics force readers/listeners to make contextual guesses to make "sense" of what they hear and read. Using deictic elements to refer to large chunks of previous discourse assumes an extremely friendly reader who is willing to do much of the writer's work. Not only is such usage lazy writing (or speaking), but it taxes the already fragile bond between writers and their audience.

Exactly how much work must readers and listeners do in order to interpret what they read or hear? Apparently quite a bit, particularly in emotional contexts, where we use false deixis often. Like advertising copywriters, song lyricists have found false deixis to be useful for creating gaps that hearers must fill from their own imaginations. Remember "I Did *It* My Way"? "Shake *it*, baby"? "What's Love Got to Do with *It*?"? "*It*'s Gonna Get Better"? We seem too willing to invest such gaps with the emotional content of our own experiences.

False deixis is a language strategy frequently resorted to in arguments among people who share a strong emotional bond, and deictic pronouns—*it* and *this/that*—figure prominently in statements intended to be *ultimatums*. Do we, perhaps, actually expect others to be so psychically attuned to our thoughts and feelings that we think we have only to vaguely invoke them in order to be understood? The more aware we become of false deixis, the more conscious we are of how often *it* and *this* are used to refer to a wide range of emotions, feelings, reactions to people and events as though such things existed somewhere "out there," and all we have to do is "tune in" psychically to figure out what someone is trying to tell us.

Maybe, in emotionally tense situations, we don't *want* to be understood at some level. Or, maybe we don't understand ourselves what we mean or want to communicate. False deixis is the verbal equivalent of flailing arms, and we use pseudo-reference many times in the course of a single day. Consider, for example, familiar statements in which *it* substitutes for underlying, unacknowledged feelings:

8.7 *It* doesn't matter.
   It's not worth talking about.
   It's what's happening.
   I can't bear *it* without you.
   That's *it*!
   I've had *it*!
   It's over, done, finished!
   Get *it* together!
   This can't continue!
   That does *it*!

Readers can add some of their own favorites to that list. I've provided only a few recognizable samples to show how we use *it* and *this* or *that* to refer to an accumulation of grievances, the habits of a lifetime, aggravating behavior patterns, a subject, still unmentioned, that the speaker wants to talk about, but, perhaps, wants to be coaxed into discussing. Notice that, especially in the statements that function as ultimatums, *this* and *that* are easier to figure out than *it*, perhaps because they seem to refer to something that hearers/ listeners are persuaded they should know about. For example, "*This* can't continue" may be uttered in reference to some behavior or action that's occurring at the moment, and "*That* does *it*" surely refers to something that has occurred just before the statement is made. But what can *it* mean? Even uses of deictics that appear to refer to elements in the immediate context force us to guess what the offending behavior or action might be, and our guesses aren't always accurate.

The apparently close association between the common uses of *it* in 8.7 and euphemism is reflected in 8.8, uttered by the female host of *Entertain-*

ment Tonight (January 21, 1989). In this example, given to me by Kate Moran, *it* seems to function as an emotional cover for the speaker's vicarious interest.

8.8 "Find out if *it was sexy* when Kathleen Turner teamed up with William Hurt."

In this imperative, *it* replaced not a single NP, but an entire sentence that was never said! The adjective *sexy* betrayed the speaker, because its use implied someone who experiences a specific set of stimuli that are sexually arousing and thus earn the description "sexy." In the sentence, the only candidate for such arousal was Kathleen Turner, so I can rephrase the imperative as: *Find out if Kathleen Turner felt sexually stimulated when she teamed up with William Hurt.* But this explicit revision sounds strange. Why would the female host want to know if playing opposite William Hurt (in the movie *The Accidental Tourist*) felt "sexy" to Kathleen Turner? Probably because she imagined that **she** would feel sexually aroused if she co-starred with Hurt. Of course, she isn't supposed to say such things on television, so she used the false deictic, *it*, to disguise her own voyeuristic interest in what Turner might have felt that she might have felt, and viewers had to read in two submerged conceptual levels to make sense of what she said.

As I introduce larger portions of discourse, readers will sense how false deictics sound euphemistic, as though there's something the speaker considers too personal, too unpleasant or "nasty" to mention out loud. Such uses are a species of denial, a refusal to name specific actions. The example in 8.9 is innocuous, because no one is harmed or coerced; the response illustrates how we use *it* to skip over several conceptual links between a question and its answer in casual conversations.

8.9 Q: What happened with Marion and Terry? I thought they broke up.
    A: *It* got better.

The questioner has requested clarification about the status of a relationship; had believed, on the basis of other information, that the two individuals involved had ended, or changed, the relationship; had recently noted that the relationship is apparently continuing as it had previously. In the answer, *It* clearly refers to the relationship, which the questioner didn't mention explicitly. In fact, the question was framed to focus on the two individuals, not the relationship *per se*. More obliquely, then, *it* referred to all the factors involved in the success or failure of the relationship: personality conflicts, differences in how the individuals wanted to structure the relationship, differences in the way they wanted to live, one individual's disapproval of the other's occupation, political disagreements, and underlying emotional insecurities. Instead of going into the details of how every problem was (or was not) resolved, the person responding opted for *it* to refer to the relationship, which had only been implied, leaving the processes hinted at by "got better" to the questioner's imagination.

A speaker's use of false deixis doesn't mean that the utterance is uninterpretable or impossible to understand. False deixis is the use of a deictic word, a word that's supposed to have an antecedent within the immediate context, when there is no explicit antecedent available to the hearer or reader. As a result, nonreferential *it* has a wide range of euphemistic uses, as do *this* and *that*. We may have difficulty identifying false deixis in the midst of our own arguments and disagreements, but television and newspaper reports provide numerous examples of how speakers resort to false deixis when they want to evade naming specific kinds of actions. The Virginia LaLonde case, for example, was widely reported in the media. (Briefly, Virginia LaLonde believed that her husband had sexually molested their daughter, Nicole. When government agencies refused to deny her husband access to Nicole, LaLonde fled with her daughter and went underground in order to protect Nicole.)[6] The excerpted quotes in 8.10 are from a story printed in the *Boston Globe* (Oct. 13, 1987, 20).

8.10 Husband: "*It* comes down to my word against her word, when you *do it* in the press."

LaLonde's attorney: "*It*'s an interesting question as to why now, when this child is safe and under evaluation, that he feels he needs to raise all *this*."

Husband: "Nicole was fine. She said *that* didn't happen, *it* wasn't true."

It, *this*, and *that* occur in these sentences as substitutes for more explicit descriptions which the speakers avoided. In the first quote from the husband, he used *it* twice with vague, implicational scope: (1) "How one decides whether or not I molested my daughter" comes down to my word against her [Virginia LaLonde's] word, when you [*we*?] (2) "discuss the specifics of this case" in the press. (He distracted us from his own involvement by using the second person, *you*, instead of *I* or *we*.)

Virginia LaLonde's attorney, Beth Herr, used *it* and *this* once apiece. The *it* that began her statement may or may not be false deixis. The structure of her assertion suggests that *it* refers forward (cataphoric reference) to "that he feels he needs to raise all *this*." *This*, however, is an example of how false deixis can be used to avoid being direct and specific, referring broadly to everything the husband had done and was saying. She expected the reporter and the audience to understand what "all this" referred to without describing what the husband was doing explicitly.

False deixis is a tactic for submerging relevant information. The husband's use of *that* and *it* when he quoted his daughter, Nicole, again gave him a way to avoid naming the actions of which he was accused, sexual molestation and rape. Oh yes, we can guess at what the husband refused to say out loud, but why should the burden of "communication" fall on us? False deixis makes us responsible for imagining what he "meant." We aren't merely "interpreting" in such cases, we're helping speakers maintain silence about actions they're responsible for. We become accomplices to their denial. The speaker who resorts to false deixis usually has the information they're suppressing; refusing to provide accessible information denies the reality of specific actions and one's responsibility for them.

Clearly, what we don't say is often more important than what we do say! False deixis serves male discourse strategies; it enables them to deny responsibility for the crimes they commit daily against women and children. As women, we must take responsibility for breaking the "agreement" of PUD, for saying out loud all the unspoken words we hear in our minds, and refuse to ignore the atrocities we wake up to every day.

WHAT KIDS DON'T TELL

A television documentary on family rape, *Kids Don't Tell*, illustrated how we use false deixis to avoid naming specific types of behavior, in particular behaviors that many people want to pretend don't occur, at least not to them or not in their family. Apparently, no one, not the reporter interviewing people, not the perpetrators, not the wives of the perpetrators, and not the victims themselves, wanted to name the crime out loud. The way of talking used by those interviewed on *Kids Don't Tell* isn't unusual. It typifies what passes for communication in many families. One of the child molesters interviewed, claiming that he raped his daughter because his wife refused to engage in sex with him, reported the following dialogue:

8.11 Husband: "How long has *it* been?"
    Wife: "Has *what* been?"
    Husband: "You know *what* I mean."

The vagueness of this conversation, its indirectness, is due as much to the use of questions as it is to *it* and *what* as false deictics. By asking a question, the husband put the responsibility for directness on his wife. The male speaker refused to come out and say that he wasn't getting enough sex from his wife, and she used his obliqueness against him. She answered his question with one of her own. Since he refused to be direct about what he wanted, she pretended that she didn't know what his use of *it* referred to. This dialogue would have had very different consequences had the wife refused to go along with her husband's strategy of suppressing the topic he seemed to want to talk about. If she'd responded instead "About six months," or, better yet, "I haven't let you touch me for six months," she'd have challenged him to say out loud what he meant, as well as broken the agreement about unspoken words, which her question accomplished. From another perspective, the wife deflected her husband's attempt to place blame on her by refusing to acknowledge that she understood his question. Had she answered in a specific way, "about six months," most people might have thought that length of

time "too long" to "deprive" a man of sex and accepted it as a *valid* justification for raping his daughter.

In the following exchanges from *Kids Don't Tell*, readers will notice other
words, such as *what*, used as false deictics in addition to the three I've
discussed so far, and how particular phrases are repeated, especially with the
verb *happen*. A brief portion of the dialogue represents three perspectives in
8.12: the reporter, the wife/mother, and the raped child (also called "the
victim"). These abbreviations indicate who's speaking: R = the reporter/inter-
viewer; FR = fatherly rapist; WOR = wife of rapist; CVOR = child victim of
rape/molestation.

8.12 CVOR: "*It* started when I was ten."
　　R: "You'll get in trouble if you tell anyone [about *it*]."
　　CVOR: "I thought the kids at school could smell *it*, that they knew *what*
　　　　we were doing."

Two processes create the obliqueness of this dialogue: deletion and substitution. The verbs used by the CVOR and R, *start* and *tell*, usually have objects,
but those objects have been suppressed.[7] In order to fully restore all of the
information omitted by the female speaker, we have to replace both *it* and the
unmentioned object of *started*. Filling in the suppressed references, I can
paraphrase the statement as "My father started raping me when I was ten."
The male reporter's following statement then successfully distanced him
from the situation, at the same time that he tried to show he understood the
victim's feelings by saying what he imagined the father rapist might have said
to her. By supplying an object for *tell*, "that I'm forcing you to have sex with
me," (*anyone* is the indirect object of *tell*) in that sentence, I derive: " . . . if
you tell anyone *that I'm forcing you to have sex with me.*" (Again, note his
use of *you* instead of *I*.)

Are such omissions the result of fear, shame, or disgust on the victim's
part, and delicacy, consideration, empathy on the part of the reporter? We
could interpret them as such, and I won't rule out those explanations for the
refusal to say out loud that a father raped his daughter. But the rapist and his
wife, who pretended not to know that her husband was raping her daughter,
have other motivations for their use of false deixis. They're trying to maintain
the "happy family" illusion and, perhaps, in the wife's case, a false description of her world. But what is the reporter's motivation for abetting their
refusal to take responsibility for their actions, or lack of actions, in the following dialogue with the father?

8.13 R: "You must know *what* you're doing."
　　FR: "Of course."
　　R: "Why does *it* keep happening?"

Remember, *Kids Don't Tell* was advertised as a documentary. It was supposed
to dig out previously unavailable information and provide some kind of

explanation of the behaviors being "documented." The reporter/interviewer, by adopting the language of the people he talked to, allowed them to draw him into their denial. He let the rapist off by not pushing him to describe his crimes against his daughter. Consider, for example, how much information was submerged by the reporter's use of *what* in his first question: "You must know *that you're continuing to rape your daughter over and over again, that you're taking advantage of your access to her, her dependence on you, her love for you, and that your rape is doing physical and emotional damage that will probably ruin her life and her ability to trust another person.*" Imagine how different the film would have been if the reporter's questions had **named** the multiple rapes this man had committed.

In order to understand what the reporter omitted in his second question, we have to revise the phrase, " . . . it keep[s] happening," because people use the verb *happening* when they don't want to admit responsibility for their actions, attitudes, and behaviors. A bumper sticker humorously points to how the verb *happen* gives us a way of describing our lives as though we're utterly passive and powerless to change our situation: "Shit happens." If we're responsible for certain aspects of our lives, and we acknowledge that fact, then we're also responsible for changing what we do have control over. We say, "this happened to me" and "that happened to me," and cast ourselves as the objects of the verb *happen*, always acted **upon** by the malevolence of other people or inanimate objects. When we stoop to honor such language, to treat it as meaningful, we deny our agency in the world.

The question I'm discussing here must be rewritten if we're to get at the acts the reporter refused to name. "Why does **it keep happening**?" must become a very different description: "Why do you persist in forcing your daughter to have sex with you over and over again?" As the explicit, direct version of the reporter's question shows, instead of pushing these men to take responsibility for raping their daughters and offering some account for their actions, to tell us, the viewers, exactly how they managed to rationalize raping their children for years, he gave them the means to avoid taking responsibility for sexually using a child's body. He talked about daughter rape the way **they** do.

The wives of the rapists, mothers of daughters raped in their homes, didn't want to talk explicitly about rape any more than the men. These women were particularly anxious to go on ignoring the acts and their consequences. Not surprisingly, they also resorted to false deixis.

8.14 WOR: "When *it* came out, I thought to myself, '*This* isn't *happening*.
          . . . I thought '*This* doesn't *happen* to people like us.'"
      R: "Where were you when *this* was *happening*?"

Again, the reporter allowed himself to be drawn into the woman's denial of her role in the seduction and rape of her daughter, by using exactly the same language she did. She, at least, had an understandable, if reprehensible, reason for denying her responsibility, and gave us a glimpse of why she thinks the way she does when she said, "people like us." This woman accepted all the patriarchal descriptions of who she is, who her husband is, and who they're supposed to be together. She's bought the illusions packaged for her by parents, religious dogma, and educators, the delusions served up by the men who would rule us: the ideal of wedded bliss and the "happy" nuclear family in which everyone is protected, safe, and loved unconditionally. If she admitted to herself that her husband raped their child for years, day in and day out, then she might have to consciously acknowledge that her life is based on a lie.

None of the assumptions she believed and acted on prepared her to deal with the reality she tried so hard to avoid and still wanted to ignore. Her language tells us how she thinks. She said, "When *it* came out," a description that reveals two features of her approach to the raping of her daughter. Her use of the verb *came out* treats what her husband did to her daughter as though it were a secret, and should have remained so, and that verb also forces us to imagine those actions as occurring in a vacuum or a closed container. *Came out* presupposes that the "secret" was "in" something from which it has now exited, and, now that "it" is "out," rape and its consequences are taken care of; the "problem" is solved.

Idyllic fantasies attract our loyalty more strongly than reality and the principles to which we pay lipservice. When the woman said she thought, *"This isn't happening,"* we must believe she meant exactly that. Her first impulse, once the raping of her daughter could no longer be kept a secret, followed the way she's habitually dealt with the reality of her life all along: whatever is going on really **isn't** going on. Deny, deny, deny. And, there is, of course, the repeated use of the verb *happen*, which described the raping as an action that no one is responsible for. Her husband isn't a rapist; her daughter isn't his victim; she isn't an accomplice, willing or otherwise.

Finally, I want to discuss the reporter/interviewer's contribution to the film. I've noted along the way that he used the same language as those directly responsible for and involved in the serial rapes. We can guess why mother, father, and daughter were reluctant to name "it," but what could have been the reporter's motivation for resorting to the tactic of false deixis? What was his investment in the scenario that made him reluctant to describe explicitly what the film was supposed to document? Perhaps he didn't want to keep repeating words and phrases like *rape, incest, forced sex, sexual molestation,* and *sexual abuse*, not a one of which accurately describes what the father did to his daughter.[8]

If I give credit to the reporter and assume that he might have been aware of the inadequacy of English for describing what it **means** for a male adult to force, cajole, one (or more) of his children to engage in sex acts with him, does that explain why he used the deceptive language of those who had reasons to do so? I don't think so. I think the reporter had an investment in refusing to deal explicitly with his subject: he was male. Maybe he was reluctant to name abhorrent acts committed by another man; not just one other, in fact, but approximately 50% of the male population: grandfathers, uncles, and brothers as well as fathers regularly force children related to them to engage in sex. As a man, perhaps the reporter simply could not bring himself to grant authenticity to such a crime. If he did, what might it mean about him?

If we step back, and look at the film *Kids Don't Tell* as a whole, another motivation emerges. First, the title itself didn't name "the act" that was its subject. *What* don't kids *tell*? They don't tell *that a member of their own family, someone who's supposed to be caring for and protecting them, is forcing them into sexual relations.* They don't tell *that their brother rapes them every time parents are gone*, that *grandaddy rubs against them when they sit on his lap*, that *daddy makes them pretend that his penis is a lollipop and suck on it.* That sort of information is what "kids don't tell." But it wasn't in the title. Maybe the suppressed information was intended to awaken our interest in the documentary's subject, to make us listen harder to what was said, but there were alternative titles that would have broken the silence about the rape of children.

Second, during the introductory narration, the film's subject was described as "child sexual abuse in the home." "In the home"? By naming the place where parents molest their children, that description suppressed the fact that an adult human being, someone assumed to have control of their behavior, capable of exercising choice, making decisions, acting of their own will, and being responsible for those dependent on them, took advantage of a child (probably not just one time, but many times). The phrase, "in the home," also made it sound as though both parents were equally guilty, as though women decide to molest children as frequently as men do, as though women are just as likely to be child molesters, which isn't true. (Compared to the percentage of male molesters, only 2% of mothers molest their children, a very low percentage when one remembers how much time women spend with children compared to men.) Given that women have much more access to children on a daily basis, the phrase "in the home" suggested generic responsibility for what is clearly a male activity.

Third, at the end of the introduction, the narrator said, "The wounds are very deep. The problems are very deep." The repetition and rhythm of those two parallel sentences was intended to make them sound profound, "deep" themselves. But, note that, again, the human beings involved disappeared. The first time *deep* was used, it was literal, not metaphorical. Men who rape children hurt them physically and emotionally. But when the literal reference of *deep* became metaphorical in reference to "problems," it admitted that we have no idea how to prevent or stop men from committing these crimes. The script focused our attention on someone's "wounds" (the children?) and someone's "problems" (the children's? the criminal father's? the complicit mother's?). If we don't name the guilty and their victims, we won't find ways of stopping men from raping whatever children they have access to.

I've discussed false deixis and its frequent use in *Kids Don't Tell* at some length because the language of the film illustrates how contemporary uses of English indicate that something is very wrong in u.s. society. False deixis, and the prevalence of its use, especially in a documentary on the rape of children by male relatives, indicates that we prefer delusion to reality—that we refuse to acknowledge our responsibility for acts committed in homes every day. We prefer fantasy, illusion, delusion, and deception to squarely facing the fact that children aren't safe in at least half of the families they depend upon for their survival, and the frequency with which false deixis occurs in discussions of male sexual abuse of children betrays our wish to ignore the violent reality of childhood. We don't want to hear about it, we don't want to know about it, we don't want to talk about it. If we did face the facts of children's lives, we'd have to change the entire social structure, organize another way of raising children, and develop some way of screening and licensing those who want to be parents. The nuclear family is a failure, and a trap for generations of children. The reporter/interviewer simply gave his audience what they wanted—avoidance, obliqueness, omission, denial.

Do television documentaries and talk shows change anything? Are we more aware of what the world created by men is like? I doubt it. The media often brag to us that we live in "The Age of Information," but we must question that description. Television provides only a little of some kinds of information and the point of view from which we are to interpret the information we get. My analysis of false deixis indicates that in the world of conversation ruled by PUD, it is "inconvenient" to discuss any ideas that would expose the reality of male culture. Television tells us what we can bear to hear in mind-numbing ways. What we hear on television is the oblique mode of conversation we ourselves practice.

The only culturally significant topics in PUD are those that maintain male hegemony; false deixis is one of many conversational strategies that continually force us to conceptualize what only a few seem willing to say aloud. Women cannot continue to assent to language that covers up the violence men enact on women and children. When we allow such descriptions to go unchallenged, we aren't protecting ourselves or children. We are protecting men and helping them to maintain their lies and deceits as "consensus reality."

Chapter 9

The Agents Within

Within the Patriarchal Universe of Discourse, speakers frequently find it expedient to omit reference to those responsible for carrying out the diverse activities necessary to maintaining male dominance. "Dummy *it*" is only one example of how speakers and writers suppress important information and force us to guess at what they omitted when we attempt to interpret utterances. Learning to identify and question the suppressed reference of false deictics is one way of breaking the tacit rules of PUD and challenging male descriptions of the world. But false deictics aren't the only syntactic maneuvers that suppress human agency in descriptions of events. As speakers of English, we can choose from a wide range of constructions when we want to deceive ourselves or someone else. English allows us to suppress reference to the agents who commit specific acts, particularly when the speaker/writer wishes to deny or cover up responsibility.

The agents who maintain PUD reside invisible and unnamed below our awareness, directing our thought processes, steering us away from ideas men would have us believe are unthinkable and unspeakable. We are powerless against these agents within unless and until we recognize the world view they represent and limit the ways they influence our thinking.

MISSING AGENTS

Theoretically, we're supposed to omit agency only when it is already explicit in the context and can, therefore, be easily recovered from what has already been said. However, the information omitted in sentences isn't always redundant and it isn't always recoverable. We suppress human agency and, sometimes, try to imply grander forces at work by doing so, appealing to an unspecified, perhaps illusory, universality or evading the issue of who will be or is responsible for some action. In 9.1, (a) asserts the universality of an experience, while in (b) the speaker avoided taking responsibility for "ordering" that a war be escalated and specifying exactly *who* might "end it."

9.1 a. Love is hard *to find*.
   b. There is only one reason for *ordering* an escalation of the war, and that is *to end* it.

In statements like "Love is hard to find," no explicit NP is a plausible candidate as the omitted agent of "to find." *Love*, the only explicit NP, is the suppressed object of *to find* and so cannot also be the agent of the infinitive. When we interpret this sentence, the only conceivable agent of *to find* would be an indefinite pronoun, *everyone* or *someone*. The indefiniteness of the implied agency asserts the universality of the experience.

The syntactic structure in 9.1.b illustrates another way of omitting agency: a gerund, *ordering*. This assertion implies that only a u.s. president can order that war be escalated, and only a president has the power to end a war. (Not true.) By reading in the suppressed agent, we can revise the sentence as follows: "There is only one reason for *my* ordering an escalation of the war, and that is *for me* to end it." If the speaker's agency is so easily identified, what did he gain by suppressing information that's so obvious? At a superficial level, the omission of direct and explicit reference to himself made the events seem far removed from our immediate experience, occurring in some abstract realm where human beings are not responsible for their actions. The omission of human agency in b. encouraged us to disassociate ourselves from what was being talked about, to think of wars as events no one is responsible for. War becomes an idea so abstract that we can distance ourselves from its reality, as though it had nothing to do with killing and maiming people. More insidiously, however, such omissions assert that the individual speaking has the power and authority to act as he has (or has not). By not referring explicitly to himself, the speaker left gaps that we filled in for him. We were so busy guessing at the missing references that we didn't realize that they were false implications, allowing the speaker to deny that he claimed any such authority.

Suppressing agency surrounds us with hosts of secret agents hovering invisibly at the periphery of consciousness. Nameless, they do the dirty work of patriarchy; named, we can know how men manipulate our perceptions of reality. English has several ways of omitting agents in sentences, but the most popular syntactic structure is the truncated **passive**, so-called because suppressing agency shortens the sentence. The passive and its related constructions are primary linguistic structures in the maintenance of male power over women and the perpetuation of the political *status quo* in the u.s. They keep our attention focused on what men want us to perceive. In this chapter, I will analyze several different uses of the agentless passive, including what I call the "victim's stance," in which an oppressed group describes its situation without naming those who oppress them. Women's knowledge begins by identifying and uprooting the agents within.

THE PASSIVE VOICE

Active and passive constructions (called the active and passive "voices" in traditional grammars) are alternative ways of making statements. Where a passive structure occurs, it might just as easily have been active. Once we understand this relationship, we can express any active sentence by an equivalent passive sentence. In active sentences, basic elements occur in the following order: Agent—Verb—Object. In passive sentences, the agent and object NPs exchange positions, becoming: Object—Verb—(by) Agent. For every passive sentence, there is an active, and vice versa. We know this without consciously recognizing it.

The sentences in 9.2 illustrate the structural relationship between the active and passive versions of a statement.

9.2   Agent   Verb   Object
                     Five men   raped   the housewife.
                       Object   Verb   Agent
                    The housewife   *was raped*   by five men.

In passive structures, we alter the form of the transitive verb, making it a past **participle** by adding -ed (or another appropriate ending) and inserting some form of be before the past participle (e.g., raped > was raped). The agent in a passive sentence is indicated with the preposition by. Once we've inserted by in front of the agent, in this example, five men, we have a grammatical passive construction, The housewife was raped by five men. But many of the passive sentences we say and hear provide no identifiable agent, for example, The housewife was raped. Once an agent follows its verb, we can suppress it, creating a truncated passive. Both the passive structure and the choice of omitting the agent are optional: there is no grammatical requirement that obligates us to use either of them.[1]

The process of **agent-deletion** leaves us with only the objects of the acts described by the verbs. Passives without agents foreground the objects (victims) in our minds so that we tend to forget that some human agent is responsible for performing the action: Hanoi was bombed, Grenada was invaded, Foodstamps have been cut, The price of fuel has been raised. The rhetorical reasons for the popularity of the passive are obvious: remove the agent, shift the hearer/reader's focus to the victim. The option of deleting agency is probably the most attractive rhetorical consequence of passive structures because speakers/writers can use them for several deceptive purposes. In order to defeat these deceptions, we have to learn to ask "by whom?" when we hear an agentless passive. All it takes is a little practice.

One important characteristic of agentless passives is their vagueness and ambiguity, especially when they force us to read in a missing agent on the basis of our real-world knowledge. Indeed, we may not often experience difficulty when we have to supply agency from what we believe we know, but such descriptions quickly turn our assumptions against us. We often find this kind of ambiguity in assertions that imply authority, and it isn't until we stop and ask "**by whom?**" that we realize what we allow to pass without scrutiny.

9.3 a. The thief *was arrested.*
    b. The vehicle has *been impounded.*
    c. Children should *be spanked.*
    d. Air attacks *were authorized.*
    e. Students *designated* as trouble-makers will *be* carefully *supervised.*

Reading these examples, you may have experienced an increasing difficulty or lack of certainty about the implied agents. In a. and b. maybe you assumed that the agents were obvious and noncontroversial: police arrest thieves and impound cars. Likewise, perhaps the agentless verb of c. initially seemed innocuous: parents spank children; but you might also have hesitated because other authority figures also spank children, and recalled the notoriety of the New Jersey principal who reinstated physical punishment in the public schools. We ought to pause before we accept the assumed authority of such agentless passives. As you read d. and e. you may have come to a full stop when you asked BY WHOM? Why? After all, some kind of military or governmental authority must be the agent of d. and some educational authority was implied in e. But those interpretations, based on our real-world experience, may arouse a vague malaise because such statements often signal authority run amok, power exercised without conscience or responsibility. We should want to know who authorized those air attacks and who has designated some students as "trouble-makers."

Of course, there are reasonable uses of agentless passives: when we don't know who is responsible for a given action, and they occur frequently in news stories or police reports when a criminal's identity is unknown (e.g., *the store was broken into, a downtown bank was robbed, a woman was raped last night*). We also use them when we're speaking hypothetically and have no specific individual or group in mind, or when the agency is already clear in the immediate context.

Identifying the suppressed agents of passive sentences, however, isn't always easy or automatic. Our relative facility as we supply missing agents depends on the context, how much information we have, the kind of action or event being described, and who is giving us the information. When we encounter agentless passives in our reading or conversations, we should weigh all of these factors. Too often, we don't notice how much we're being asked to assume, and agentless passives slip right past our awareness without hesitation on our part. We treat the passive participle as "just another word" without stopping to wonder exactly **who** was responsible for this or that action.

Of course, as English speakers, we know that the potential agents of the sentences in 9.3 belong to restricted categories, and if we try to guess "whodunit," our guesses will be limited by our "real-world" knowledge. We won't consider potted plants, jelly beans, or flies as agents that might have impounded a car or arrested a thief, and we wouldn't think of avocados, salami, or six-month-old babies (even though human) as possible agents who might authorize air attacks or supervise students.

Because we can omit the agents of passive descriptions, they provide PUD speakers with a simple way to present male claims about the world as accurate and authoritative. Because they're so useful, agentless passives turn up frequently in contexts in which men want to hide or deny their responsibility for or justify the world as they create it. Try to identify the agent suppressed in a passive sentence, and in many cases you'll find that some man or group of men is the only logical possibility. The examples in 9.4 illustrate this point.

9.4 a. Power *is* never *bestowed*, it *is taken*.
   b. It has often *been said* that giving women the right to vote would destroy the republic.
   c. The masculinity complex *found* in many women as a result of defeminization trends in modern society must *be dealt with*.

If we ask "whodunit?" for these examples, the male identity of the suppressed agents isn't hard to guess. In a., power "is taken" by men from those who are in a position to "bestow" it: other men. (Women would do well to read ourselves in as the suppressed agents.) In b. the invisible agents saying "that giving women the right to vote would destroy the republic" are just those who have given themselves the power to bestow or withhold that right from women: men. And in c., it is Frank Caprio, author of *Female Homosexuality*, who "found" what he chose to describe as a "masculinity complex . . . in many women," but it is assuredly men he's urging to "deal with" it. Once men have described something as a problem that endangers their view of reality, they get busy constructing elaborate ways to eradicate it. In a recent article, "Telling the Truth" (*Trivia* [Fall 1986]), Sonia Johnson described her own realization of how agentless passives "often absolve men from responsibility for their violent behavior toward women."

> Suddenly I realized that in my campaign [for u.s. president] speech I had been saying, 'Today over 2,000 women in this country will be raped.' By using the passive voice, I made rape sound as innocuous as 'today it will rain,' as if rape just falls out of the sky on women, just 'happens' to us. As though there were no rapists. (19)

PASSIVE MOTIVATIONS

Like any other kind of PUD description, agentless passives claim to be accurate statements about events in the world. More frequently they tell us the conceptual framework within which speakers perceive and comprehend actions, people, and events. A line from one of George Michael's hit songs illustrates how an agentless passive reveals the speaker's perspective.

9.5 "Sometimes love can *be mistaken* for a crime."

In this example, the male perspective dictated even the choice of the **direct** and **indirect objects:** *love* is the direct object of *mistake, crime* the indirect object. There is no agent. Because the description occurs in a song about a man wanting to be some woman's "father figure," *crime* hints at rape or incest, and tells listeners, many of them girls and young women, that describing forced heterosexuality as "a crime" is a "mistake." If we accept the proposition as a true and accurate description of what forced heterosexuality means, we come to believe such false descriptions, remaining unconsciously loyal to them even when we consciously reject them.

In PUD, agentless passives conceal and deceive when it doesn't suit speakers' or writers' purposes to make agency explicit.[2] This simple structure makes it easy to suppress responsibility and forces hearers or readers to supply the missing agents from a range of possibilities that is often too broad. These less-than-honest motivations for agent-deletion fall into several rhetorical categories: (1) appeals to various kinds of authority as defined by male societies; (2) protection of the guilty and denial of responsibility; (3) the pretense of objectivity; (4) laziness, ignorance, or intellectual pretension, based on familiarity with motivation; (5) the victim's stance; (6) exhortation (urging an audience to some action); and, (7) trivialization.

Appeals To Authority

When someone uses a passive as a covert appeal to an unspecified authority, they either assume that we share their assumptions of what constitutes legitimate authority, or hope that they can persuade us to do so. The agent omitted from such assertions may be an institution (educational, military, governmental), supposed divine intent, or a specious "universality" (popular consensus). However we identify the suppressed agent of such passives, the speaker/writer is betting that we'll accept the assertion as a true statement. With each type below, I give two examples of each of these appeals to implied authority.

Institutional Authority:
a. We develop greater power only by attempting to understand that which needs *to be controlled.*
b. There's too much *being said* about fiber and health for me to ignore.

Divine Intention:

c. "This love *was meant* to be."

d. Woman *is intended* for reproduction; she has *been appointed* to take an active part in the reproduction of the race by pregnancy and child-birth.

Universality:

e. The true heroes of the feminist movement can *be found* more easily in a kitchen in Dorchester than on a platform in the person of a weeper like Pat Schroeder.

f. It *is* widely *understood* that the process of impeachment [of Richard M. Nixon] would throw our country into chaos and make a mockery of the presidency.

Examining these statements reveals facets of our interpretive processes not immediately obvious. The contexts of both a. and b. suggest the probable identities of their missing agents, but interpretation must take into account other aspects of the assertions. In a., from B. F. Skinner's *Beyond Freedom and Dignity*, we should question the reference of "we" even though we guess that the suppressed agents of *to be controlled* are behavioral psychologists: exactly **who** will "develop greater power" if they understand what Skinner claims should "be controlled"? Does his "we" include his readers, everyone in a society, or only behavioral psychologists? "Needs" implies that whatever the method of control, control itself is a necessity and, therefore, beyond his readers' challenge. Again, who will determine the reference of "that which"? Psychologists? Finally, the *by* of "by attempting to understand" isn't functioning here to mark the agent of a passive construction. Instead, like *by* in d., "by pregnancy and child-birth," it introduces a preposi-tional phrase functioning as an adverb of manner. That is, it tells us how someone can "develop greater power" in a., and, in d., how women "take an active part in the reproduction of the race."

The context of b., a television commercial, encourages us to identify the deleted agents of "being said" as medical authorities, because what the unnamed "experts" are talking about is fiber and health. Because this com-mercial is televised, it quickly passes through short-term memory and is filed unanalyzed in our long-term memories. We might assume that the sup-pressed agents the speaker can't ignore are people who know what they're talking about, and forget that many people have opinions on subjects about which they know nothing. The context thus leads us to an interpretation of the assertion that is probably inaccurate. We remember our interpretations unconsciously, especially the information we supply, and those interpreta-tions, accurate or distorted, influence our actions.

The suppressed agency in examples c. and d. urges us to accept the idea that a supernatural power has absolute control over our lives. Frank Caprio, the author of d., used agentless passives, *is intended* and *been appointed*, to deny his investment in restricting the scope of women's lives and to pretend that he was merely passing along the "revelation," in which the implied agency of god's will and biological determinism simultaneously justify his misogyny. The appeal in d. may be to divine intention, the workings of destiny, or a variety of otherworldly influences. Whatever we read in for the omitted agent, we are told to believe that love is an emotion we can't control. God, the stars, tea leaves decree it.

Appeals to universality or an imagined consensus are similarly obvious once they're pointed out, but they add an interpretive aspect that may not be immediately apparent. Both *be found* and *is . . . understood* (in e. and f., respectively) imply that there is consensus among those who agree with the author's statement, for example, "all right-thinking people," "all intelligent (or well-informed) people," or "anyone who, like me, really knows what they're talking about." We are subtly informed that, should we have the bad taste to disagree with this assertion, we are in a minority, uninformed, or stupid. Because we don't want other people to perceive us as wrong-minded, such agentless passives attempt to make us distrust our own perceptions and intimidate us into accepting without question whatever we're told.

Agentless passives hinder readers from inquiring further into the implied authority behind questionable declarations. Any sentence that begins with *it* as the topic of a truncated passive, such as "It is known," "It is hypothesized," "It is understood," should be a signal to us that whatever follows is something we don't want to file away without careful, thorough examination. Whenever someone says, speaking about a relationship, "It's meant to be," as though an omniscient deity or personified destiny had nothing better to do than monitor our lives and make our choices for us, we have to wonder WHO intends for this relationship to exist or continue? Questioning such fundamentally empty assertions is unlikely to increase our popularity, and we run the risk of alienating those we dare to challenge, but people will persist in mouthing inanities unless (and until) each of us takes responsibility for improving the substance and quality of our talk, however casual it is.

Protecting the Guilty

Agentless passives are also useful for *denying responsibility* in a first-person assertion or *protecting the guilty* if the speaker is describing an individual or group in the third person. In either situation, descriptions without explicit human agency can sound authoritative and convincing. Such passives provide politicians and bureaucrats with a way of protecting themselves and their friends, and we've become accustomed to hearing the construction routinely in news releases and congressional investigations. They also serve the purposes of male writers, particularly when they're trying to justify their continued oppression of women, as the examples in 9.4 illustrated. In 9.6, example a. protects the class of men as the oppressors of women, and b. denies strikers' responsibility for a threatened confrontation.

9.6 a. As long as the issues *are conceptualized* and *allowed* to remain as women's alone (e.g., women's liberation, women's movement, women's issue, feminism, etc.) men will *be forced* to be reactive to women's pressures and fail to identify their own issues as men.
   b. We are going to have a confrontation situation *generated* if they do what they say they are going to do.

These examples reveal how suppressed agency obscures, disguises, or denies responsibility for some action. The first quotation intrigued me because it has three passives for which the reader must find a plausible agent: *are conceptualized, allowed,* and *be forced*; it's not at all clear, however, that the implied agent is identical for all three verbs. The indeterminacy of agency frustrates our efforts to figure out exactly who is responsible for the alleged state of affairs. I'm guessing that the suppressed agents of *conceptualized* and *allowed* are identical. Paraphrasing them as actives, filling in possible agents, my first revision takes one possibility suggested by "women's":

As long as **women** conceptualize the issues and **women** allow them to remain as women's alone . . .

Alternatively, maybe we're supposed to construe the omitted agent as "men," the topic of the entire sentence, who conceptualize the issues as women's alone. But it's equally possible that the intended agency was generic, including women and men, in which case we should infer "people" as the missing agent. Which group is responsible for what the author implies is **mis**conceptualization: the women who have described the movement and issues as ours, or the men who have no interest in anything labeled as "women's"? Or is it actually "everybody in general"? Then again, perhaps the deleted agents aren't identical, and it is women who have (mis)*conceptualized* the issues as ours, and men who have *allowed* that (mis)conceptualization to go unchallenged.

However we interpret those unidentified agents, it will not help us determine who is responsible for "forcing" men to be "reactive." Whoever the guilty party (or parties) might be, they are also responsible for men's failure to "identify their own issues." Perhaps the causes that are forcing men are some nominal form of the preceding passive verbs. Revising the statement to illustrate this possibility, I arrive at the following paraphrase: "*Conceptualizing* the issues as women's alone and *allowing* them to remain so forces men . . ." Some readers may be satisfied with that revision, but it moves us no closer to identifying the human agents alleged to be responsible for the situation. In fact, the description, "men will be forced" casts them as a group victimized by the earlier unknown agents, a group the writer wants us to pity and sympathize with, as though men are powerless in the situation being described.

The author accomplished something else by suppressing the agents: the situation and its consequences are described as though they're occurring in a social vacuum, somewhere "out there," disconnected from the cultural, social, and historical context from which they arise. Indeed, the same can be said of b., in which the railwaymen's union leader described a "confrontation" as though the actions of his opponents would "generate" it. The speaker was protecting himself and the union members by denying that they would be responsible for generating the confrontation.

Speakers omit agency from descriptions to protect themselves even when the imputed agency appears to belong to someone else. For example, I invited a friend to dinner while an out-of-town guest was going to be visiting. It so happened that my friend had, on a previous occasion, unintentionally offended my guest-to-be, and she was still angry with herself for doing something she thought was "stupid." To avoid talking about her feelings and appear to reject the invitation for a justifiable reason, she said:

9.7 "I know I'd *be expected* to apologize."

Instead of hiding her anger, though, her statement made it obvious to me, because the only possible candidate in the context for the suppressed agent of *be expected* was **me**. But I had no such expectation when I issued the invitation! Now I was angry! Why? Because she had implied, in a devious way, that I had caused her feelings, that my invitation would somehow force her to admit that she had done something offensive. In an effort to make herself feel righteous and justified, she attributed thoughts to me that I didn't have. She used an agentless passive in an attempt at verbal self-protection. In this case, though, her omission of agency denied her own responsibility by covertly shifting it to me.

Pseudo-Objectivity

Like my friend, other writers and speakers know very well that omitting human agency from their descriptions of the world imbues their most distorted assertions with an aura of truth. Refusing to name those responsible for actions and events removes them from the mundane level on which they occur and makes our descriptions appear to be objective. The pretense of objectivity is highly favored in PUD, because suppressing agency turns the most absurd opinions into "facts" that few are willing to challenge. As a result, academics and those who want to sound like experts leave us numb and dazed, striving to interpret and comprehend their descriptions of an unreal world. The examples below illustrate a few of the ways agentless passives create the pretense of objectivity.

9.8 a. The history of anger is the history of mankind. Man has *been exposed* to the effects of anger, others' as well his own, since he *was* first *placed* on earth.

b. Power, however *obtained, is maintained* either through consent or violence. Although his heavier musculature has traditionally *been cited* as the basis for male dominance, it is not the use of force which has kept women subordinate.

c. Mouth–genital contacts can *be explained* on the hypothesis that a person wants someone else to do what he is unable to do.

d. A baby grows in a world that is wondrously *made*.

Such examples will not bear close scrutiny, but the reasons each author needed to be heard as speaking objectively are clear. From the missing agent who has "exposed" men to the effects of anger in a. to the fatuous description of the world in which children grow in d., we are asked to accept subjective descriptions as statements of incontrovertible "fact." The assertions about anger in a., for example, turn out to be circular when we question them. *Mankind* and *man* refer exclusively to men; if they were being used generically to include women, then we have to wonder who the "others" are who have "exposed" men to the effects of their anger. Angels? Fairies? Maybe sharks or rattlesnakes? *Was placed*, of course, implies that divine agency has been at work again, but the deity invoked isn't the obvious agent of *exposed*. Men don't tolerate overt expressions of anger from women, reserving that privilege to themselves; women resort to expressing it obliquely. So, the only logical agent of *exposed* is *man*.

The writer of b. used a variety of structures to cloak his opinions in objectivity, and the most plausible agent of both *obtained* and *is maintained* is explicit, albeit in the possessive pronoun *his* that precedes "heavier musculature." Filling in nongeneric *man* as the missing agent produces a much more intelligible assertion: "Man obtains and maintains his power either through consent or violence." That revision does have the ring of truth to it, although it restricts our explanation to those offered by the writer. ("Consent," of course, might cover anything from seduction to bribery or intimidation, and "violence" nicely hides the forms it takes: rape, assault, and battery.) We have no way of guessing the identity of those who "traditionally" cite men's heavier musculature as the "basis" of their persistent subordination of women, but I want to draw your attention to two phrases, "the use of force" and "kept women subordinate." The first is a **nominal** phrase, used instead of the clause "men use force." In place of a structure that names the agent of *use*, we find an abstract description, which has then been used as the pseudo-agent of *kept*. **Men** have used force so that they can keep women subordinate. And note the adjectival form of *subordinate*. The adjective lacks the participial marker -*ed* so we don't even have an explicit passive to caution us, warning us to look for a suppressed agent. "Subordinate" again obscures what men do to women and forces us to interpret it as an attribute of women, disconnected now from the assertion that men obtain and maintain power and so are the culpable agents who subordinate women. And, if we accept the implied claim that men haven't used force to subordinate women, then the context manipulates us to infer that women consent to male oppression. These syntactic manipulations coerce us to accept "consent" as the explanation for men's oppression of women without looking too closely at what they disguise.

I won't keep you in suspense about the identity of the implied agent of *be explained* in c. The author of this hypothesis, from *Female Homosexuality*, is Frank Caprio, who believes that our anatomical inflexibility and the fact that most of us aren't contortionists "explains" why we enjoy having our genitals sucked on. How obtuse can one be? Aired on the radio, the anti-abortion ad quoted in d. shows how suppressed agency creates multiple readings. How we interpret "a world" depends upon how we identify the agent of *made*, all that remains of a passive structure. If we interpret "a world" literally, as referring to this one, then the secret agent of *made* has to be either *people* or *men*, depending on the extent of our humanism. If we understand that the world referred to is "man's world," the adverb *"wondrously"* is simply incongruous in the context. More likely, however, "a world" was intended to refer metaphorically to the womb, in which case the description is merely another appeal to divine agency: God wondrously made wombs. Women, who must carry babies for nine months and assume primary responsibility for their well-being, are reduced to a nameless, faceless "world" of some deity's making, invisible incubators detached from personality and the right to control of their bodies.

INTELLECTUAL PRETENSION

Writers and speakers often suppress agents because they're too lazy to look up a reference, they don't actually know of a source for an assertion they want to make, or they think that they will sound intellectually credible if they make a claim in the passive voice. The use of *been cited* in b. above is a good example of laziness; the writer didn't want to name the implied experts who cite men's musculature as the cause of their oppression of women. The active voice would have forced him to provide information that might have distracted his readers from the interpretation he was leading them to. Given motives like these for omitting agency, constructions starting with "dummy *it*" should warn us to remain alert to the assertions that follow: *"It is believed," "It is thought," "It is understood," "It has been demonstrated."* The claims that follow such an opening should be read with extreme caution. The writer or speaker may be making a sweeping generalization for which there is no evidence whatsoever, or, if there is evidence, may be too lazy to provide references. In many cases, though, they may not even know or care whether any evidence for their claims exist, and use an agentless passive to make readers believe that they could supply evidence if they wanted to.

THE VICTIM'S STANCE

Suppressed agency is also a rhetorical strategy often exploited by spokespersons of oppressed groups, but it serves oppressors equally well in descriptions which they construct to make themselves appear to be victims. In example 9.6.a., the phrase "men will *be forced*" encouraged us to accept the idea that men are the victims of women's efforts to become independent of them, rather than the agents of women's oppression. The examples of 9.9 show how suppressed agency perpetuates internalized oppression when its victims fail to identify explicitly who benefits from their oppression. If we refuse to name our oppressors, we find it difficult to figure out how we might go about redefining and identifying ourselves.

9.9 a. We have all *been condemned* to living out our lives in troublesome toil and despair.
   b. You wonder how the power you once had *was* suddenly *taken* away from you.
   c. After all, males do not behave differently from females in similar situations. Men on the make have plenty of intuition and are very good at monitoring their environment for threatening signals, and the major difference in aggression is that men *are allowed* to be aggressive in ways that are more remunerative.

In 9.9.a. someone condemns "us" to toil and despair. In b., someone takes away the power "we" once had, while in c. someone allows men to be aggressive in ways that someone doesn't permit to women. Who are these invisible agents who exercise such destructive control over our lives? Who are we so reluctant to name as the agents of so much power? The description of culturally-condoned behaviors in c., written by a professor at Georgetown University, illustrates how far women will go to absolve men from responsibility, to make it seem that men, too, are the victims of oppression by "society." But a society is a system, a structure with regulated processes and predictable outcomes. This writer's primary objective was avoiding recognition of the fact that men control and regulate social structures and benefit directly and indirectly from the outcomes they engineer. Women do not enjoy this kind of control or benefit from it to the extent men do. (In a racist society, the u.s., white women benefit indirectly from white men's oppression of African-Americans in the public sphere. But since most white women are excluded as a class from the exercise of power in the public sphere, we cannot benefit directly from skin privilege.)[3] There is a more accurate description of the way men define and control sex roles: "White men have defined sex roles in such a way as to deny social and personal space to women and all others they perceive as inferior to themselves; by successful intimidation and domination, they control the earth's known resources and maintain the structures that systematically exclude everyone else from access to those resources."

We cannot extricate ourselves from the unspoken manipulations of the agents within unless we identify our oppressors. We perceive the world—and ourselves in the world—only as white men describe our situation, and fail to conceive of acting as agents on our own behalf. Whether we attribute control of our lives to some deity or supernatural agency, as the speaker of a. does, or to a collective entity, probably "society," as the speakers in b. and c. do, we perpetuate our status as victims, vulnerable to perpetual predation. Victims cannot act; conceptually restrained by the agents within, they are unable to think of themselves in any way but as acted upon . . . *by whom*?

The last two motivations served by the agentless passive, exhortation and trivialization, also de-emphasize our capacity to act as agents. We hear exhortatory passives from politicians who imply that they will perform the actions they describe. Since they neglect, however, to name themselves as the agents, their audience can't hold them accountable when the promise fails to materialize. We hear exhortatory passives often, too, in women's groups from someone who is willing to act as a spokesperson but unwilling to do anything specific in the world, like fundraising, collating newsletters, or organizing a demonstration. Whatever the context in which we hear exhortatory passives, we interpret the agent as someone other than the individual speaking.

9.10 a. There is vital work to *be done* in moving to curb inflation.

     b. Except for certain offices in the church that *are set* aside for men, women should *be given* equal opportunity to obtain and hold the same positions as men.

     c. Newspaper articles like that shouldn't *be permitted*.

Exhortatory passives describe an action that the speaker may have no intention of carrying out, and they are often preceded by a modal that posits future obligation, such as *should, ought to*, or *must*: Something *ought* to *be done* about those disgusting people! The speaker in b. absolved himself from responsibility by first using the passive "are set aside," thereby refusing to name the agents who determine which church offices women will "be allowed" to hold, then saying that those unknown agents "should" also "give" women "equal opportunity" to hold what are clearly insignificant positions. There's no way the speaker will be held responsible for either action. In some cases, as in c., a speaker disclaims the power to censor the offending newspaper articles, placing the responsibility on someone who "should" do it.

Too often, we find it convenient to pass on responsibility and power that we should take for our own.

The desire to trivialize someone else's ideas or actions is another motivation for using passives. Those who use them present themselves as authoritative and more knowledgeable than the person they trivialize, so they usually deliver such assertions in a recognizably condescending tone: "It's already *been done,*" "That's *been said* before, and better," or "Your help *isn't wanted* or *needed.*" Such statements discourage us from acting and speaking. If, instead of accepting or ignoring these assertions, we stopped the person speaking and asked, "by whom?" the motivations themselves would be revealed.

Before I move on to other passive constructions, I want to illustrate the cumulative effects of agentless passives in larger segments of texts than I have used up to this point. The excerpts in 9.11 and 9.12 illustrate the underlying motives served by agent-suppression and the strategies we must use to interpret passages in which there are multiple missing agents. I'll start with a paragraph excerpted from a newspaper story about Virginia LaLonde and her daughter, Nicole, in which all of the deleted agents are different; yet we can make educated guesses for most of them.

9.11   Virginia LaLonde *was released* from Framingham State Prison last Thursday after Nicole *was returned* to Massachusetts from Durham, N.C., where she had *been found* the week before in the care of a local woman. The girl *is being evaluated* at Cambridge Hospital. The results of the tests *are expected* within the next week. (John H. Kennedy, "Stephen LaLonde asserts his innocence," *Boston Globe,* Oct. 13, 1987, 19)

Most of the agents omitted in this paragraph call upon us to supply the missing information from our "real world knowledge," and we can do so without much hesitation. Most of the deleted agents are institutional figures with authority for carrying out specific acts. Virginia LaLonde could only *be released* from a prison by prison officials; Nicole LaLonde *was found* and, undoubtedly, *returned* to Massachusetts by some branch of the local or state police in North Carolina, and was *being evaluated* by doctors and nurses in the Cambridge Hospital. However, even though our assumptions may be accurate, they necessarily fail to include information about behind-the-scenes activities. For example, did Stephen LaLonde hire private detectives, and was it they who found Nicole? Was the release of Virginia LaLonde arranged by the state social service and merely carried out by prison officials? We may be able to construct a rough interpretation of the events, but its accuracy will be limited. The missing agent of the passive in the final sentence of the paragraph, *are expected,* is the most difficult to identify. We can rule out all but one of the identified missing agents (the social workers), but that leaves several other reasonable guesses: that it's the reporter who expects the test results, the social workers and lawyers involved in the case, the judge who will decide Nicole LaLonde's fate. Or, the writer might be telling us that we, his readers, can expect to know the results of the test (because they'll be reported to us). It's also conceivable that all of these people expect the test results; we don't have enough information to choose among the several possibilities.

I've excerpted the next example from two paragraphs of Doris Lessing's 1971 Introduction to her popular novel, *The Golden Notebook*, in which she responded to those who read the novel as a feminist polemic. It shows how useful agentless passives are in suppressing agents one doesn't want to name explicitly, and how tricky it is for readers to guess at them even when we're fairly sure we understand what is being said. I have provided enough of the text to include the part with explicit agency.

9.12   To get the subject of Women's Liberation over with—I support it, of
       course, because women are second-class citizens, as they are saying
       energetically and competently in many countries. *It can be said* that
       they are succeeding, if only to the extent they *are being seriously lis-
       tened to*. . . . [R]eformers must expect to *be disowned* by those who are
       only too happy to enjoy what *has been won* for them. . . .
           But this novel was not a trumpet for Women's Liberation. It described
       many female emotions of aggression, hostility, resentment. It put them
       into print. Apparently what many women were thinking, feeling, experi-
       encing, came as a great surprise. Instantly a lot of very ancient weapons
       were unleashed, the main ones, as usual, being on the theme of "She is
       unfeminine," "She is a man-hater" . . . Men—and many women—said
       that the suffragettes *were defeminised*, masculine, *brutalised*. (viii–ix)

As we read this excerpt, we have to supply several missing agents, guessing as we go along. The agent of the first truncated passive, *be said*, could well be Lessing herself, because she's the author. If that's the case, why didn't she simply say, "I think they're succeeding"? Because deleting the agent of *said* makes the reference multiply ambiguous. The agent might be Lessing, but we could equally well read it as an appeal to universality or consensus, and interpret the deleted agent as "all right-thinking people," "everyone who agrees with me," or simply "anyone," With the exception of Lessing, any of these could be the agent of the next passive construction, *are being seriously listened to*. I suggest, however, that these indefinite agents are made explicit later in the quotation: "Men—and many women." Lessing then spoke more generally of "reformers," the suppressed agents of *been won*, but I want to point out that the explicit agent of *be disowned*, "by those who are only too happy to enjoy," is as nonspecific as the universal agents *everyone* and *anyone*, which are not explicit. Here, though, I suggest that Lessing's virtual, if not intended, referent should be interpreted as female-specific rather than generic. I think she was alluding to the fact that women are as vocal as men in disowning Feminists, but have been, as Lessing implied, more than willing to enjoy any benefits for women in general which have resulted from the work of Feminists. We might not be conscious of this implication unless we were reading critically. In this case, the vagueness of an explicit agent served as well to suppress the identity of a plausible referent as deletion would have.

Continuing on to the next paragraph of Lessing's Introduction, I want to discuss the passive, *were unleashed*. To do so, however, I must direct my readers back to the last phrase of the preceding sentence, "came as a great surprise." This structure omitted not an agent but the experiencer of "great surprise." (I will talk about suppressed experiencers in chapter 11, but it is necessary to bring it up here in order to get at the identity of the missing agent of *were unleashed*.) The fact that many women were hostile and felt resentment (toward whom?) "came as a great surprise" to some segment of the population, but it cannot have been women themselves. (Or could it? Surely they would know what they were feeling.) If these revelations didn't surprise women, then the deleted experiencer must be *men*, and men must also be the suppressed agents who unleashed "a lot of very ancient weapons," namely, the two accusations Lessing used as examples of those weapons. Yet, Lessing then qualified the identity of her attackers by saying, "Men—and many women—said," suggesting that she wanted to block the interpretation that men, and men alone, were the intended agents of *unleashed*.

Doris Lessing took great pains to suppress explicit references to agency in these paragraphs. She's a skilled writer; her syntactic choices were deliberate. What could her motivations have been? I'm not a mindreader, but I can suggest a rhetorical motivation for her choices. The first thing Lessing wanted to do in this portion of her Introduction was to put a lot of distance between herself, the women she wrote about, and the women and men who comprise her readership. She began glibly, wanting "to get the subject of Women's Liberation over with," saying, "I support it, of course," then talking about women in the third person, removing herself from the group. The first passive, "It can be said," cast Lessing as an objective, disinterested observer with no personal stake in Women's Liberation. Was the agent of *being listened to* intended to be read as a generic like "people"? Was Lessing one of the outside listeners taking women seriously?

Men and women, according to her account, had attacked Lessing for writing *The Golden Notebook*. But she wasn't going to back down and deny the accuracy of the novel and the feelings of her characters; she was equally determined to describe the politics of women's lives as she perceived them. In both cases, her primary motivation was the accurate description of the world as she saw it. Her vision is complex, and she was unwilling to simplify it in order to make it more palatable. On the other hand, I think she must have felt protective of men—and many women—to some extent, and it was this protectiveness that dictated the use of so many agentless passives. On the one hand, she implied some hard truths—that antifeminist women have not hesitated to collect the benefits won for them by Feminists and many women joined with men in attacking her—without, on the other hand, alienating men by naming them as the sole agents of verbs like *listened to* and *unleashed*. The crux of my interpretation is the phrase, "came as a great surprise," in which I think the only plausible agent was men. Lessing made the choices she did so that she could have her say without being called a man-hater, an epithet that still terrorizes many women.

I've excerpted my last illustration of the cumulative effects of agentless passives from a *60 Minutes* segment, "Machismo," (CBS, August 7, 1988), in which Morley Safer reported that Brazilian men can murder their wives with impunity. The following excerpts occurred early in the story.

9.13   Each year they celebrate Carnival in Rio de Janeiro, a celebration that goes way beyond marking the beginning of Lent. . . . Central to Carnival is the body beautiful, where men celebrate female beauty and, at the same time, enforce their dominance of women. Throughout Latin America, it is called "machismo." It suggests manliness, pride, honor and perhaps, most of all, the use and abuse of women. . . .

There's no place like Brazil, no place that seems to celebrate women quite the way Brazil does. She *is flaunted* and *admired* and *idolized*. The beaches of Rio are the playgrounds, the strutting grounds for this national obsession. In fact, no place on earth degrades women quite the way Brazil does. (2–3)

Throughout, Safer's tone suggests a curious ambivalence. At first, he didn't try to hide male agency. He was explicit about that: "[men] enforce their dominance of women"; and he noted that the word *machismo* suggests "the use and abuse of women." (Note, however, the agentless nominals *use* and *abuse*.) In spite of the fact that Safer named men, I sense a reluctance to do so. It's as though he had to report the facts—men regularly murder their wives in Brazil and aren't held responsible for it—but he repeatedly retreated from such explicitness.

Two aspects of "Machismo" suggest what I interpret as reluctance on Safer's part: the way he opposed "men celebrate female beauty" with "enforce their domination," as though the two attitudes toward women contradict each other, and his repeated use of inanimate nouns where the word *men* was the logical choice. He began by talking about Carnival in Rio: "Central to Carnival is *the body beautiful*." "The body beautiful," which viewers might have interpreted as a generic reference (since men as well as women have bodies) quickly turned out to exclude men as referents. "The body beautiful" referred exclusively to women, reducing them to bodies that men want to fuck. Carnival, Safer implied, is a large-scale orgy of male sexual aggression.

The relevance of Carnival to an exposé of wife-murdering in Brazil may seem dubious at first, but Safer used it to introduce what he perceived as a contradiction: on the one hand, Brazilian men "celebrate female beauty," but, on the other, they "enforce their dominance of women." He implied that these two aspects of Brazilian culture contradict each other, and he may have intended his audience to think to themselves: "How can Brazilian men reconcile celebrating female beauty with murdering their wives?"

If this was what Safer was implying, if he perceived the two activities as incompatible, then he had every reason to feel uneasy. "Celebrating female beauty" puts a shine on the male habit of objectifying women, thinking of women as objects of their sexual predations: prey, meat, the hunted. The assumption that women are men's legitimate prey is a prominent feature of PUD by no means unique to Brazil. Beauty contests, pornography, and advertising reflect and maintain the equation of women with meat in the u.s., and describe such activities as "celebrating female beauty" to justify men's enjoyment of exploiting women. As a representative of united states patriarchy, Safer may have intuited that perceiving women as bodies, as sexual objects, is one aspect of the patriarchal premise that men have the right to use women in any way and to do anything to women they wish, as their whims move them. Maybe he sensed that his own rationale for using women was threatened by that juxtaposition.

Clearly, if the two activities are conceptually related, then the one touted as harmless is in danger of being exposed. Murdering one's wife because she is offensive or too independent is unjustifiable; that may mean that sexually objectifying women is also unconscionable. Safer may have glimpsed in his subject an intimation that his own perceptions of women were threatened. In order to protect and maintain his views about women, he resorted to a standard PUD rhetorical ploy: he equated the country of Brazil with its male citizens and erased the women of that nation, who are mentioned only as bodies. The *place* became responsible for what men to do women, implying that only Brazilian law tacitly condones male violence against women. His selection of several different agentless structures reflects how carefully he constructed the description in 9.13.

Safer began with an assertion that foregrounded Brazil as "a place," apparently inhabited only by men. "Brazil" "celebrate[s] women," not men. "Women" surface as "the body beautiful," and this sentence is followed by three truncated passives, *is flaunted* and *admired* and *idolized*. (There was no antecedent for *she*.) Although viewers knew perfectly well from the beginning that men were the only logical agents in the sentence, the immediate context encouraged them to substitute either *Brazil* or *the place* as the suppressed agent of *flaunted, admired,* and *idolized.* The rest of the excerpt did nothing to contradict that interpretation. Someone must *strut* the beaches of Rio. Someone *obsesses* on women's bodies, but this was described with a pseudo-generic nominal, "national obsession," implying that women are also the agents, rather than the objects, of the obsession. Then Safer switched back to Brazil as the explicit agent of "degrades women." Again, the inanimate nation was responsible; obliquely, men became the sole inhabitants of Brazil. The endangered women were invisible.

Safer's use of Brazil as an explicit agent implied that women also celebrate, flaunt, admire, idolize, strut, obsess, and degrade themselves, since they are, conceivably, citizens of Brazil, but I don't think Safer thought of that. Women were explicitly mentioned as the objects of most of those verbs, and the context itself suggested that we identify Brazil only with its male inhabitants. But we arrived at this interpretation only if we recognized his switch. By suppressing the male agents and referring to Brazil, Safer probably distracted most of his audience, successfully guiding them away from realizing that, when men give themselves the "natural right" to identify a woman as nothing more than a hole designed (by god) for their use, they simultaneously assume the "right" to use, abuse, exploit, violate, degrade, humiliate, and murder her. They act as they have entitled themselves to act.

Safer was properly repelled by the fact that Brazilian law condones the murder of women by their husbands. But men rule Brazil. They make and enforce laws that serve their purposes, which makes them no different from any other men. They are, perhaps, more explicit about the meaning of patriarchy, taking male possession and domination of women to its logical conclusion. It was the overt endorsement of and legal support for this logical conclusion that Safer reacted to.

Agentless passives serve many rhetorical strategies, and women who speak within the conceptual framework of PUD find them as useful as men do. I cited excerpts from Doris Lessing's Introduction to *The Golden Notebook* to illustrate how women use truncated passives to avoid acknowledging that men are the agents and beneficiaries of our oppression. Using truncated passives, however, has other dangerous consequences, binding us to the limits imposed by patriarchal consensus reality.

Among Lesbians, for example, there are several publications devoted to creating a subspecies of pornography, as though imitating men's sadism and voyeurism might be liberating. Pornography, including what is called "erotica," is highly profitable because it validates and endlessly reproduces the pleasure men experience when they hurt women, children, and animals. Pornography thrives because it caters to and exploits two fundamental premises of PUD: (1) there are two kinds of people in the world, FUCKERS and FUCKEES; (2) women are the primary fuckees and men are the only fuckers. When Lesbians attempt to use the heteropatriarchal framework as a viable description, the resulting frame conflicts and conceptual confusion turn up in assertions like those in 9.14.

9.14   [L]esbian porn is not well *funded*, widely *distributed*, or *recognized by the mainstream*. . . . Women's sexuality *is given* zero recognition; it *is feared, despised*, and pointedly *ignored*. (Excerpt from letter written by Susie Bright, editor of *On Our Backs*, to *Sojourner* [January, 1989], p. 3, in response to Nicki Leone's letter published in *Sojourner* [December 1988].)

The confusion caused by trying to use PUD as a descriptive framework for Lesbians is evident in 9.14 in two different ways. First, there is Bright's equation of "lesbian porn" in the first sentence with "[w]omen's sexuality" in the second. (I'm assuming that, by "lesbian porn," Bright means 'pornography produced by lesbians for a lesbian audience,' since Lesbianism itself has been a staple of male pornography for hundreds of years.) Without any clear connection between the two, she wanted her readers to make the conceptual leaps her assertion required: (1) that pornography in general is directly connected with sexuality; (2) that lesbian porn differs significantly from male pornography in its assumptions, descriptions, and visual representations; and (3) that lesbian porn somehow reflects the sexuality of all women.

Second, the two sequences of passives revealed Bright's confused thinking about pornography and her failure to examine her own assumptions. In the first sentence, she provided an explicit agent for the passive participles *funded, distributed* and *recognized*: "the mainstream," an inanimate, abstract agent, and a negative overtone as well that is open to interpretation (because we are reading) as condemnation, bitterness, disappointment, or some combination of all three. Bright sounded displeased that the mainstream (read: heterosexual society) doesn't recognize, distribute, or financially support "lesbian porn." Her displeasure implied that she assumes that the pornography she publishes should be supported by men. Why lesbian pornographers would want men to seek out and buy "lesbian porn" is a question I won't address.

The second passive sequence, *is given, is feared, despised*, and *ignored*, had no identifiable agent in the context, but I'd guess that Bright intended "the mainstream" to serve as the nonhuman agent of these passives as well. Again, we should interpret *mainstream* as a euphemistic way of talking about heterosexual men. (Of course, heterosexual women belong to the mainstream, too, but men are the primary producers and consumers of pornography in the u.s.) Furthermore, men are the likely intended agents of these passives because heterosexual women may "fear" and "despise" their sexuality, but I don't think they give it "zero recognition" or "ignor[e]" it, "pointedly" or otherwise. Bright's agentless passives are only the overt manifestation of her conceptual mess.

She failed to distinguish between the sexuality of Lesbians and hetero-sexual women because, apparently, she didn't think there is a difference. Since the only agent available in the context was "the mainstream," and heterosexual women and men constitute a significant majority of the popula-tion (as far as I know), Bright didn't distinguish the sexualities of heterosex-uals. She refused to acknowledge that any of us is different, but managed this reduction only by implication.

1. women and men possess and express identical sexual feelings and behav-iors;
2. lesbians and heterosexual women share identical sexual feelings and be-haviors;
3. heterosexual women are sexually identical to heterosexual men; therefore: Lesbians are "just like" all heterosexuals.

But what is the relationship she implied between "porn" and "women"? She posited a causal relationship: "lesbian porn" isn't "funded," "distrib-uted," or "recognized" by men (disguised as "the mainstream") because men "fear," "despise," "ignore," and "give zero recognition" to "women's sexuality." Conversely, if men didn't fear and despise women's sexuality, they'd recognize it, not ignore it, and then they'd fund, distribute, and recog-nize lesbian porn. Underneath these assumptions is yet another one: there is a "real" women's sexuality conceptually contrasted with an "unreal" women's (and Lesbian's?) sexuality. I say this because the four passives of her second sentence don't even hold true for men. Men do "recognize" a spe-cific sort of "women's sexuality" and they certainly do not "ignore" it. Men have paid a lot of attention to what they describe as women's sexuality. In fact, it is their descriptions of what they want to believe is women's sexuality that provides most of the fantasy fodder produced by pornographers. Main-taining men's beliefs about "what women want" sexually is the purpose of pornography. That's what turns men on. If it didn't work, pornography wouldn't exist, and it's a billion-dollar industry. It is the pornographer's busi-ness to portray women behaving sexually as men want them to.

Men are "turned on" by pornography because it represents women's sexuality as men describe it, a desperate sexuality in which their penises are the only significant element. Whatever isn't fucking is labeled "foreplay." Fucking is the main event, and nothing else counts on the PUD scoreboard. Men, and most women, believe that there is no sexuality without a penis. What men "fear" and "despise," then, is Bright's hypothesized "real" women's sexuality, which is . . . Lesbian?

What Bright might have been trying to say was that the patriarchal main-stream doesn't support lesbian pornography; therefore, the fact that lesbian pornography isn't supported by the patriarchy proves that it's different and cannot be perceived as "like" male pornography. By women's sexuality she may have meant women's "real" sexuality in contrast to our sexuality as men have perceived and defined it. But her equations indicate that she believes that all people are the same. I hope she's wrong.

Agentless passives make murky what might otherwise be clear, confuse where one hopes for clarity. I've said throughout this chapter that the passive construction is a danger signal. When we encounter agentless passives, in particular, we should be on guard. Whether the individual suppressing human responsibility is a president, a general, a psychologist, a woman trying to ignore male agency, or a lesbian attempting to fool herself (and a few others besides), the structure indicates that there is more going on beneath the surface of the statement than appears at first reading (or hearing). Sometimes, stopping and listening for what is not being said reveals more than the words actually uttered.

GETTING THINGS DONE

For some reason, prescriptive grammarians and linguists concentrate their attention on the *be*-passive and overlook other kinds of passive. In addition to the familiar *be*-passive, there are *get*-passives, *have*-passives, and *become*-passives, which serve the same rhetorical motivations that make *be*-passives so useful to PUD speakers, although each has unique characteristics.

In 1972, Robin Lakoff identified *get*-passives and demonstrated how they differ from *be*-passives.[4] *Get*-passives imply that objects of the verb are responsible for whatever happens to them. That is, *get* forces us to read such assertions as though the object is also the agent, as though the object were looking for trouble. Because of this implication, *get*-passives often turn up in "blaming the victim" descriptions. When the agent and object of a verb are interpreted as identical, that identity relation is said to be reflexive. Reading sentences with *be*- and *get*-passives reveals the very different ways we interpret them.

9.15 a. The rebellious students *were attacked*.
        The rebellious students *got attacked*.
     b. Many women *are raped* every day.
        Many women *get raped* every day.
     c. Lots of people *are killed* in their homes.
        Lots of people *get killed* in their homes.

The *be*-passives clearly assume that whoever committed the action is also solely responsible for it. Responsibility isn't imputed to the victims. But the *get*-passives force us to read them as if they had an implied reflexive pronoun: *The rebellious students got **themselves** attacked, Many women get **themselves** raped every day; Lots of people get **themselves** killed in their homes.* The *get*-passive forces us to allot responsibility to the victim(s).

Speakers of English intuitively sense that *get* shifts responsibility to the object/victim. A sportscaster's impulse to revise an incipient *get*-passive demonstrates that we can catch ourselves making such false attributions if we listen to what we're saying.

9.16 "Of course, Florida is *getting . . . being beaten up* at LSU."

Rather than imply either that the University of Florida team was incompetent or that Louisiana State wasn't a stronger team, the reporter quickly switched to the *be*-passive to acknowledge the quality of the LSU team. *Getting* would have implied that the Florida Gators were at fault.

The implied reflexive agency of the *get*-passive makes it particularly attractive when speakers wish to disavow their responsibility for an event. In the 1987 movie *Pack of Lies*, a british secret service agent used 9.17 to avoid taking responsibility for knocking over a bottle of perfume on her unwilling host's dresser:

9.17 "It just *got knocked over.*"

In the movie, British spies have coerced a family to let them use their home to observe suspects living across the street. The family members cooperate, but are obviously unhappy about having government spies sharing their home. When one of the spies accidentally knocked over a perfume bottle, spilling its contents, she was reluctant to take responsibility for her clumsiness. Anxious for the family to accept her presence, she substituted *it* for the perfume, used the adverb *just* (meaning 'merely') to downplay the importance of the accident, and polished the sentence off with a *get*-passive, attributing responsibility to the inanimate bottle.

Using the *get*-passive to eliminate oneself as the responsible agent for accidental events is a common rhetorical maneuver. A friend once used the construction to tell me about a horrible mess she'd caused in my refrigerator: "You had that little thing of gravy in the frig? [significant pause awaiting acknowledgment] It *got dumped.*" "It got dumped" may sound abrupt, but two linguistic "alerts" prepared me: her use of the past *had*, meaning 'you no longer have it', and the fact that she asked a question instead of saying, "I knocked over that little thing of gravy you had in the frig." The question set me up for the *get*-passive description.

Like many *be*-passives, *get*-passives are useful when men want to deny their responsibility for or involvement in specific events, especially pregnancy. Unlike a *be*-passive, a *get*-passive describes pregnancy as though it were something women willed upon themselves without male participation. The following example from a 1976 episode of the television series *Maude* (brought to my attention by Susan J. Wolfe) indicates how the reflexivity inherent in the *get*-passive shifts responsibility to victims, a popular PUD tactic. The father of the pregnant woman made the statement.

9.18 "Why is marriage the first thing everybody thinks of when a girl *gets herself knocked up?*"

Because *Maude* was marketed as a "liberal" sitcom, this description was probably intended to show how "progressive" the male character was: just because a woman is pregnant doesn't mean she has to marry the man responsible; she could raise the child by herself! Ironically, even a *get*-passive is preferable to the pseudo-active version we hear more often, "She got pregnant," in which the woman is the only individual responsible and makes it sound as though the fetus is something she bought on sale at a mall. *Got* in such statements means 'obtained', "She got a new sweater," "She got the flu," so we interpret "She got pregnant" as parallel to other sentences in which *got* signals purposeful action on the part of the woman.

Have-passives, in contrast, imply that the object of the passivized verb cannot also be the suppressed agent. They point our attention away from the named object and toward some unnamed individual or group specifically hired or called upon to perform some action. We say, "I *had* my car *washed*," "We *had* the carpet *cleaned*," "They *had* our broken windows *replaced*." In each sentence, the speaker implies that someone else performed the action described. One of my most incriminating examples came out of my own mouth. One night, having undressed and stacked my clothes on a chair, I carefully took off my glasses and put them on top of my clothes. Then I sat on them. I crushed them, totally. The next day, when someone wanted to know why I wasn't wearing my glasses, I said, "I had them smashed," a ludicrous description that made it sound as though I went out and purposely hired someone else to smash my glasses to avoid saying that I'd broken them.

By saying "I had my glasses smashed," I disavowed my own responsibility. *Have*-passives not only hide speakers' agency but describe their acts as though their victims actively, purposely invited the acts to be done to them. In the December, 1987 *Boston Globe*, a bureaucrat's description explaining why old people had been evicted from their homes contained "dummy *it*," a missing experiencer (with *seems*), and the comparative adjective *easier* used speciously, as well as a *have*-passive.

9.19 "I think because they are older people who don't have much in the way of resources, it *seems* it was easier for them and people like them *to have* their rights *violated*," Doty added.

As transparently false as the statement is, it's typical of what we are expected to accept as reasonable, rational, logical explanation in PUD. Doty, the bureaucrat who said this, started off honestly enough with "I think," predisposing us to accept it as his honest opinion. The first *it* replaced the entire clause that follows *seems*. The experiencer that should have followed *seems—to me* [Doty]—was suppressed. Logically, the comparative *easier* requires an agent, which Doty supplied, "for them and people like them," but the basis for the comparison was missing, and I wondered, "easier than what"?

Doty's use of *easier* forced readers to accept two covert implications of his description: First, that the older people had choices among alternatives, that they knew about them and decided that having their rights violated was "easier" than some implied alternative; second, that they also decided that the options they were allegedly aware of were harder than having their rights violated! Because he did not tell us what those alternatives were, we couldn't examine them to determine if his description was accurate. The *have*-passive, following other deceptive uses of language, was the final element that cast the victims as responsible for what other people did to them. This, Doty would have us believe, described the "reality" of the elderly!

BURIED PROPOSITIONS

As the preceding examples suggest, agentless passives serve a variety of rhetorical strategies, most often those of men who want to avoid explicit responsibility for the consequences of the power they exercise. Once we have selected a passive structure, there are additional ways we can use passives for other structural functions: as **adjectives, nominals,** and **adverbs.** The flexibility of the passive increases its usefulness.

Adjectives are said to modify a noun. Cognitively, in terms of what *modify* means to our interpretive processes, adjectives *change* the character of a noun, describing it as the speaker wants us to perceive it. They coerce us to agree with and confirm the speaker's judgment. For this reason, modifiers are functionally important in PUD descriptions because they reflect individual perceptions, casting objects, events, and people as the speaker perceives they are. In "*sexy* clothes," "a *tasteful* decor," "*poor* judgment," "*true* believer," "an *ugly* disposition," and "*beautiful* painting," for example, the modifiers require us to agree with a value judgment.

Attributive adjectives, which modify nouns, occur frequently in PUD, because the speaker/writer can bury a proposition, along with all its presuppositions, inside an NP. Adjectives present us with someone else's judgment as inherent in the nouns they modify. When we interpret sentences, we use superficial form to decide how words and phrases function. The position of a word or phrase determines how we interpret its function within the sentence. Speakers position words in phrases and sentences so that they function in specific ways, and their functions dictate how we interpret what we hear and read. Consequently, when someone uses an agentless passive participle before a noun, we treat it as though it were an adjective, "modifying" the noun. Their position forces us to interpret them as adjectives, hence as inherent characteristics of the nouns they precede.[5]

Some readers may think that I'm not being fair here about the use of passives as attributive adjectives, that there's no evidence for a suppressed agent, and that such structures are merely adjectives, period. That we are subliminally aware of suppressed agents in such constructions makes them a productive source of humor. The multiple interpretations introduced by adjectival passives creates a surprise element that we find funny. The humor of one of the daily "Blondie" strips, for example, depended on an agentless, prenominal passive in the phrase "*paid* vacation."

Blondie (to Dagwood):	"The weather is so nice, we ought to take a little trip. Didn't Mr. Dithers agree to a *paid vacation* this year?"
Dagwood:	"Sure . . . as long as *I* paid for it!"

Mr. Dithers might have agreed to a "paid" vacation, but he didn't say that he would pay for it. Here, Mr. Dithers' use of an agentless prenominal passive modifier reminded readers of the ongoing hostilities between Dagwood and his boss. Like Blondie, we assumed that the missing agent of "paid vacation" was Mr. Dithers. But that assumption misled us, because there was no explicit agency. Revealing the agent of the adjectival passive, *paid*, in the last frame was funny because our expectations were turned against us.

Passives functioning as noun modifiers serve the same rhetorical strategies of passive sentences, but the resulting structures are additionally useful to speakers and writers in other ways because of how we have to interpret them. When a passive participle is used prenominally, it states a hidden claim, a buried proposition, that the speaker/writer is making about the noun that the participle precedes. These participles look like adjectives, they seem to be attributes inherent in the character of the noun, and they constitute hidden, and therefore unsupported, claims.

The italicized words in the following NPs are passive participles that we treat as attributes because of their position, overlooking the agency that underlies the NP: "*distressed* wood," "*disturbed* prairie," "scientifically *selected* sample." Someone marred or mistreated wood described as "distressed" or chemically altered it to look antique; the men who "conquered the west" did more than "disturb" the prairie—they destroyed the native flora and fauna. In the third example, someone selected the sample referred to, and the adverb *scientifically* asked us to assume that whoever chose it did so according to scientific methods, which implied that the suppressed agent was a scientist, an "expert."

The buried propositions characteristic of prenominal passives make them particularly useful for copywriters eager to promote their clients' products and politicians who have things to hide. Many spurious claims turn up as agentless, prenominal passives. A popular antacid informs us that "Inside packages comply with *prescribed* specifications"; a well-known aspirin man-

ufacturer advertises its product as a *"Doctor-recommended* pain reliever."
Both suggest the superior quality of the advertised products. Although the
adjectival passive in *[d]octor-recommended* retains its agent, we're no better
informed about the quality of the product. Indeed, the aspirin may be an
excellent pain reliever, but not because the advertising copy tells us that it's
"doctor-recommended." That alleged trait is simply an appeal to anonymous
authority intended to persuade us to buy the product.

The federal government, among the worst linguistic offenders, numbs our
sensibilities by talking about *"limited* resources" and *"neutralized* forces,"
phrases that hide the perceptual framework they serve. By whom, by what,
are resources limited? Who chose this description? What skullduggery does
limited hide from us? The NP "neutralized forces" illustrates how the position of *neutralized* coerces us to interpret it as an attribute of the dead
soldiers rather than the agentless passive it is.

Once we recognize the rhetorical potential of prenominal passives, it
comes as no surprise when we find them in familiar phrases that direct our
attention away from the men who rape, batter, and maim women and children. Phrases like *"battered* women" and *"abused* children" force us to
interpret the agentless passives as defining characteristics of women and
children, as though men battering women and abusing children are inherent
properties of being a woman or a child. Other contemporary phrases, such as
"liberated woman," are no less suspect, because we have no way of identifying the missing agent. Can women liberate ourselves, or must we wait upon
the benevolence of men or the agency of male control euphemized and
abstracted as "society"? The contemporary media equation of "liberated
woman" with 'heterosexually active' doesn't encourage optimism, either. In
"Chatter," one of *People* magazine's regular features, Peter Castro equated
liberated with **wanton** when he contrasted Andrea Evans with one of her
roles: "Despite her character's **wanton** ways, Andrea herself isn't as **liberated**" (100). Women who allow men to fuck them are liberated; those who
don't, aren't. Using *liberated* in this way is a typical PUD description that
perverts and trivializes our desire for freedom by turning the participle into a
pejorative. Just as *housewife* pejorated into *hussy*, men use *liberated* instead
of *promiscuous* because the latter adjective is now treated as an archaic
attribute that represents unenlightened eras when men had to marry women
before they could fuck them and a woman who didn't wait for marriage was
"promiscuous," ergo bad and immoral. Men's attitudes haven't changed.
They're adapting what originated as a rebellious description among women
to lure them back into the heteropatriarchal fold. If women say they want to
be liberated, then men equate liberation with fucking, and the women whose
minds they seduce linguistically have changed their lives, but for the worse.
Men detest the women they fuck, whether they say *liberated* or *promiscuous*.

Because we interpret prenominal passives attributively, they allow speakers and writers to present subjective opinions without explaining or defending them. The examples in 9.20 illustrate how writers use this structure to slip their assertions past our conscious mind, force their opinions on us without arguing their validity, and bury their prejudices as "modification."

9.20 a. The computer helps management cut *unneeded* labor costs.
     b. At least it [Carter's "New Foundation"] will distract attention from the *overused* "human rights."
     c. I admit there is danger of *misdirected* violence.
     d. Men regard as amusing this *exaggerated* fad of trying to substitute the "Ms." for "Mrs."

The appeal to authority associated with the agentless passive rings in all these examples but it is now more difficult to question. Like true adjectives, such modifiers imply the existence of their semantic opposites. *Unneeded* in 9.20.a. suggests that there are also *needed* labor costs, implying by negation that those costs won't be affected by cuts. Workers correctly listen closely whenever managers talk about "unneeded labor costs" because the phrase means that those identified as "unneeded" will lose their jobs. "Labor costs" is a euphemism for 'workers' salaries'. This phrase not only attempts to sugarcoat a decision that will mean hard times and poverty for workers; it also protects the managers, denying us access to the identity of those who make the distinction between needed and unneeded costs and act in terms of it.

How the phrase "human rights" mentioned in 9.20.b. could be "overused" is a matter for speculation, but the description is alarming. Suggesting that a president's program might usefully "distract" attention from human rights is a contradiction in a democracy, but describing people's claims to human rights as "overused," however many times they repeat them, identified the author as someone who finds those claims an unwelcome nuisance, unworthy of his recognition. The negative connotations of "overused" hint that the author is tired of hearing about inequalities in the u.s., and that he would like oppressed groups to shut up. Furthermore, the phrase implied that some human rights are more justifiable than others and that the writer had some method of measuring these claims. How does one decide that a phrase like "human rights" has been uttered too many times? How much is too much?

Similarly, in 9.20.c., saying that there is such a thing as "misdirected violence," as a character in the television mini-series, *Roots*, did, implied simultaneously that there also exists well-directed violence which is a good thing, or, at least, not a dangerous thing. The character implicitly condemned violence directed at the wrong people or institutions, but tacitly condoned violence directed toward those who deserve it.

The quotation in 9.20.d. illustrates how men wield power rhetorically. The author, Dr. Crane (in his nationally syndicated "Worry Clinic"), asserted that replacing "Mrs." with "Ms." was "a fad," and then asserted that someone has "exaggerated" what he described as a fad. How does "someone" exaggerate a fad? The statement sounds even more ludicrous when we question the hidden proposition: Who is exaggerating the fad? In 9.21 I've italicized some possible identities, and arranged them in the order of likelihood that I think Crane implied. His intended agents might be one or all of the first three or four.

9.21 a. Men regard as amusing this fad which *women* have exaggerated . . .
　　 b. Men regard as amusing this fad which *feminists* have exaggerated . . .
　　 c. Men regard as amusing this fad which *someone* has exaggerated . . .
　　 d. Men regard as amusing this fad which *everyone* has exaggerated . . .
　　 e. Men regard as amusing this fad which *they* have exaggerated . . .
　　 f. Men regard as amusing this fad which *Dr. Crane* has exaggerated . . .

I suspect that the actual, rather than the intended agents are probably five, because Crane is a man, and six, because he's the speaker. Such are the profundities of PUD.

Another group of passive modifiers, "true" adjectives, end with -*able* (e.g., *respectable, controllable, available, accessible*). (I'm using -*able* to talk generally about these adjectives, but the vowel can be "i," too.) Like agent-less -*ed* modifiers, these adjectives attribute inherent traits to the nouns they precede, but -*able* incorporates the concept of potentiality. In English we have two choices for assertions of this kind: a passive construction with the modal *can* or one of these adjectives. Describing someone as *respectable* means that the speaker can respect them; saying that certain variables are *controllable* means that someone can control them. The -*able* adjectives may have experiencers (*to me*) like *seem* and *appear*, or agents, more frequently covert than explicit, and their suppression makes them especially useful for making a speaker's perceptions sound general or universal. These two features of the -*able* adjectives, when combined, produce claims that may be easy to interpret but extremely difficult to challenge.

9.22 a. A *collectible* is something that's *able to be collected*.
　　 b. Violent crime is down, but *forcible* rape is up.
　　 c. Konrad Lorenz: Man is a very *conditionable* animal, and we don't know just how far you can train man to fit another environment.
　　 d. ABC has the most *watchable* news.

With this class of modifiers, the full import of how English implants what Kate Moran has called "the terrorists of the mind" and the extent of the power wielded by the invisible agents of the passive is now clear, although it may not seem so in my first example, which is fairly innocuous. In his column of August 14, 1979, Russell Baker explained the "meaning" of passive adjectives, and, in the process, illustrated the potentiality inherent in the ending -*able* and how the activity of the suppressed experiencer becomes an attribute of a noun. (In this case, the adjective functioned as a noun, a common usage e.g., *the poor, the quick and the dead, the homeless,* with something like "objects" or "items" understood.) The transference of the concept of 'potential' from the human agent (or perceiver) to the objects themselves was explicit in Baker's paraphrase: the objects *are able* [to be collected]. If I rephrase his explanation of what "a collectible" is as an active with an indefinite agent ('someone can collect such objects'), the modal *can* and its position before the verb *collect* reveal that the 'potential' belongs to the human activity, not to the objects. Whatever potential is attributed to inanimate objects originates in the patriarchal system of values and human perceptions, not in the objects themselves, but these adjectives can be used to suggest that such potential is absolute or a universal perception.

The NP, "forcible rape," in 9.22.b., shows how -*ible* covertly transfers the idea of 'capability' to the suppressed female victims, and exactly how men use passive structures to terrorize women by implication. With these constructions, men don't need to threaten or coerce us explicitly. We internalize this information and carry it with us through every day of our lives. *Forcible* means 'capable of being raped', certainly a male perception of women, but the adjective attributes that description to women as though it inheres in our very being, and simultaneously erases the men who perceive women in that way and rape them. (Note that the description itself distinguished "violent crime" from "forcible rape," as though rape were not a violent crime and, therefore, not among the statistics that should have been included as violent crimes!)

Lorenz's description in 9.22.c. accomplished exactly the same things, erasing the human agency inherent in the verb *control* and attributing the potential of being controlled to "man," as though it were an innate characteristic, not an externally imposed desire of the psychologists who seek to control people and spend their lives figuring out how to do so.

In my last example, in which ABC News advertised itself as "the most *watchable*," copywriters exploited the conceptual contrast between explicit passives and their adjectival cousins. ABC didn't say that a lot of people watched its news broadcasts; that might have been a false claim. Instead, they used a passive adjective, *watchable*, which asserted only that their news has the potential for being the most watched, not that it actually is! Passive adjectives provide PUD speakers with a way of implying a distinction between "what is" and "what might be" that erases male agency and how men perceive the world, instead attributing the feature of potential or capability to women, objects, and events.

SPEAKING ADVISEDLY

There are additional ways of utilizing truncated passives—as adverbs, for example—to create more complicated passive constructions, and as nominals (noun phrases into which an entire sentence has been condensed). Once we've taken a passive participle and used it in positions other than those usually occupied by verbs, its rhetorical potential increases. Like what I'm calling the "true" adjectives, passive modifiers have the same potential for conversion into adverbs by the addition of *-ly*. Just as we can turn the adjectives *careful* and *warm* into adverbs by attaching the suffix *-ly* to them (e.g., *carefully, warmly*), we can make further use of agentless passives as adverbs: *alleged > allegedly, reported > reportedly, demonstrable > demonstrably, remarkable > remarkably*. English is such a resourceful language that we can shrink an entire assertion into a single word that functions as a modifier within another proposition. And these words are as useful to speakers and writers as the agentless passives themselves. The following examples illustrate a few possibilities.

9.23 a. This soft, fluid little restaurant dress is *understatedly* dressy for afternoon and evening wear.
   b. He felt a little guilty to be enjoying himself so much, to be here so *unexpectedly* alone . . .
   c. A woman was raped and *allegedly* assaulted.

Passive adverbs are compressed propositions that hearers and readers have difficulty challenging. In a., *understatedly* is actually metaphorical. We commonly hear that clothes make fashion "statements," a metaphor in which what we wear is treated as communication. (A television commercial for a new perfume, ex-clam-a-tion!, exploits this metaphor.) So the way we choose to attire ourselves can be "overstated," that is, flashy, gaudy, "inappropriate" for an occasion, or "understated," that is, subtle. Saying too much is, of course, bad taste, for women; withholding information, saying little or nothing, is good taste.

The context in which one uses a passive adverb determines how accurately we can guess the suppressed agency. Sometimes we have no problem at all, other times the speaker leaves us wildly speculating. Again, the speaker's motivations govern how much help we'll get interpreting a passive adverb. In 9.23.b., the agency of *unexpectedly* is clear from the context. It is the speaker who didn't expect to be alone. In other contexts, however, such as *Stock prices dropped unexpectedly*, a host of possible agents suggest themselves as those who were caught off guard: investors, stock brokers, economists, businesses, and the Federal Reserve Bank, among others.

The use of *allegedly* in 9.23.c. is a familiar adverb in newspaper, radio, and television reporting because it protects members of the media from being sued by those accused of crimes. In this case, though, its use is strange because of its placement. In the sentence, that "a woman was raped" is a fact about which there is no hedging. What the adverb casts doubt on is whether the woman was assaulted. Someone has said that a woman was definitely raped, but someone, not necessarily the same speaker, has merely *alleged* that she was also assaulted. What, then, is rape, if not an assault? Since the woman was raped, how can there be any question of whether she was assaulted? Who wrote that description, and who did it protect? The construction itself suggested a description that simultaneously denied the violence of rape, making the act seem less harmful than it is, and, thereby, coercing us to perceive rape and assault as coexisting on an implied continuum of violence. Without knowing who did the alleging, one can interpret the sentence to mean that the police, the public, or the reporter didn't believe that the woman's description of what a man did to her was true.

FROM ACT TO ABSTRACT

Like passive modifiers, passive nominals[6] may or may not occur with explicit agency; the proposition describing some action now functions as an NP in another full sentence. In English, which is becoming increasingly "nouny," passive nominals serve an important function often overlooked. Because they lack grammatical information like tense and aspect, the actions and events they describe are presented to us as abstract, immutable facts.[7] Such condensed abstraction makes it extremely difficult for readers/listeners to question assertions so stated, for example, "the destruction of the city," "the liberation of women," "the elimination of racism."

Challenging the presuppositions of nominal constructions requires an alert hearer/reader. Suppressing agency makes these structures particularly popular in deceptive and coercive descriptions. When a proposition is condensed into a noun, it loses all reference to time and forces us to interpret what it describes as a fact. Conceptually, we treat nouns as though they have an indubitable factual status, as though they refer to actual people, events, or activities. Compare, for example, the difference in meaning between the sentences and NPs in 9.24. (The a. examples are passive sentences; the nominal versions are in b.) Note that the object of the verb in each case becomes the object of a preposition in the nominalized passive, usually *of*.

9.24 1. a. The union's offer to negotiate was *refused.*
　　　　b. *Refusal* of the union's offer to negotiate . . .
　　　2. a. The Indian way of life has been *destroyed.*
　　　　b. *Destruction* of the Indian way of life . . .
　　　3. a. English can be *used* to deceive.
　　　　b. The *use* of English to deceive . . .

Descriptions that might be open to question in a full sentence are unquestionable assertions of fact as noun phrases; actions marked for time become timeless, fixed events. Since the noun phrases are placed in other propositions as topics, objects, and agents, for example, *The refusal of the union's offer to negotiate resulted in a strike*, we focus on the more accessible verb phrase during the interpretive process, in this case, *resulted in a strike*, and neglect to question what the nominal presented to us as an incontrovertible fact.

If we accept the assertion in 9.24.1., we also believe that whoever refused the union's offer to negotiate is responsible for its decision to strike. The range of conceivable agents for the noun *refusal* is narrowed by our knowledge of labor negotiations, and we may deduce, on the basis of that knowledge, that the corporate management of a company refused to negotiate. But can we be sure that only their refusal caused the union to strike? Didn't the union and its members have some responsibility for the occurrence of a strike?

Likewise, in 9.24.2., what we know about the conquest and settlement of North and South America restricts the possible agents of the nominal *[d]estruction*; we might choose agents such as *Europeans, white men* or *Caucasians*, but the generality of the statement prompts us to reject both specific agents, *the English* or *the Spanish*, and generics, *people*, as potential candidates. In contrast, identifying the agency of *[t]he use*, in 9.24.3., is virtually unrestricted. Anyone who speaks English can use it deceptively.

Even when we find explicit agents with passive nominals, however, the agency can turn out to be less specific than it at first appears. In 9.25, examples from newspaper articles describing the gradual exposure of Nixon's Watergate coverup illustrate pseudo-agency with passive nominals.

9.25 a. *Impoundment* of billions of dollars of allocated funds represents an unparalleled *seizure* of power *by the White House*.
   b. *Our* almost blind *obedience* to the Presidency has acted to sanction each successive *usurpation* of power and authority *by this institution*.

The explicit agents of *[i]mpoundment of billions of dollars* and *seizure of power* (a.) and *usurpation of power and authority* (b.) refer to the dwelling of presidents, *the White House*, and the institution of the presidency itself in b., thereby avoiding naming the specific individual responsible for seizing and usurping political power in the u.s. during his terms in office, Richard M. Nixon. Those of us who remember the months of investigation as the extent of Nixon's criminal actions was uncovered can supply his name, but will history remember? The frequency of passive nominals in media descriptions of Nixon's crimes suggested that u.s. citizens would forget, and his reappearance on the political stage as a credible figure shows that many have.

UNLEARNING PUD

A language, any language, is a coherent system of interdependent rules. I've illustrated one portion of the English system, the structural properties of the passive voice, and explained both the rhetorical motivations served by such structures and the interpretive gymnastics they force on readers and hearers. When speakers and writers resort to passives in order to protect those responsible, including themselves, from identification, their audiences must then creatively engage in a nonverbal game to guess "whodunit?"

The u.s. is a nation of hypocrites and liars, and the passive and its related structures do, indeed, serve the purposes of men's descriptions and the conceptual framework of PUD, either omitting identification of the agents responsible for perpetrating the violence we live with or providing distorted descriptions that preserve male "consensus reality," including assertions that demean and trivialize women. If we don't question assertions that maintain white male power, we participate in the conceptual conspiracy that oppresses so many people. Worse, we allow the hidden agents of patriarchy to roam our consciousness freely, manipulating, controlling, and terrorizing us. The *be*-passive and its manifestations as modifiers, adverbs, and as noun phrases, as well as the *get*- and *have*-passives, illustrate only some of the rhetorical possibilities inherent in the grammatical processes available to all speakers of English. In particular, these structures provide those with something to hide with ways of withholding information from their audience.

I've sketched some of the interpretive strategies we must use in our efforts to identify the agents omitted from typical examples. If we are to protect ourselves against deceptive and misleading uses of English, we need to attune ourselves to passive structures. More importantly, we must expel the mind terrorists of patriarchy patrolling the corridors of our minds, and free ourselves from the unspoken fear they instill in us. Not that we don't have plenty of reasons to fear men. But we must do two things to eradicate the unconscious fear that keeps us from acting as agents in the world:

1. we must identify explicitly the male agency that rapes our bodies and our minds;
2. we must destroy the patriarchal programming that tells us we are weak and incapable of fighting back against men and their institutions.

Then we can start to reclaim our lives and minds from male control and violence.

We can also choose not to use passive structures in situations in which we know we're trying to suppress agency; the active version of an assertion is always available to us. Other English constructions, however, especially those that describe internal psychological experiences and perceptions, don't leave us options, and these are more psychologically insidious than the agentless passives we hear daily. What should be clear at this point is the necessity of breaking the hold on our minds that patriarchal English sustains. We must challenge patriarchal descriptions of the world and replace them with our own.

Chapter 10

Acting in the World

In this chapter I will continue my explanation of how English syntax organizes discourse to serve PUD descriptions of the world. My concern will be twofold: first, to describe the structures (such as the passive) we use to place NPs in topic position; second, to analyze examples of several predicate types, both adjectives and verbs, to show how selection of a predicate determines its potential agents and objects. Two different levels of language interact in the creation of topics and objects: syntax and semantics. The semantics of verbs and adjectives (predicates) limits our selection of agents and objects; syntactic processes create topics.

PREDICATE SEMANTICS

Predicates are the most important choice speakers make when they construct sentences. Because they are the structural core of sentences, other options become impossible, or at least awkward, once we decide on a predicate. Because verbs and adjectives are semantically biased, limiting the types of noun phrase that can occur with them in sentences, our decision to use one predicate rather than another (e.g., *happen*) determines our choice of agent and whether or not there will be an object. Most of us probably don't think about such things because these semantic properties seem to inhere in the "real" world. That is, we have accepted the semantic restrictions of English as though they were inherent features of the world.

The semantic structure of predicates in English determines the kinds of statements we can make about the world. We would not, for example, ordinarily say "She drank the sandpaper" or "The sandpaper drank the sawdust." We don't think sandpaper can be the agent or object of the verb *drink*. While it is unlikely that we would want to drink sandpaper, our inclination to follow paths already set before us, as is the case with the structures imposed by predicate semantics, would keep us from making statements that "make sense," such as those in 10.1.

10.1 a. Maria fondled the slab of schist.
   b. We ate cotton bolls with great relish.
   c. I kicked aside the dilapidated house.
   d. The alligator hated high heels.

The probability of saying sentences like those in 10.1 is low, but it's one thing not to say sentences because we have no context in which they might be meaningful and another to be forced to say specific kinds of things in the only way provided by the grammar of English. It's the difference between the innocuous, the inadequate (or distorting), and the damaging. The semantic properties of some predicate sets are dangerous to our well-being, and, if we assume that the descriptions they force us into are inherent in people and events in the world, we find ourselves having trouble communicating without knowing why.

The "Impersonal" Verbs

The verb *happen* frequently has *it* as its topic and its implied experiencer as the grammatical object, for example, *It happened to Mary again! Seem* and *appear* (hereafter EPs, experiencer-predicates), two familiar verbs we use to qualify our perceptions or to indicate that an observation is an opinion, not a "fact," also require that the experiencer (or perceiver) function syntactically as an object. Grammarians call such predicates "impersonal" because their structure puts perceptual distance between the human experiencer and the subjective observations they describe. Sentences in which we use *seem* or *appear* often begin with "dummy *it*," but other NPs can occupy the topic slot as well. (In 10.2.c. and d., I've indicated that the experiencers are optional with parentheses.)

10.2 a. It seemed *to Maude* that I was angry for no reason.
   b. It appeared *to us* that our manager would be late again.
   c. Mary seemed preoccupied (to me) yesterday.
   d. Your endless ranting appeared (to my friends) to be an overreaction.

We can't automatically interpret an omitted experiencer as *I* or *we*. As a. and d. indicate, both *seem* and *appear* allow speakers to attribute hypothetical feelings that may or may not have been experienced by someone else. The syntax of such EPs casts the one who perceives what is reported as a bystander, and we shouldn't readily accept indirect attributions of experience, especially internal ones, as accurate. In d., suppressing the experiencer "to my friends" would encourage us to supply an indefinite pronoun, *everyone*, and interpret the description as a statement of universal consensus.

Other EPs demonstrate the same characteristics: experiencers can be suppressed with some predicates (but not *strike* or *occur*), and speakers attribute feelings or perceptions to others. Like passive agents, experiencers can be omitted at the option of the speaker.[1] Instead of "by whom?," we should ask "to whom?" when an experiencer has been suppressed.

10.3 a. It *struck* us that you haven't talked much about Leslie lately.
   b. It was *clear* that she didn't want to be there.
   c. Janet *looks* tired these days.
   d. You *sounded* out of sorts on the telephone yesterday.

Although we often use *seem* and *appear* to indicate that we aren't sure of our perceptions, these verbs permit a wide range of false descriptions, some of them similar to the strategic uses of agentless passives. When speakers suppress the experiencer in sentences with *seem, appear,* or any of the sensation verbs (*look, feel, taste, sound, smell*), their assertions imply an imaginary consensus or authority. By varying the intonation with which a sentence is delivered, speakers can use such statements to insult, trivialize, or patronize.

10.4 a. You seem to be overeating again.
   b. Mary looks like she's at her wits' end.
   c. Mark always smells bad!
   d. That salmon tasted funny.

As the examples in 10.4 suggest, suppressed experiencers serve exactly the same rhetorical purposes as missing agents, implying consensus or authority, for example. But omitting experiencers has some persuasive motivations of its own. In *Beyond Freedom and Dignity*, B. F. Skinner challenged the idea that people have minds, relying heavily on *seem* and omitting experiencers. As identified by Donald Smith (1975), missing experiencers enable us to "appeal to indeterminate authority," creating "referential chaos." Especially tricky, though, is what Smith called "the-other-guy's use of doubly subjective" reference, which Skinner used to attribute ideas he didn't like to indefinite others so that he could attack them. The examples in 10.5 are those excerpted from *Beyond Freedom and Dignity* in Smith's analysis.

10.5 a. By questioning the control exercised by autonomous man [sic] and demonstrating the control exercised by the environment, a science of behavior also *seems* to question dignity or worth.
   b. A scientific conception *seems* demeaning because nothing is eventually left for which autonomous man can take credit. (58)

As Smith observed, the lack of experiencers in Skinner's prose was so systematic as to be deliberate, a linguistic tactic to coerce his readers to share his views by excluding them as potential experiencers or sharers of the ideas he attacked. By suppressing experiencers, Skinner accomplished two rhetorical aims with one structure: he didn't have to identify any of the people whose ideas he attacked, and, by exclusion, encouraged his readers to be on the "right" side: his. Ambiguous non-reference to the experiencer making claims excludes "[t]he reader [who] does not stand accused of the thoughts being described and at the same time is invited to entertain them and possibly join" Skinner in his attack on them (Smith, 198).

Psych-Predicates[2]

The psych-predicates, verbs and adjectives that describe a speaker's emotional reactions to someone else's actions or behavior (e.g., *amuse, annoy, frighten, nauseate, surprise, astonish, excite, gratify, disgust, horrify, irritate, mystify, bore, threaten, puzzle, rile,* and *worry*) are distinguished in several ways. Superficially, they occur as syntactic structures similar to the active and passive voices, with one important difference: like the EPs, the NP that performs the predicate action is an experiencer, not an agent. Because psych-predicates describe internal emotional responses, the experiencer NP must be animate, usually human, and the syntax of these verbs forces the experiencer to function as the object acted upon.

10.6 a. Your behavior repulsed me.
    a'. I was repulsed by your behavior.
    b. You intimidated me.
    b'. I was intimidated by you.
    c. Your sudden appearance frightened me.
    c'. I was frightened by your sudden appearance.

Unlike true passives, however, the agency alleged by psych-predicates can be preceded by a number of different prepositions, including *by*, but also *at, with, about,* and *of.*

10.7 a. I was bored *with* (*at, by*) your antics.
    b. I am confused *about* (*at, by*) her motives.
    c. They were amused *at* (*by, with*) our confusion.
    d. She is irritated *by* (*at, with*) Miguel.
    e. We are frightened *of* (*by*) loud talk.

The event, action, or behavior pointed to as the cause of an individual's psychological response can be phrased as a clause that starts with *because* or *when*, or introduced by a preposition:

10.8 a. I was excited *because she called today*.
    b. I was excited *when you called on time*.
    c. They were amazed *at how easily we changed the tire*.
    d. I was horrified *when they got married*.

Psych-predicates describe an internal, psycho-social response to some event, situation, or individual; the experiencer identifies the feeling and the person or behavior that evoked it and decides which predicate most accurately describes their reaction. I am distinguishing between verbs that describe emotions or emotional states—e.g., *hate, love, despise, loathe*—and the psych-predicates, which describe feelings. By this distinction, I want to separate emotions, which I believe to be relatively permanent internal states, and feelings, which I think are more transient responses to actions and behaviors in a specific situation. We may love an individual and yet be repulsed by one of their behaviors or frightened by them at a particular time.

Distinguishing feelings and emotions may sound bizarre at first, but we make the distinction because English syntax does. When we use a predicate that describes one of our emotions, we have to identify ourselves as the agent, for example, "I love you," "I loathe getting out of bed," "I hate the smell of perfume." The psych-predicates, in contrast, allow us greater flexibility for assigning responsibility for our feelings to people and their behaviors, and, as with passives, we can use *get/got* or *become/became* instead of *be* with the verb. Either auxiliary verb emphasizes the process of feeling, but places it within the individual.

10.9 a. I get excited when you enter a room.
    b. They got irritated at your constant chatter.
    c. She becomes confused with so much noise.
    d. We became frightened at his wild gesturing.

These predicates, like passive participles, can also be used as prenominal modifiers, forcing us to interpret them as characteristics of the noun they precede. Because they describe internal feelings, however, their use as modifiers produces a phrase in which feelings become attributes of a noun denoting the human face or its expressions (10.10 a. and b.), although they can modify other kinds of noun (c. and d.)

10.10 a. Sarah's *puzzled expression* alarmed me.
    b. The child pressed her *worried face* against the window.
    c. The travelers lay sprawled in *exhausted sleep*.
    d. Her face registered *shocked desperation*.

In noun phrases, psych-predicate modifiers describe our interpretations, inferred from their movements, gestures, expressions, and body posture, of what others are feeling. What such NPs report are our projected guesses of the correspondence between what people are feeling and wrinkled foreheads, knitted brows, shoulder shrugs or head turns. Although the significance of body language and facial expressions is culturally determined, motions and gestures can have several possible interpretations unless accompanied by some verbal signal. For example, I might shrug my shoulders to indicate disappointment, indifference, or tension, and someone trying to interpret my shrug would have to guess at its meaning and might misinterpret it.

Because the correspondence between our feelings and what we do with our bodies isn't clear-cut, novelists use psych-predicates as noun modifiers to control our responses as we read. Narrators or characters report their or others' feelings to us, and we use those descriptions to interpret character and plot development. So we are often surprised, and forced to revise our interpretations when we later discover that one character's interpretation and resulting description of another's behavior were wrong.

Understanding the psych-predicates and how they restrict us psychologically is crucial for women if we want to change the way we think; they reveal how the syntax and semantics of English require specific kinds of description. Regardless of the form the psych-predicate takes, the experiencer of the psychological response can only be the object, the person acted upon by someone else, who cannot be held responsible for their emotional/physical reactions. The psych-predicates freeze internal psychological experiences into two roles, the victim and whoever or whatever is to blame, and locate the sources of our psychological responses outside of us.

Sex-Marked Predicates[3]

In earlier chapters, I discussed sex-specific nouns in several different languages (chapter 5), the historical development of [+human] nouns in English (chapter 6), and the semantic structure revealed by their present-day usage (chapter 7). Certainly, the semantic restrictions of those nouns limit their reference, but the sex-marked predicates have more binding consequences: they determine the sex of the nouns we can use with them, as agents, objects, or, in some cases, both. Violating the semantic properties of these predicates results in sentences that listeners find peculiar, ridiculous, or downright nonsensical because the violations contradict PUD's version of the "real" world. While English lacks predicates that are explicitly marked for biological sex, the semantics of sex-marked predicates is no less specific. Consider, for example, the perceived anomaly of the sentences in 10.11.

10.11 a. Before she died, Hilda *fathered* eight children.
     b. Avoid Sam today. He's *menstruating*.
     c. Sally *impregnated* her childhood sweetheart.
     d. Richard is *pregnant* again.

To many speakers of English, such statements are simply absurd. The events they describe are unreal, counter-factual, impossible. The predicates of a. and c., *father* and *impregnate*, require [+male] agents, while those of b. and d., *menstruate* and *pregnant*, require agents semantically [−male]. The semantic features of *father* proscribe its use in a., but the same restriction doesn't seem to apply to *Harry is wonderful about mothering the children.* To say that a man is "menstruating" strikes us as impossible, but we now know that men experience monthly cycles like those of women,[4] and people say, "He's on the rag," to describe a man when they want to attribute to him the irritability associated with menstruating women because English lacks a [+male] term. Because of artificial insemination, the statement of c. is not only possible, it now occurs frequently. If I'd said, "Sally impregnated a cow," not another human, few readers would object to it. They might assume that she's a veterinarian. And reproductive engineers would like d. to make sense in the near future. It might seem bizarre to us now, but utterly commonplace in a mere ten years. What our knowledge of English semantics tells us is nonsense is, in fact, perfectly sensible if we think outside of the limitations of the language.[5]

Like the sex-specific nouns, sex-marked predicates show the same semantic asymmetry, with a significant difference. Sex-specific nouns, are more susceptible to change than the predicates. When men enter occupations stereotyped as "women's work," the associated terms receive [+male] markers. When women enter male domains, the nouns either remain [+male] or are given a [−male] marker. The same isn't true of the [+male] predicates, which are semantically closed to women. Although the [−male] predicates can be used with [+male] nouns as agents, using [+male] predicates with [−male] agents is nearly impossible. In contrast, men have freely appropriated [+female] predicates when it suited them. Furthermore, predicates marked [+male] clearly predominate in the vocabulary and there are numerous gaps where one might expect (or hope) to find equivalent [−male] predicates. English speakers have a set of [+male] predicates for penile activities and what can be done to the penis: *father, sire, beget, impregnate, penetrate, ejaculate, castrate, fertilize, deflower, inseminate* and *emasculate*. There is no semantically symmetrical set of predicates for activities performed by or to the clitoris, labia majora or minora. Male perceptions and activities dominate the sex-marked predicates, which is, perhaps, the structural reason they are a fixed set, closed to women. The semantic structure reflects social reality: men take over whatever they like from the women's sphere with impunity. Indeed, they think of such acquisitiveness as their right and prerogative.

Shut out of agency in sex-marked predicates, women must rely on nouns and multisyllabic phrases to describe our experiences. What we have are nominals—*clitoridectomy, infibulation, excision*, and *hysterectomy* (since women's genitalia are categorized not as sexual parts of our anatomy but as reproductive "equipment," "plumbing")—or phrases in which the predicate is one of the helping or semantically empty verbs: *to get/be aroused, to get/ be excited, to get/be hot, to have an orgasm*. But none of those phrases is uniquely [−male]. If anything, they are sex-neutral, and both sexes use them. I would suggest, however, that as women have acknowledged they have sexual feelings and decided they want to talk about them, they have borrowed already available, formerly [+male] terms. Thus, lacking a female-specific word like *ejaculate*, women have begun to use the noun *orgasm* as a verb: "I orgasmed all night."

In fact, a woman's sexual experience and feelings are nonexistent if we believe that the English vocabulary describes reality, because there are no [−male] words for sexuality. There are hundreds of words and phrases for male sexuality and what men do to women; the slang vocabulary of English reflects the male's obsession with his penis and its "personality." Men even name their penises and talk about them as though they lead an independent existence. Men's obsession with their penises and its structural centrality in PUD is a given, rarely worthy of comment. Men are "supposed" to be obsessed with fucking women. (Men who aren't are deviant.) One can say of a woman, "She's oversexed," but we rarely hear that adjective used to describe a man. Instead, the categorial dichotomy—men have the predicates, women get nouns—again applies. There is a predicate for describing the male activity of fucking lots of women, "womanize," and a noun, "womanizer." A woman obsessed with letting men fuck her is a "nymphomaniac," not a "*mannizer." There is no such [−male] agentive noun; it would be a semantic contradiction because PUD assumes that agency is inherently [+male]. *Womanizer* and *nymphomaniac* both express negative judgments, as Gary Hart, Jimmy Bakker, and Jimmy Swaggert could testify, but unless a womanizing man lives in the public arena, his "weakness" is more likely to be overlooked or tacitly condoned. A woman, however, once branded as a "nymphomaniac," is condemned to a more marginal life than most heterosexuals.

To the best of my knowledge, women have not shown the exaggerated regard for their clitorises men give to their penises. When women talk about their genitals, they say "down there." Whereas men's genitalia are objects, women's are described as a location. In contrast to the penile vocabulary [−male] words and phrases focus on the place where men stick their penises or the end result of heterosexual coitus for women, having babies. An exception to this is the verb *menstruate*, which is intransitive (there is no object) and requires a [−male] agent. Other female biological processes, however, can be talked about only as states, as nouns. Women "go through *menopause*," we "have a *climacteric*," even though menopause is a process that continues for years, sometimes a decade or more. And, to avoid using the one verb we do have, women have an extensive vocabulary of euphemisms: *fall off the roof, be on the rag, Aunt Jane is visiting, red Herbie has come, to be unwell, have a period, be on the mattress, it's that time of the month,* and *have the monthlies.* Women do not act; we have a function: reproduction. PUD describes our lives as nouns, nouns, and more nouns.

Specifically female predicates disappear from English, to be replaced by phrases in the passive voice; women become the objects on which men perform actions. The verb *bear*, as in "She bore four children," "My mother bore me," is now virtually obsolete except, perhaps, among older speakers in rural communities, replaced by the agency of medicine men or euphemisms. (Patriarchal medicine continues to fight legitimating midwives.) Doctors "deliver babies," women "are delivered of" them. Women "carry a fetus to term," are "in labor," "have labor pains," "have children," "give birth." Doctors "perform abortions," women "have" them. Only anti-abortionists talk about "aborting fetuses" as an action requiring human agency.

Women "conceive," but even that verb is used intransitively. Instead, women "become pregnant," "get pregnant," "get knocked up," "have a loaf in the oven," "have one on the way," "are with child," "are in trouble," "get in trouble," are "in a family way," have "been pumped up." Like the vocabulary for menstruation, most of these expressions are euphemisms and passives, and several imply guilt on the woman's part, but without describing her as active sexually. (At one time, the language had a gerund that meant 'the act of conception', OE *geeacnung*.)

Two verbs show how thoroughly the dichotomy between the male as sexual actor and the female as breeder structures the syntax of the reproductive process: *mother* and *father*. One might expect these verbs to be semantically and syntactically symmetrical, but they aren't. As a verb, *father* denotes the act of fertilization, implying no responsibility toward a child on the part of the male parent. Semantically, it refers only to a momentary spasm, yet, the adverb *fatherly*, to describe men as nurturers, has the same descriptive range as *motherly*.

The verb *mother* describes the actions said to inhere in the noun: (1) 'to give birth to', 'to be the mother of', (2) 'to create', 'to care for', (3) 'to watch over, nourish, and protect', and (4) 'to love'. Unlike *father, mother* doesn't describe the act of conceiving. Unlike other female animals, women don't have a unique verb that describes the process of ejecting a baby from the womb. Cows *calve*, mares *foal*, sows *farrow*. Women "become mothers" and men simultaneously "become fathers," expressions that erase female agency and the physical experiences of women.

Predicates that denote behaviors thought of, within PUD, as processes extending over time have distinctive syntactic characteristics. As a verb, *mother* is treated as a process; *father* is not. Linguists use two tests to determine whether a verb is a **process** or **stative** predicate: (1) can it be used in the progressive **aspect**; and (2) can it occur with adverbs of frequency (e.g., *frequently, often*). We use process predicates in the progressive aspect (*be + -ing*): *I am eating breakfast, We're being careful.* Predicates that we can't use with the progressive aspect are called stative because they describe something thought of as a state. In spite of recent efforts to convert *father* into a process predicate with *-ing*, we hear it used as a noun, not a verb. The strangeness of the b. sentences in 10.12 and .13 shows that the conversion has yet to take hold.

10.12 a.   She has been mothering her children for years.

     b. ? He has been fathering his children for years.

10.13 a.   She has frequently (always) mothered her children.

     b. ? He has frequently (always) fathered his children.

The asymmetry of these paired descriptions indicates that English speakers continue to think of mothering and fathering as semantically asymmetrical. In fact, when men decide that they want to impose themselves on a context or situation, the word for the related action or idea is more likely to be a pseudo-generic than a sex-specific term. In this case, what has occurred linguistically is a sudden preference for the sex-neutral word *parenting*. Men aren't explicit in it, but its use succeeds in erasing women's agency.

If we place both verbs in identical sentences, *mother* clearly denotes nurturance, a nonbiological process, while *father* denotes fertilization, a biological process. We can say the sentences in 10.14:

10.14 a. She mothers her sister.

    b. She mothers her grandfather.

    c. She mothers her dog.

    d. She mothers her vegetables.

But the parallel sentences of 10.15, with *father*, make very different, even criminal assertions:

10.15 a.   He fathers his sister.

    b.   He fathers his grandfather.

    c. ? He fathers his dog.

    d. ? He fathers his vegetables.

The sentence in a., if it is possible, refers to a sexual relationship, and b. is a paradoxical assertion, contradicting the chronological relationship we presume for the two kinship terms. Both c. and d. are biological impossibilities.

If we say, *She didn't mother her children*, we are making a negative judgment about a woman with respect to social expectations of her, but we haven't denied her biological relationship to them. In contrast, if we say of a man, *He didn't father his children*, we've asserted that he has no biological relationship to them, that it wasn't his sperm that contributed to the genetic make-up of the children we're talking about. That sperm is perceived as more important than eggs is evident when we say *He was cuckolded*. English has no parallel word for women, nor is there a way to deny maternity. A woman is a mother or she isn't; it isn't a debatable subject. These asymmetries underscore the PUD significance of descent from the fathers, in spite of the fact that the verb *father* is a stative predicate.

The sex-marked predicates, some of which only take [−male] subjects (*menstruate, be pregnant*), [+male] subjects (*impregnate, ejaculate*), and [+male] objects (*emasculate, castrate*) reveal how patriarchal assumptions about the biological origins of the female and male social roles have produced the extreme degree of semantic asymmetry in the English vocabulary. Male sexuality is perceived as agentive, active, aggressive, and often violent; female sexuality as passive, objectified, or nonexistent. It is sufficient for a man to provide sperm to fertilize an egg. After that, the years-long process of mothering takes over. Most of the ways heterosexual women can talk about their sexuality aren't sexual at all, but reproductive. Furthermore, a majority are phrases with empty verbs like *have* or *make* (Women "have orgasms," "have babies," "have clitoridectomies"). Even during the process of giving birth, women are cast as the often invisible objects of male action: *The doctor* **delivered** *the baby*. Heterosexual women can talk about themselves only as sexually acted upon, and the only experience connected with their sexuality validated by English is the reproductive consequence. There is no vocabulary for Lesbian sexuality.[6]

As the terms for cutting off penises suggest, the presence or absence of a male organ has to be distinguished in English. We can *emasculate* a man, but the word *effeminate*, an adjective, isn't semantically parallel. It is used only to describe men. We don't **effeminate* a woman. In PUD, a woman's womanliness inheres in her behavior, clothes, and hairdo, not her clitoris; a man's manliness is located in his genitals. The abstract attribute of courage is described as residing in a man's balls, and, in those rare instances when one wants to talk about a woman's courage or nerve, we don't say, "She has ovaries" or "she has vulva," and when a woman is said "to have balls," it isn't intended as a compliment. Even the [+male] Yiddish word *chutzpah*, which English speakers have borrowed and often apply to women, retains the sense that a woman so described has transgressed into male territory. Any references to women's biological sex, as we saw in chapter 7, is negative. A woman who defies male assumptions of superiority is said to be a "cunt."

Men have, however, appropriated for themselves positive references for the female-specific reproductive process in metaphorical extensions of the vocabulary that they attribute to thinking and learning. Given the fact that men have cherished for millenia the idea that they alone are capable of thinking, it is ironic that they should preempt birth as a vehicle. Men say that they "conceive ideas" and "give birth" to inventions. For example, in his Introduction to the *Oresteia*, Robert Fagles (1975) described what he called "the pregnancies of Aeschylus's style" and characterized the language of the play as "giving birth to a new drama and a new poetic voice" (36–37).

In spite of this appropriation of the birth process, other common metaphors simply extend the cultural asymmetries of *mother* and *father* as verbs. Although some countries are called "the motherland," others, like Germany, are "the fatherland," and the primacy of fatherhood is emphasized in numerous expressions so common we forget that they're figures of speech. Once men "conceive" of ideas, they are described as *seminal*. Men *dissemi-*

nate information to students attending their *seminars*. There are no "ovular ideas" and we don't "ovulate information," even though the [– male] metaphor would be more accurate. In those long genealogical lists of the old testament, only the males who "begat" and their sons are named; the women and daughters who must have participated remain nameless and invisible.

Men talk about "the fathers" of a country, wax eloquent about building on the "wisdom of their fathers and forefathers" and living by "the rules set down by their fathers." They honor each other's "brainchildren" by saying so-and-so was "the father of American parasitologists" or "the father of the Cocktail Age." Although the predicate semantics of English treats the verb as a single, instantaneous event, the noun extends metaphorically throughout the social structure. The fathers become the creators, like Zeus, who bring forth and define ideas and objects for all time, whereas the verb *mother* is socially defined as a nurturing activity that takes place within the limited, localized context of the female domain. Rarely, if at all, is an outstanding woman similarly hailed. "Necessity may be the mother of invention" but invention, according to PUD, belongs to men. The male domain, in contrast, isn't only global, it's cosmic. C. S. Lewis (1964) admired the novelist George MacDonald because he learned from his father that "Fatherhood must be at the core of the universe" and taught that "the relation of Father and Son is of all relations the most central" (5).

So thorough-going is the assumption of men's importance and women's insignificance in the world that PUD abounds with examples in which the female role in reproduction—carrying a fetus for nine months—disappears. Bearing and raising children may be one of the most significant kinds of agency that men allocate to women, but even those abilities are easily attributed to men. The following exchange, from Zenna Henderson's collection of stories, *Holding Wonder* (1972), attributed reproduction to male reflexivity.

10.16 "I'm only one man and, alas! have but one life to give for Science!"
      "Only one man. . . . But *man reproduces himself. You will have children.*" (249)

The interpretive problems with this exchange originate in the author's unsuccessful attempt to persuade us that "man . . . himself" has the scope of generic reference following her character's first use of *man*. The phrase, *have children*, eradicates women. Never mind that *have* in the sentence functions only to denote male ownership!

The semantics of sex-marked predicates reveals how men perceive the reproductive cycle more explicitly, perhaps, than they like. A Tennessee man, giving his reason for perceiving abortion as "murder," described a fetus as "a male sperm that has gotten bigger." Shades of Aristotle! But Jerome Hamer, a roman catholic archbishop, made still better use of the deceptive resources of

English syntax in his "Declaration on Abortion" (1975), at once placing the burden of responsibility on women and denying their right to choose abortion. Note particularly where he used agentless nominals and the noun *persons*.

10.17 [T]*hose who practice abortion* very often are the same *persons who habitually practice contraception*, but without satisfactory results. *Persons* who have a contraceptive mentality, that is *a determination to avoid fertilization at any cost*. [sic] This contraceptive mentality is a *worrisome* phenomenon and it, in fact, *threatens to destroy man by inverting his order of values*.

It would be hard to be clearer about why men deny women's right to decide whether or not they will bear children, yet Hamer's construction of the statement is a masterpiece of PUD doublethink. In the first partial sentence, the verb phrase *practice abortion* nests the action with the fairly innocuous verb *practice*. One "practices" the piano, yoga, dancing, medicine, or law. The act Hamer deplores, *abort*, becomes a noun, the object of *practice*. The agents of *practice*, "the same persons" (*those*), also unsuccessfully "practice contraception." Because *practice* is indeterminate with respect to sex, his use of *persons* may not, at first, bother us. As medical doctors, men "practice abortion"; as fuckers, they sometimes "practice contraception."

In a sentence fragment lacking a main verb, Hamer puts together a complicated NP that contains a clause with another explanatory clause tacked onto it. The "head noun" of the clause is the same seemingly innocuous *persons* (unmarked for sex). 'People in general', then, "have a contraceptive mentality." The telling omissions are then further buried in a clause that defines what Hamer means by "contraceptive mentality": *a determination to avoid fertilization*. The male agents are hidden in the noun *fertilization*, the bipedal sperm factories that "fertilize" eggs: sperm fertilize eggs. Women are the invisible objects of *fertilize*, men its secret agents.

Hamer's nominals enable him to make the suppressed objects of *fertilize*, women, the **agents** who "have a contraceptive mentality." Women are the intended agents of both the nominal *determination* and the infinitive clause, "to avoid fertilization." Replacing the omitted agents and objects in his sentence fragment produces "Women determine . . . women avoid . . . men fertilize women." Hamer's former use of "persons" turns out to have female-specific reference, and was not intended as a generic. The "contraceptive mentality" belongs solely to women who refuse to allow men to "fertilize" them as though they were cornfields. Hamer managed to make women the culpable agents of *abort* and, simultaneously, denied them agency.

In his final sentence, he enrolled "contraceptive mentality" as the abstract, inanimate agent of *threaten*, *destroy*, and *invert*. Women are again denied agency in the world, but "man," *men*, are presented as the objects/

victims of female non-agency. The "contraceptive mentality . . . threatens to destroy *man* by *inverting* **his** order of values." Hamer doesn't bother to attribute the "order of values" to some deity. This appeal is intended to scare men, to make them feel as though they'll lose something if women abort their sperm (that's "gotten bigger"). He doesn't explain why a woman's decision to abort a fetus would "threaten to destroy" men's "order of values" (but not succeed!).

Hamer's use of language is PUD at its finest—clear without being clear, specific while vague and abstract. What would destroy men's values is women acting as agents in the world, women seizing control of their lives and refusing to allow men to persist in their pathological domination.

CREATING TOPICS IN PUD

English syntax allows us to move virtually any NP to the beginning of a sentence. The rhetorical motivations of speakers and writers and their skill at manipulating the rules determine where an NP will end up in a sentence.[7] Because one NP, rather than another, occurs first in a sentence doesn't mean we have to accept a description as it's presented to us. Yet, once an idea has been syntactically organized in a certain way, we treat that organization as the only way of describing it. Believing that there's only one way to say something is dangerous to our minds because the way speakers organize information in sentences is nothing less than deceptive packaging. They select their syntactic structures, and topic NPs, in terms of what they want their listeners to buy.

Speakers assess the gullibility and attentiveness of their audience, and determine, on that basis, how much they can get away with. The selection of non-agentive topics serves two related rhetorical purposes: it focuses the reader's/listener's attention on what writers and speakers want to foreground, and backgrounds information they have decided to downplay. Backgrounded information is usually agency or responsibility, as the following sentences, which provide almost the same information, show. Typically, none of us is conscious, when we hear or read texts, of authors' selection process which determined the position of NPs in sentences. As you read sentences a. through c., note how the syntax pushes the human agency responsible for having questions further and further into the background.

10.18 a. I would like to raise two questions about your analysis.
    b. Your analysis raises two questions (for me).
    c. Two questions arise as a result of your analysis.

In a. the speaker's responsibility for raising the questions is explicit; version b. attributes responsibility to the analysis itself, with explicit mention of the speaker (*for me*) an optional element. Without the experiencer, the assertion is presented as a general perception. In c., typical of so-called objective (or scientific) writing, the questions have become the topic, denying the subjectivity of the perception and leaving only the analysis as a putative cause of the speaker's concern.

As a method of packaging, selecting a topic is an effective method of damage control; speakers suppress potentially incriminating information, forcing their audience to attend to what is explicit. In such cases, it's difficult to listen for what is not being said, yet what is unspoken is often more important than the actual words we hear. Deciding which NP will be the topic of a sentence is a strategy only for speakers, foregrounding what they want to focus our attention on and backgrounding, by suppression or position, the information they hope we won't think to listen for. We treat topics as givens, as if there were some inevitability in their privileged position. We may not think about it consciously, but we know how to select topics for damage control and how packaging manipulates attention and affects interpretation. As children we know this, although our earliest efforts sometimes fail. The sentences in 10.19 illustrate some of the syntactic options available to a child called upon to explain how a toy "came to be broken." I've ordered them from most honest to most deceptive.

10.19 a. I broke my toy.
        b. The toy was broken by me.
        c. The toy was broken.
        d. The toy got broken.
        e. The toy broke.

However the child decides to package the information, whoever has asked about the toy will probably believe that the child did it. If someone else had broken the toy, the child wouldn't hesitate to name the agent responsible: "Mary did it!"

As we grow older, though, our grasp of the least incriminating ways of presenting damaging information increases, keeping pace with the enormity of the crimes we describe. The sentence in 10.20 was spoken by a psychologist discussing a child raped by her father.

10.20 "She *had* sexual abuse." (Oprah Winfrey Show, February 19, 1988)

That statement shows how the speaker selected her topic to suggest false agency, blaming the victim. The woman raped as a child was foregrounded as the topic, *she*. Her father, the rapist, was deep-backgrounded; his agency was nonexistent in the sentence, buried somewhere in the nominal "sexual abuse." The predicate *had* added several insidious implications. Used as a main verb, *have* denotes possession of objects or characteristics: We **had** *ten dollars*, *She* **had** *a lot of energy*. It also has extended meanings: 'to produce', as in *My dog* **had** *four puppies*; 'to receive', *I* **had** *a letter from Betty*; 'to obtain', *We* **had** *the breakfast special*; 'to suffer from', *She* **had** *chicken pox*;

'to be subject to the experience of', *We* **had** *a lot of trouble last winter*; 'to perform or execute', *We* **had** *an argument*. There are, in addition, uses of *have* with sexual interpretations, for example, *They* **had** *sex*.

All these meanings of *have* are potential in 10.20, and because the speaker topicalized the victim, we were forced by the structure to treat her, erroneously, as the agent. The diverse interpretations of *had* include the possibilities that she "suffered" sexual abuse, or "experienced" it, but without the male agency explicit; the statement also suggested that she "permitted," "received," "obtained," and "performed" the rape. Her agency and, therefore, blameworthiness was strengthened by the sexual implication of *have*, particularly in its common occurrence as an agentless passive: "She was *had.*" Because the speaker foregrounded the female victim as the sentence topic, her description served the purposes of PUD very well, suppressing the male agent of sexual abuse and forcing the interpretation that the child "consented to" the sexual intercourse her father coerced her into.

In 10.21, topic selection erased all human agency from an event, in particular the speaker who said it; it was an effort to divert the listener's attention from the specific action being talked about to a generalization.

10.21 "Errors do happen."

As I mentioned in chapter 8, *happen* occurs frequently in statements that remove human agents from the acts they commit. Because it is impersonal, *happen* cannot properly have an agent, human or otherwise. It means, 'to come to pass', 'to come into being, take place', 'to take place or occur by chance', 'to appear by chance, turn up'. In this case, the speaker intended to imply by foregrounding with *happen* that her act was an "accident of fate," thereby further distancing herself, not only shifting the discussion to an abstract level, but also suggesting a subtle contrast: we "make mistakes," "errors happen." She could have said, "I made a mistake." By choosing *happen*, which cannot take an agent, and using "errors" as her topic, she tacitly acknowledged that she might have done something wrong but simultaneously implied that she should not be held responsible. Had the tactic worked, she might have managed yet a third implication, namely, that anyone who held her responsible for her action was a "bad person."

Non-agentive topics are often the construction of choice for those who want to deny responsibility (and, therefore, culpability) for their actions in the world. Moving now from single statements to longer stretches of discourse, I'll show how speakers choose topics to suppress human agency, foreground what they want us to pay attention to, and limit the damage to themselves, their reputations, and their credibility. The quotation in 10.22 illustrates a telling topic shift performed by an Omaha zookeeper trying to explain, without incriminating himself, how some tigers had died. I've italicized the NPs that figured in his decision process.

10.22 "It appeared that *the tigers* were reacting to *a drug they* had been
    injected with . . . [pause] *that* had been injected in *them*."

How did this topic shift serve specific rhetorical strategies for the
zookeeper? His job may have been on the line. Minimally, he needed a
superficially credible explanation without implying his own responsibility,
and he had at least three ways of explaining why the tigers died. He tried two
of them. Any one of the three NPs in the sentence could have been its topic:
(1) *they* (referring to the tigers), (2) *a drug*, and (3) the omitted agent of *had
been injected*, either *we* or *I* (depending on the actual responsibility for
administering the drug to the tigers, information conveniently omitted from
the zookeeper's description).

In the zookeeper's first version of 10.22, *they* does appear as the topic of
the relative clause. But, after a thoughtful pause, he re-evaluated the situation, made the drug the topic, and moved the pronoun referring to the tigers
into **focus** position[8] at the end of the sentence as an object, *them*. In order to
answer my question fully, we must first consider the third topic option, the
one rejected by the zookeeper from the beginning. The passive provided a
useful syntactic structure for his maneuver, but there's more going on.

If we return to the beginning of the sentence, we notice first that the topic
is nonreferential *it*, substituted for everything following the verb *appear* ("that
the tigers were reacting . . . " and so on). This structural decision enabled the
zookeeper to delay the information he had been asked for, which we proc-
essed as a complex clause. It also made *appear* the main verb of the entire
sentence. It is the suppressed experiencer of *appear*, "to someone," that
should have been explicit in the potential third version of the sentence: *It
appeared to* **me/us** *that the tigers were reacting to a drug* **I/we** *had injected
them with*. Had the experiencer been explicit in the main clause of the
sentence, however, the zookeeper would have had to name the human
agency responsible for the death of the tigers.

I can now return to the rhetorical strategies that motivated the topic shift
from the tigers (*they*) to the drug (*that*). The agentless passive, *had been
injected*, stable in both versions of the sentence, suppressed one candidate
for topic, the agent/experiencer. That left only two NPs to choose from: the
drug or the dead tigers. Having done what he could to suppress reference to
himself, the zookeeper made the inanimate instrument (the drug) the topic,
in order to avoid rementioning the dead tigers, likely forgotten after *appeared*. Furthermore, substituting the pronoun *that* for "a drug" eliminated
any need to mention the drug! If listeners missed the explicit reference to the
drug that killed the tigers in the first version of the sentence, they learned
almost nothing from the zookeeper's revision.

As the zookeeper's sentence illustrates, maneuvering topic shifts during
speech is easy because hearers must process and interpret language more

quickly than we do when we're reading. As a consequence, we often lose track of earlier segments of discourse, forgetting antecedents that we can go back and recover when we're reading. Even in prose, however, topic shifts can be managed unobtrusively as long as the audience goes along with the writer's assumptions. The excerpt of 10.23 demonstrates how topic selection foregrounds only some information and controls our interpretive processes over a brief span of discourse. I've italicized both logical topics and NPs that have been made topics so readers can follow the writer's topic shifts.

10.23 *Middle East harems* are inherited. . . . *Not every potentate's son* is glad of *that*. *The youth* bequeathed a *houseful of heavyweights*, did not always admire his *father's* choices. In bygone years, *the harem women* were fed *oils*. *Fat* was the fashion. (*Sioux City Journal*, 8 July, 1979, A–13)

Speakers and writers choose their topics not on the basis of what they think their audience might know, but on the basis of what they want us to notice. Selection of a topic in a first sentence determines what kinds of statements can or cannot follow in the remainder of the sequence. The author of 10.23 guessed that his audience would share his belief system and be willing to read in all the connecting material he omitted. The topic of the first sentence is *Middle East harems*, while that of the last one is *[f]at*. Not only did the readers of this story have to work hard to make sense of it; they had to interpret it with naive credulity. How did the writer get from harems to the alleged fatness of the women in harems?

The shifts in topic were managed by three agentless passives, *are inherited, bequeathed,* and *are fed*. The agent of one passive, *are inherited,* had to be *potentate's son*, but it wasn't overt until the next sentence, where it was the topic of the predicate *is glad*. "Potentate's son" became "[t]he youth" in the third sentence, the topic (logically, the object) of another agentless passive verb, *bequeathed,* but also the agent of the main verb *admires*. The agent of *bequeathed* appeared later in the sentence, but only as a possessive, *father's choices*. Although the agents of the first two passives were available in the context, those structures enabled the writer to manipulate sentence topics so that readers internalized only the most accessible information.

The transition from focus to topic in the last two sentences illustrates how this strategic use of structure controls our interpretation. The direct object of the fourth sentence, *oils* (in "focus" position), provided the conceptual link to *[f]at*, the topic of the last sentence, and the idea we are left with at the end of the paragraph, "Fat was the fashion." The discourse antecedent for both *oils* and *fat* occurred in an earlier clause, *heavyweights*. Although the apparent topic of the paragraph was harem women, the agency was entirely male. The writer used agentless passives to foreground the women and their alleged fatness, and to background the male agency controlling their lives.

The agents of the first two truncated passives were explicit, but separated from their verbs. There was no overt agent, however, for *were fed*, something we may not register because the writer moved immediately to "[f]at" in the following sentence, in which there is no sex-specific reference whatsoever. Who fed oils to the women in the harem?

I can supply the sex obliterated by the inanimate nouns *fat* and *fashion*. *Fat*, of course, referred to the women's bodies, and *fashion* to the male perceptions (called "beauty") that required the women to be fattened in order to please their masters. Although the immediate agents of *fed* were probably male attendants, the one who commanded the act(s) was undoubtedly the potentate who owned the women and then bequeathed them to his son. The principal agent throughout this paragraph is the potentate father, who appeared explicitly only in possessives ('he who owns'), "potentate's" and "father's," and was conveniently erased from awareness in the final two sentences.

In order to read this passage without wincing, one must share the writer's point of view. That is, one must be a white man. The way the author set the objectified women up as topics in 10.23 illustrates what feminists have called the "objectification of women." It appeals to western men's voyeurism and fantasies about eastern women and the exoticness of middle eastern women in particular, as represented in stereotypical depictions of the harem. A condescending male tone pervades this paragraph because it was written as a "male interest" story, and it reflects the writer's sense of his own superiority to the women he wrote about. The writer foregrounded the women living in harems. The specifically male agency that acts on these women was **backgrounded**, the men moving quietly behind the verbs, shadowy agents who elude our awareness. Only the women's "fat" bodies and whether they're pleasing to the potentate's son concerned the writer. The passage also implied, however, that readers were expected to sympathize with the son who inherits fat women as property from his father.

My next example illustrates how we may miss syntactic maneuvers that expose the male conceptual framework when we interpret PUD descriptions.

10.24 *A two-hour special* starts *the giant saga of two soldiers*—*one* compassionate, *one* ruthless. *The women they* loved, betrayed, and *were betrayed by*.

The topic shift in this *TV Guide* description of the mini-series *Once an Eagle* (1976) may have been constructed to get the attention of the television audience, but it also reveals how the writer conceived of that audience and the assumptions they would go along with. The topic of the first sentence is *[a] two-hour special*; the object of the verb is *the giant saga*, with *two soldiers* as the object of the preposition *of*. The male characters are salvaged from their syntactic unimportance by the description of them that ends the sen-

tence, "one compassionate, one ruthless." What follows is a sentence fragment, a lone noun phrase composed of the topic NP, [t]he women, and a
clause, they loved, betrayed, and were betrayed by. Replaced by the pronoun
they, the soldiers were the agents of two of the verbs in that clause, loved and
betrayed, but the **object** of the third, a passive with its agent, the women,
moved back to topic position.

Bear in mind that we are looking at a passive clause. It could have been an
active ("The women betrayed them") in which "the women" would have
been both agent of the verb and topic of the clause. What, then, is the
rhetorical purpose for the passive? Two propositions, "the soldiers loved the
women" and "the soldiers betrayed the women," are barely visible in that
clause. The ordering of the propositions suggests a chronological interpretation: 'the soldiers loved the women, betrayed the women, and then the women
betrayed the soldiers.' (Note that whether or not the women loved the soldiers is irrelevant!) The mini-series was about the two soldiers, but retopical-
izing the women foregrounded their betrayal, and, simultaneously, backgrounded the implication that the soldiers betrayed the women first. In
10.24, retopicalization of an agent enabled the writer to cast the female
characters as the ultimate betrayers, and de-emphasized the behavior and
responsibility of the soldiers. The control of our interpretive processes thus
exercised extended to the way we viewed the mini-series: the women and
their lives and feelings were backgrounded. Their only significance in the
development of the plot was their function as the objects of the soldiers' love
and, as agents, in the role of betrayers. The syntactic structure of the fragment
dictated that we perceive the women only in relation to the soldiers, and the
men as the victims of the women's betrayal.

Sentence structures package information to divert, mislead, and distract
us. As the preceding examples indicate, the selection of topics is one of the
syntactic processes that gives speakers greater power in speech situations
because they can control how we process and interpret information by fore-
gounding what they want us to remember while backgrounding what they
hope we won't pay attention to. Speakers choose one NP rather than another
as a topic by assessing our willingness to buy what they're selling. If they
judge us to be resistant to some degree, they choose "packaging" that they
think will be alluring enough to get us to let down our guard.

There are also several different ways sentence topics are created, and this
syntactic variety makes identifying coercive uses more difficult. The examples in 10.25 illustrate four cases in which topic selection, combined with
other structures I've already discussed, packaged information to downplay or
hide facts.

10.25 a. What Sheehan [author of A Bright Shining Lie] later discovered was
        that Vann [u.s. proconsul in Viet Nam, 1962–72] suffered from a

sexual compulsion that led him to seduce hundreds of young women. His career was permanently stained even before he arrived in Viet Nam when he narrowly averted being court-martialed for the statutory rape of a 15-year-old baby-sitter. (Laurence Zuckerman's review of *A Bright Shining Lie, Time*, 17 October, 1988, 80)

b. As Jack the Ripper attacked women's wombs, nuclear war will attack the whole earth. (Radical Feminist's summation of Jane Caputi's presentation at the W.I.T.C.H. Forum)

c. The bank [Bank of Credit and Commerce International, located in Luxembourg] allegedly laundered drug profits for cocaine kingpins Escobar and Ochoa, handled political payoffs for Noriega and funneled money for Khashoggi's Iran-*contra* arms deals. (Caption beneath photos accompanying Janice Castro's report, "The Cash Cleaners," *Time*, 24 October, 1988, 66)

d. "Try a subscription now, and if not satisfied, cancel any time." (Television advertisement for *Prevention* magazine)

Each of these examples focuses our attention on the immediate context provided by the writer/speaker and, thereby, encourages us to "forget" contradictory information. In a., John Paul Vann was described as a victim who "suffered from a sexual compulsion," and the nominal *compulsion* became the agent "that led him to seduce hundreds of young women." Even the verb *seduce* disguised what was probably rape by suppressing any suggestion of coercion or violence. Consider, for example, the distinction made between *rape* and *seduce* in 10.25.a. Although *rape* was used as noun in that quotation, the semantic contrast between *rape*, as a verb, and *seduce* remains. To rape someone necessarily involves force; the verb specifies that the individuals who have been raped were forced to engage in sex against their will. *Seduce*, in contrast, implies persuasion on the agent's part. The verb presupposes that the human object, having initially said "no" to sexual intercourse, was persuaded by the agent's persistence, generosity, and/or debating skills and willingly agreed to fucking. The patriarchal idea of what can be interpreted as consent determines which verb is chosen. *Seduce* distinguishes verbal coercion (pressure) from *rape*, physical violence (force). Ordinarily, only men are the suppressed agents of rape, but either sex can be said to seduce the other, so it is thought of as nonviolent and less coercive. Furthermore, the use of *statutory* to modify *rape* in this example indicates that Vann's victims said or did something that he could interpret as consent, but their age negated it.

In b., the topic "nuclear war" erased the fact that men invented nuclear weapons, spend trillions of dollars manufacturing them, and sit before the buttons that will send them on their murderous trajectories. "Nuclear war" will "attack" nothing. It will be the consequence of men's stupidity, greed, and arrogance. They will attack each other. Jack the Ripper, in contrast, was cast as an aberrant man, an individual responsible for his actions, while the men who wage and profit from war or the threat of war weren't held responsible. This erasure of male agency protected them.

In c., the possessive noun *Khashoggi's* forced us to make him responsible for the Iran-*contra* deals engineered by Oliver North and condoned by John Poindexter and Robert MacFarlane, Ronald Reagan's advisors. The example in d. is an imperative, a command in which the agent/topic *you* is ordinarily suppressed (understood), for example, *Close the door, Get out of here.* The result of this omission is that, in the second part of the sentence, the object/topic/experiencer of *satisfied*, also *you*, was suppressed. Chances are, the viewers, busily processing the imperative and awkward psych-predicate, failed to hear the end of the sentence, "simply cancel." If they "try a subscription" (instead of "subscribe"), they'll be stuck with paying for something they didn't really want.

Once we grasp the idea that promoting a given noun to topic position doesn't reflect inherent properties of the noun, isn't necessarily an accurate description of what the sentence purports to talk about or the "inevitable" way of making a statement, challenging such descriptions becomes easier. As readers probably noticed, though, the predicates and sentence structures I've analyzed occur together: "dummy *it*" is often the topic of agentless passives and impersonal verbs; specifically female descriptions are often nouns, while male activities are described by verbs; and, in general, the structure of English ignores or erases the agency of men and focuses our attention on their female victims when it suits their purposes. As a corollary of these patterns, the language enables men to deny women's capacity to act as agents except when they want to blame us for their stupidity and malice.

Chapter 11

Speaking Out

Throughout *Speaking Freely* I've described specific examples of how English semantics and syntax reflect the assumptions of the Patriarchal Universe of Discourse and, thereby, perpetuate male dominance and women's oppression. Yet, I've written an entire book in English. How can I write in a language I want to change? Isn't there a contradiction when I use structures I've described as patriarchal?

Yes. I have made a choice between silence and risk. Communicating what I know about PUD was more important to me than silence. I made compromises in order to describe how English reflects and perpetuates men's versions of reality. I could have written innovatively, making up words or constructing sentences in new ways, but linguistic innovation can try readers' patience and willingness to try something new, without convincing them to undertake such changes themselves. So I elected a middle course: I stayed with the familiar structure of English and avoided, as much as possible, typically patriarchal words. Because my purpose is communicating information, linguistic innovation could have limited my book's intelligibility.

Speaking Freely has other contradictions as well. Our lives are built around many contradictions that we negotiate and renegotiate to the best of our ability. Trying to live as a free agent in a patriarchy is an essential contradiction for any woman. One cannot be free and live subordinate to men, yet we continue to act on the choices we have and resist men's efforts to proscribe them. Just as we must fight for control of our bodies, we must fight to be speakers, to construct a woman-centered universe of discourse.

LANGUAGE AND THOUGHT

What we say *is* who we are. Creating a universe of discourse that reflects a different way of perceiving the world requires understanding how the language we use indicates how we think and our awareness of the conceptual

202

framework we've learned. My concern for the structures that perpetuate patriarchy is founded on two assumptions: (1) that a language reflects the dominant culture and the speakers who define "legitimate" discourse; (2) that our conceptual structure is largely determined by our first language. My assumptions about the relationship between the language we speak and the way we think are known as the Sapir-Whorf Hypothesis.

The Sapir-Whorf Hypothesis, named for Edward Sapir and Benjamin Lee Whorf,[1] is often represented as claiming that we are incapable of thinking beyond the limits set by our native language, but Sapir didn't say that. He distinguished between the flow of thought and the linguistic symbols that represent ideas, and suggested that "language is . . . a prepared road or groove" (1921, 15) into which our thoughts "slip." Do we think the way we talk? I think we do. I'm sure that Sapir's "grooves" limit the options available to us for describing our perceptions. Many people ridicule Feminist attempts to change the structural properties of English, and some women claim that they don't feel excluded by words like *he* and *man*.[2] That others of us do feel excluded and invisible seems irrelevant to them. They refuse to question why they interpret male words as including them and perceive efforts like mine as hostile. That their resistance to questioning how they think originated in their linguistic socialization doesn't occur to them. For such readers, my discussion of how English forces us to describe people who are differently abled, later in this chapter, and my own difficulty finding descriptions that aren't inherently negative illustrate how language limits thought.

Some can tolerate more contradictions than others. If we were utterly incapable of thinking outside PUD I would have had no reason to write this book. Yet, the language we speak does restrict our range of conceptual exploration, and I am sure that we will continue to think as we do as long as we accept, and perpetuate through our own use, descriptions of the world based on PUD. As part of our project of redefining ourselves as agents in the world, we must resist allowing our thinking to flow into the man-made channels that eat away at the larger masses of thought lying outside them. Language focuses our attention on what we believe we know, because we can talk about it, and we neglect to glance aside at what borders the patriarchal grooves—the much larger, but apparently formless lands of all that we do not, but might know if we stepped outside the mainstream.

For those of us who can hear, language is only patterned noise we have learned to associate with specific ideas; it structures our thinking in ways similar to other foregrounding devices. Like a road map, it foregrounds those aspects of experience deemed significant by a culture and, simultaneously, backgrounds concepts for which it provides no labels. As a topographical map highlights aspects different from those of a road map, each culture's map provides a few descriptions of experience from possibilities we remain unconscious of.

Language draws our attention to only some experiences in some ways, making it difficult to grasp and articulate those it doesn't provide labels or descriptions for. We can describe feelings and perceptions English doesn't provide words for, but finding an accurate description takes time and patience and some fluency with the language. Because English foregrounds only some aspects of experience as possibilities, we have a repertoire of specific gestures, sounds, words, sentence structures, metaphors, that focus our attention on just those activities named by patriarchy: the "naturalness" of heterosexuality, the "natural" inferiority of women and superiority of men, the "naturalness" and "inevitability" of war, the earth as an object to be conquered and controlled and its resources as "ours" by "right," and the inherent superiority of *homo sapiens* and the inferiority of other species. These descriptions present but one possible version of our world and how we can perceive and relate to it.

Patriarchal culture presents us with these ready-made descriptions as though they are accurate. When we learn patriarchal descriptions as children, we abandon perceptions we have no way of describing. Eventually, we perceive what the culture has taught us to perceive, because we perceive only what we expect to. If we believe that what we perceive is all there is, we miss all the activity going on beyond the descriptions permitted by patriarchal discourse. The adult daughter raped by her father, convinced by the repeated assertion of the innocence of children and the happy childhood myth, for example, either forgets her experience altogether or comes to believe that she was responsible for her father's actions. She assumes she could have controlled a situation in which she was powerless.

I've already discussed some of the structural properties of English that make it a superb patriarchal language: the semantic organization of human nouns that forces us to think of men as quintessential "humanity" and women as subhuman; the sentence patterns that allow men to suppress their agency (passives, impersonal verbs, psych-predicates); verbs converted into nominals, a process that makes actions in the world into abstractions; the sex-marked predicates, which describe men as the only actors who count heterosexually. There are, in addition, structural ambiguities inherent in compounds like *father rape* and *daughter rape*, descriptions which, despite the word *rape*, incorporate the idea of mutuality suggested by *incest*. Structurally, English makes it impossible to identify the perpetrator and his victim unless we make the effort to do so in every instance.

English presents us with other problems in discourse I haven't described, and I'll indicate only a few of them here. Deictic elements, for example, which are supposed to provide means for uniquely identifying people or objects without ambiguity, fail to be specific enough in numerous contexts. We find ourselves in a quandary whenever we describe situations in which all the participants are same-sex, for example. Unless we know and use individuals' proper names every time we mention them, we end up with descriptions in which the identity of the persons involved is confusing. The sentences in 11.1 illustrate the unavoidable ambiguity of *she* in such contexts.

11.1 a. While Mary took a shower, Joan pondered where *she* wanted to eat.
   b. Theresa went to the store and Marge vacuumed the mess *she*'d made in the kitchen.
   c. When Terry left the room, Anita thought about what
      she $\begin{Bmatrix} \text{would} \\ \text{might} \end{Bmatrix}$ do.

Having only a single pronoun to refer to individuals of the same sex makes it hard to attribute agency without ambiguity. In both a. and b., *she* can refer equally appropriately to Joan or Mary or Theresa or Marge, respectively. This inherent ambiguity is somewhat lessened if we add modals, as I've done in c. Because Anita is doing the thinking, *would* inclines us to interpret *she* as referring to her, whereas *might* sways us toward Terry as the agent of *do* (at least in my dialect). The modals suggest one or the other woman more strongly, but the reference of *she* in c. remains uncertain.

Similarly, the deictic specificity attributed to *the* fails to function in contexts in which there are two or more identical objects or people. In 11.2, both individuals have a truck parked in the same driveway.

11.2 Speaker A: "I left my wallet in *the* truck."
   Speaker B: "Which truck."

Here, Speaker A was thinking specifically of her truck as the logical place where she might have left her wallet. For her, *the* was clear. For Speaker B, however, *the* referred to B's truck. Because A travels frequently in B's truck as well as her own, and because A leaves her wallet in many places, B's truck among them, she thought A was saying she'd left her wallet in B's truck. In this case, *the* underspecifies its reference. The intended reference of A and the ambiguity pointed out by B are both accurate. In the context, and given knowledge of the other factors involved, either interpretation is equally plausible, and *the* fails to provide unique identification.

In other contexts, unexpected modification betrays a speaker's conceptual framework. In chapter 4, I described how the semantic structure of English human nouns reflects the assumption of heterosexuality. Behaviors assumed to be normal are taken for granted. In popular usage, for example, the word *sex* refers to heterosexual sex as though it were the only variety. When someone mentions heterosexuality explicitly, however, we are reminded of other possibilities. A closeted Lesbian found herself unexpectedly "out" when she talked about "heterosexual couples" and "heterosexual households" in a sociology class. The heterosexual students listening to her knew immediately that she was a Lesbian, because none of them would have felt it necessary to modify *couples* or *households*. By modifying nouns that the heterosexual students didn't think required qualification, the student drew attention to the fact that her conceptual framework differed from that of her classmates. Heterosexuals assume their sexuality, Lesbians and gays make the distinction because we think differently. What appears initially to be overspecification is, in fact, necessary.

Euphemizing what speakers perceive to be negative or repugnant aspects of the world is a familiar discourse tactic, and I've discussed it at various points in this book. Euphemisms pretty up people, objects, behaviors, and events perceived by members of a culture as bad, immoral, or terrible, and they allow us to distance ourselves conceptually from "them." We forget that we are "they." To gauge the degree of repugnance with which people perceive someone or something, we need only count how many euphemisms are available in the language. Death and dying, for example, aren't perceived as celebratory events in western cultures, and we have numerous euphemisms to avoid mentioning death explicitly: "pass away," "gone to one's reward," "pushing up daisies," "gone to heaven," "meeting St. Peter," "crossed the final bridge."

Poverty and aging are also aspects of the real world speakers euphemize. In a society that boasts of the wealth only a few actually enjoy, poor people are a repugnant embarrassment, and expressions that suppress explicit reference to the people who live in poverty proliferate apace with superficial attempts to provide them with better living conditions: "the poor," "the poverty-stricken," "the homeless," "the economically disadvantaged." These descriptions make both victims and agents invisible as people and hide the fact that the structure of u.s. society perpetuates poverty. Poverty itself is an abstraction made purposeful agent in *poverty-stricken*, in which the human agents and victims are suppressed, as though the condition "struck" the unnamed. Because PUD values youth, or the appearance of youth, especially in women, English provides euphemisms for aging that hide our underlying fear of the process: "the elderly," "senior citizens," "advanced in age," and "over the hill." Many people believe that whatever they refuse to talk about doesn't exist or is less real and euphemism is one device for avoiding whatever realities they wish to deny.

Neil Postman has maintained that "euphemisms are a means through which a culture may alter its imagery and by doing so change its style, its priorities, and its values" (1982, 262), but, as the editors of *Time* magazine observed, "the persistent growth of euphemism . . . represents a danger to thought and action, since its fundamental intent is to deceive" (1982, 256).[3] But western culture perceives some aspects of reality as so horrible that euphemizing them is virtually impossible, and the descriptions that follow these negative concepts dehumanize the people victimized by them. One of those things-that-cannot-be-euphemized is the idea of being incapacitated or

disabled in some way. The words and phrases that describe physical limitations reflect the negative attitudes we've learned. We think of being able to
do something as normal, and being incapable as inherently negative. Mobility is positively valued; immobility is negative. Conceptually, *able/not able*
are fixed in a binary, either/or relation in which ability to perform is assumed.
The way we conceptualize abilities focuses our vocabulary negatively on
what we cannot do, on what we lack, rather than what we can do. When all
or part of our bodies can't perform in ways thought of as normal, we are
described as *dis*abled. There are no positive ways of thinking or talking about
the abilities of people who have physical or anatomical limitations; what they
can't do becomes their only identifying characteristic and their many other
qualities are conceptually suppressed.

People who cannot perform one physical activity or another are thought of
as "defective" or "deformed." They are "disabled," "crippled," "handi-
capped," or "physically-challenged." We have no positive ways to describe
something we cannot do. There aren't even any neutral terms in the English
vocabulary. The only phrases that point us toward a different way of thinking
about the range of human abilities are "differently abled," and the acronym
T.A.B.s, 'temporarily able-bodied', which reminds the able-bodied that an
automobile accident, a fire or disease may make them suddenly unable to
perform acts they take for granted. Being able is good; being unable is bad,
and the idea that there are events in our lives we cannot control frightens us.
Yet, there are areas of our lives over which we don't have control, and some
disabled people consider the phrase "*differently abled*" to be a ridiculous
euphemism because there are things they cannot do and this fact is a reality
of their lives they have to deal with every day. Euphemizing their reality
doesn't change their lives; shifting the focus away from what they can't do to
what they can is a useless pretense. As Catherine Odette has commented,
saying that she is "differently abled" suggests that she's able to perform
differently, that, instead of walking up a hill, she can fly to the top.

Yet, we must confront how we think and examine the meaning of what we
say. Recognizing how our language hurts others and admitting that we don't
know how to change begin the process of confronting the conceptual restrictions that determine the language we use. We can certainly refuse to use
words and phrases that extend the language of disability metaphorically as
negative descriptions of events and situations. In common usage, both
cripple and *paralyze* are used negatively to describe an inability to act:
"Losing their best wide receiver has *crippled* Chicago's offense," "I was
paralyzed by fear." Chicago's offense wasn't crippled; it wasn't as good as it
would have been with their best wide receiver in the line-up. We may be
unable to move or act because we're afraid, but we aren't paralyzed. Similarly, because both seeing and hearing metaphorically represent knowledge
or understanding in common expressions (e.g., "I *see* what you mean," "I

hear you") *blind* and *deaf* are frequently used metaphorically to mean ignorant or unaware.[4] Such changes aren't difficult, and thinking about what we
say commits us to changing how we think.

Less obvious immediately are syntactic maneuvers in descriptions of disabilities. One in particular, the phrase "hidden disabilities," was brought to
my attention by Anne Leighton when she gave a workshop on the subject
called "Who's Doing the Hiding?" Her title challenges the distortion created
by the agentless passive *hidden* which seems to "modify" *disabilities* as
though someone were hiding a disability. The buried proposition of *hidden*
suggests that individuals purposely hide their disabilities and implies a secre-
tive intent on their part. In fact, this passive modifier functions as a perceptual
reversal, making disabled people responsible for the act of hiding when what
is meant is that others are unable to perceive the disability. That is, there are
no apparent visual signals to cue people who are strangers to someone who
is deaf or chronically ill or has heart trouble, diabetes, or arthritis. The
description reflects the assumption that everyone is able-bodied unless they
tell us otherwise, and puts responsibility for declaring the existence of disabilities on those who have them rather than on the individuals who don't
perceive them. As more and more of us are disabled by chemicals in our
food, poisons in our water, and the toxicity of our environment, the practice
of assuming able-bodiedness becomes less supportable as the probability
increases that we, or someone we know, has Epstein-Barr Syndrome or some
other type of environmental illness (EI).

Regardless of the specifics of disabilities, this area of our vocabulary requires complete restructuring, as my own descriptive efforts indicate. There is
probably no good reason to think positively of disabilities, but perpetuating
negative descriptions serves no useful purpose either. As the numbers of
those disabled by war, automobile accidents, job-related illnesses, malnutrition, drugs, and neurological diseases increase, the most feasible approach is
accepting the idea that being disabled is a permanent aspect of our reality.
Although I've tried to avoid the negative descriptions of PUD, I haven't
succeeded nearly as well as I wanted to, at least in part because I am writing
generally. Kate Moran has pointed out to me that one way of avoiding the
negative structures I'm discussing is to speak specifically—"She has cerebral
palsy," "The child was born with club feet," "I use sign language to communicate with those who can't hear." If we're to change our thinking about
physical inabilities, we'll have to change the way we describe them, and my
futile efforts should convince readers of the need to unlearn PUD ways of
thinking as well as illustrating the difficulties involved. Until we achieve that,
however, we must seek ways of describing our bodies that acknowledge the
existence of disabilities without attempting to euphemize or ignore them. We
may not be able to learn to think differently about abilities immediately, but
we can refuse to use words like *blind, deaf, cripple*, and *lame* as negative
metaphors. We don't need to call someone "blind" when we mean they're

unaware of something, or to talk about "lame excuses" and a "crippled economy."

Euphemism may properly fail as a way to describe people who are disabled, but in other areas of our lives, equally insupportable euphemistic expressions proliferate. In my analysis of sex-specific nouns and verbs, I showed how actions and behaviors attributed to women are thought of as inherently negative. Yet, there are certain acts and behaviors identified as both negative and primarily male, such as rape and battering. In contrast to the negative vocabularies that describe women and physical abilities, euphemisms abound for male violence. In these cases, men have created a plethora of euphemisms to downplay their violence and hide their sexual exploitation of women and children, and these expressions quickly find their way into common usage. Men beat their wives, but the media talk about *spouse abuse, battered spouses*, and *domestic violence*. In the last phrase, *domestic* hides male agency and focuses our attention on the places where men beat their wives and children, dwellings, disguising violent acts as well as erasing the male agents. Men rape children, but we talk about *incest, sexual abuse* and *molestation*, making the men who commit crimes of violence against children invisible. The most euphemistic word for describing how men exploit children sexually we inherited from the Greeks: *pedophilia*. Translated literally, it means 'love of children'; 'love' not only euphemizes sexual activities but disguises male predation.

Men create euphemisms to control how we perceive and interpret their actions. These aren't descriptions we should emulate because they distort reality, making the bad seem good and the merely innocuous seem wonderful. Yet, some women prefer euphemisms for the same reason. A booth selling turkey-basters at the Michigan Womyn's Music Festival, for example, advertised "parthenogenetic wands" for sale, fostering the illusion that sperm aren't involved in Lesbian pregnancies. Sado-masochists are now describing themselves as "differently pleasured," a description that accomplishes several conceptual tricks at once. First, it exploits the positive phrase "differently abled" and the oppressed people it refers to by linking sado-masochists to them. Because being differently abled isn't a matter of choice, "differently pleasured" suggests that sado-masochists haven't chosen their sexual behaviors and that they are oppressed for something they can't help. Second, it obliterates the fact that pain is the defining element of sado-masochism, and that its sexuality requires humiliation, degradation, and elaborate "scenes" based on stereotyped power-over relationships: teacher/student, parent/child, master/slave, nazi/Jew. Third, the phrase uses women's attempts to value differences (such as class, race, and ethnic background) positively to suggest that sado-masochism is nothing more than another difference we should not only tolerate but think of as a good thing.

There is a point at which we identify the function of euphemism in our speech with politeness and kindness because PUD describes truth-telling as making waves or being mean and rude. Honesty is not valued positively, so we increasingly use an oblique mode of speaking in which we disconnect what we say from what we are thinking or what we mean. In public discourse, rape has become "unconsented sexual activity," murder is "neutralizing someone," and a man who beats his wife commits "domestic violence." We are so numbed to dishonest uses of language that the oblique mode permeates our private discourse, too. Sometimes speaking obliquely is harmful, sometimes it's not. But it is always dishonest, even when it is a defensive tactic for avoiding emotional conflict and physical violence.

A couple of examples will illustrate my point. A friend casually described a pleasant phone conversation with an acquaintance, saying, "I had a warm encounter with her." She didn't "have an encounter." Two women talked to each other by telephone, perhaps with mutual pleasure. What the speaker avoided saying was that she had *enjoyed* her conversation with the other woman. No one was harmed by her description, but the lack of motivation for it shows how thoroughly the oblique mode has become our linguistic habit.

My next example is more complex. I arranged to have lunch with an acquaintance to discuss her comments on a manuscript of mine. A couple of days after we'd made the appointment, the manuscript and her comments appeared in my mailbox with a note that said, "Thought I'd just send these and make it easier all around." Because I wanted to be sure that I was accurately interpreting the meaning of her statement, I called her to confirm my guess that what she'd meant was, "I'm cancelling our lunch date."

What factors do we consider when we choose to say something other than exactly what we mean? I can understand why men prefer the word "pedophilia" to saying "I rape children," why generals talk about "neutralizing the enemy" instead of how many soldiers were killed, why politicians prefer legislation that deals with "domestic violence" rather than "wife beating." Euphemism and other forms of oblique discourse serve the interests of the powerful. Any use of language that directs our attention away from the violence men do when they assert their power over other people enables them to deny their agency and responsibility for what they do. At the same time, oblique language enables women to pretend that they don't know what men are doing. If we remain "unaware" of male violence, we don't have to challenge them and, in this way, avoid the possibility of yet more male violence.

But what motivates us to use oblique language among ourselves, particularly in private situations where there is no audience to judge the relative merits of our behaviors? Why should those of us who are without social and political power perpetuate male forms of discourse? What is our investment in not saying what we mean? Using my friend's statement, I'll speculate. We don't say what we mean when we don't want to be honest. We don't want to be honest if we believe we won't like the results. Lying is a way of avoiding conflict. My friend didn't want to discuss whether or not we'd have lunch. As a discourse tactic, not saying what she meant was a way of exercising power over me without having to be responsible for her decision. She had decided she didn't want to have lunch with me, knew that she had to inform me of her decision without giving me an opportunity to ask her why she'd changed her mind, and was confident that I'd decipher her intention accurately. Being oblique gave her a way to inform me of her decision without discussing it; she made a unilateral decision that involved both of us without giving me an opportunity to argue whether we should have lunch. She reserved to herself all the power in the situation and invalidated any idea I might have had that we had a relationship in which we could discuss the pros and cons of having lunch together.

The meanings and results of her language are clearer than her motivations for it, but indicating some of the possibilities will illustrate why we have to say what we mean to each other. Two elements of her statement alerted me to hidden meaning: *just*, which downplayed the significance of her decision, and *make it easier all around*. With "all around" she suppressed explicit mention of the two of us. Her omission of explicit reference to her own agency was also important, but it didn't affect my interpretation. It was her choice of the adjective *easier*, because she didn't explain who her decision made "it easier" for, that told me she was trying to avoid saying something. Since I had had no part in the decision, I wasn't the beneficiary of *easier*. She was. How did her decision make "it" easier for her, though? Maybe she didn't want to have lunch on that day or something more important had come up and she didn't want to discuss the change in plans. Maybe she thought I'd be angry, disappointed, or annoyed by a change in plans, and she didn't want to deal with how I might feel about her decision. Maybe she doesn't like me and spoke obliquely to put me off; that way, she didn't have to be responsible for what she felt. Maybe she was angry at me about something I'd done or said and being oblique enabled her to cancel our lunch without discussing her feelings with me. Perhaps she thought I didn't want to have lunch with her, and using *easier* was her way of claiming that her decision was motivated by concern for me. Or, her self-esteem may be so low that she thought I didn't want to have lunch with her and, in order to avoid my hypothetical rejection, she cancelled our lunch before I could. Whatever her motivation, her goal was avoiding a situation she believed would be painful for her, and she succeeded.

TALKING OUR WAY OUT OF PUD

What we say reflects how we think, and there is no biological determinism that justifies the habits of thought revealed in our language use. Yet, our experience with unlearning racist language indicates that simply avoiding prejudiced and harmful ways of talking won't necessarily change our assumptions or how we think. Suppressing language that reflects racist attitudes seems to leave racist ideas in place and functioning, submerging them where, like polluted ground water, they become invisible but more dangerous. Because we don't know they're there and so can't eradicate them, they gradually seep into our behaviors and poison our best intentions and our will to change.

There are at least four different ways our language use may signal our attitudes I want to distinguish, based on the intentions that motivate our linguistic choices. Racism isn't a simple either/or, and there are white people who believe people of color are inferior to them and those of us who don't believe that we should judge anyone on the basis of their skin color. White people of the first type I consider racists because they choose to believe that they are superior to people of color (and anyone else who is different from them, including queers, atheists, conscientious objectors, environmental activists). They have no intention of changing their language or their beliefs and they condone violence done to others who differ from them. They believe that they have the "right" to kill "niggers," "queers," and "pinko commies," and what they say is what they think.

Then there are the "closet racists" who are harder to identify. They also believe that anyone who isn't white, male, and heterosexual is inferior to them, but, realizing how their language can betray them, choose to scrupulously avoid racist words and phrases. The fact that someone doesn't use the word *nigger* or the word *black* to mean 'evil' or 'dangerous', avoids anti-Semitic expressions like *to jew someone down* or the insulting label *Indian-giver*, doesn't mean they have unlearned the racist assumptions they grew up with. They have only realized that, in order to retain their white, male, heterosexual power over others, they should give the appearance of being fair and unbiased. This second type is, I believe, a majority of the population in the u.s.

I belong in the third category, people who believe that any prejudice based on difference is wrong, who have chosen to change our language, yet who, in spite of our best intentions, retain vestiges of the institutionalized racism we learned as children. Because, however, we reject racism and disapprove of racist assumptions, choosing to avoid expressions that reflect prejudice forces us to confront, on a day-to-day basis, the racism entrenched in our minds. The fourth category differs from the third in only one way: they are people of color whose usage reflects the racist attitudes of English-speaking societies. (Michael Jackson's use of *black* in his lyrics is one example.) None of us is immune to the damaging conceptual structures of PUD even if our own interest would have it otherwise.

What I have said about institutionalized racism and racist language is also true of misogyny and sexist usage. I know from my own experience that many men continue to believe that women are inferior to them although they don't use *man* as a generic and no longer tell jokes that expose their misogyny. Dropping overtly racist or sexist usage from our speech suppresses evidence of our prejudices, but the assumptions themselves remain unexamined and securely entrenched in our thinking. We cannot simply stop thinking in PUD terms and suddenly begin to think in woman-centered ways, but there are a number of ways we can disrupt PUD and begin to loosen its hold on our minds.

I remain convinced that becoming self-conscious about our linguistic choices gives us immediate access to our thought processes and that continual monitoring of what we are about to say will gradually enable us to unlearn patriarchal ways of thinking and create new conceptual patterns in their place. Ceasing to use racist, anti-Semitic, and sexist language at least indicates our willingness to change, even if we are indistinguishable from the closet type who pays lipservice to change without commitment to it. Self-conscious language use requires us to conscientiously examine virtually every word that comes to mind *before* we say it and confront the PUD conceptual structures we're striving to supplant and, simultaneously, create new ways of thinking. In this transitional endeavor, we have to rethink, un-think, and creatively think anew. We have to resist men's efforts to hold us within the boundaries of the world as they describe it and, at the same time, find our own ways to conceive the world. Other thinkers than I have already provided specific ways we can accomplish both conceptual feats, from re-claiming old words to the creation of a new language altogether. Some Feminist writers, like Mary Daly (1978, 1984, 1987) and Judith Fetterley (1978), to name only two, have described different aspects of the "reading in" process as it affects women and suggested how we can resist the demands of male subjectivity. Men strut, posture, and exhort upon the world they perceive as stage, now yelling, now muttering, gesturing all the while: "See me, feel me, touch me, heal me," luring us to identify with them. For our own well-being, we must resist their demands for attention.

Language is power, in ways more literal than most people think. When we speak, we exercise the power of language to transform reality. Why don't more of us realize the connection between language and power? Suzette Haden Elgin attributes our lack of awareness to the "bill of goods" about English sold to us by male grammarians (1989, 5), who have convinced us that

1. skilled uses of language are either innate or the result of years of training;
2. our own language skills are "ordinary" and that people who are linguistically skilled are geniuses, people with doctorates, or people who "have charisma."

Elgin states that these beliefs are false, and I agree with her. However, al-though I debunked the claims of patriarchal grammarians in chapter 1 and

discussed some of the falsehoods their descriptions of English have perpetrated, I disagree with Elgin's assertion that "Language is the only source of
real power" (1989, 5). It's an important way we can exercise power within a
limited sphere, but it isn't the only source or, perhaps, the most important
one.

   Elgin's claim echoes the simplistic linguistic advice being urged on us by
New Age rhetoricians, namely, that what we say will make some aspects of
reality appear and others disappear, as though changing our descriptions
might visibly alter the reality in which we live. This is good advice, properly
taken, but it is also dangerous, especially to the self-esteem of oppressed
people, because it implies that we are responsible for our oppression, that, if
we really wanted to, we could end our experience of oppression by describing it out of existence. Obviously, a disabled woman can change the way
she describes and thinks about her disability, but neither will alter her physical reality or enable her to do more than what her body can do. Likewise,
such claims not only trivialize oppression and the social structures that maintain it, they also blame the victims by ignoring the fact that differences in
power among African-Americans, Native Americans, Latinas, Chicanas and
whites, women and men, Lesbians and gays and heterosexuals, the differently
abled and the able-bodied, the poor and the rich, the powerless and the
powerful, are institutionally supported and that those who benefit directly
and indirectly from such differences in economic and political power have
investments in keeping for themselves the privileges they enjoy. Changing
our descriptions won't immediately change reality or eliminate white supremacy or male dominance, but it will change the way we perceive power
imbalances and the conceptual structures that make them appear to make
sense to us. Only then will we act to end white male heterosexual control of
this society. The rhetoric of New Age thinking isn't new. It's the same old
androcentric thinking repackaged in the framework of quantum physics.

   Unfortunately, there is no quick fix that will reorganize for us the ways we
perceive and act in the world. The world needs more than love. Putting "a
little love in our hearts" isn't enough. We'll have to take the difficult, uncertain approach and learn new ways of talking about who we are and the way
we act. As my previous discussion suggests, there are two levels involved as
we learn to wield language in gynecentric ways, and each level has visible
and abstract consequences: (1) specific words and the conceptual structures
they represent, and (2) the syntactic structures that organize our descriptions
and the mode of thinking they reflect.

   To date, Feminist efforts to change English have concentrated on the vocabulary, on specific words and phrases that keep our thinking within the
boundaries of PUD, and they have suggested how we might make the vocabulary of English more amenable for describing our experiences: (1) reclamation of negative and pejorative words (*dyke, cunt, bitch*), (2) going back to

earlier positive or neutral meanings of words (*crone, hag, witch*), (3) creating new words (e.g., sex-neutral pronouns, *per* in Marge Piercy's *Woman on the Edge of Time* [1976], and *na* in June Arnold's *The Cook and the Carpenter* [1973]) or using already existing roots (*gynecology, gynergy*).

All three methods focus on words as a way into the reconstruction of English, so they are also limited by the pre-existing boundaries of the language itself. Sapir (1921) described this situation when he talked about the relationship between language and thought:

> The birth of a new concept is invariably foreshadowed by a more or less strained or extended use of old linguistic material; the concept does not attain to individual and independent life until it has found a distinctive linguistic embodiment. In most cases the new symbol is but a thing wrought from linguistic material already in existence in ways mapped out by crushingly despotic precedents. As soon as the word is at hand, we instinctively feel, with something of a sigh of relief, that the concept is ours for the handling. Not until we own the symbol do we feel that we hold a key to the immediate knowledge or understanding of the concept. . . . And the word, as we know, is not only a key; it may also be a fetter. (17)

Although each approach to rethinking the world has its merits and its limitations, all three attempt to shape a new conceptual structure using the materials already available in English. Reclaiming specific words, for example, isn't simple, and numerous problems present themselves as we contemplate the choices we have. How should we decide which words we can reclaim without also reenforcing the patriarchal ideas they denote? There is a sifting process that involves talking among ourselves and arguing about the relative effects each has on our thinking and our behaviors. I would argue, for example, that we can reclaim words like *dyke* and *bitch*, but not *slut* or *fuck*. The first two have been used as insults because the idea that we are out of our place inheres in their meaning. We can take the strength and defiance of such words for ourselves and be proud of our refusal to stay within the confines of behavior assigned to us by men. We cannot, in contrast, reclaim specifically patriarchal words like *feminine* and *wife*, without further enslaving ourselves to the passive and subjugated virtues they name, because the concepts and institutions they describe are "despotic precedents."

The words we decide to reclaim should be those that name a behavior or attitude that enables us to move outside the world as men have named it. They should denote actions and ways of being that reflect a radical valuation of ourselves and of which we can be proud. We will reject words that denote the behaviors and traits men believe are positive for women because they are the fetters of which Sapir spoke. They keep us dependent on male approval and mirror PUD stereotypes. Reclaiming the features of our subordination denoted by *femininity* and all its external trappings (cosmetics, high heels, women's dialect) and treating them as virtues within our own framework reaffirms meanings we want to destroy. Likewise, words such as *coy, sultry, sexy* or *seductive* denote behaviors that function to objectify or trivialize us in PUD. That advertising refurbishes women's stereotypes and links them to liberated rhetoric should be a warning to us. Nor should we assume that, when we reject the adjective *feminine* and the behaviors it names, our only choice is being **masculine**. That assumption, too, reflects the either/or thinking of patriarchal "logic." Stepping into that conceptual trap deludes us, making it seem that we have only two options and restraining us from examining the horizon of possibilities just beyond the edges of PUD's map of the world.

Although we can reclaim some words because of their negative meaning in PUD, there are other elements of the language of misogyny we cannot use. During the sifting process, we have to consider not only the negative intent of words but what they denote as well. I would argue that we cannot reclaim words such as *slut, whore, gash* and *slit* because, although they are as insulting as *dyke, bitch* and *queer*, men use the first two to describe women who are "too easy," who enjoy fucking with them too much, and the last two use the female genitals to refer to women. They objectify us: our only significance is as holes men can fuck and they degrade us because that is how men perceive us. We will gain no strength or pride by perpetuating words men created to signal their hatred of us. *Dyke* and *bitch* label things we do that break patriarchal rules and place us outside men's control. *Slut, whore, slit* and *gash* all refer to us as objects of male predation and, like men's compliments, are fetters that hold us within their conceptual framework. They are names whose meanings and values exist only because we live in a patriarchy.

Since the late 1960s, this "sifting process" has engaged the attention of many Lesbians and women as we've tried to change our language use so that what we say reflects the way we think, and there has been an ongoing dialogue about which words to keep and which ones to abandon. Sonia Johnson, for example, in *Wildfire: Igniting the She/volution* (1989, 130) has suggested in a footnote that we stop using the word *survivor*; offering the following rationale:

> As a relational word that throws the mind instantly back into some dread, powerless past experience(s), the word 'survivor' perpetuates women's feelings of powerlessness and their perceptions of themselves as victims. Words are energy. I would like to see us use them to create our own powerful, free reality. For instance, Susan Horwitz suggests that we use the word 'thrival' instead of survival.

What may sound at first like a positive, empowering suggestion becomes less so when one considers several objections to Johnson's interpretation of the word *survivor* and its relation to *victim*. First, the two words, taken together, distinguish between those who survive their victimization and those who don't. An incest "victim" continues to function and perceive herself within the context of her rape experience(s); that is, she merges past and present contexts and interprets events and actions in the present only on the basis of her past experience(s). A "survivor," in contrast, is aware of how her past influences her behavior in the present and consciously attempts not to confuse it with present situations. Although we can never erase our past, we can lessen the degree to which it controls our lives. The word *victim* does throw us "back into some dread, powerless past," and I'm surprised that Johnson suggested dropping *survivor* but not *victim*, given her explanation. Dropping either word from our vocabulary, however, trivializes the experiences of those whom white men victimize, as well as tempting us to forget the many forms of male violence women and children are subjected to. While we might look forward to "thrival" in some unimaginable, utopian future, survival remains a significant accomplishment for many people and this is not something we can afford to drop. As long as there are victims and survivors, both words serve to remind us of our pain, our anger, and the strengths that enable us to survive.

What we must attend to, then, is not whether a specific word is insulting because it labels us as within or outside the world conceived by men, but which strategies will best accomplish our goal—freeing ourselves from men's control. Any reclamation project can fail, preserving ideas better destroyed and losing some of those it seeks to preserve. As we weigh our words, we must bear in mind the function of each word as it is used in PUD, and judge its potential for enabling us to imagine ourselves as different. Which words are fetters, which are not? *Dyke, bitch* (as in "castrating bitch"), *crone, witch,* and *hag* all seem capable of fostering our reconceptualization process because men perceive their meanings as inherently negative; men use them to warn women that we are out of our assigned place in their world. If we limit ourselves to only those concepts men have left to us, they will keep our attention focused on the world as they present it. Every time we use a word created by PUD thinking, we reenforce the structures of PUD and strengthen its control of our thought processes. When we speak the language of PUD, we agree to remain in men's shadows.

WORDS AND WOMEN

Dictionaries record cultural meanings and we must be careful how we use them as we try to determine what we can use and what we must avoid in order to change our thinking. As Cheris Kramarae has pointed out (in press), dictionaries promote the myth of standard English (14) and their claims to authority have persuaded a majority of English speakers that their definitions are objective and complete (4–11). Yet, when Kramarae examined the lists of "authoritative sources" provided by dictionary editors, she found that only the works of anglo men had been consulted for usage while women's works, as well as those of other oppressed people, were ignored (11,17). She concluded: "Women are not to coin words or to muck about the language" (5). Dictionaries elevate white men's usage to "authoritative" status. They are, as the editor of *Webster's Third International Dictionary* bragged, "a prime linguistic aid to interpreting the culture and civilization of today" (1981; cited in Kramarae, in press, 10).

The culture "of today" recorded by English dictionaries is patriarchal. The coherence of a culture's vocabulary lies in how words are categorized as classes, and the distinctions among the words in a class that create sub–classes. Together, the categories, classes, and sub-classes that structure the vocabulary tell us what is valued, devalued or utterly ignored by dominant members of a culture.[5] The dictionary, as a repository of these categories and classifications, reflects a culture's world view and standardizes it for its preservation and perpetuation. This back-and-forth interplay of valuation and repetition is clear in the historical development of dictionaries for patriarchal languages like English.

Feminist and Radical Feminist dictionaries challenge our ideas about the function of dictionaries: standardization is not only *not* the purpose, implied or otherwise, of their definitions, it is simply unworkable, as is any pretense to completeness. Women and Lesbians, recognizing that the words and definitions printed in dictionaries record the meanings and distinctions of a culture's conceptual framework, have prepared numerous dictionaries to document our linguistic creativity. These dictionaries are radically different from standard dictionaries in the information they present and the way they treat it. Among the most widely known are *A Feminist Dictionary* by Cheris Kramarae, Paula Treichler, and Ann Russo, *Lesbian Peoples: Material for a Dictionary* by Monique Wittig and Sande Zeig, now out of print, and *Websters' First New Intergalactic Wickedary of the English Language* (1987) by Mary Daly In Cahoots with Jane Caputi.

There are several others of course, of varying intention and ambition,[6] but the three I've mentioned will illustrate how some women are rethinking the vocabulary of English and how we can introduce our own meanings into the language. These dictionaries serve a politically important function for us because they incorporate the approaches to language change I suggested earlier:

1. negative words can be redefined to reflect our use and interpretations of them;
2. what male dictionaries describe as the obsolete meanings of words can be reintroduced in our usage;
3. the new words we coin to describe our experiences and aspirations can be recorded and, thereby, preserved.

The most striking thing about women's dictionaries is that they are unlike the patriarchal dictionaries whose ill-gotten authority they challenge. Kramarae, describing Capek's achievement in *A Women's Thesaurus* (1987), might have been speaking of *A Feminist Dictionary* and the work of Daly and Caputi and Wittig and Zeig as well: "Knowledge looks and sounds different in this system" (in press, 20). Just as men's dictionaries reflect their world view, the internal organization of PUD and male institutions, so women's knowledge requires very different principles of categorization and definition. Our knowledge doesn't simply look and sound different, it *is* different. When we're brazen enough to muck about with male languages, we push their world view aside and put our own in its place. What's more, each of these dictionaries is quite unlike the other two, and they demonstrate that there are many descriptions of the world we can choose from.

Of the three, *A Feminist Dictionary*, by Kramarae and Treichler with Russo (KTR), comes closest to functioning in the way most people use patriarchal dictionaries: one can look up a word to see how other women have used it. There the resemblance ends. Initially, KTR "collected citations and tried to write" the kinds of definitions we expect to find in a dictionary. They "quickly found that this process [writing definitions that briefly summarize the 'allowable' meanings of a word] hid the very kind of value judgments which had prompted [their] work in the first place" (Kramarae, in press, 14). Rather than write the pseudo-objective definitions typical of men's dictionaries, KTR chose to emphasize the *tensions* among the possible meanings of a word. They selected words and definitions "for their controversial nature, for their ability to undermine, unmask, and overturn ruling definitions and paradigms" (KTR, 1985, 16).

The idea fostered by patriarchal dictionary makers, that words have a basic, central meaning extended gradually by usage, is contradicted by KTR's selection of multiple uses of words which illustrate how our political perspective determines how we understand what words mean. Gone is the idea that we have only to consult the "best" thinkers for an authoritative settlement of semantic disputes. The result is a compendious, if not comprehensive, dictionary of women's meanings. Here, the ways women use words set up reverberations in a field charged with urgency. Cross-references send readers from *mental health*, for example, to *gaslighting, madness, marriage, personality disorders*, and *yellow wallpaper*. Whereas white men claim that their dictionaries list all or most of the words in English, KTR say, in their "Words on a Feminist Dictionary," that their work is "suggestive, certainly not comprehensive" (16). Whereas patriarchal dictionaries "promote the illusion of a general agreement of speakers and writers about word meanings" (Kramarae, in press, 12), there is no pretense to agreement among us. The quotations contradict and reflect and echo and contend among themselves; the possible meanings of our meanings jostle and nudge each other in a most disputatious fashion.

The *Wickedary*, by Mary Daly In Cahoots with Jane Caputi, is about perspective and how the way we think determines how we describe and interpret events in the world. As we read the definitions, the logic and accuracy of a Feminist world view becomes coherent and real. The effect is cumulative. Of course, one can read it as one reads patriarchal dictionaries, looking up words whenever it seems necessary, but, like *A Feminist Dictionary*, the credibility of the *Wickedary's* definitions relies on women's interpretations and perceptions of the world. The effect is encyclopedic.

The *Wickedary* is composed of three phases: (1) *Preliminary Webs*, (2) *The Core of the Wickedary: Word-Webs*, (3) *Appendicular Webs*. The First Phase establishes the Radical Feminist perspective of the methodology and definitions and prepares readers to use the *Wickedary* itself. Specific sections describe how men have controlled English to maintain their versions of reality and how women can wield words to free ourselves from the mind-binding framework of androcentrism. *The Casting of Spells* describes how changing the shape of words transforms them so that they can "convey Super Natural meanings . . . masked and muted by man's mysteries" (14) and enables us to "break the Great Silence imposed on us" (18). Grammar, rooted out of its patriarchal bindings, becomes *Our Wicked Witches' Hammer*, a means for "unfixing the fixations of phallogrammar" (24), and Pronunciation is stripped of its "authoritative" trappings and elaborated as *Denouncing, Pronouncing, Announcing*, exercises in authentic Naming (33).

The heart of the *Wickedary*, its *Core*, isn't one list of words alphabetized from A to Z, but three: Word-Web One: *Elemental Philosophical Words and Phrases and Other Key Words*; Word-Web Two: *The Inhabitants of the Background. Their Activities and Characteristics*; Word-Web Three: *The inhabitants of the foreground, their activities and characteristics*. Word-Web One, for example, contains the key terms of the Background perspective and establishes the contrast between the Feminist Background and the patriarchal foreground. Here, the *Wickedary* itself is gleefully defined:

> Wicked/Wiccen dictionary; dictionary for Wicked/Wiccen Women; Metamysterious Web-Work Spun by Websters; Guidebook for the Intergalactic Galloping of Nag-Gnostic Voyagers; Book of Guide Words for Wayward, Weirdward Wanderers. (100)

The *Wickedary* is a guidebook that maps territories beyond patriarchal thinking, describing the vocabulary necessary for articulating the perceptions of Background Inhabitants. As readers consult the Word-Webs woven by Daly and Caputi, the conceptual boundaries of our Background perspective become clearer as familiar words are animated with woman-centered meanings.

Lesbian Peoples: Material for a Dictionary, by Monique Wittig and Sande Zeig, demonstrates the mutually reenforcing relationship described by Kramarae between a culture and its dictionaries. As with *A Feminist Dictionary* and the *Wickedary*, in which the method and definitions are grounded in women's perceptions and experiences, the effect is gradual and cumulative but the perspective and purpose of *Lesbian Peoples* move readers beyond the world of PUD, positing a chronology of events and an interpretation of them uniquely Lesbian. Its achievement is a coherent Lesbian conceptual framework distinct, not only from men's descriptions of the world, but from heterosexual women's as well.

At the center of *Lesbian Peoples* is the Lesbian perceiver who describes the events of a world that was and the world as it might be. Wittig and Zeig have made coherent the perspective of an invisible, colonized group so fragmented and isolated that its members argue about the meaning of the word *community* and whether or not they do, can, or will form one. How does one construct a lexicon for which there is no continuous historical tradition or connection and, therefore, no etymologies from which cultural changes might be drawn out? Monique Wittig has answered those questions twice, first in *Les Guérillères* (1969):

> There was a time when you were not a slave,
>   remember that.
> You walked alone, full of laughter,
> You bathed bare-bellied.
> You say you have lost all recollection of it,
>   remember . . .
> You say there are no words to describe this time,
> You say it does not exist.
> But remember.
> Make an effort to remember,
> Or, failing that, invent. (89)

What we cannot remember, we must invent. *Lesbian Peoples* is Wittig's second, concrete answer—the dictionary she created with Sande Zeig. *Invent* is what they did, creating a comprehensive framework gleaned from the marginalia of patriarchal histories. Although *Lesbian Peoples* is a slim dictionary, containing only a few terms (364), readers close the book feeling they've glimpsed portions of a vast mural or mosaic whose individual strokes or tiles are so intricate they can be comprehended only in relation to the grand design of which they are details.

Again, the effect is cumulative. Wittig and Zeig gathered the stray threads of Lesbian continuity and wove them into a visionary tapestry of time and territories. A few long entries, *age, history, irreals*, provide much of the information that constructs the dictionary's coherence. The first entry, *age*, establishes the chronology:

> After harmony had been destroyed in the terrestrial garden, the end of the Golden Age followed. And things have gone from bad to worse. After the Golden Age came the Silver Age (sometimes mistaken for the Golden Age), after the Silver Age came the Bronze Age, and after the Bronze Age came the most terrible of all, the origin of chaos, the Iron Age. With the last age, there

came numerous dark ages to darken it even more, casting the greatest confusion over what for too long a time has been called history.
    From the chaos of the Iron Age emerged such ages as the Soft Stone Age, the
Steam Age, the Concrete Age, the High-Speed Steel Age (the same as the
preceding one). The Lesbian peoples do not hold themselves responsible for
the confusions, contradictions, incoherences of that history.
    We have now entered the Glorious Age. This was not achieved without
difficulty. (1)

Starting from this definition, a cultural history is gradually elaborated by
more specific entries. The amazons, still dismissed as impossible legends,
even by women, are identified as the original people of Lesbian tradition: "In
the beginning, if there ever was such a time, all the companion lovers called
themselves amazons" (5).[7] How women forgot themselves and men came to
rule must be explained; some daughters, and some mothers, preferred living
in cities to a wandering, nomadic life, and ceased to call themselves amazons. "At that time . . . the mothers and the amazons began to live sepa-
rately" (108–09). Wittig and Zeig describe the activities of the amazons
between the Golden and Glorious Ages in the definition of *history*. This
"plausible interpretation," attributed to Julienne Bourge (*Dialectics*, Gaul,
Glorious Age), provides differing interpretations of events, and concludes:
"Others say that it is impossible to know because there are too many gaps in
our history" (74–79).

Specific gaps in Lesbian continuity, who, when and where, are filled in
with geographical and biographical information about the "companion
lovers." Placed alphabetically throughout *Lesbian Peoples* are the names and
descriptions of various amazon tribes (Bedjas, Carians, Chaldeans, Da-
naides, Furies, Gagans, Gorgons, Harpies, Numidians, Volscians), and well-
known companion lovers (Agrippina and Livia, Britomartis and Artemis,
Christina and Ebba Sparre, Damia and Auxesis, Evadne and Pasiphae, Hippo-
lyte and Antiope, Joan of Arc and Haiviette, Thelis and Melita). In this way,
Wittig and Zeig people their chronology with numerous Lesbians.

Just as they explained the demise of the Golden Age, they describe how
the amazons re-emerged at the end of the High-Speed Steel Age in the entry
for *powder*, the catalyst that brought on the Glorious Age:

Two strikes with one powder, as it is said of the vanishing powder since the
Glorious Age. This powder permitted an explosive operation at the end of the
Concrete Age, when half of the population took it. From which comes the
expression "to take a powder." It therefore caused a double disappearance
through which both parties forgot each other, did well and continue to do so.
The vanishing powder was invented by a small group of companion lovers who
called themselves the Red Dykes, in sheer modesty. Its instantaneous diffusion
was accomplished through the Irreals who distributed all kinds of dreams the
same night. The day after when exulting companion lovers wanted to compliment them for their trick and hug them tightly, the Red Dykes said as modestly
as ever "taking a powder is easy, it is staying which has been hard." (128)

Other entries, *innocent, joy, kaleidoscope, kaolin, antenna,* and *rain,* contribute to the coherence of *Lesbian Peoples,* adding details of the culture and daily lives of the companion lovers in the Glorious Age. Like *A Feminist Dictionary* and the *Wickedary,* the word *dictionary* itself is defined, its organization explained, and the selection process—why some words were included and others omitted—described:

> The arrangement of the dictionary allows us to eliminate those elements which have distorted our history during the dark ages, from the Iron Age to the Glorious Age. This arrangement could be called lacunary. The assemblage of words, what dictated their choice, the fiction of the fables also constitute lacunae and therefore are acting upon reality. The dictionary is, however, only a rough draft. (43)

Lesbian Peoples, as its subtitle tells us, is "materials for a dictionary," the substance out of which we can construct and reconstruct the continuity men have destroyed.

The writers who compiled the dictionaries described here, realizing the cultural function of patriarchal dictionaries, have enlarged that purpose to name the perceptions and customs of an emergent Feminist/Lesbian society and articulate a vocabulary of meanings that reflects the self-awareness of a woman-centered social order. These vocabularies reorient the conceptual structure of English, suggesting new uses of existing resources without confronting the syntactic structures that organize words. I haven't been able to do justice to any of them here, but each succeeds in its radical purpose.

Suzette Haden Elgin, however, decided that, instead of talking about the creation of a women's language, she would do it. Rather than remain within the linguistic boundaries of English, Elgin used her knowledge of non-I-E languages to construct a new language "for women, for the specific purpose of expressing the perceptions of women" (1988, 1). The result is Láadan, the 'language of those who perceive'. She began work on Láadan when ideas from several concurrent projects converged. She was writing a review of Cheris Kramarae's *Women and Men Speaking* (1981), preparing a speech for the 1982 WisCon science fiction convention, studying Douglas Hofstadter's *Gödel, Escher, Bach: An Eternal Golden Braid* (1979), and reading research papers on lexicalization processes by Cecil Brown and his colleagues. Kramarae's book brought to Elgin's attention the paradox with which this chapter began: "Existing human languages are inadequate to express the perceptions of women . . . " but the only way women can discuss the problem "is the very same language(s) alleged to be inadequate for the purpose," while the work of Brown *et al.* made her realize that what they were describing was "the *male* way to create words" and that "women would have done it differently" (3).

The most radical element in Elgin's work came from *Gödel, Escher, Bach,* in which Hofstadter suggested that "for every record player there were rec-

ords it could not play because they would lead to its indirect self-destruction." Reformulating the proposal as it applies to language, "for every language there [are] perceptions it could not express because they would lead to
its indirect self-destruction," she took the idea to another level of abstraction:
"for every culture there are *languages* it could not use because they would
lead to its indirect self-destruction. This made me wonder: what would
happen to American culture if women did have and did use a language that
expressed their perceptions? Would it self-destruct?" (4). In 1982, she began
work on Láadan, and described how women might proceed with its development and dispersal in her novel, *Native Tongue* (1984).

Creating a language based on the perceptions of women underlies the
most significant structural assumption of Láadan: *inner sensory information
becomes as important as outwardly obvious material phenomena if we have
the words to describe it.* I won't go into detail about the structure or vocabulary of Láadan, but illustrating a few of the ways it differs from English and
other I-E languages will give my readers some specific information about
how properties of the language reflect a different world view. Every Láadan
utterance, for example, indicates both the speaker's intention and the perceived reliability of its claims. Speech act morphemes, which inform hearers
of a speaker's intentions for saying something, are almost always required at
the beginning of sentences:

Speech Act Morphemes:

Declarative:	Bíi (usually optional)
Question:	Báa
Command:	Bó (very rare, except to small children)
Request:	Bóo (usual 'command' form)
Promise:	Bé
Warning:	Bée

Every sentence ends with an evidence morpheme which tells hearers how
confident a speaker is about her source of information and the accuracy of a
description:

Evidence Morphemes:

1.	wa:	known to X because perceived by X, exter- nally or internally
2.	wi:	known to X because self-evident
3.	we:	perceived by X in a dream
4.	wáa:	assumed true by X because X trusts source

5. waá: assumed false by X because X distrusts
                                  source; if evil intent is also assumed, the form
                                  is *waálh*
6. wo: imagined or invented by X, hypothetical
7. wóo: used to indicate that X states a total lack of
                                  knowledge as to the validity of the matter
8. ∅ (no overt marker):   used when X makes no comment on validity,
                                  either because of personal preference or be-
                                  cause no comment is needed (as in a series of
                                  sentences in connected discourse) (131)

In addition, Láadan provides speakers with a set of suffixes which they can attach to speech act morphemes to indicate how they feel about what they're saying:

1. said neutrally: ∅
2. said in anger: -d
3. said in pain: -th
4. said in love: -li
5. said in celebration: -lan
6. said in jest: -da
7. said in fear: -ya
8. said in narrative: -de
9. said in teaching: -di (132)

Using a limited vocabulary, *be*, 'she,' and *hal*, 'to work,' the following sentences illustrate how the structure of Láadan enables speakers to make their intentions and perceptions explicit. (Note: verbs come before nouns in Láadan sentences.)

11.3 a. Bíi hal be wa.
        I say to you (neutrally) she works (I perceive this)
     b. Bíili hal be wi.
        I say to you (lovingly) she works (self-evident perception)
     c. Báad hal be?
        I ask you (in anger) does she work? (Because questions request infor-
        mation, no evidence morpheme is needed.)
     d. Bélan hal be wáa.
        I promise you (in celebration) she works (I trust my source for this
        assertion)

Other morphemes provide Láadan speakers with more refined methods to communicate their perceptions accurately: degree markers, repetition morphemes, and state of consciousness morphemes. The perceptual information made explicit by these morphemes suggests the extent to which Láadan's conceptual framework differs from that of English.

Degree Markers:

1.	to a trivial degree, slightly:	-hel
2.	to a minor degree, rather:	-hil
3.	to an ordinary degree:	∅
4.	to an unusual degree, very:	-hal
5.	to an extreme degree:	-hul
6.	to an extraordinary degree:	-háalish

Repetition Morphemes:

1. bada: repeatedly, at random
2. badan: repeatedly, in a pattern over which humans have no control
3. brada: repeatedly, in a pattern fixed arbitrarily by human beings
4. bradan: repeatedly, in a pattern fixed by humans by analogy to some phenomenon (such as the seasons)
5. bradá: repeatedly, in what appears to be a pattern but cannot be demonstrated or proved to be one

State of Consciousness Morphemes:

(The state of consciousness morphemes are suffixed to the root
hahod, 'to be in a state of'.)

1.	neutral	∅
2.	ecstasy	-iyon
3.	deliberately shut off to all feeling	-ib
4.	in a state of shock, numb	-ihed
5.	linked empathically with others	-itha
6.	in meditation	-o
7.	in hypnotic trance	-óo
8.	in bewilderment/astonishment, positive	-imi
9.	in bewilderment/astonishment, negative	-imilh (130–32)

The vocabulary of Láadan also indicates some of the differences between thinking in Láadan or in English. There are, for example, eleven words that distinguish as many kinds of 'love', five words for describing how a woman feels during pregnancy, six verbs for describing menstruation, a word that means 'science of peace' (*eshon*), formal and informal terms for 'mother', a verb meaning 'to manifest', *dam* (which replaces English *seem*), and a word for 'lover' that cannot be used of males, *lilahá*. There are words for jesus of nazareth, penis, and testicle, but none for clitoris or Lesbian. So, although the conceptual framework of Láadan differs in significant ways from that of English, what one can think about in it conforms snugly to the thinking of conventional folks. The end result is yet another language governed by patriarchal conceptual structures. At this point, it's too early to know whether or not north american culture will self-destruct if women use Láadan instead of English as Elgin hypothesized. In spite of its limitations, the descriptions it makes possible, even requires, indicate how significant changes in consciousness, social structure, and empowerment for women could become the structural bases of a new language.

To date, with the exception of Láadan, the focus of suggested linguistic change has been on new words, and new meanings for old words. While having new words can alter the semantic structure of a vocabulary, simply dropping them into the existing syntactic structures doesn't radically change the way we organize our perceptions. Syntactic structures must change, too, and that has been my purpose in the latter chapters of this book. By describing the sentence patterns that reflect androcentric ways of perceiving the world and exposing the purposes those structures serve in PUD, I encourage women to avoid using them and seek more accurate sentence patterns to communicate our thoughts and feelings.

Whichever aspects of English we try to change, promoting them won't be easy, as we already know. Those of us who want to change the language confront the entrenched and powerful class of men whose interest and control we threaten, and the indifference and inertia of the conventional majority who either don't understand the importance of change or who once did care but have retreated into the safety of apathy. *Ms.*, for example, has caught on with many women, at least as an alternative to *Miss* and *Mrs.*, but without displacing them. Other efforts, however, have been less successful. Some of the approaches to correcting the androcentrism of English that I've described haven't caught on, such as sex-neutral pronouns, and speakers persist in using *he* and *man* as pseudo-generics at least 50% of the time, especially in mainstream media such as television. Some reclamation efforts have gained some popularity among women, *hag* and *crone* as positive ways of describing themselves. More radical solutions, like using Láadan instead of patriarchal languages, have received limited attention. (The magazine *Hotwire* regularly publishes information on Láadan.)[8] I can't downplay the strenuous effort we must expend to change our individual language use. Urging widespread adoption of those changes for others is even more difficult. Until, however, we are convinced that English-as-it-is is inadequate for describing our experiences and perceptions, and work together to promote linguistic change, we'll remain the prisoners of PUD. We must change not only the semantic and syntactic structures of English but its underlying assumptions about discourse and meaning as well.

In order to proceed, we have to understand our role in PUD and reconceive ourselves as speakers. Feminists of the twentieth century have often said that men are the subjects of male discourse and that women are its objects.[9] Learning PUD rules socializes us, making us the docile objects of male control. But this analysis doesn't do justice to the complexity of our oppression or the reality of male domination. Returning to the distinction I made in chapter 8 among the terms *subject, topic,* and *agent,* the relationship between men's control of language and their subjugation of women can be described.

When we examine how men fashion and maintain their versions of reality, we need to identify which sex functions as agent and which one as topic. In PUD, men are the only credible speakers;[10] the major premise of PUD is that only men have anything worthwhile to say, and only their descriptions are valid. A television ad for a cereal made by Kellogg, S. W. Grahams, exemplifies how males assume themselves to be the only speakers who "count" and women's supportive complicity in that assumption. Two white children, one female and one male, are seated next to each other eating cereal and debating what the initials S. W. in the cereal's name stand for. They take turns speaking. The girl initiates the discussion by saying, "S. W. stands for So Wholesome," and the boy says, "Stanley Willis. The outfielder for the Blazers." Then the girl chirps, "They stand for Simply Wonderful," to which the boy responds, "So What. It tastes good." The girl shrugs, looking puzzled, and ends the commercial by asking, "How does he *do* that?"[11]

What each child talks about reflects the experiential spheres of PUD: the girl focuses on nutrition, the boy on baseball. The girl speaks in the feminine mode, using two intensifiers, *so* and *simply.* The boy asserts his opinion without acknowledging that the girl has said anything or recognizing the context she established as the first speaker. The final utterances of the two children capsulize bisexual discourse in patriarchal society. As the only significant speaker, the boy dismisses what the girl has said and the girl wonders "how" he controlled the discourse, pretending she doesn't understand what is, in fact, a stereotyped discourse pattern which the creators of the ad could assume viewers would recognize. The male asserts, the female questions, but also allows his dismissal of her opinions to stand without challenge or contradiction.

Although the male dominance portrayed in this commercial should be questioned, I'm less concerned with it than I am with the girl's pretense. Just as women know what men are doing in similar conversational situations, we understand that her behavior is sheer pretense. She knows perfectly well what the boy has done. He's ignored and dismissed everything she said; she's only superficially a participant in the "dialogue," there to supply lines so that he can "take the floor." She "plays dumb" so that he can feel superior. She speaks only so that he can ignore her. Her opinions are shunted aside so that his description stands.

The intent and predictable effects of the commercial maintain PUD. Whoever wrote it intended its effect to be funny, counting on adult viewers to identify with the sex-specific roles. The humorous effect depends upon viewers' identifying with the two children's respective speech behaviors. If the writer's portrayals are successful and viewers find it funny and identify with the children, the validity of PUD has been acknowledged and reenforced. Nonadult members of the audience, however, would miss the humor of the ad and accept it as a discourse model they ought to emulate. Of course, the copywriter and parents do expect them to imitate it, and, in this way, all of us conspire to perpetuate PUD.

As the only speakers in PUD, men cast themselves as **agents** of the important events in the world and determine whether women appear as agents or topics in the sentences they construct on the basis of what they want to foreground in our awareness and what they want to relegate to the background. Women cooperate in the perpetuation of PUD by pretending that we don't know what men are doing, and the surest way to end our complicity in the construction of male discourse is to stop pretending we're dumb.

But we must do more than this. We must also reject our roles in PUD. Although it is true that women are frequently topics in PUD, we aren't perpetually cast as utterly passive objects. We do have two agentive roles, represented in judeo-xtian myth as Eve and Lilith: (1) as nurturers of men and children, and (2) as the destroyers (literal or figurative) of men and their lives. Men condone our agency as long as we adhere to our role as Eve, the supportive nurturer. When we conceive of ourselves as independent agents and act on our behalf, however, men describe us as "evil," Liliths out to "do them in." Both female roles serve to perpetuate male versions of reality. When we act in their terms, we confirm their descriptions.

In contrast, men determine the contexts in which they acknowledge their agency. When men have beaten or raped a woman, they omit explicit reference to their own agency, leaving themselves in the background of their descriptions so that their responsibility isn't directly accessible to our conscious minds. Readers may recall, for example, Morley Safer's substitution of the nation Brazil, in "Machismo," for the agency of men who murder their wives. Safer's syntax equated maleness with the country, as though women aren't citizens, but his sentences also erased men as murderers of women. Starting with simple sentences, the male authors of PUD have filled the shelves of thousands of libraries with their descriptions of what they would have us believe. And they continue to do so.

We must refuse to be docile PUD speakers and listeners, and choose, instead, to create an active discourse in which we are agents acting on our own behalf. We must stop pretending we don't know what men are doing and become the purposeful and conscious creators of a women-centered universe of discourse. We cannot accomplish this by relying on the dichotomies and descriptions inherent in PUD. That includes all of the so-called virtues that PUD allocates to women: nurturing (men), being the emotional (or feeling) sex, accepting our status as the objects/victims of men's actions.

Language doesn't describe how the world is. Rather, it imposes the perceptions of men as descriptions, which are more often inaccurate and distorting than not. If we are reluctant to break the rules and break out of the limitations imposed on us by PUD, there are still specific tactics we can use to change reality by changing how we talk about our experiences. Language mediates between cognition and the semantic level of language. If we wish, we can abandon patriarchal categorizations and refuse to use language grounded in those categories. Change in our usage or the categories will change both. G. Lakoff's "domain of experience" isn't "out there." It's inside our minds and determines how we think and act unless we abandon it and learn other ways of being. Consider the predicate sets I discussed in chapter 10, the sex-marked predicates, "impersonal" verbs and psych-predicates as examples of the male categorizations and structures we must reject. The sex-marked predicates of English represent the cognitive categories that men impose on the world, the values of patriarchal cultures maintained and perpetuated by PUD.

It is the purpose of PUD structures to contradict our perceptions of the world, to deny us as agents in the world, and to coerce us into accepting the roles assigned to us in PUD. If we ignore how English serves the patriarchal world view, we find ourselves victimized by our best intentions, tyrannized by a tactic we thought would empower us. This has already happened. During the early years of the Women's Liberation Movement, we affirmed the validity of every woman's perceptions. Whatever a woman said she felt or perceived, we accepted as necessarily true. Our desire to affirm every woman's perceptions was a lofty aspiration, and our own experiences of the social/political realities of oppression convinced us that we should not question, challenge, or deny each other's perceptions. We had good reasons for wanting to validate each other and desiring the same acceptance for ourselves, but none of us realized how patriarchal language could undermine the integrity of the perceptions we sought to affirm. The psych-predicates are the language in which we describe our perceptions of situations and interactions, and they illustrate how semantics and syntax are interrelated. The semantic structure that determines their syntax forces us to place responsibility (and blame) outside ourselves, thereby maintaining the PUD fiction that we are emotionally dependent.

Psych-predicates require the experiencer to be described as an object acted upon by someone else's attitude or behavior. *Intimidate*, for example, is a verb women use often to describe how they feel about someone else's carriage, speech or "presence": "She intimidates me," "I'm intimidated by you," "You're intimidating." All three descriptions locate the source of the speaker's feelings in the behavior of another person and assume that the behavior itself is (a) intentional, (b) an expression of "power over," and (c) that the speaker's interpretation and response are the only possible reactions because any other response is inconceivable to her. She denies responsibility for her feelings and "explains" them by blaming someone else's way of talking, standing, or walking, as though the actions in and of themselves were "intimidating."

With verbs that describe a negative emotional response, like *intimidate*, the structure encourages experiencers to perceive themselves as the victims of others' behaviors and to treat that description as though it were valid. The third description, "You're intimidating," allows the speaker to remove herself entirely from the action and attribute the underlying motivation and behavior to the individual she blames. What the speaker feels can no longer be interpreted as an individual response. It becomes an allegation of malevolent intent on the other person's part, an inherent attribute of her personality, and the experiencer's response is generalized, as though anyone who interacts with the individual so accused will also be intimidated.

When we use psych-predicate descriptions, we forget that any habitual gesture or movement has several possible interpretations; we forget that our internal responses to physical or verbal expressions are often located in our personal histories and experiences with parents and other adults who had power over us and probably did *intimidate* us, intentionally or not. Relative physical size, for example, can arouse feelings of intimidation remembered from our childhood, and we may feel intimidated around people who are larger than we are. But those feelings are ours and may not be intentional on the other person's part or inhere in their behaviors. We cannot assume that our perceptions of mannerisms and behaviors are accurate, and we certainly cannot assume that the malevolence of another woman inheres in the situation. Of course, there are people who do set out to intimidate women, who want to assert their power over us. A verb like *intimidate* may accurately describe what is happening, but we simply cannot take for granted that our descriptions and the assumptions such verbs express are accurate, and we have to be careful about our use of psych-predicates and related structures. As we empower ourselves linguistically, this is one area of the English vocabulary that we'll have to rethink, redefine, and redescribe for ourselves.

The psych-predicates trap English speakers. In English there is no way for us to use one of these predicates actively, to name ourselves as responsible for our feelings. In every instance, when we feel repulsion, fright, disgust, or irritation the psych-predicate forces us to describe ourselves as acted upon by

some person or event. More insidiously, however, the psych-predicates enable us to blame someone else for our internal, psychological responses, as
though they cause us to feel as we say we do and are, therefore, responsible
for our responses to them. The psych-predicates locate the origin of and
responsibility for our feelings and emotional responses outside of us. If only
so-and-so hadn't done this or that, we think, we wouldn't feel like we do.
Likewise, if these verbs force us to blame what someone else does or says for
our feelings, they simultaneously provide us with a handy way of erasing our
own responsibility, whether or not we're aware of it. That is, although something external to us may trigger our psychological response, that response
comes from inside us. It is a consequence of our accumulated experiences.
More unfortunately, our emotional response may be utterly unrelated to the
individual or behavior that we blame for it; our feelings may originate with
something done to us years before, and not in the immediate context to
which we're responding. As long as we rely on psych-predicate constructions, we remain unaware of how our personal history determines our responses to specific contexts, and we continue to perceive ourselves as the
victims of others' actions. If we believe that psych-predicates accurately describe our perceptions of situations and other people's behavior in them, we
won't examine the internal sources of our feelings or take responsibility for
them, and we'll continue to think and act as victims.

I'm not saying that our anger, fear, and pain aren't real. I'm saying that the
syntax and semantics of the psych-predicates force us to find someone else
to blame for our feelings, and that we may falsely accuse them of causing us
anger or pain when the responsibility for what we feel belongs to someone in
our past. To say to another woman, "You intimidate me," and believe what
that description implies about her intentions in a situation makes us the
helpless victims of the malevolence we ascribe to her. When we force her
into the role of oppressor and make her the culpable agent of the way we feel
in her presence, we simultaneously disguise our internalized feelings of
weakness and our sense of powerlessness and insecurity. Some women do set
out intentionally to intimidate other women, but the description hides the
fact that we could react differently and we fail to realize the behavioral
options we have. We don't have to allow her to succeed in intimidating us,
just as we can resist men's attempts to intimidate us. This is one area in which
we can control situations by conceiving ourselves and others differently. No
one can "intimidate" us if we cease to accept the description itself.

There are other problems we can trace to psych-predicate descriptions.
Readers may have detected a slight difference in meaning in my examples in
chapter 10, for example, *Your sudden appearance frightened me* and *I was
frightened by your sudden appearance*. This apparent difference in meaning
is determined by which NP is the topic: the experiencer or the individual
said to be responsible for the feeling. Either the victim or the alleged perpe-

trator becomes the topic of subsequent discourse, but the feeling of fright will be hard to challenge for the accused individual. If you tell me, "You intimidate me," there is no simple way for me to prove different intentions on my part or ask why you feel as you do.

Simply refusing to use psych-predicates won't change the way we think in and of itself. Omitting them from our vocabularies would be a significant advance, but English is full of similar cognitive traps. We have to learn new ways of thinking by self-consciously attending to the words we choose. The semantics of psych-predicates represent a way of thinking that attributes agency for individual feelings to someone or something outside of themselves, and that conceptual structure has other ways of finding expression. One of its most familiar manifestations involves the causative use of the verb *make*, as in "You *make* me angry" (or nervous, or jealous—whatever). In the sentences of 11.4, *make* is used to attribute agency to someone or something else described as responsible for *causing* our feelings. Here, again, we externalize the sources of our responses.

11.4 a. You make me feel insignificant.
    b. You make me feel wonderful.
    c. Rainy days make me feel depressed.
    d. Your indecision makes me angry.

We have no integrity when we say such things. Again, we attribute agency for our feelings and emotions to someone else, their behavior, or the weather, none of which we can control, and cast ourselves as the objects/victims of their malevolence, denying our own ability to choose alternative behaviors. It's not that other people don't treat us badly, but that we need to imagine ways of describing events and our perceptions of them so that we do have control in a situation. Consider, for example, the alternative ways of talking about our feelings in 11.5, which describe us as agents and provide specific information at the same time.

11.5 a. I feel insignificant when you trivialize my opinions.
    b. I feel wonderful when we hold hands.
    c. I feel depressed when it rains.
    d. I become angry when you refuse to decide.

Now, the sentences in 11.5 are longer than their counterparts in 11.4, and most of us were taught to omit qualifying phrases like "I feel," "I think," "I believe," on the assumption that they're redundant, but we regain a measure of integrity when we become responsible for our feelings and specify the behaviors and events that we're reacting to.

Like uses of the verb *make* and the psych-predicates, English has many descriptive methods we can use to remove ourselves as agents and experiencers in the world. One familiar description substitutes the second person pronoun, *you*, for the first person *I*, projecting our feelings and experiences onto our audience. Instead of saying "I," which is surely what we mean, we omit ourselves and, at the same time, attempt to generalize our experiences to other people.

11.6 a. "There *I* was, 35,000 feet in the air. *You* feel elation and fear at the same time, and *you* want it to go on, but *you* don't."

   b. "It's just a horrible, horrible thing to go to school and watch *your* friends study for three hours and be done. And *you* know that *you* can't get near them unless *you* study fourteen, fifteen, or maybe twenty-four hours."

   c. "*You* know, when *you're* charging the kind of prices *we* have to charge today, that's the kind of attention *you* have to provide," he said. "*We're* a hands on business. It's not a factory. *You* can't slop a mop around like a factory."

These are the kinds of descriptions we must resist although we hear this usage so often we've stopped noticing it. The speaker in a. was a man who had taken up sky-diving. Although he started with *I*, when he described his experience he projected his fear and elation onto his listeners. In b., Jack Horner (who revolutionized thinking about the dinosaurs) projected his frustrations with studying onto readers of an interview (*Omni*, 1989, 112), as though their experience were identical to his. The owner of a motel in Boston provided the quotation of c., which is of special interest for two reasons. First, he used *you* in two different ways, as a direct address to readers ("You know") and then in the self-erasing sense ("you're charging"). Second, he switched from *you* to *we* twice, as though his listeners would identify with the problems he described. At no point did he use *I*.

There is no reason to impose our feelings on others as Jack Horner, the motel owner, and the sky-diver did. This device follows the pattern established by other syntactic structures, creating an illusory universe of discourse peopled with disembodied agents and experiencers. Even as a discourse tactic, the use of *you* to project pseudo-agency is transparently manipulative. As hearers, we need not buy the deceptive packaging of PUD descriptions. As speakers, we cannot rely on PUD structures to describe what we feel and what we perceive. The English language contains many linguistic resources, and we can become resourceful and conscious speakers of English (or any other language). We start by steadfastly insisting upon our own agency in the world, and then acting on what we think and say.

WORDY WOMEN

If we want to think beyond the conceptual grooves of PUD, we can learn to avoid using verbs like the psych-predicates altogether, choosing instead other ways to describe ourselves. The result will be lengthy sentences in which we make explicit every internal and external factor we perceive as relevant in a situation, supplying the kinds of information, for example, provided by speech act, evidence, and state of consciousness morphemes in Láadan. Instead of saying either "You intimidated me" or "I was intimidated by you," our descriptions will be longer and more explanatory. We might say, "I feel that you intentionally set out to intimidate me because you wanted to feel like you are stronger or more important than I am," when we're confronting someone who ought to take responsibility for bullying others, or "I set myself up to feel intimidated by your self-assertiveness because I still don't have much self-confidence and my self-esteem was pretty low that day," when we acknowledge our own responsibility in such an interaction. We'll become "wordy."

We have to start rejecting the descriptions English provides, or we'll be forever trapped by them. There are worse consequences than being wordy. We'll do far less damage to ourselves and others if we take the time to construct sentences that describe, as accurately as possible, what we perceive and feel. More importantly, as we engage in the mental processes necessary for creating alternative descriptions we'll begin to reconceptualize who we are in relation to others. Rewording our perceptions will lead us to rethinking, and rethinking will lead to a self-knowledge that's impossible within the boundaries of PUD.

As we undertake this project of conceptual exploration and restructuring, our contradictory position requires that we live by a linguistic double standard. Our minds will have to live simultaneously in two universes of discourse: the patriarchal world we want to change and the woman-centered world we seek to create. On the one hand, because we live in a male-dominated society, we will have to improve our ability to use the structures of PUD in our dealings with men. That is, we must become better liars, better verbal acrobats, in order to sustain ourselves in the world as men have made it. On the other, we must create radically different ways of perceiving and describing events in the world. We will have to live in transition, between what is and what we want.

We'll make mistakes, yes. But the difference in the way we feel and act when we say what we mean is, I think, worth the effort. If we are serious about freeing ourselves from male oppression and the many forms it takes, we must be willing to commit ourselves to unlearning the map of reality presented to us as children. If women want to work together for our mutual liberation, we cannot go on speaking to each other in destructive, self-eroding ways. We must turn our attention from patriarchal linguistic distortions and learn to focus on the features of our experiential landscape barely perceptible outside the boundaries of the known.

We are not power*less*. We can act. Men may control discourse, but we don't promote our self-interest by acceding to their power. One way of developing our own power is to laugh at theirs, to refuse to take their posturing and deceits seriously. For example, many Feminists refuse to watch television, listen to the radio, or read mainstream newspapers and magazines because they believe that the images are so irresistible they can invade our minds, like contagious bacteria—invisible, overwhelming, corrupting. But patriarchal discourse has only the power we give it. Yes, we can passively accept patriarchal messages, but we can also become an active, critical, laughing audience. In order to collect the examples in this book, I've watched months of television, listened to the lyrics of popular songs for years, read the print media, including the backs of cereal boxes, studiously. I figured out how English preserves and perpetuates PUD by analyzing the language, not by ignoring it. Men may control the information we get, but we can control how we interpret and use it.

More importantly, we must find new ways to perceive our world and new words and descriptions for articulating those perceptions. In order to change the way we describe the world and talk among ourselves, we will have to find words that fit our perceptions and structures that organize our experiences with as little distortion as possible. As we find ways to describe our own perspective, the act of naming events and relationships as we perceive them will be the first step toward making our realities visible and functional in the world. Lack of ways to talk about our perceptions keeps them in the realm of the invisible, the unreal. If we do not learn to speak freely, imagining ourselves into an age where oppression is obsolete will remain an unaccomplished "perhaps" in the long sentence of patriarchy.

Endnotes

INTRODUCTION

1 Linguists have recorded and analyzed the spectrum of regional and social dialects of u.s. English, and the following books contain nontechnical articles on language variation for readers interested in more detailed discussion: Klaus R. Scherer and Howard Giles, eds., *Social Markers in Speech* (Cambridge: Cambridge UP, 1979); Geneva Smitherman, "White English in Blackface, or Who Do I Be?" in *Exploring Language*, ed. Gary Goshgarian, 3rd ed. (Boston: Little, Brown and Co., 1983), 330–41, and "Black Idiom and White Institutions," *Negro American Literature Forum* Fall 1971); Lorenzo D. Turner, [1949], *Africanisms in the Gullah Dialect*, (New York: Arno Press and The New York Times, 1969); Juanita V. Williamson and Virginia M. Burke, eds., *A Various Language: Perspectives on American Dialects*, (New York: Holt, Rinehart and Winston, 1971); William Raspberry, "Should Ghettoese Be Accepted?" in *Language Awareness*, eds. Paul Eschholz, Alfred Rosa, and Virginia Clark, 3rd ed. (New York: St. Martin's Press, 1982), 226–31.

2 Although opinions regarding the "best" usage were divided for some time, the condemnation of *between you and I* and *It's me* also originated with the eighteenth-century grammarians (Baugh, 335–36).

3 This particular "rule" fails to recognize the three distinct functions of these little words, which can be used as prepositions, adverbs, and, increasingly, verbal particles. The conflict for English speakers resulting from this confusion led Winston Churchill to comment humorously, "That is something *up with* which I will not put." Accepting the prescriptivists' rule as accurate for English has been the cause of innumerable awkward sentences. Either one "breaks" the rule in the interests of intelligibility, or subverts clarity by following it.

4 The so-called irregular verbs in traditional grammars are, by and large, the remnants of a shift from the vowel mutations typical of the Germanic "strong" verbs to the "weak" verbs that mark tense with a dental preterite (*-ed*), a change in English that continues. For example, the verb *dive* has two acceptable past tense forms, the weak, *dived*, and the strong, *dove*. The "problem" with using *brang*, rather than *brought*, as the past tense of *bring* is that *brang* is based on a false analogy to familiar strong verbs such as *ring* and *sing*. *Bring*, however, like *seek*, belongs to a class of weak verbs that, like the strong verbs, formed their past tenses by vowel mutation. Analogy is among our most fruitful methods of conceptualizing, and we would do better to use such occurrences as an opportunity to teach children that analogy can lead to faulty conclusions rather than "correcting" their "bad grammar."

5 Regional dialect forms of the second person nominative, like *y'all, you'uns,* and *youse,* fill a gap in the pronominal system of Modern English created by the fact that a single form, *you,* serves as both the singular and plural of the second person nominative.

6 Albert C. Baugh credited Bishop Robert Lowth with stating the rule forbidding double negatives "that we are now bound by": "Two Negatives in English destroy one another, or are equivalent to an Affirmative" (*Short Introduction to English Grammar* [1762], 336). Lowth's grammar was extremely influential, going through at least 22 editions during the eighteenth century; among his many imitators was Lindley Murray (Baugh, 334).

7 Linguists use the terms *traditional, normative,* and *prescriptive* to refer to the eighteenth- and nineteenth-century grammars and their twentieth-century descendants.

8 In the 1960s, African-Americans began to specify how racism dictates the curricula of white educational systems. Among many areas in the English curriculum cited was treating Black English as a sub-standard and unacceptable dialect, the imposition of white English as the only acceptable dialect, and the practice of forcing African-Americans to learn white English by marking uses of Black English "wrong." Liberal educators, in an effort to deflect these charges of racism, changed tactics. They substituted covert for overt racism and began to argue the advantages of *bidialectalism* in schools of education. Bidialectalism required African-Americans to learn a second dialect, white English. Black English, they were told, was fine for talking among themselves but not good enough to get them the jobs they needed. This tactic enabled school boards to continue using the same prescriptive grammars, and the teachers continued teaching white English as the only "acceptable" dialect for mainstream communication.

That is, nothing really changed, including the racist attitudes of the majority white teachers. James Sledd, in a stinging condemnation of such educational hypocrisy, exposed the racism of bidialectalism in "Bi-Dialectalism: The Linguistics of White Supremacy," *English Journal* (December, 1969). His article is more accessible in a number of anthologies prepared for teaching introductory linguistic courses, and I recommend *Language: Introductory Readings,* eds. Virginia P. Clark, Paul A. Eschholz, and Alfred F. Rosa (New York: St. Martin's Press), 418–29, which contains other essays on the English language that are worth reading and considering.

The fact is that white north americans are proudly ignorant of other languages, arrogantly maintaining a steadfast monolingualism that assumes people of other nations "ought" to learn English if they want to talk to us. The irony of our arrogance isn't lost on them: most white americans don't speak the dialect they subscribe to as the only permissible "standard," or speak it poorly, and are as ignorant of their own social and regional dialects as they are of Black English.

Black English (BE), in fact, is as systematic as any other dialect, although, as Madelon E. Heatherington has commented, "it is strikingly different from other ethnic dialects" because its speakers didn't learn it from an already existing community. They had to create it from scratch (1980, 118). BE is unique in another way: most of its distinguishing features are structural; rather than simply sounding different, the syntactic rules of BE differ markedly from white English (WE). For example, Heatherington mentions the omission of *be,* e.g., BE: "They going," WE: "They are going"; BE: "He cool," WE: "He is cool"; BE: "I cold," WE: "I am cold." BE syntax differs from WE in other ways, e.g., there is no plural marker on nouns in phrases like "three sister" or "five month." Such features of BE, which ignorant whites have used to justify their condemnation of it, and others as well, are systematic and predictable, giving BE a linguistic status quite apart and distinct from WE. It is a dialect; it is made up of rules; the rules function regularly to promote communication. Only white ears seem not to notice.

This information has been available in linguistics texts and courses for years now. There is no acceptable reason for remaining ignorant about Black English or taking pride in one's ignorance, and this is especially true of the publishers who continue to print handbooks of white English presenting it as "standard," the school boards who determine the content of English language curricula, and the English teachers who persist in teaching only what the prescriptive handbooks say. There is no excuse for any of this. It is racism of the most vicious kind because it is lazy. The information about social and regional dialects, including Black English, has been available for years and ignored. The "back to the basics" movement has sought to bury such information in order to delay the thorough-going overhaul of the u.s. educational system that must, eventually, occur. If we don't acknowledge that we have a social and political problem too large for outdated solutions and act quickly to change educational curricula, starting with pedagogy and proceeding through every textbook and teachers' manual, we will end up living in an intellectually impoverished nation. We have to scrap every lie in every textbook and rewrite them. There is no excuse for perpetuating what we know to be lies or for punishing students who refuse to learn the lies, and whites are going to have to take responsibility for helping to create an educational system that honors the linguistic and cultural differences of all children and for educating new generations of teachers committed to eradicating linguistic and social inequalities.

9 For an excellent review of the literature purporting to be "evidence" of biologically innate sex differences and how it supports and promotes the socially constructed sex-specific behaviors, see Janice G. Raymond, *The Transsexual Empire: The Making of the She-Male* (Boston: Beacon Press, 1979), esp. her Introduction, 1–18.

10 Although linguists perpetuate the fuddy-duddy stereotype of the English teacher, the label "Miss Fidditch" was made up by Mr. J. Donald Adams in his article, "Does Anyone Know What Creative Writing Is?" *Saturday Review* 18 September 1965: 23. The first use by a linguist that I know of is in "English Usage: The Views of the Literati," by Thomas Pyles (*College English* March, 1967: 453).

11 In general, when linguists prepare a grammar of a language, they divide their data for that language into four distinct levels: the sound system (phonology), how words are constructed (morphology), the internal structure of sentences (syntax), and the abstract features of the vocabulary (semantics). Treating language structures as discrete levels has an advantage for beginning as well as advanced students of linguistics. It provides a way to analyze language starting with the most accessible linguistic rules, phonology, leading to the most abstract and, therefore, difficult level of language, semantics. Linguists readily admit that these "levels" of language are artificial, reminding those encountering this stratification that it is one way of making linguistic structures easier to analyze and more accessible to describe, but that one must always bear in mind that all four aspects of language structure work simultaneously when we speak or listen.

Phonology and morphology are the most familiar levels of language. The sound system of a language is the most immediately apparent to linguist and non-linguist alike. Whether we understand a language or not, whether we know the language-specific rules that govern sound production, we can hear the sounds even if they mean nothing to us. The next level, morphology (word construction), along with etymology, the histories of words, are also familiar to non-linguists. Many people enjoy playing with words and sounds and speculating about how a particular word or phrase came to be, and linguists often use Lewis Carroll's "Jabberwocky" to illustrate how we use our knowledge of English morphology to "understand" the non-sense of the poem.

12 Betty Lou Dubois and Isabel Crouch challenged Robin Lakoff's claim that women use tag–questions more than men do and that these questions indicate a speaker's uncertainty in "The question of tag–questions in women's speech: they don't use more of them, do they?" (1976). They point out that tag–questions can be used in several ways, including as genuine requests and to "forestall opposition" (292). They collected 33 examples of tag–questions during an on-campus workshop, all used by men. None of the women used a tag–question. They concluded that "Stereotyping hypotheses from folk linguistics must not be accepted arbitrarily because they appear plausible; they cannot in any case be verified by unsystematic observation" (294).

13 Among the women whose work must be constantly re-discovered are Aphra Behn, Mary Astell, Catherine Macauley, and Mary Wollstonecraft. In the seventeenth century, Aphra Behn (1640–1689) served as a spy for Charles II, invented the novel as a long prose narrative,

Oroonoko: or, the Royal Slave (1688), long before Defoe wrote *Robinson Crusoe* (alleged to be the "first" novel in patriarchal literary histories), and argued that women were entitled to an education. In 1694, well before the Inquisition ceased its vile activities, Mary Astell anonymously published *A Serious Proposal to the Ladies*, and, along with Lady Mary Wortley Montagu, developed a new frame of reference from their experience as women, that "conceptualised women as an independent category" (Spender, 40). As Dale Spender argues, Mary Wollstonecraft wasn't alone when she wrote *A Vindication of the Rights of Women* in 1792, only seven scant years after Sarah Bradshaw agreed to allow her persecutors to "swim" her.

[14] This is as true of the various sign languages, such as American Sign Language (AMSLAN), as it is of verbal language. Sign and its dialects also develop within patriarchal cultures and incorporate the misogynist assumptions of the spoken language.

[15] Suzette Haden Elgin has written four books describing the five basic modes of communication and the eight primary forms of verbal attack: *The Gentle Art of Verbal Self-Defense* (Englewood Cliffs, NJ: Prentice-Hall, 1980); *More on the Gentle Art of Verbal Self-Defense* (Englewood Cliffs, NJ: Prentice-Hall, 1983); *The Last Word on The Gentle Art of Verbal Self-Defense* (New York: Prentice Hall Press, 1987); and *Success with the Gentle Art of Verbal Self-Defense* (Englewood Cliffs, NJ: Prentice-Hall, 1989). A workbook, *The Gentle Art of Verbal Self-Defense Workbook* (1986), and an audio cassette of the same title, are available from Dorset Press, which has reprinted the first book in the series. For information about the *Gentle Art of Verbal Self-Defense Newsletter*, write to Suzette Haden Elgin, Route 4, Box 192E, Huntsville, Arkansas 72740.

[16] The quotation, "Failure is personal," comes from Andrea Dworkin's "A Battered Wife Survives" (1978), published in *Letters from a War Zone: Writings 1976–1987* (London: Secker and Warburg, 1988), in which she described how the contradictions between a woman's experience and the PUD version of reality make her conceptually immobile.

A battered wife has a life smaller than the terror that destroys her over time.

Marriage circumscribes her life. Law, social convention, and economic necessity encircle her. She is roped in. Her pride depends on projecting her own satisfaction with her lot to family and friends. Her pride depends on believing that her husband is devoted to her and, when that is no longer possible, convincing others anyway.

The husband's violence against her contradicts everything she has been taught about life, marriage, love, and the sanctity of the family. Regardless of the circumstances in which she grew up, she has been taught to believe in romantic love and the essential perfection of married life. Failure is personal. Individuals fail because of what is wrong with them. The troubles of individuals, pervasive as they are, do not reflect on the institution of marriage, nor do they negate her belief in the happy ending, promised everywhere as the final result of male-female conflict. Marriage is intrinsically good. Marriage is a woman's proper goal. Wife-beating is not on a woman's map of the world when she marries. It is, quite literally, beyond her imagination. Because she does not believe that it could have happened, that *he* could have done that to *her*, she cannot believe that it will happen again. He is her *husband*. No, it did not happen. And when it happens again, she still denies it. It was an accident, a mistake. And when it happens again, she blames the hardships of his life outside the home. There he experiences terrible hurts and frustrations. These account for his mistreatment of her. She will find a way to comfort him, to make it up to him. And when it happens again, she blames herself. She will be better, kinder, quieter, more of whatever he likes, less of whatever he dislikes. And when it happens again, and when it happens again, and when it happens again, she learns that she has nowhere to go, no one to turn to, no one who will believe her, no one who will help her, no one who will protect her. If she leaves, she will return. She will leave and return and leave and return. She will find that her parents, doctor, the police, her best friend, the neighbors upstairs and across the hall and next door, all despise the woman who cannot keep her own house in order, her injuries hidden, her despair to herself, her smile amiable and convincing. She will find that society loves its central lie—that marriage means happiness—and hates the woman who stops telling it even to save her own life. (102–03)

Letters from a War Zone had been unavailable in the u.s., but E. P. Dutton has now reprinted it here.

17 Readers who wish additional information on the inadequacy of English for expressing women's experiences and perceptions will enjoy the following works: Dale Spender, *Man Made Language* (London: Routledge & Kegan Paul, 1980), esp. 60–64; Cheris Kramarae, *Women and Men Speaking* (1981); Suzette Haden Elgin's Introduction, "The Construction of Láadan" in *A First Dictionary and Grammar of Láadan*, 2nd ed. (Madison, WI: SF³, 1988), 3–6.

18 Those interested in nonsexist writing should consult *The Handbook of Nonsexist Writing for Writers, Editors and Speakers* by Casey Miller and Kate Swift (New York: Lippincott & Crowell, 1980).

CHAPTER ONE:
THE GLAMOUR OF GRAMMAR

1 The phonological process of vowel reduction has caused many of the changes between Old and Modern English. For example, it was probably vowel reduction in final syllables that set in motion the gradual loss of case endings and, as a result, the loss of "grammatical gender." During rapid speech, vowels that occur in the last syllable of a word are often reduced to the mid-central vowel called *schwa*, /ə/. As its final vowel was gradually lowered, *hēo* would have been pronounced [heə], and, eventually, the vowel would have been dropped entirely during speech.

2 The introduction of the /š/ forms of the third person female nominative and the question of its origin are discussed in Stanley and Wolfe, "Going through the Changes: The Pronoun *she* in Middle English," *Papers in Linguistics* 11, 1–2 (1978): 71–88.

3 For an examination of the conflicting evidence for literacy in early English society, especially among women, see Christine Fell, *Women in Anglo-Saxon England* (London: Basil Blackwell, 1984).

4 The Chinese had discovered how to make paper in the first century A. D. and invented the process of block printing in the tenth (Robins, 111).

5 It wasn't until the nineteenth century that male scholars applied the term *renaissance* to the period, but it stuck.

6 In spite of the lack of congruence between the terminology of Greek and Latin grammars and the English language, I will, with some exceptions discussed later in the book, use the terms that most of my readers are familiar with. If those words are often imprecise, I hope that a majority will still be able to follow my discussions.

7 Discussions of the history of the grammatical tradition in English and its classical sources are common in linguistics texts. Here, I've relied on Albert C. Baugh's *A History of the English Language* (New York: Appleton-Century-Crofts, 1963) and R. H. Robins, *A Short History of Linguistics* (London: Longmans, Green and Co., 1967). There is also an informative article by Karl W. Dykema, "Where Our Grammar Came From," *College English* April 1961: 455–65. In *Grammar* (London: Penguin Books, 1971), Frank Palmer discusses how the categories and terminology of prescriptive grammars have influenced twentieth-century linguistics, esp. 13–20 and 41–106.

8 Vowel reduction (see en. 1) in final syllables has probably led to the notion among native speakers that *would've* is a contracted form of *would of*, rather than *would have*, an interpretation of the contraction that prescriptive grammarians have condemned (unsuccessfully) since the eighteenth century.

9 In the case of *gotta*, what may appear to be a spelling eccentricity on my part is a necessary way of distinguishing two different senses of *got to*. *Gotta* functions as a modal, e.g., "I *gotta* leave now," and its pronunciation contrasts with *got to* [gat'tu], as in "I got to go to the movies tonight," which some may find still ambiguous. Both *get to* and *got to* imply that permission was required for an event to occur and that it was granted. The external agency granting permission is seldom explicit.

10 I'm indebted to Lowell Bouma for sharing his analysis of the Modern German modal system, with which my analysis of the Modern English modals began (unpublished paper delivered to the Linguistic Society of America, December, 1968). Because the two systems are dissimilar, in particular the ambiguity with respect to internal agency versus external pressure of the English modals, I've reworked his description of German to represent the English system. For a fuller treatment of the English modals from a linguistic point of view, see F. R. Palmer, *Modality and the English Modals* (London: Longman, 1979).

11 In *The Road to Gandolfo* (Bantam Books, 1982, 272), Robert Ludlum uses *will* as an imperative with the form of a question, and his narrator comments on how it should be interpreted: "'*Will* you keep quiet!' The Hawk did not ask a question."

12 The cover of *TV Guide* (April 18–22, 1988), however, used *may* in what is clearly intended to indicate present, or, perhaps, continuative time: "What You *May* Not Be Noticing About TV News—and Should."

CHAPTER TWO:
LANGUAGE IS A WOMAN

1 For an analysis of the protection/predation axis in patriarchal logic and its function in holding together patriarchal descriptions of reality, see Sarah Lucia Hoagland's article, "Coercive Consensus," *Sinister Wisdom* Summer 1978: 86–92.

2 As cited in Janice G. Raymond, *A Passion for Friends: Toward a Philosophy of Female Affection* (Boston: Beacon Press, 1986), 151.

3 In her Introduction to *Gyn/Ecology: The Metaethics of Radical Feminism*, Mary Daly identified the patriarchal dichotomies that make textiles female and reserve "texts" for men, cf. especially 4–6.

4 I discovered Hildegard of Bingen in *Pure Lust* by Mary Daly (1984, 99). A benedictine nun, she was born at Böckelheim on the Nahe in 1098, and died in 1178. Known as the "Sibyl of the Rhine" because of her visions, she founded a new convent near Bingen around 1147. In addition to being a well-respected abbess, she was a poet who also wrote numerous treatises on a wide range of subjects, including medicine and natural history. Readers who want to learn more about Hildegard and her work can now consult Barbara Newman, *Sister of Wisdom: St. Hildegard's Theology of the Feminine* (Berkeley: University of California Press, 1987). Of the language created by Hildegard, mentioned specifically in Daly's *Pure Lust*, Newman has only this to say:

> Perhaps the oddest of all her works is the so-called *Unknown Language*, a list of about nine hundred artificial nouns and other words with an accompanying German glossary. The purpose of this invented language is unclear, although it includes many names for plants and herbs and may have been related to Hildegard's medical work. (12)

5 "Framing" is one of the essential processes in problem solving. (The other is naming.) When we identify what we perceive to be the significant aspects of a problem we wish to solve, we use metaphors (and analogies) to *frame* our perceptions. When we attempt to use two different metaphors to frame a problem (usually without being aware that we're using two metaphors), the metaphors may be incompatible. Two (or more) metaphors that don't work together create a "frame conflict." For further discussion of framing and frame conflict, see Schön (1979, 264–67).

6 My discussion of the metaphorical concept LANGUAGE IS A WOMAN and how it under-lies the prescriptivism of men like John Simon draws on two of my earlier essays, "John Simon and the 'Dragons of Eden'," *College English* December 1982: 848–54, and ""'Users and Abusers: On the Death of English," *The English Language Today*, ed. Sidney Greenbaum (Oxford: Pergamon, 1985), 80–91.

CHAPTER THREE: THE PATRIARCHAL UNIVERSE OF DISCOURSE

1 Charles F. Hockett begins "The Origin of Speech" (*Scientific American* September 1960: 3–10) by mentioning that the Linguistic Society of Paris banned papers speculating on the origins of language in its constitution (1865) because there was no way to prove or disprove hypotheses on the subject. James H. Stam examined the history of the issue in *Inquiries·into the Origin of Language: The Fate of a Question* (New York: Harper & Row, 1976).

In spite of his awareness of the problems, Hockett formulated a pragmatic hypothesis about how language might have arisen among proto-hominoids as their communication signals gradu-ally developed the 13 "design features" that distinguish human language from animal call systems. Hockett's theory of language origin was controversial, as he knew it would be. In 1964, the journal *Current Anthropology* June: 135–68, published an expanded version of Hockett's proposal, co-authored by anthropologist Robert Ascher, as well as critical responses from other scholars. (For a Feminist theory of evolution that includes a different hypothesis about how language originated, see Elaine Morgan, *The Descent of Woman* [New York: Stein and Day, 1972].)

2 Several Feminists have written analytical books about the cultural and social implications of the metaphorical concept, NATURE IS A WOMAN, and readers interested in exploring how the patriarchal conceptual framework has intertwined the two will want to read their books: Susan Griffin, *Woman and Nature: The Roaring Inside Her* (New York: Harper & Row, 1978); Annette Kolodny, *The Lay of the Land: Metaphor as Experience in American Life and Letters* (Chapel Hill: University of North Carolina Press, 1975); Carolyn Merchant, *The Death of Nature: Women, Ecology, and the Scientific Revolution* (San Francisco: Harper & Row, 1980).

3 There aren't many exemplary pairs of this particular contrast in English. The positive words that would be antonymous to those beginning with the Latin prefix *ab–* don't exist in the language, e.g., **-scond* < Lat. *abscondere, ab* 'away' + *condere* 'to put'; **-stract* < Lat. *abstractus*, p. part. of *abstrahere, ab* 'away' + *trahere* 'to draw'.

4 My thanks to Liza Cowan for passing this ad on to me.

5 The words in English forbidden to women include terms for bodily functions (*shit, piss*) parts of the body (*cunt, prick*), and heterosexual intercourse (*fuck, hairpie*); they are often lumped together as "obscenities," subjects that "ladies" aren't supposed to know or talk about. Because this segment of PUD has been declared "Off Limits" for us, we may feel "powerful" when we say them. Especially as children or teenagers, saying *fuck* or *eat shit* may have been an act of defiance, a way of rebelling against authority figures who told us how to behave and what we could do.

Because these taboo words are as much a part of PUD as any other set, however, and serve the masculist description of the world, we are understandably ambivalent about them as we become aware of their poisonous effect on our minds. For women, then, it becomes a question of exactly which words are susceptible to reclamation, that is, which words can we feel comfort-able saying because they express our perceptions and feelings about the world? *Cunt, slut*, and *fuck*, for example, may be fine words for women to utter if we identify contexts in which they seem to be the most accurate way of describing someone or something. I reserve the word *fuck*, for instance, to name what men do *to* women, restricting its reference to the universe of discourse in which it "makes sense."

In general, however, I think that patriarchal words express only men's perceptions. To the extent that women may feel as though such terms also express their perceptions, I would say that this sense is derivative; lacking a vocabulary of our own to name our bodies and what we feel, we use what is accessible to us, with or without some awareness of the self-derogation inherent in men's ways of talking about us.

6 In their analysis of the relationship between industrialization and the color terminologies of languages, Brent Berlin and Paul Kay identified Swahili as a Stage II language (1969, 59–60), one whose speakers don't require a large vocabulary of color terms. The three colors named by single words in Swahili are black (–eusi/nyeusi, and neusi used for dark shades), white (–eupe/nyeupe, and nyeupe for light shades), and red (ekundu, and nyekundu, for reddish shades, orange, rose, and brown).

In addition, Swahili has several color terms based on analogy to other phenomena or borrowed from other languages: kijani ('leaf-green'), kijivu ('grey' < 'ashes'), chungwa ('orange' < 'orange fruit'), kimanjano ('yellow' < 'turmeric'); from Arabic, khudhurungi ('brown'), from English, bulu ('blue'), and from Persian, urujuani ('purple').

7 This count of the number of synonyms for fuck in English is attributed to Eric Partridge by Peter Fryer in Mrs. Grundy: Studies in English Prudery (London: Dennis Dobson, 1963) on p. 75. The full quotation reads as follows:

Over 1,200 English synonyms for this word [fuck] have been recorded; their 'vivid expressiveness' and 'vigorous ingenuity' . . . .'bear witness to the fertility of English and to the enthusiastic English participation in the universal fascination of the creative act.'

8 This section draws on the semantic analysis in my article, "Heteropatriarchal Semantics: 'Just Two Kinds of People in the World,'"in Lesbian Ethics Fall 1986: 58–80.

9 In The Lonesome Node January/February 1982: 3–4, Suzette Haden Elgin commented, after reading a series of papers by Stanley R. Witkowski, Cecil H. Brown, and Paul K. Chase on how things get named (lexicalization), that she believed that the vocabulary would be very different if women had done the naming. Granting that they are "exceptionally fine articles on what things get named in human languages and why they are named as they are," she said:

After reading them several times, I realized that they offer the most extraordinarily MALE view of the lexicalization process! Not that I think they are wrong—on the contrary, given the dominance of males in language development, they are probably absolutely right. But I was fascinated by the fact that there is a quite different way of looking at their data.

10 Gregory Bateson was the first to describe "the double bind" in "A Theory of Play and Fantasy," where he identified a message, "This is play," as "a negative statement containing an implicit negative metastatement," comparable to Epimenides' paradox, "This statement is untrue." He interpreted the sentence "This is play" to mean something like, "These actions in which we now engage do not denote what those actions for which they stand would denote" (1972, 180) [His emphasis]. In "Epidemiology of a Schizophrenia" (1972, 194–200), he linked such messages to a case of schizophrenia in which the patient's mother habitually reclassified messages: "An endless taking of the other person's message and replying to it as if it were either a statement of weakness on the part of the speaker or an attack on her which should be turned into a weakness on the part of the speaker; . . . " (199). In "Toward a Theory of Schizophrenia," co-authored with Don D. Jackson, Jay Haley, and John H. Weakland, this moebius-like communication process was called the "double bind" (1972, 120–27).

11 Although it was first published in 1960, I chose to use the definitions provided by the Random House Dictionary because, where other dictionaries rely on our experience and knowl-

edge of social mores to infer which behaviors are "appropriate," "fitting," and "proper" for women and men, *RHD* is explicit.

CHAPTER FOUR:
GENDER: THE SEX OF NOUNS

1 The Indo-European language group includes German, French, Russian, Spanish, Portuguese, Italian, Welsh, Irish, Norwegian, Swedish, and English, to name a few, including the Indo-Iranian sub-group.

2 "Case," as a grammatical term, refers to the various functions a noun can serve in a sentence; these functions are determined by the relationship between a verb and the nouns that occur with it. Obviously, a noun can function many ways, depending on the sentence in which it occurs, so the case labels Nominative, Dative, Genitive, and Accusative name the four most frequent ways that nouns function in the sentences of I-E languages. Thus, a noun that functions as the "subject" of a verb, what I call, following linguistic terminology, the agent or topic, is said to be in the Nominative case. Nouns that function as the "direct object" of a verb are in the Accusative case, and the Dative case more or less corresponds to what you may know as the "indirect object" of a verb. Finally, one of the functions of nouns in the Genitive case is probably familiar as "possessive."

Unlike Latin, German, and other languages, English nouns are no longer inflected for case, with the exception of possessives, e.g., *Mary's* book. The *–s* at the end of *Mary* is all that remains of the Old English inflections, the genitive, and the apostrophe represents a long-forgotten vowel. In Modern English, some prepositions have been specialized to mark case relationships, e.g., *to* and *for* precede indirect objects of a verb, and *by* precedes agents when they occur after the verb in the passive voice. Ordinarily, agents and direct objects (patients) are unmarked in English, as they were in I-E. The sentence below contains four nouns, each of which has a different role in the sentence (agent, object, indirect object, possessive). (Only some English verbs can occur with agents, direct, and indirect objects. *Give* is one of them.) Above each noun phrase (NP), I've provided the classical case label.

Nominative	Verb	Genitive	Accusative	Dative
Hermione	gave	Gertrude's	book	to Madge.

If we change this sentence from the active to the passive voice, we have to insert the preposition *by* before the agent of the verb, e.g., Gertrude's book was given to Madge *by Hermione*.

3 In his critique of the semantic theory proposed by Jerrold J. Katz and Jerry A. Fodor (1964), "Explorations in Semantic Theory" (1971), Uriel Weinreich observed that their account of English semantics failed "to represent *as a productive process* the reference (especially by men) to lovingly handled objects by means of *she*. The patent fact is that any physical object can in English be referred to by *she* with a special semantic effect" (316–17).

4 Elizabeth S. Sklar attributed this observation to André Joly's "Toward a Theory of Gender in Modern English," *Studies in English Grammar*, eds. A. Joly and T. Fraser (Paris: Editions Universitaires, 1975), 245–48, in "Sexist Grammar Revisited," *College English* April 1983, 348–58. Sklar's essay corroborated, to a large extent, my analysis in "Sexist Grammar," and included, as well, evidence that "approximately fifteen grammar texts were published by women" between 1750 and 1800 (351).

5 My reference for the grammars of English written prior to 1800 is the facsimile edition, *English Linguistics, 1500–1800*, ed. R. C. Alston (Mentson: Scolar Press, 1967).

CHAPTER FIVE:
WOMAN'S PLACE IS IN THE HOME

1 But there is Láadan, a language of women's perceptions, created by Suzette Haden Elgin in June of 1982; a fictional account of its development was described in her novel *Native Tongue* (New York: DAW, 1984). Its newness and incompleteness, however, and the fact that it was created by an anglo, heterosexual, xtian woman mean that its accuracy for the expression of all women's perceptions will be severely limited for some time to come. These shortcomings can, theoretically, be eliminated by future developments in the language.

2 A case in point is William Labov's *The Social Stratification of English in New York City* (Washington, DC: Center for Applied Linguistics, 1966), which included one of the first linguistic descriptions of the Black English grammatical system and firmly established the relationship between one's social/economic class and dialect. Labov's study is regarded by many linguists as a landmark in sociolinguistics, but his analysis is based on male speech because he didn't identify sex as a linguistic variable.

3 See the work of Otto Jespersen, *Language: Its Nature, Development and Origin* (1921) and Mary Ritchie Key, *Male/Female Language* (1975) for differing accounts of the ways women's speech contrasts with men's in a variety of languages.

4 Key based her description of sex-specific linguistic differences on the following evidence: (1) for Cham, Doris Blood, "Women's Speech Differences in Cham," *Asian Culture* 3 (1962):3–4, 139–143; (2) for Gros Ventre, Regina Flannery, "Men's and Women's Speech in Gros Ventre," *International Journal of American Linguistics* 12 (1946), 133–135; (3) for Koasati, Mary R. Haas, "Men's and Women's Speech in Koasati," *Language* 20 (1944), 142–49 (reprinted in Dell Hymes, *Language in Culture and Society: A Reader in Linguistics and Anthropology* [New York: Harper and Row, 1964] 228–233); (4) for Yana, Edward Sapir, "Male and Female Forms of Speech in Yana," in St. W. J. Teeuwen, ed., *Donum natalicium schrijnen* (Nijmegan-Utrecht: Dekker and Van de Vegt, (n.d.): 79–85) (reprinted in *Selected Writings of Edward Sapir in Language, Culture and Personality* [Berkeley: University of California Press, 1968] 206–212).

5 The field of historical linguistics was inaugurated by Sir William Jones's observation of similarities among Sanskrit, Greek, Latin, Gothic, Celtic, and Old Persian in 1786, and he was the first to speculate that the similarities could be explained if those languages had a common ancestor. After several scholars (among them Grimm, Rask, and Schlegel) had attributed the observed similarities to regular sound shifts (e.g., Grimm's Law), the hypothesized proto-language came to be called "Indo-Aryan" or "Indo-Germanic," because most, but not all, of the scholars were Germans, cf. Brugmann's three-volume *Elements of the Comparative Grammar of the Indo-Germanic Languages*, first published in 1888. The German ethnocentricity and accompanying anti-Semitism which assumed that the ancestor language was aryan was erased in the twentieth century when linguists changed the name to "Indo-European" after Hitler's rise to power and attempts to eradicate the Jews. Jespersen, however, wrote in the tradition of the nineteenth-century historical linguists before Hitler undertook his program of genocide.

6 Linguists do not agree about how many languages exist, and the exact number of known languages on earth remains a matter for speculation. Some say there are 3,000 different languages, others say more. Mary Ritchie Key, for example, says that there are between four and five thousand languages (1975, 13). Here, I've decided to give a figure between the low of 3,000 and the high of 5,000.

7 The term *superordinate* may not be as familiar to readers as its antonym, *subordinate*. That relation of opposition explains much. Linguists use *superordinate* to refer to the semantic relationship between generic terms, which nonspecifically designate classes of objects or people, and the more specific words included in their scope of reference as subsets. Thus, *dwelling* is a *superordinate* term that includes the following *subordinate* words: *cabin, hut, palace, condominium; glass* is a superordinate term, and *goblet, pilsner,* and *shotglass* are its

subordinate terms; *vehicle* is a superordinate word, and *car, truck, van, bus, tank,* and *jeep* are subordinate words.

8 For my discussion of the Chinese radical *nu*[3] I am indebted to the generosity of Professor Louie Crew, who first shared Geoffrey Wade's essay with me, and to Mr. Chan Wing Cheung who transliterated the Chinese characters for me, explained the Mandarin tone system to me, and corrected errors in Wade's original. Geoffrey Wade's essay was published in the Hong Kong University Students' magazine, *Undergrad* August 1987: 21. Any errors of presentation or interpretation are my own.

9 The "words" listed in 5.2–5.6 are transliterations of the Chinese ideographs; that is, they are the "words" that the Chinese characters represent. As Chan Wing Cheung explained to me, the transliterations presented here are those of the Mandarin dialect, *pinyin*. The superscript number that follows each transliteration (1, 2, 3, 4) indicates the tone with which each "word" is pronounced:

1 = high tone
2 = rising tone
3 = dipping tone
4 = falling tone.

Speakers of English who want some idea of the differences in sound these numbers indicate can say two different types of question in English, one that can be answered either by "yes" or "no," the other that requires a more specific answer, e.g.,

yes/no question: [2]*Can I leave* [3]*nów*[3] ↗
wh-question: [2]*When can I expect* [3]*yóu?*[1] ↘

In English, yes/no questions typically end with what is called "rising intonation," whereas wh-questions end with "falling intonation."

CHAPTER SIX: THE PLACE OF WOMEN IN ENGLISH: HISTORY

1 Berlin and Kay's "map" of how the Swahili color vocabulary is used by its speakers (1969, 120) showed that, for what an English speaker might label 'aqua' or 'turquoise', a Swahili speaker might use *kijani* ('leaf-green'), or *neusi* or *meupe*, depending on its brightness. Swahili speakers may perceive what we call *aqua*, but they have no cultural use for the distinction.

2 Portions of the analysis presented in this chapter were first explored in two articles of mine, "*Woman* and *Wife*: Social and Semantic Shifts in English," *Papers in Linguistics* 12, 3–4 (1979), 491–502, with C. McGowan, and "Lexical Gaps and Lexicalization: A Diachronic Analysis," *Proceedings of the Tenth LACUS Forum*, 296–304.

3 In her discussion of existing approaches to representing the semantic features of human nouns, Key used the work of D. Terence Langendoen (1969) and James D. McCawley (1968). Also relevant to understanding how linguists arrive at their representations is John Lyons (1969; discussed in chapter 7).

4 Among the linguists cited by Key who have proposed the features [+male]/[+masculine] and [+female]/[+feminine] are Katz and Fodor (1964), Jacobs and Rosenbaum (1968), Gruber (1967), and Alyeshmerni and Taubr (1970). She quoted the last collaborators as they explained why they decided to use positive features:

> [the +male analysis] defines *woman* as "an adult human being without maleness," but it says nothing, for instance, about the fact that a woman has female reproductive organs and not simply an absence of male reproductive organs. We could define '−male' as '+female,' but this would be an ad hoc definition. It would not simplify the grids of such groups as *child, pup, kitten,* and *fawn*. To avoid the ad hoc definition, one must make *female* a feature here, as well as male. (80)

⁵ The word *war* entered English through borrowing from Norman French *werre*, which is, however, Gmc. in origin.

⁶ Many of the terms and their senses which I discuss in this section are based on Hilding Bäck's semasiological study (1933).

⁷ Readers interested in tracing the development of female-specific words from Proto-Indo-European may wish to peruse Carl Darling Buck's *A Dictionary of Selected Synonyms in the Principal Indo-European Languages*, (Chicago: University of Chicago Press, 1949), in which he organized synonyms from the I-E languages by category and sub-class. He noted, for example, that at one time New High German *weib* was considered a derogatory term and, as a consequence, was replaced by *frau*, permanently in the sense of 'wife', while for the sense 'female human being' it has regained respectability (82).

In section 2.2, Buck listed the following synonyms of *woman* as also meaning 'wife':

French: femme, épouse
Spanish: mujer, esposa
Irish: ben
Welsh: gwraig
Old Norse: kona
Old English: wīf, cwēn
Dutch: vrouw
Old High German: wīb, quena
Middle High German: wīp
New High German: frau

Serbo-Croatian: žena
Bohemian: žena
Sanskrit: janī-
Avestan: nāirī-
Lithuanian: žmona
Lettish: sieva
Church Slavonic: žena

(82–95)

According to Buck, the I-E words for 'man' and 'woman' were most commonly used to mean 'husband' and 'wife' (95).

CHAPTER SEVEN: THE PLACE OF WOMEN IN ENGLISH: TODAY

¹ In 1926, Vilem Mathesius founded the Linguistic Circle of Prague, a group that has influenced the development of linguistics in the twentieth century even though its members have produced no general conceptual model of language (Bolinger, 1975, 515–16). Both markedness and the use of binary features to represent contrast were introduced by scholars of the Prague Circle and are generally accepted among linguists.

² Diagram 7.1 expands Chomsky's partial representation of the common nouns in English (1965, 83) to analyze that portion of the vocabulary his analysis omitted. The section of Chomsky's diagram relevant to my discussion looked like this:

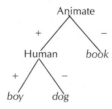

Without explaining why he diagrammed ModE nouns in this way, Chomsky managed to avoid saying that all nouns marked [+human] are interpreted as [+male]; to be "human" in English is to be [+male].

3 Her discussion of the semantic contrast between *lady* and *woman* is among Robin Lakoff's (1975) most perceptive analyses. Acknowledging that the contrast may derive from the sexual connotations of *woman*, she reminded her readers that, when people are asked why they used *lady* instead of *woman*, they say that *lady* seems "more polite."

> The concept of politeness thus invoked is the politeness used in dignifying or ennobling a concept that normally is not thought of as having dignity or nobility. It is this notion of politeness that explains why we have *cleaning lady*, but not, normally, *lady doctor*. (24)

I don't know what Lakoff had in mind when she said that *lady doctor* doesn't "normally" occur, but my evidence indicates that she was wrong in believing that a doctor didn't "need to be exalted by conventional expressions" because her professional status bestowed all the dignity she needed (24–25). Women are so degraded and demeaned in ModE that even *lady* fails to confer dignity upon us, no matter what we do or say.

Because *lady* is "devoid of sexual connotation," Lakoff continued, it is the euphemism for *woman*, which is "too blatantly sexual." Illustrating the sexual connotations of *woman*, she provided three contexts in which *woman*, but not *lady*, because of its hint of "politeness," sounds appropriate.

a. She's only twelve, but she's already a { woman / *lady. }

b. After ten years in jail, Harry wanted to find a { woman / *lady. }

c. She's my { woman / *lady } , see, so don't mess around with her. (25–26)

4 J. L. Austin introduced the idea of "illocutionary mistakes" in *How to Do Things with Words* (1970, 10–11) although he was writing explicitly about what he called "Infelicities" in the uttering of performative statements. A "performative" sentence is one in which the action of the verb is *executed* by uttering the sentence, as in "I *christen* this ship . . . ," "I *pronounce* you . . . ," or "I *vow* to avenge. . . . "

Promise is a performative verb in Austin's sense: the speaker must be the first person, *I*; the verb must be in the present tense; and the adverb *hereby* can be optionally explicit in the utterance. When the comedian said "I promised my banker that I wouldn't cash checks and he wouldn't cook meals," only the first part of the promise can be executed because no one can make a promise on behalf of someone else. This type of mistake Austin called "infelicitous." Whether her audience laughed at her "mistake" as well as her use of the dumb woman stereotype I don't know.

5 Much of the analysis of pseudo-generics, occupational terms and other "human" nouns is based on my article "Gender-Marking in American English: Usage and Reference," *Sexism in Language*, eds. Alleen Pace Nilsen et al. (Urbana: National Council of Teachers of English, 1977), 43–74.

6 Several studies have demonstrated that both *he* and *man* are conceptually confusing even when they are interpreted as encompassing women as well as men. Most often, however, pseudo-generics are interpreted as exclusively referring to males among adults and children. See, for example, "The Case for Nonsexist Language" (1983) and "What Does 'he' Mean? Use of the Generic Masculine" (1978), both by Wendy Martyna; "Does Sex-biased Job Advertising 'aid and abet' Sex Discrimination?" by Sandra and Daryl Bem (1973); Joan Huber's "On the Generic Use of Male Pronouns" (1976); and Alleen Pace Nilsen's "Sexism in Children's Books and Elementary Classroom Materials" (1977).

7 The information regarding the prescriptivists' method of condemning plural *they* and substituting *he* as the "correct" pronoun draws on my article "Sexist Grammar" (1978).

8 Ann Bodine concluded, after her search of prescriptive grammars, that Lindley Murray was the first grammarian to declare *they* "ungrammatical" when it referred to *anyone, everyone,* or

everybody and to assert that *he* was the "correct" pronoun to replace an indefinite antecedent because it agreed in "number" (1975, esp. 131–36).

9 I collected the terms analyzed in "Paradigmatic Woman: The Prostitute" from a variety of sources. In addition to examples brought to me by colleagues, students, and friends who knew about my research, I combed numerous slang dictionaries and books, including the *OED*, Eric Partridge's *Dictionary of Slang and Unconventional English* (1961), Hyman E. Goldin et al., eds., *Dictionary of American Underworld Lingo* (1962), Harold Greenwald, *The Elegant Prostitute* (1970), Xaviera Hollander, *The Happy Hooker* (1972), John Barth, *The Sot-Weed Factor* (1966), Vance Randolph and George P. Wilson, *Down in the Holler: A Gallery of Ozark Folk Speech* (1953), Eugene Landy, *The Underground Dictionary* (1971), J. Redding Ware, *Passing English of the Victorian Era* (n.d.), Harold Wentworth and Stuart Berg Flexner, eds., *Dictionary of American Slang* (1931), and Maurice H. Weseen, *A Dictionary of American Slang* (1960).

CHAPTER EIGHT: *THAT'S* HOW *IT* IS!

1 The prescriptive definition of pronouns, "A pronoun replaces a noun," is another inaccuracy we memorized in school. This is a functional definition; it tells us what a pronoun does, not what a pronoun is. Even as a functional definition, it describes only some cases, those instances when a noun occurs without determiners or modifiers, e.g., so-called proper nouns, such as the ubiquitous *John* and *Mary*, and fails to cover several other common types of pronominal replacement. In fact, pronouns replace entire NPs, not just nouns, whether the NP consists of a single noun or a larger syntactic unit functioning as an NP. In the following sentence, *it* in the second clause replaces *the ball*.

a. I hit *the ball*, and Tina caught *it*.

If we followed the prescriptive rule instead of our own knowledge of English, we'd end up with a non-sentence: *I hit the ball, and Tina caught the it*.

Other varieties of NPs that pronouns replace are illustrated in the next three examples.

b. *Joan and Jill* had dinner and then *they*** went home.

c. I saw *the cows lying* in the pasture yesterday, but *they* weren't there today. (*There* replaces *in the pasture*.)

d. *Doing nothing all day* may be fine for some people, but I don't like *it*.

**In sentences like b., the pronoun may not appear at all, e.g., *Joan and Jill had dinner and then went home*, without any loss of intelligibility.

2 English provides numerous ways of replacing repetitions with single words, usually very short ones. In endnote 1 above I illustrated how pronouns replace a variety of NPs. Similarly, we replace verb phrase repetitions with "proverbs," such as *do* and *do so*. In the following examples, it's also possible to omit *do* in b. and *so* in c.

a. I had grocery shopping to do and *so did* Jane.

b. Tulips bloom later than daffodils *do*.

c. Don't spit on the sidewalk even though others *do so*.

3 For example, Halliday and Hasan, in *Cohesion in English* (1976), presented a comprehensive analysis of how various kinds of substitution provide cohesion within a text by enabling us to refer back and forth across discourse.

4 A word of caution: I'm not talking about sentences like *It's raining*, *It's snowing*, or *It's too bad you missed the party* and *It's a good thing I came along just now*. The first two examples show a peculiarity of many languages; apparently anomalous constructions for talking about the weather. In the second pair of sentences *it* has been substituted for whole clauses, *that you missed the party* and *that I came along just now*.

5 Richard A. Spears, in *Slang and Euphemism* (1981), says that the use of *it* without an explicit antecedent to refer to both the female and male genitals is a "very old euphemism." Hugh Rawson, in *A Dictionary of Euphemisms and Other Doubletalk* (1981), cited Randle

Cotgrave's 1611 definition of *fretiller*, "to lust to be at it," as an early example of *it*'s use to refer to heterosexual copulation, and D. G. Kehl suggested that the Cotgrave example precurses the contemporary spate of bumper stickers. In his article, "Doublespeak, Double-Entendre, and the Case of the Ambiguous 'It'" (1982), Kehl described the intentional use of ambiguous *it* as having a dual purpose, "either to *cloak* any unpleasantness one prefers not to divulge or to *evoke* associations of pleasantness one cannot overtly claim to produce." These functions merge, according to Kehl, in the "literary double-entendre" which cloaks "indecorous" or "indecent" meanings at the same time that it seeks to evoke them" (3).

6 In June, 1989, a Massachusetts court awarded custody to LaLonde's ex-husband because she hadn't proved that he molested their daughter Nicole.

7 The line between transitive and intransitive verbs in English is virtually nonexistent. A verb is transitive if it has an explicit object and intransitive if it doesn't, and most verbs in English allow optional omission of their objects. Verbs like *dance, sing*, and *dream*, for example, take a limited set of objects. *Tell*, in 8.12, belongs to this class of verbs. We dance dances and jigs, we sing songs, airs, and tunes, we dream dreams, and objects of *tell* are NPs describing a linguistic act, e.g., a lie, a story. Similarly, the objects of verbs like *bake* and *cook* are predictable unless the verb is used in a metaphorical sense. Only a few English verbs are inherently intransitive, e.g., *disappear*, yet I've found several examples of its use as a transitive (*I disappeared the cookies*).

The verb *start* is usually transitive; we *start* something, a car, singing, watching TV. In 8.12, however, *start* is used by the incest victim as an intransitive verb (a verb without an object) in order to suppress the identity of its agent. So she omitted any reference to her father, substituted *it* for the object of the verb (what he did to her), *raping me*, and made *it* the topic.

8 The word *incest* is a euphemism that protects men. It suggests that the sexuality is mutual, reciprocal, equally voluntary and beneficent for child and parent, and is silent about the father's betrayal of his daughter's trust and love, silent about the difference in power between the adult and the child. The violence inherent in the word *rape* makes it an accurate description but, again, it fails to describe the horrors of children betrayed, used, then threatened into silence by an adult who is supposed to protect them. *Forced sex* borders on euphemism and omits the male perpetrator who violates the child's body and trust. *Sexual molestation* and *sexual abuse* are not only euphemistic, but make the violence abstract and erase both the victim and the perpetrator from consciousness. Yet, even the repetition of those expressions would fail to represent adequately the pain, humiliation, shame, deceit, and betrayal the father is responsible for causing. After a while, we become inured to repeated horrors.

Two other compounds have been suggested to replace the word *incest* by survivors of rape as children, *father rape* and *daughter rape*. Neither of these is satisfactory because both are ambiguous. The compounding rules of English we use to create such phrases make them structurally ambiguous because the first nouns in those phrases can be either the subject or object of the verb *rape*. That is, we can interpret *father rape* as 'rape by a father' or 'the rape of a father', and *daughter rape* as 'the rape of a daughter' or 'rape by a daughter'. Both structures tell the same lie as the word *incest*, and trying to make visible either the male agent or the female victim fails to say what we want to say. Furthermore, using the terms for a specific familial relationship isn't fully accurate. These compounds hide the fact that ANY male relative considers ANY female (or male) child his legitimate *prey*. It isn't "just" fathers who rape children they have access to, and it isn't "just" their daughters that they rape.

Yes, we may "know" that daughters don't rape their fathers, but our knowledge of the real world doesn't make those phrases nonambiguous. It is an ambiguity we cannot allow to exist. Here, the English language is fully exposed as collaborating in the protection of men: there doesn't seem to be a way, using the rules of the language, that we can create a word or phrase that expresses accurately, fully, and explicitly the horror of the violence men do to children.

Yet another syntactic euphemism for rape evidences men's determination to deny their responsibility for rape. On the program *20/20* in June, 1989, Kate Moran heard the following description of "date rape": "The rise of AIDS on college campuses is due to *unconsented sexual activity."* The phrase "sexual activity" suggests that nothing violent or harmful has occurred; it hides RAPE. The modifier *unconsented,* if one accepts it as an English word, utterly erases the agency of the male rapist and, instead, implicitly focuses our attention on the woman who didn't "consent" to rape! Men are getting desperate.

CHAPTER NINE: THE AGENTS WITHIN

[1] Not all instances of passive use are evil. There are some occasions, for example, when using the passive rule produces better sentences than the active versions. Such sentences usually involve nesting one sentence within another. For example, the b. sentences below are clearer than their a. versions, although both are grammatical.

1. a. The punch bowl *the party-goers had emptied by midnight* suddenly crashed to the floor.
   b. The punch bowl *emptied by midnight* suddenly crashed to the floor.
2. a. The floor *I had carefully scrubbed and polished earlier that day* was now a mess.
   b. The floor, *carefully scrubbed and polished earlier that day,* was now a mess.

[2] My discussion and analysis of the rhetorical motivations served by the truncated passive is an expanded version of the information I first presented in "Passive Motivation," *Foundations of Language* 13 (1975): 25–39 and, later, in "The Stylistics of Belief," *Teaching About Doublespeak,* ed. Daniel J. Dieterich (Urbana, IL: National Council of Teachers of English, 1976), 175–87.

[3] To the best of my knowledge, Anna Lee first defined and explained the idea of "revokable privilege" in "A Black Separatist," in *For Lesbians Only,* eds. Sarah Lucia Hoagland and Julia Penelope (London: Onlywomen Press, 1988), 87. In that article, she distinguished between *power* and *privilege*: white men have power, white women have privilege derived from white male power. Furthermore, according to Lee, white women's privilege is "revokable" because it is derived. When a white woman exercises her privilege in a manner that defies or threatens white male dominance, white men can "revoke" her privilege, i.e., ignore her white skin and treat her as outcast.

[4] Robin Lakoff introduced her analysis of the *get*-passive in a paper presented to the Chicago Linguistic Society in April, 1971, in which she pointed out that the *get*-passive, unlike the *be*-passive, betrays the speaker's negative judgment of an event, person, or object.

[5] The fact that the prenominal position of passive adjectives forces us to interpret them as attributes of the noun they precede I have called *syntactic exploitation,* first in a paper entitled "Syntactic Exploitation: Passive Adjectives in English" (1972), then as one of several rhetorically useful syntactic structures in "The Stylistics of Belief" (1976). Later, I presented a more thorough analysis of how we interpret both pre- and post-nominal truncated passives in "Style and Choice in English Syntax: Target Structures and Rule Conspiracies" (1979).

[6] I first identified the rhetorical uses of nominalized passives in my paper, "Nominalized Passives" (1972), and later included them in "The Stylistics of Belief" (1976). In *The Syntax and Semantics of Complex Nominals* (1978), Judith N. Levi attempted a comprehensive, if unresolved, analysis of the morphology and syntax of every type of nominalization in English.

[7] In "Grammar, Society and the Noun," British linguist M. A. K. Halliday, discussing "the function of language in establishing value systems and systems of social control" (4), described nominalization as the means of reducing a process to a simple equation (22). He maintained, however, that nominalizations, although they require the omission of tense and person, also mean "freedom of movement," because "[w]hen processes, qualities, states, relations, or attributes are 'objectified' they take on the potentialities otherwise reserved to persons and objects" (24).

Unfortunately, when Halliday spoke about "objectification," he defined it as patterning "on (some aspect of) the outer world rather than on our subjective experience" (22), and this cannot be the case. I would say, in fact, that the opposite would be a more accurate description: The processes (verbs) we choose to treat as nouns by nominalizing them represent, not patterns inherent in the outside world, but patterns we impose on the world, patterns based on our subjective experience, that is, how we believe we perceive the world. What Halliday called "freedom of movement" I would describe as the imposition of male ways of thinking.

However, I agree in a qualified way with Halliday's conclusions about the relationship between the structure of English and how we learn to perceive the world. Halliday said:

> All the various distinctions that the child learns to associate with nouns, such as common or proper, general or specific, count or mass, concrete or abstract, definite or indefinite, as well as the various roles occupied by nouns in clause structure, provide a part of the conceptual framework for his [sic] mental development, and thus for the formation of his [sic] ideas about himself [sic] and society. (26)

The distinctions made by nouns, including nominalizations, not only contribute to our conceptual structure; they are the basis for our ideas about ourselves and the society we live in. But those distinctions do not inhere in objects and people in the world; they are not "objective." They are subjective, and inhere in the heteropatriarchal values we learned as children. As such, nouns represent an important element in the maintenance and perpetuation of the "consensus reality" promulgated by PUD.

CHAPTER TEN: ACTING IN THE WORLD

1 Donald Smith's analysis of the syntactic structure of experiencer-predicates and the rhetorical implications of suppressed experiencers appeared in "Experiencer Deletion," *Glossa* 9, 2 (1975): 182–201.

2 In *Cross-Over Phenomena* (Holt, Rinehart and Winston, 1971), Paul Postal described psychological predicates as "a class of verbal/adjectival stems containing several hundred members that refer to psychological features of animate beings" (41). Postal was the first linguist to show their behavior to be consistent with other syntactic phenomena in English, although others had previously described some of their features, e.g., G. Lakoff (1968), Chapin (1967), and Rosenbaum (1967).

3 Much of my analysis of sex-marked predicates here is based on an earlier article, co-authored by Susan J. Wolfe and me, "Sex-marked Predicates in English," *Papers in Linguistics* Fall–Winter 1978: 487–516.

4 I was first made aware of the fact that men experience monthly cycles similar to those of women by Mary Brown Parlee's article, "The Rhythms in Men's Lives," *Psychology Today* April 1978: 82; 85–6; 91. Parlee lists among her references the following: Doering, C. H., Kraemer, H. C., Brodie, H. K. H., and Hamburg, D. A., "A Cycle of Plasma Testosterone in the Human Male," *Journal of Endocrinology and Metabolism* 1975; Hersey, R. B., "Emotional Cycles in Man," *Journal of Mental Science* 1931; Luce, Gay B., *Body Time* (New York: Bantam, 1973); Richter, Curt, "Periodic Phenomena in Man and Animals: Their Relations to Endocrine Mechanisms (A Monthly or Near-Monthly Cycle)," in *Endocrinology and Human Behavior: Proceedings*, ed. R. P. Michael (London: Oxford University Press, 1968).

5 Most people have known for some time that talking about the sun "rising" or "setting" falsely describes the events, that the descriptions represent the way we perceive the sun's movement. What is not as well known, or talked about, is how the semantic structure of a language encodes speaker perceptions, not what may actually be happening. The distinction between what is perceived as animate or inanimate is demonstrably false, because words like *tree, bush, plant* and *cauliflower* are marked as [-animate] in the English vocabulary, and other things we perceive to be inanimate may be alive, too. In the October, 1988, issue of *Omni*, Ed Regis and Tom Dworetzky reported on the research now being conducted on the creation of artificial life forms (ALF), which indicates that what we had previously thought to be inanimate matter may, in fact, be animate. What we perceive as alive, carbon-based organisms, have several

traits: they are born, they grow, (some) reproduce, they die; they evolve, mutate, create (sometimes) more successful versions, they interact with their environment, eat, and excrete the resulting waste.

But these characteristics we identify with animacy are shared by soil, crystals, membranes composed of inert chemicals. Now scientists think that what we call "being" is "a system that orders random matter in a specific way. As long as it follows certain patterns and rules . . . any sort of thing could be alive . . . All that counts is that these materials—whatever they may be—have the right organization, the right logic." They quote Richard Dawkins, a biologist at Oxford University: "Life is not a substance; there's no 'living material.' . . . It's just an incidental fact that real living things happen to be made of organic, soft, squishy stuff" (96).

The descriptions we assume to be accurate reflections of the world we live in are products of how our brains interpret the information we get from our biased, barely adequate senses.

6 Marilyn Frye has discussed the cognitive limitations Lesbians accept when we use words borrowed from heterosexual language to describe our most intimate physical experiences with other Lesbians, starting with the word sex. She suggests, instead, "creating a vocabulary that elaborates and expands our meanings, a fine-tuned descriptive vocabulary that maps and expresses the differences and distinctions among the things we do, the kinds of pleasure we get, . . . and so on" ("Lesbian 'Sex,'" Sinister Wisdom Summer/Fall, 1988: 53–54).

7 My presentation in this chapter extends my analysis of the rhetorical uses of topic selection published previously in "Topicalization: The Rhetorical Strategies It Serves and the Interpretive Strategies It Imposes," Linguistics 20 (1982): 683–95.

8 Linguists use the term focus (also "sentence focus") to label an NP that occurs at the end of a sentence, because the intonation pattern of declarative sentences in English requires us to say them with maximum stress and relatively high pitch (3) at the end. NPs that end declarative sentences are said to be in "focus position" because linguists believe that this position forces listeners to pay more attention to them. How this correlates with the rhetorical purposes of topicalization, the occurrence of agents at the end of passivized sentences, and the alleged correlation between "new" versus "old" information and sentence position has yet to be explained.

CHAPTER ELEVEN: SPEAKING OUT

1 Edward Sapir (1921), one of the first linguists in the u.s., and his student, Benjamin Lee Whorf (1956), gave their names to the hypothesis that the structural properties of languages determine how we conceptualize the world. Since the 1950s, linguists, especially the transformationalists, have made numerous attempts to discredit the stipulated relationship between language and thought, and continue to analyze languages as though their cultural and social contexts were irrelevant in order, they say, to discover linguistic "universals." The resulting descriptions of language are simplistic, based almost exclusively on men's interpretations of linguistic evidence gathered mostly from male informants. Having determined that the purpose of linguistics is the discovery and elucidation of universal properties of language, mainstream linguists have dismissed research on language use with the result that the field of linguistics, without formal notice, is now dominated by theoretical proclamations about language abstracted from its social context, while those of us who study language use are marginalized as somehow less "respectable."

2 In the first of "Two Essays on Language and Change: I: Power and the Opposition to Feminist Proposals for Language Change," College English December 1982: 840–48, I described the six basic arguments against feminist proposals for changing the English language. Each argument takes a variety of forms, but none of them refutes the claim that English is sexist; each accepts that claim as valid and proceeds to argue that change itself is undesirable. Briefly, they are

1. DENIAL: The language itself is neutral. It is speakers who use language in sexist ways because they have sexist attitudes. Therefore, we have to change people's attitudes, not the language.
2. CREATIVITY: Even if there are sexist expressions in English, asking us to refrain from using them is asking us to deprive ourselves of "the expressive possibilities in which English is so rich." Therefore, asking us to change the ways we use language stifles our creativity.
3. TRIVIALIZATION: The problem of sexism in language is not a "real" issue at all. It is a "red herring" introduced by feminists who don't know what they're talking about. Therefore, let's work on "substantial" issues, such as "equal pay for equal work."
4. ESTHETIC: Granted there is sexism in language, all of the alternative suggestions are "awkward," "clumsy," "wordy," and, besides, "they don't sound right." Therefore, because nonsexist language is lacking in "esthetic appeal," we are entitled to resist changes in language on the grounds of "taste."
5. NEGATIVITY: Because sexism in language is a result of sexism in society at large, we cannot change attitudes by changing language. Therefore, let's concentrate on changing social structures, then language change will follow as a consequence.
6. CENSORSHIP: Given that specific uses of English are sexist, each author has the "right" to write in a sexist way, and editorial policies that require nonsexist forms of expression constitute censorship that threatens the writer's "freedom of speech." (842–43)

3There are several excellent collections of articles on the relationship between language and thought, class, race, and sex, and any one of them will provide interested readers with more information about how language reflects the way we think. Among the most readable are *Language*, ed. Virginia P. Clark, Paul A. Eschholz, and Alfred A. Rosa, 4th ed. (New York: St. Martin's Press, 1985); *Language Awareness*, ed. Paul Eschholz, Alfred Rosa, and Virginia Clark, 3rd ed. (New York: St. Martins' Press, 1982); *Language Power*, ed. Carol J. Boltz and Dorothy U. Seyler (New York: Random House, 1982); *Speaking of Words: A Language Reader*, ed. James MacKillop and Donna Woolfolk Cross, 2nd ed. (New York: Holt, Rinehart and Winston, 1982); and *Exploring Language*, ed. Gary Goshgarian (Boston: Little, Brown and Co., 1983). There are also single-author books analyzing contemporary language use: *How Language Works* by Madelon E. Heatherington (Cambridge, MA: Winthrop Publishers, 1980) and *Language: The Loaded Weapon* by Dwight Bolinger (London: Longman, 1980).

4 Words like *crippled* and *blind* continue to be used as metaphors in contexts where one might hope for more sensitivity to the implications of language use. In the January 23, 1989, issue of *Time*, for example, Susan Tifft quoted the trustees of Dartmouth College as denouncing the editors of *Dartmouth Review* for "ignorance and moral *blindness*" ("Bigots in the Ivory Tower," 56), and, in a letter soliciting contributions, a lobbyist for the National Gay and Lesbian Task Force described Jesse Helms as wanting "to add *crippling* amendments" to the congressional bill against hate crimes (August, 1989). Apparently, sensitivity to prejudiced language in one situation doesn't carry over into other contexts.

5 In an article in *Natural History* (April, 1989), "This-Fellow Frog, Name Belong-Him Dakwo," Jared Diamond attributed the naming process of the Foré people of the New Guinea Highlands to their "economic view": The Foré distinguish hundreds of plants, birds, and insects not recognized by western naturalists on the basis of what is or is not worth hunting.

> This ultimately economic view of Foré naming is borne out by what the Foré do not name. I was surprised that the Foré had no names for individual stars or constellations, which were all lumped as *norí*. Surely, I thought, the constellations are much more distinctive than Guinea's species of little green warblers. . . . In the rugged terrain of New Guinea's mountains, it's impossible to go anywhere in a straight line, and following a compass direction is futile. . . . Besides, you can't see stars when you're inside the jungle . . . the Foré don't clutter their minds with useless names. (18–19)

As with other analyses of naming, the hunting model accounts for which objects of the world are lexicalized by Foré men. No women are mentioned in this article, as though the only interesting aspects of the Foré vocabulary are those significant to men.

6 In addition to the dictionaries discussed in this chapter, interested readers may be able to find copies of the following: Varda One's columns on *Manglish* (1970–71) in *Everywoman*, discussed in the Introduction to Kramarae, Treichler, and Russo's *A Feminist Dictionary*, 10; Ingrid Bengis, *A Woman's New World Dictionary* (in Special Collections at Northwestern University, Evanston, Illinois); Marleen Dixon and Joreen, "A Dictionary of Women's Liberation," *Everywoman* August 1970: 16–17; Bina Goldfield, *The Efemcipated English Handbook* (New York: Westover Press, 1983); Midge Lennert and Norma Willson, eds., *A Woman's New World Dictionary* (Lomita, CA: 51% Publications); Ruth Todasco, ed., *An Intelligent Woman's Guide to Dirty Words* (Chicago: Loop Center YWCA).

7 The historical connection between Lesbians and the Amazons was chosen as the title of the Radical Lesbian journal *Amazones d'hier/Lesbiennes d'aujourd'hui*.

8 Readers who want additional information about *Hotwire* can write to the Editor, Toni Armstrong, at 5210 N. Wayne, Chicago, IL 60640. The 64-page journal carries news about women's music, festivals, interviews, and much more. It appears three times a year and subscriptions are $14/US, $17 Canada (US $).

9 The conceptual connection between women as sexual objects and men's sexual aggression and the grammatical categories of "subject" and object has been discussed in numerous Feminist books and periodicals. Among the most prominent are Kate Millet, *Sexual Politics* (New York: Equinox Books, 1980), esp. 26–58; Phyllis Chesler, *Women & Madness* (Garden City, NY: Doubleday & Co., 1972), esp. 276–83; three books by Andrea Dworkin, *Woman Hating* (New York: E. P. Dutton, 1974), *Our Blood* (New York: Harper & Row, 1976), esp. chapter 9, "The Root Cause," 96–111, and *Pornography: Men Possessing Women* (New York: Perigee Books, 1981), esp. 102–28; Susan Griffin's *Rape: The Power of Consciousness* (San Francisco: Harper & Row, 1979) and *Pornography and Silence: Culture's Revenge Against Nature* (New York: Harper & Row, 1981), esp. 211–32; Mary Daly's *Gyn/Ecology: The Metaethics of Radical Feminism* (Boston: Beacon Press, 1978), and *Pure Lust: Elemental Feminist Philosophy* (Boston: Beacon Press, 1984); Michelle Cliff, "Object into Subject: Some Thoughts on the Work of Black Women Artists," *Heresies* 4, 3: 34–40; *Feminism & Institutions: Dialogues on Feminist Theory*, ed. Linda Kauffman (Cambridge, MA: Basil Blackwell, 1989), esp. "Criticus Interruptus: Uncoupling Feminism and Deconstruction" by Bella Brodzki and Celeste Schenck, 194–208; "Writing Against Writing and Other Disruptions in Recent French Lesbian Texts," Alice Parker, 211–39; "Negotiating Subject Positions in an Uneven World," R. Radhakrishnan, 276–90.

10 For a thorough examination of this point, I recommend Cheris Kramarae's book, *Women and Men Speaking* (Rowley, MA: Newbury House, 1981).

11 Diane M. Dickey, Senior Communications Coordinator, Corporate Communications at the Kellogg Co. denied me permission to quote the entire S. W. Grahams commercial because, in her view, my interpretation of it wasn't fair.

> The provocative interpretations of dialogue in your book will certainly start good discussions . . . However, Kellogg commercials are intended to be used to fairly and accurately portray our products to consumers. This is not the usage intended by your interpretation, so we must decline permission to quote the copy in your book. (Letter, November, 1989)

Kellogg's refusal of my request to quote one of their advertisements is a subtle, hard-to-define form of censorship: if we are unable to analyze advertisements critically in print, especially if the results posit a relationship between the ad as a structured discourse and the social expectations of its intended audience, how are we to seek accountability from the corporations whose advertising dollars determine the quality of programming available to us?

Because I was denied permission to quote the advertisement, I have paraphrased all but the essential statements.

Glossary

accusative: In classical grammars, the case name for noun phrases functioning as objects of a verb in inflected languages. ("Inflected" means that such languages have special morphemes that are suffixed to nouns to signal their case relationship to the verb.) See also **declension**.

adjective: A type of predicate which, in English, requires a tense-marked form of *be*, e.g., *true, yellow, edible*; when an adjective occurs before a noun, in prenominal position, it is interpreted as an attribute, an inherent characteristic, of that noun.

adverb: A category of words that qualify predicates (verbs, adjectives) or entire clauses and sentences, e.g., *fairly, usually, now*, adding information regarding the time, place, or manner of the action described by the predicate.

agent: The grammatical role of a noun phrase functioning as the instigator of whatever action a verb describes. Agents must be animate and are usually [+human]. In the sentence, *Mary caught the ball, Mary* is the agent of the verb *caught*.

agent-deletion: In English, speakers can suppress the agent of a verb in a variety of syntactic structures. For example, the agent can be omitted in infinitive clauses *Mary liked **to drink** soda*), passive sentences (*The car **was totaled***), and reduced relative clauses (*the jewels **stolen last night***). When a passive verb becomes a prenominal modifier, however, agent-deletion is obligatory (*this **ravaged** earth*).

ambiguity: An inherent property of language resulting from the fact that apparently identical words and syntactic structures are produced by different processes or rules. Lexical ambiguity occurs when a word refers to more than one thing, e.g., *bank*. When the position of a clause or phrase suggests two or more possible interpretations, **syntactic ambiguity** is the result, e.g., **Driving home** *I saw an empty bus*.

animate/inanimate: The semantic feature of nouns that represents the conceptual dichotomy between things that are thought of as living and things that are not, e.g., *cat, lizard*, and *person* are [+animate] nouns; *rock, tree*, and *star* are [−animate] in English. Mobility, the ability to move voluntarily, appears to be the perceptual basis for categorization.

antecedent: The noun phrase, usually preceding, for which a pronoun is substituted in subsequent discourse. In the sentence, *Elaine cooked the pasta and we ate **it**, pasta* is the **antecedent** of *it*.

antonym: One of a pair of words conceptualized as representing semantically opposite properties; e.g., *up/down, forward/backward, female/male, black/white*.

article: See **determiner**.

aspect: Aspect is a temporal category that indicates whether the action of a verb is considered to be completed or ongoing, habitual or momentary. English is said to have two aspects, each of which is indicated by an auxiliary verb that precedes the main verb and a suffix attached to the main verb: the *progressive, be* + *–ing* and the *perfect, have* + *–ed*. We use the progressive aspect to describe actions going on at the time we speak, e.g., *I am leaving.* The perfect aspect indicates actions that occurred prior to the time we speak, e.g., *I have eaten.*

aspiration: An expulsion of breath during speech, especially characteristic of the pronunciation of consonants in certain phonological environments.

background: Wilson Bryan Key (1972, 1977) and Mary Daly (1978, 2–3) describe the Background as consisting of those suppressesd (or hidden) objects, actions and people that members of a culture try to ignore. In the u.s., for example, *aging, incest, lesbians*, and the *clitoris* are background subjects.

bilingual: The ability to speak two different languages.

conceptual metaphor: A conceptual metaphor is the abstract, cognitive equation of two otherwise unrelated ideas. Conceptual metaphors structure the way we think and talk about our behaviors and actions. In English, we describe feeling good as "up" and feeling bad as "down"; many sports provide conceptual metaphors used to describe political events. Following Lakoff and Johnson, I represent conceptual metaphors in capital letters: UP IS GOOD, DOWN IS BAD, POLITICS IS FOOTBALL, LANGUAGE IS A WOMAN.

dative: The case of a noun phrase that functions as the indirect object of a verb or, in some instances, as its direct object. In English, noun phrases functioning as indirect objects are often preceded by the prepositions *to* or *for* when they follow the direct object, e.g., *I gave the book* **to Mary** but *I gave* **Mary** *the book; I bought the car* **for Lisa** but *I bought* **Lisa** *the car.*

declension: In inflected languages, a class of words that share identical or similar endings to mark their case relationship with verbs.

deixis: The function of some classes of words is to *point out* and identify specific objects. Adverbs, for example, can function deictically to identify objects or events in location or time; pronouns are supposed to function deictically in discourse by referring to preceding or following noun phrases; definite determiners specify one item in a class of identical or similar objects.

deletion: The omission or suppression of some grammatical element, either because it's already been mentioned or because the speaker doesn't want to mention it explicitly.

demonstrative pronoun: See **pronoun**.

determiner: In English grammars, articles are also called determiners. There are two: the indefinite determiner *a* or *an*, and the definite determiner, *the*. In addition, the **demonstrative pronouns**, *this/these* and *that/those*, and numbers, *one, two, nine*, can also function as determiners, e.g., *I only ate* **one** *cookie.*

devoicing: When speakers drop the feature *voice* from a consonant in some speech environments, that sound is described as devoiced; the process is devoicing. In German, for example, some consonants, like /d/, must be devoiced when they occur at the end of words. What is spelled as "Bund" is pronounced "boont."

dialect: Every language has identifiable *regional* and *social dialects* characterized by distinct pronunciations, vocabularies, and grammatical structures. "Regional dialects" often identify the people who share a geographic location; "social dialects" are varieties of a language that identify members of a class or occupation. Habits of speech regarded as specifically male or female are also social dialects.

discourse: Any verbal text, written or spoken.

dummy _it_ : Any use of the pronoun _it_ when there is no explicit mention of what _it_ refers to in the immediate context.

dysphemism: A word or phrase that highlights or emphasizes what members of a culture consider the unpleasant or distasteful features of an object or person, e.g., _slut_ for a woman who enjoys sex with a lot of men or _ballbuster_ for a woman who behaves aggressively and independently.

entailment: A necessary requirement or consequence. In this book, the logical relationship between two (or more) ideas or assumptions involved in the coherence of a conceptual framework; the "necessary" connection between ideas so that they appear to "make sense."

euphemism: A word or phrase speakers use to avoid mentioning something they perceive as bad or unpleasant or to downplay the negative or offensive features of someone or something, e.g., "gone to her reward" for _died_, "neutralized the opposing units" for _killed men_.

experiencer: The human subject who perceives or experiences the feeling or attitude described by a predicate, preceded by the preposition _to_ but usually omitted: _You seemed (to me) rather grouchy yesterday_.

experiencer-deletion: Suppressing the experiencer of a psych-predicate or "impersonal" verb: _Her attitude was surprising, They seemed unwilling to reciprocate_.

experiential domain (or **sphere**): Metaphorically, a cluster of conditions—boundaries, activities, restrictions—that characterize the typical (or assumed) experiences of one sex.

false deixis: Using a pronoun, or some other deictic element, as though it had a specific reference or pointed to something already explicit or understood in the context.

focus: A noun phrase placed at the end of a clause or sentence is said to be in focus because its position requires speakers to use a higher pitch and greater stress relative to other elements when pronouncing it. In the sentence, _I went to the movies, movies_ would be described as the focus because we pronounce it with a higher pitch and more emphasis than the other words.

foreground: Those people, activities, events and assumptions considered "relevant," "significant," and "normal" in a culture. In the u.s., _motherhood, consumerism, upward mobility, heterosexuality_, and _men_ occupy the foreground of public discourse.

gap, lexical: Lexical gaps are "holes" in the vocabularies of languages where one might expect, because of the structure of a category, to find a word for an idea, event, person, or activity. As a result of historical processes in English, for example, we don't have a distinct word for the second person plural; this is a "lexical gap" because we have unique pronouns everywhere else in the system. We've filled this lexical gap by using _you_ for plural as well as singular reference, but some dialects have unique ways of distinguishing the plural second person from the singular, e.g., _youse, y'all, you'uns_.

gender: Gender refers to the distinctions among noun categories that determine, in inflected languages, their declension and agreement with determiners, modifiers, and pronouns that refer back to them. In western patriarchal grammars, gender is construed as "sex," so the noun categories of Indo-European languages have been labeled "feminine," "neuter," and "masculine."

generic: Generic terms refer to an entire group or class. Just as _people_ is a generic, so are _chicken, goose, flower, tree_, and _rock_, for they refer to entire groups of beings and things without distinction.

genitive: In the grammars of inflected languages, nouns are marked as functioning as genitives when they signal possession, measurement, or source.

gerund: In grammars of Latin, a _gerund_ is a verbal form that functions as a noun. In English, gerunds are marked with the _-ing_ suffix (for example, _speaking, lying, shouting_) associated with the progressive aspect.

grammar: In its broadest sense, *grammar* refers to the system of rules that every native speaker of a given language begins to learn during their first year of life. These "rules" are abstract and reflect the structural properties of the language, including the sound system, how words are pronounced, how words are formed, including affixes, how words must be grouped together to form a sentence, and how two or more sentences may be combined to form more complex sentences. In this book, two types of grammar are discussed. The first, which most readers identify with the word *grammar*, are **prescriptive** or **normative** grammars, which set forth the "rules" of the "standard" or "prestige" dialect of a language. The second kind of grammar, which I use throughout the book, is a **linguistic** or **descriptive** grammar. Such grammars attempt to describe languages as they are spoken by native speakers and discover the internal structural properties of languages; these descriptions of native speaker linguistic knowledge are the "rules" of descriptive grammars.

head noun: A head noun is the defining element of a noun phrase. For example, *emerald* is the head noun of "a beautiful deep green *emerald*," *boa constrictor* is the head noun of "the fully grown *boa constrictor*," and *wall* is the head noun of "an ivy-covered *wall*."

homonym: The term *homonym* can refer either to words that sound and are often spelled the same but differ in meaning or to a single word used to designate several different things.

homophone: One of two or more words that sound the same but differ in spelling, etymology, and meaning.

ideograph: A character or symbol, as in the Chinese writing system, not a word or phrase, that represents an idea or thing.

illocutionary act: J. L. Austin identified "performative utterances" (or "speech acts") in *How to Do Things with Words* (1962). An illocutionary act is an utterance that accomplishes a specific act; usually these utterances are fixed and institutionalized: "I now pronounce you husband and wife;" "I christen this ship _____;" "I sentence you to twenty years in prison." In order for illocutionary acts to be valid, certain grammatical and social conventions must be observed.

imperative: In traditional grammars, the "mood" that expresses a command or polite request. In English, the person addressed, *you*, is usually suppressed.

implication: Something intimately connected or entwined, usually implied or inferred, with explicit ideas or assertions in a text.

Indo-European: The language group consisting of most of the languages of Europe, and those of Iran, India, and other parts of Asia as well. **Proto**-Indo-European is the hypothetical, reconstructed language from which languages such as Latin, Greek, Sanskrit, Gothic and their modern descendants developed as dialects.

inflection: The addition of suffixes (morphemes) to a word's base; these suffixes bear information about grammatical relationships, semantic categories, discourse roles and social status.

intonation: Patterns of pitch (or tone) quality produced by voice modulations that carry grammatical information essential to speaker intention and hearer interpretation; **intonation contours** distinguish statements from questions or commands, for example, and can override syntactic structure as when we use the intonation contour typical of a question when we utter a statement.

instrument: The case relationship (or "role") of a noun phrase, usually inanimate, to a verb, when the noun phrase refers to the instrument with which the action was performed. In *We killed two birds* **with one stone,** *with one stone* is the instrument.

kinship system: That portion of a language's vocabulary used to refer to those institutional relationships among people recognized by the members of a society. Kinship terms may be either *consanguineal*, based on biological relatedness and common ancestry—e.g., *mother, sister, grandmother, niece*—or institutionally sanctioned—e.g., *wife, mother-in-law, husband.*

lexicalization: Creating words that describe or refer to ideas, objects, events, or people.

marked/unmarked: A feature, whether phonological or syntactic, which is assumed to be present unless otherwise specified is said to be **unmarked**. Features that are unmarked are the *usual* values of sounds or words. **Marked** features contrast with the usual values of sounds and words and must be explicitly specified. In English, for example, the feature [+male] is unmarked for words like *doctor, carpenter,* and *lawyer,* but marked for *nurse, secretary,* and *prostitute.*

markedness: A linguistic method for expressing the quantity of information carried by a specific form. Phonologically, the sound /d/ carries more information than /t/ because it has an additional feature, [+voice]. Semantically, the situation in English is more complex and varies with the denotation of a word. If I say "That's a cow," the word *cow* is *unmarked* for sex because it's a generic term. If I say "That's a cow, not a bull," however, the word *cow* is said to be marked for sex because it now has the feature [+female].

meaning: This is a difficult word to define because its sense differs according to the context in which it's being used. Here, I reserve the word to refer to the combined effects of every level of language: the sound and intonation, the words, and their syntactic order relative to each other all combine to produce a hearer's interpretation of what a speaker intended to say. For example, the intonation contour with which I say something can determine its "meaning."

1. a. ²Ré ³ady¹ ↘ = statement
   b. ²Ré ³ady³ ↗ = question

Likewise, the position of words in sentences determines their meaning:

2. a. I *only* know the time.

   b. I know *only* the time.

3. a. I painted the *blue* room.

   b. I painted the room *blue.*

The meaning, then, of a given utterance depends upon a hearer's ability to interpret all the linguistic cues provided by a speaker, from the phonological to the semantic.

metalinguistic: Literally, "beyond [or above] language," a word used in several ways. When the meaning of what we say is accompanied by gestures, facial expressions or body signals, our hearer's interpretation is affected by these metalinguistic signals. *Metalinguistic* also refers to the terminology linguists use to talk about language as an object of study and to the language all of us use in conversation to talk about the process of communication.

metaphor: An analogical use of language in which the features and characteristics of one thing are transferred to another. When I say, "Your speech was brittle," I've compared your speech to something fragile and concrete, such as porcelain, which metaphorically **transfers** the features of fragile objects to your speech.

metonym: A figure of speech in which a characteristic or feature associated with an object or person is used to refer to the object or person, e.g., *pussy* is a metonym for referring to a woman; *prick* is a metonym for referring to a man.

modal: An auxiliary verb, such as *can, shall, or must,* that precedes a main verb and indicates both the likelihood that the verb's action will occur and the source, either internal or external, of determining factors (or control) regarding its occurrence. The "semi-modals" are verbs that function both as main verbs and as auxiliaries. In English, these include *oughta, dareta, needta, wanta, hafta, get/got.*

modifier: A word, phrase, or clause that somehow qualifies another word, phrase, or entire sentence by adding information. For example, the adverb *suddenly* modifies the verb *arrived* in 1., and, in 2., the clause, *As I was getting ready for bed,* modifies the rest of the sentence, *the phone rang.*

1. Marge and Elaine arrived *suddenly*.
2. *As I was getting ready for bed*, the phone rang.

morpheme: A word, such as *rabbit*, or a word element, such as the *–s* used to make *rabbit* plural (*rabbits*), that cannot be broken down further into smaller meaningful units. Thus, although we say that *rabbit* and *rabbits* are both "words," *rabbit* is a single morpheme while *rabbits* contains two morphemes.

morphology: The study of morphemes, i.e., the systematic ways words are constructed in a language. In English, for example, there are free and bound morphemes. The plural *–s* of *rabbits* is a "bound morpheme," while *rabbit* is a "free morpheme"; it can occur with or without the *–s* and still be meaningful.

neologism: A recently created word, phrase, or expression, or the use of an already existing word or phrase to mean something new.

nominalization: The linguistic process of reducing a sentence so that what remains functions as a noun phrase in another sentence, e.g., in the sentence *The destruction of Nagasaki was a bad decision,* [t]he destruction of Nagasaki is the nominalized version of the sentence. [The U. S.] destroyed Nagasaki.

nominative: In inflected languages, the case of a noun phrase functioning as the topic of a sentence.

noun (N): A word that names and is used to refer to any object, event, action, or person. **Proper nouns** are the specific names of individual people, objects, or places, e.g., *Maria, Grant's Tomb, Nicaragua*; **common nouns** refer to whole classes, categories, groups or any member of them.

noun phrase (NP): A noun phrase is any word or group of words occupying a position and serving a function that a noun can serve. Thus, *the red hat, the poverty-stricken, the rich*, and *the destruction of Nagasaki* are all noun phrases because they can function as topics, objects, and indirect objects in sentences.

number (singular, plural): In many languages, number is the grammatical indication of a distinction between one and more than one object belonging to a class. English and other Indo-European languages distinguish between singular and plural (more than one) objects. Some languages also distinguish *two, three* or *four* objects; Old English, for example, had pronouns that referred to one, two, and more than two individuals.

object: In general, an object is a noun phrase functioning as the event, thing, or person at which the action described by the verb is directed. Although some verbs don't occur with objects at all, many verbs can have one object, called the **direct object**, and some can have two objects; the second object is called the **indirect object**. In the sentence, *Mary made lunch for all of us, lunch* is the direct object and *for all of us* is the indirect object.

participle: A verb form that occurs with an auxiliary verb (*be* or *have*) to signal the time at which an act happened that can also be used by itself as a modifier or part of a modifying phrase. In *the growing deficit*, the participle *growing* modifies *deficit*; in *While driving home from work yesterday I stopped to admire the foliage, driving home from work yesterday* is a participial phrase modifying the sentence *I stopped to admire the foliage*.

passive voice: A sentence in which the topic is actually the direct or indirect object of the verb, the agent is preceded by the preposition *by* and has been placed at the end of the sentence or omitted entirely, and the main verb is preceded by some form of *be* and has the suffix *–ed* or some other past ending attached to it. The sentences, *The pond was drained by the army* and *The pond was drained* are both in the passive voice.

pejorative: A word or phrase that emphasizes the negative aspects or expresses a negative valuation of an object, event, or person.

phoneme: A single speech sound, or a group of similar or related speech sounds, that makes a difference in meaning. For example, in the two words *pore* and *bore*, /p/ and /b/ are the phonemes that signal the difference in meaning: /b/ is **voiced**, /p/ isn't.

phonology: The scientific study of speech sounds; also the analysis and identification of the meaningful speech sounds in a language.

possessive: A grammatical form that indicates possession. In Indo-European languages, the **genitive** case identifies a noun or pronoun of possession.

predicate: The part of a sentence or clause that says something about the topic, describes an action performed by the agent, or attributes some feature to the topic/agent. The predicates of the following three sentences are italicized.

1. The barn *was quickly burned to the ground.*
2. The frog *croaked noisily in the marsh.*
3. Your late arrival *was predictable.*

prescriptive grammar: A grammar consisting of "rules" that speakers must follow if they want to speak the "standard" dialect of a language. (Also *normative* or *traditional* grammar.)

presupposition: An unstated assumption that must be shared by both speaker and hearer if an utterance is to be interpreted literally. When speakers and hearers don't share presuppositions, an utterance intended to be interpreted as literally true may, instead, be interpreted as a metaphor or a joke.

pronoun: Pronouns are used to replace noun phrases, and refer to the people, objects, events, ideas already mentioned in a text. English has several types of pronoun: personal (*I, you, she, it, he, we, they,* and their object forms); demonstrative (*this/these, that/those*); possessive (*my, your, her, its, his, our, their*); relative (*who, that, which*).

proto-: In linguistics, the prefix *proto-* indicates that the form of a language (Proto-Germanic) or a word (**ma-*) is a reconstructed, hypothetical form, based on the available evidence. The roots postulated for a protolanguage are marked by an asterisk (*).

psych-predicates: Predicates that require a human experiencer of the internal, psychological response described by the predicate; these predicates occur in sentences that look like actives and passives; in their active versions, the experiencer functions as the object and the person, behavior, or situation that elicited the experiencer's response functions as an **agent**. In the pseudo-passive version, the experiencer functions as the topic and the pseudo-agent can be preceded by one of several prepositions, e.g., *by, at, with.*

relative clause: A clause that functions to further describe or identify a preceding noun phrase. In English, relative clauses follow the noun phrase they modify, and are introduced by a relative pronoun or adverb (*where, when*) that replaces the head noun of the noun phrase.

semantics: In common usage, semantics is understood as "the study of meaning." "Meaning," however, covers a wide variety of linguistic phenomena including sentence structure, intonation, placement of stress, word choice, as well as nonverbal elements (facial expression, gesture) that accompany verbal messages. In this text, I've used semantics in a narrow sense, restricting its reference to the features that define noun categories and distinguish one noun category from another or one noun from other members of the same category. [Human] is a feature that distinguishes human nouns from other animate nouns (*dog*); [female] distinguishes nouns referring to women from those referring to men within the [human] category. A semantic set consists of those nouns which share all but one semantic feature in common.

semi-modal: See **modal.**

sentence: A number of words organized following the syntactic rules of a language that form a grammatical sense unit. In English, for example, a sentence requires at least one noun phrase functioning as the topic or agent, and a verb phrase, which may consist of additional noun phrases functioning as objects, direct objects, and the objects of prepositions, plus a variety of adverbs.

sex-marked: Any verb or noun that speakers of a language mark with specific reference to one sex or the other. Also "sex-specific."

speaker: Here, following linguistic convention, I often use *speaker* to include not only oral users of language but writers, hearers, and readers as well.

standardization: The institutionalization of one dialect over others as the "standard," "formal," "elite" dialect in which formal texts (including speeches and proclamations) must be delivered. Standardization occurs most frequently with those languages that have writing systems.

stative: A predicate is stative, describes a state of an NP, if it cannot be used in the progressive aspect or in an imperative, or occur with adverbs of frequency.

strategies, listener: Listener strategies are those intuitive methods we use to interpret what someone has said or written, to identify ambiguities or to "make sense" of garbled utterances.

strategies, speaker: Uses of language for predictable rhetorical effects, such as the decision to suppress agency, as with truncated passives, or topicalize a noun phrase that's the logical object of a verb, as in *"Problems* arise often." Other speaker strategies include euphemism and dysphemism, metaphors, gobbledygook, and digression.

syntactic rule: Syntactic rules describe the relationships between noun phrases and the verbs with which they occur in a language, or the relationships between sentence types, e.g., the passive rule describes the relationship between active and passive sentences; question rules describe the relationship between declaratives and questions.

synonym: Two or more words in a language that may differ in nuance or connotation but have the same reference.

syntax: Syntax is the study of the internal structure of sentences in a language.

tense: Tense is the modification of a verb (in English) to indicate the time of an utterance, relative to the time at which it is said, by means of an inflectional suffix: zero or –s indicates the present (for third person verbs), –ed or its equivalent the past tense. If a sentence has only a main verb, that verb carries the tense inflection; if there is one or more auxiliaries, they carry the tense inflection, e.g., *She* **wrote** *letters* but *She* **did** *write letters.*

tone: In languages like Chinese, vocal variations in pitch (or tone) distinguish words that are otherwise phonetically identical or similar.

topic: The noun phrase that occupies the first position before the main verb in a sentence or clause. Topics cannot be preceded by a preposition.

universe of discourse: A **universe of discourse** is any ongoing written or spoken discourse in which the participants share (or assume they share) assumptions and the presuppositions they use to interpret utterances as meaningful and to distinguish literal utterances from nonliteral ones, e.g., jokes; the (usually) implicit social framework of valuation that structures meaning. Universes of discourse can be relatively small, e.g., the conversations among members of a family, or large, e.g., the discourse typical of academic disciplines in which participants are trained in jargon and methodology.

verb: Verbs describe actions, processes, states or conditions, and are traditionally classified as *transitive* or *intransitive*, whether they do or do not require an object, and *regular* or *irregular*, whether they developed from the Gmc. "weak preterite" (past tense) typically signalled, in English, by the *-ed* suffix or the so-called "strong verbs" which used vowel mutation to signal tense, e.g., *sing, sang, sung.* Transitivity, however, often depends upon the sentence in which a given verb is used, and linguists have proposed different ways of categorizing verbs, e.g., stative/ nonstative, psych-predicates, and "impersonal" verbs.

verb phrase (VP): A verb phrase consists minimally of a main verb (or predicate), plus other optional elements: auxiliary verbs, direct and indirect objects, adverbs, and prepositional phrases.

voice, active: The active voice is considered to be the most basic sentence pattern in a language. In English, an active sentence has at least an agent and a main verb, e.g., *We sang*, but the verb can have an object, *We sang* **songs**, and numerous adverbs specifying time, place, and manner, *We sang songs* **loudly in front of the White House until three** A. M.

   passive: When the **agent** and **object** of a verb have exchanged positions, a sentence is said to be in the passive voice ("passivized"). *The door was opened by Sherry* is the passive version of the active sentence, *Sherry opened the door.*

References

Adams, J. N. 1982. *The Latin Sexual Vocabulary*. London: Gerald Duckworth & Co. Ltd.

Alston, R. C., ed. *English Linguists, 1500–1800*. Mentson: Scolar Press.

Alyeshmerni, Mansoor, and Paul Taubr. 1970. *Working with Aspects of Language*. New York: Harcourt, Brace and World.

Anderson, Hans. 1968. "The Emperor's New Clothes," *Forty-two Stories*, trans. M. R. James. London: Faber and Faber, 104–07.

Arnold, June. 1973. *The Cook and the Carpenter*. Plainfield, VT: Daughters, Inc.

Austin, J. L. 1970. *How to Do Things with Words*. Ed. J. O. Urmson. New York: Oxford UP.

Bäck, Hilding. 1934. *The Synonyms for "Child", "Boy", "Girl": An Etymological-Semasiological Investigation*, Lund Studies in English. II. Lund: C. W. K. Gleerups Forlag.

Baron, Dennis. 1986. *Grammar and Gender*. New Haven: Yale UP.

Barth, John. 1966. *The Sot-Weed Factor*. New York: Grosset & Dunlap.

Barwise, Jon. 1980. "Scenes and Other Situations," *Stanford Working Papers in Semantics*, Vol. 1. Ed. Jon Barwise and Ivan Sag. Palo Alto: Stanford University.

Bateson, Gregory. 1972. *Steps to an Ecology of Mind*. New York: Ballantine Books.

Baugh, Albert C. 1963. *A History of the English Language*. 2nd ed. New York: Appleton-Century-Crofts, Inc.

Beattie, James. [1788] 1967. *The Theory of Language. English Linguistics, 1500–1800*. Ed. R. C. Alston. Mentson: Scolar Press.

Bem, Sandra, and Daryl Bem. 1973. "Does Sex-biased Job Advertising 'aid and abet' Sex Discrimination?" *Journal of Applied Social Psychology* 3, 1: 6–18.

Benét, William Rose. 1965. *The Reader's Encyclopedia*. 2nd ed. New York: Thomas Y. Crowell Co. Vol. 2.

Bengis, Ingrid. n.d. *A Woman's New World Dictionary*. Special Collections, Northwestern University, Evanston, Illinois.

Berger, Peter, and Thomas Luckmann. 1967. *The Social Construction of Reality*. New York: Anchor Books.

Berlin, Brent, and Paul Kay. 1969. *Basic Color Terms: Their Universality and Evolution*. Berkeley: U of California P.

Bodine, Ann. 1975a. "Androcentrism in Prescriptive Grammar: Singular 'they', Sex-indefinite 'he', and 'he or she'." *Language in Society* 4: 129–46.

_____. 1975b. "Sex Differentiation in Language," *Language and Sex: Difference and Dominance*, 130–151. Ed. Barrie Thorne and Nancy Henley. Rowley, MA: Newbury House Publishers.

Bolinger, Dwight. 1975. *Aspects of Language*. 2nd ed. New York: Harcourt Brace Jovanovich.

———. 1980. *Language: The Loaded Weapon*. London: Longman Group.

Boltz, Carol J., and Dorothy U. Seyler, eds. 1982. *Language Power*. New York: Random House.

Bouma, Lowell. 1968. "The Semantics of the Modal System in Contemporary German." Paper delivered to the Linguistic Society of America.

Brown, Goold. 1851. *The Grammar of English Grammars*. New York: William Wood and Co.

Buck, Carl Darling. 1949. *A Dictionary of Selected Synonyms in the Principal Indo-European Languages*. Chicago: U of Chicago P.

Cameron, Deborah. 1985. *Feminism and Linguistic Theory*. London: Macmillan.

Campbell, A. 1959. *Old English Grammar*. Oxford: Oxford UP.

Caprio, Frank. 1962. *Female Homosexuality*. New York: Grove Press.

Caputi, Jane. 1977. "The Glamour of Grammar." *Chrysalis* 4: 35–43.

Cassidy, F. G., and Richard N. Ringler. 1971. *Bright's Old English Grammar and Reader*. 3rd ed. New York: Holt, Rinehart and Winston.

Chafe, Wallace. 1976. "Givenness, Contrastiveness, Definiteness, Subjects, Topics, and Point of View." *Subject and Topic*. New York: Academic Press.

Chapin, P. B. 1967. *On the Syntax of Word Derivation in English*. Information System Language Studies No. 16. Bedford, MA: Mitre Corp.

Cherry, Kittredge. 1987. *WomansWord: What Japanese Words Say About Women*. Tokyo: Kodansha International.

Chesler, Phyllis. 1972. *Women and Madness*. Garden City, NY: Doubleday & Co.

Chomsky, N. 1965. *Aspects of the Theory of Syntax*. Cambridge, MA: M.I.T. Press.

Clark, Virginia P., Paul A. Eschholz, and Alfred F. Rosa, eds. 1985. *Language: Introductory Readings*. 4th ed. New York: St. Martin's Press.

Cliff, Michelle. 1982. "Object into Subject: Some Thoughts on the Work of Black Women Artists." *Heresies* 4, 3: 34–40.

Daly, Mary. 1978. *Gyn/Ecology: The Metaethics of Radical Feminism*. Boston: Beacon Press.

———. 1984. *Pure Lust: Elemental Feminist Philosophy*. Boston: Beacon Press.

———, in Cahoots with Jane Caputi. 1987. *Websters' First New Intergalactic Wickedary of the English Language*. Boston: Beacon Press.

De Beauvoir, Simone. 1953. *The Second Sex*. New York: Bantam Books.

Diamond, Jared. 1989. "This-Fellow Frog, Name Belong-Him Dakwo." *Natural History* (April), 16: 18–20, 22–23.

Dixon, Marlene, and Joreen. 1970. "A Dictionary of Women's Liberation." *Everywoman* 21 August: 16–17.

Dixon, R. M. W. 1982. *Where Have All the Adjectives Gone? and Other Essays in Semantics and Syntax*. Berlin: Mouton Publishers.

Dixon, Roland, and Alfred Kroeber. 1903. "The Native Languages of California." *American Anthropologist* 5: 1–26.

Dubois, Betty Lou, and Isabel Crouch. 1976. "The Question of Tag Questions in Women's Speech: They Don't Really Use More of Them, Do They?." *Language in Society* 4: 289–94.

Dworkin, Andrea. 1988. *Letters from a War Zone: Writings 1976–1987*. London: Secker & Warburg.

———. 1976. *Our Blood: Prophecies and Discourses on Sexual Politics*. New York: Harper & Row.

———. 1981. *Pornography: Men Possessing Women*. New York: Perigee Books.

———. 1974. *Woman Hating*. New York: E. P. Dutton.

Dykema, Karl W. 1961. "Where Our Grammar Came From." *College English* April: 455–65.

Elgin, Suzette Haden. 1982. "Women & Language Update." *The Lonesome Node* January/February: 3–4.

———. 1985. *A First Dictionary and Grammar of Láadan*. Madison: Society for the Furtherance and Study of Fantasy and Science Fiction, Inc. (In 1988, the second edition of the Láadan grammar and dictionary was published. For more information write to SF[3]: Box 1624, Madison, WI 53701-1624.)

_____. 1980. *The Gentle Art of Verbal Self-Defense*. Englewood Cliffs, NJ: Prentice-Hall.

_____. 1987. *The Last Word on the Gentle Art of Verbal Self-Defense*. New York: Prentice-Hall Press.

_____. 1984. *Native Tongue*. New York: Daw.

_____. 1989. *Success with the Gentle Art of Verbal Self-Defense*. Englewood Cliffs, NJ: Prentice-Hall.

Eschholz, Paul, Alfred Rosa, and Virginia Clark, eds. 1982. *Language Awareness*. 3rd ed. New York: St. Martin's Press.

Fagles, Robert, with W. B. Stanford. 1975. *Aeschylus, The Oresteia*. New York: Viking Press.

Fell, Christine, with Cecily Clark and Elizabeth Williams. 1984. *Women in Anglo-Saxon England, and the Impact of 1066*. New York: Basil Blackwell.

Fell, John. [1784] 1967. *An Essay Towards an English Grammar. English Linguistics, 1500–1800*. Ed. R. C. Alston. Mentson: Scolar Press.

Ferguson, Moira. 1985. *First Feminists: British Women Writers 1578–1799*. Bloomington, IN: Indiana UP.

Fetterley, Judith. 1978. *The Resisting Reader: A Feminist Approach to American Fiction*. Bloomington: Indiana UP.

Fodor, István. 1959. "The Origin of Grammatical Gender I." *Lingua* January: 1–41.

Frye, Marilyn. 1988. "Lesbian 'Sex'." *Sinister Wisdom* Summer/Fall: 46–54.

Fryer, Peter. 1963. *Mrs. Grundy: Studies in English Prudery*. London: Dennis Dobson.

Givón, Talmy. 1979. *Understanding Grammar*. New York: Academic Press.

Goffman, E. 1961. *Encounters: Two Studies in the Sociology of Interaction*. Indianapolis: Bobbs-Merrill.

Goldfield, Bina. 1983. *The Efemcipated English Handbook*. New York: Westover Press.

Goldin, Hyman E., et al., eds. 1962. *Dictionary of American Underworld Lingo*. New York: Citadel Press.

Goshgarian, Gary, ed. 1983. *Exploring Language*. 3rd ed. Boston: Little, Brown and Co.

Greenbaum, Sidney. 1985. *The English Language Today*. Oxford: Pergamon Press.

Greenwald, Harold. 1970. *The Elegant Prostitute*. New York: Walker & Co.

Griffin, Susan. 1981. *Pornography and Silence: Culture's Revenge Against Nature*. New York: Harper & Row.

_____. 1979. *Rape: The Power of Consciousness*. San Francisco: Harper & Row.

_____. 1978. *Woman and Nature: The Roaring Inside Her*. New York: Harper & Row.

Grimsdell, Susan. 1988. "Speaking Our Selves." *Broadsheet* March: 14–16.

Gruber, Jeffrey. 1967. "Functions of the Lexicon in Formal Descriptive Grammars." Santa Monica: System Development Corporation.

Halliday, M. A. K. 1966. *Grammar, Society and the Noun*. An Inaugural Lecture delivered at University College London, 24 November.

_____, and Ruquaiya Hasan. 1976. *Cohesion in English*. London: Longman Group Ltd.

Harrison, R. [1777] 1967. *Institutes of English Grammar. English Linguistics, 1500–1800*. Ed. R. C. Alston. Mentson: Scolar Press.

Heatherington, Madelon E. 1980. *How Language Works*. Cambridge, MA: Winthrop Publishers.

Hoagland, Sarah Lucia. 1978. "Coercive Consensus." *Sinister Wisdom* Summer: 86–92.

_____. 1980. "Androcentric Rhetoric in Sociobiology." *Women's Studies International Quarterly* 3: 285–93.

_____, and Julia Penelope, eds. 1988. *For Lesbians Only: A Separatist Anthology*. London: Onlywomen Press.

Hockett, Charles F. 1960. "The Origin of Speech," *Scientific American* September: 3–10.

_____, and Robert Ascher. 1964. "The Human Revolution." *Current Anthropology* June: 135–68.

Hofstadter, Douglas R. 1979. *Gödel, Escher, Bach: An Eternal Golden Braid*. New York: Vintage Books.

Holland, Peggy. 1978. "Jean-Paul Sartre as a NO to Women," *Sinister Wisdom* Summer: 72–9.

Hollander, Xaviera. 1972. *The Happy Hooker*. New York: Dell.

Huber, Joan. 1976. "On the Generic Use of Male Pronouns." *The American Sociologist* May: 89.

Jespersen, Otto. [1905] 1958. *Growth and Structure of the English Language*. Oxford: Basil Blackwell.

Jespersen, Otto. [1921] 1964. *Language, Its Nature, Development and Origin*. New York: W. W. Norton.

Johnson, Samuel. [1747] 1970. *The Plan of a Dictionary*. Mentson, England: Scolar Press.

_____. 1968. *The Preface to the Dictionary*. In *Samuel Johnson: Selected Writings*, 235–43. Edited with an Introduction by Patrick Cruttwell. London: Penguin Books.

Johnson, Sonia. 1989. *Wildfire: Igniting the She/volution*. Albuquerque, NM: Wildfire Books.

Katz, Jerrold J., and Jerry A. Fodor. 1964. "The Structure of a Semantic Theory." *The Structure of Language: Readings in the Philosophy of Language*, 479–518. Ed. Jerry A. Fodor and Jerrold J. Katz. Englewood Cliffs, NJ: Prentice-Hall.

Kauffman, Linda, ed. *Feminism and Institutions: Dialogues on Feminist Theory*. London: Basil Blackwell.

Kay, Paul. 1983. "Linguistic Competence and Folk Theories of Language: Two English Hedges." *Proceedings of the Ninth Annual Meeting of the Berkeley Linguistics Society* 128–37. Berkeley: Berkeley Linguistics Society.

Kehl, D. G. 1982. "Doublespeak, Double-Entendre, and the Case of the Ambiguous 'It.'" *Quarterly Review of Doublespeak* May: 3–4.

Key, Mary Ritchie. 1975. *Male/Female Language*. Metuchen, NJ: Scarecrow Press.

Key, Wilson Bryan. 1972. *Subliminal Seduction*. New York: New American Library.

_____. 1977. *Media Sexploitation*. New York: New American Library.

Kolodny, Annette. 1975. *The Lay of the Land: Metaphor as Experience and History in American Life and Letters*. Chapel Hill: U of North Carolina P.

Kramarae, Cheris. [in press]. "Punctuating the Dictionary." *Language, Sex and Society*. Eds. Tove Bull and Toril Swan. The Hague: Mouton.

_____. 1981. *Women and Men Speaking*. Rowley, MA: Newbury House.

_____, Paula Treichler, and Ann Russo. 1985. *A Feminist Dictionary*. London: Pandora Press.

Labov, William. 1966. *The Social Stratification of English in New York City*. Washington, DC: Center for Applied Linguistics.

Lakoff, George. 1968. "Instrumental Adverbs and the Concept of Deep Structure," *Foundations of Language* February.

_____. 1987. *Women, Fire, and Dangerous Things*. Chicago: U of Chicago P.

_____, and Mark Johnson. 1980. *Metaphors We Live By*. Chicago: U of Chicago P.

Lakoff, Robin. 1971. "Passive Resistance." Paper delivered to Chicago Linguistic Society, April.

_____. 1975. *Language and Woman's Place*. New York: Harper & Row.

Landy, Eugene. 1971. *The Underground Dictionary*. New York: Simon and Schuster.

Langacker, R. W. 1968. *Language and Its Structure: Some Fundamental Linguistic Concepts*. New York: Harcourt, Brace & World.

Larson, Arlene, and Carolyn Logan. 1980. *How Does Language Work?* Dubuque: Kendall/Hunt Publishing Co.

Lee, Anna. 1988. "A Black Separatist." *For Lesbians Only*, 83–92. Ed. Sarah Lucia Hoagland and Julia Penelope. London: Onlywomen Press.

Leech, G. 1969. *Towards a Semantic Description of English*. London: Longman.

Lennert, Midge, and Norma Willson, eds. 1973. *A Woman's New World Dictionary*. Lomita, CA: 51% Publications.

Leo, John. 1988. "A Glossary of Reporterspeak." *U. S. News & World Report* 3 October: 63.

Lessing, Doris. [1962] 1971. *The Golden Notebook*. New York: Bantam Books.

Levi, Judith N. 1978. *The Syntax and Semantics of Complex Nominals*. New York: Academic Press.

Li, Charles N., ed. 1976. *Subject and Topic*. New York: Academic Press.

Lipsky, Abram, and Elisabeth B. Reifler. 1938. *Easy German*. New York: Henry Holt and Co.

Lyons, John. 1969. *Introduction to Theoretical Linguistics*. Cambridge: Cambridge UP.

MacKillop, James, and Donna Woolfolk Cross. 1982. *Speaking of Words: A Language Reader*. 2nd ed. New York: Holt, Rinehart and Winston.

Martyna, Wendy. 1983. "The Case for Nonsexist Language." *Language, Gender and Society*, 25–37. Eds. Barrie Thorne, Cheris Kramarae, and Nancy Henley. Rowley, MA: Newbury House.

———. 1978. "What Does 'he' Mean? Use of the Generic Masculine." *Journal of Communication* 28, 1: 131–38.

Merchant, Carolyn. 1980. *The Death of Nature: Women, Ecology, and the Scientific Revolution*. San Francisco: Harper & Row.

Miller, Casey, and Kate Swift. 1980. *The Handbook of Nonsexist Writing for Writers, Editors and Speakers*. New York: Lippincott & Crowell.

Millett, Kate. 1970. *Sexual Politics*. New York: Equinox Books.

Mills, Anne E. 1986. *The Acquisition of Gender: A Study of English and German*. Berlin: Springer-Verlag.

Morgan, Elaine. 1972. *The Descent of Woman*. New York: Stein and Day.

Murray, Lindley. [1795] 1967. *English Grammar. English Linguistics, 1500–1800*. Ed. R. C. Alston. Mentson: Scolar Press.

National Public Radio. 1988. "Japanese Women's Language." Washington, D. C., #880213.

Newman, Barbara. 1987. *Sister of Wisdom: St. Hildegard's Theology of the Feminine*. Berkeley: U of California P.

Nilsen, Alleen Pace. 1977. "Sexism in Children's Books and Elementary Classroom Materials." *Sexism and Language*, 161–79. Ed. Alleen Pace Nilsen, Haig Bosmajian, H. Lee Gershuny, and Julia P[enelope] Stanley. Urbana: National Council of Teachers of English.

———, and Haig Bosmajian, H. Lee Gershuny, and Julia P[enelope] Stanley, eds. 1977. *Sexism and Language*. Urbana: National Council of Teachers of English.

Nilsen, Don L. F., and Alleen Pace Nilsen. 1978. *Language Play: An Introduction to Linguistics*. Rowley, MA: Newbury House.

Obayashi, Hiroshi. 1974. Personal communication [to Ann Bodine].

Ortony, Andrew, ed. 1979. *Metaphor and Thought*. Cambridge: Cambridge UP.

Palmer, F. R. 1979. *Modality and the English Modals*. London: Longman.

Palmer, Frank. 1971. *Grammar*. Middlesex: Penguin Books.

Palmer, L. R. 1954. *The Latin Language*. London: Faber and Faber.

Parlee, Mary Brown. 1978. "The Rhythms in Men's Lives." *Psychology Today* April: 82; 85–6; 91.

Partridge, Eric. 1961. *A Dictionary of Slang and Unconventional English*. New York: Macmillan.

Penelope, Julia. 1982a. "Topicalization: The Rhetorical Strategies It Serves and the Interpretive Strategies It Imposes." *Linguistics* 20: 683–95.

———. 1982b. "Two Essays on Language and Change: I: Power and the Opposition to Feminist Proposals for Language Change; II: John Simon and the 'Dragons of Eden.'" *College English* December: 840–54.

———. 1984. "Lexical Gaps and Lexicalization: A Diachronic Analysis." *Proceedings of the*

Tenth LACUS Forum, 296–304. Ed. Alan Manning, Pierre Martin, Kim McCalla. Columbia, SC: Hornbeam Press.

_____. 1985. "Users and Abusers: On the Death of English." *The English Language Today*, 80–91. Ed. Sidney Greenbaum. Oxford: Pergamon Press.

_____. 1986. "Heteropatriarchal Semantics: 'Just Two Kinds of People in the World.'" *Lesbian Ethics* Fall: 58–80.

_____. 1988. "Interpretive Strategies and Sex-marked Comparative Constructions." *Gender and Talk: The Power of Discourse*. Ed. Alexandra Dundas Todd and Sue Fisher. Norwood, NJ: Ablex Publishing Corp.

_____. [Stanley], Julia. 1972a. "Nominalized Passives." Paper delivered to Linguistic Society of America, Summer meeting.

_____. 1972b. "Syntactic Exploitation: Passive Adjectives in English." Paper delivered to Southeastern Conference on Linguistics (SECOL), Athens, GA.

_____. 1975. "Passive Motivation." *Foundations of Language* May: 25–39.

_____. 1976. "The Stylistics of Belief." *Teaching About Doublespeak*, 175–187. Ed. Daniel J. Dieterich. Urbana, IL: National Council of Teachers of English.

_____. 1977. "Gender-Marking in American English: Usage and Reference." *Sexism and Language*, 43–74. Ed. Alleen Pace Nilsen, et al. Urbana: National Council of Teachers of English.

_____. 1978. "Sexist Grammar." *College English* March: 800–11.

_____. 1979a. "Style and Choice in English Syntax: Target Structures and Rule Conspiracies." *Rhetoric 78*, Proceedings of Theory of Rhetoric, An Interdisciplinary Conference. Ed. Robert L. Brown, Jr. and Martin Steinmann, Jr. Minneapolis, MN: University Center for Advanced Studies in Language, Style, and Literary Theory.

_____, and Cynthia McGowan. 1979b. "*Woman* and *Wife*: Social and Semantic Shifts in English." *Papers in Linguistics* Fall–Winter: 491–502.

_____, and Susan W. Robbins. 1978a. "Going through the Changes: The Pronoun *She* in Middle English." *Papers in Linguistics* Spring–Summer: 71–88.

_____, and Susan W. Robbins (Wolfe). 1978b. "Sex-marked Predicates in English." *Papers in Linguistics* Fall–Winter: 487–516.

Piercy, Marge. 1976. *Woman on the Edge of Time*. New York: Alfred A. Knopf.

Poole, Joshua. [1646] 1967. *The English Accidence. English Linguistics, 1500–1800*. Ed. R. C. Alston. Mentson: Scolar Press.

Postal, Paul M. 1971. *Cross-Over Phenomena*. New York: Holt, Rinehart and Winston.

Postman, Neil. 1985. *Amusing Ourselves to Death: Public Discourse in the Age of Show Business*. New York: Viking Penguin.

Randolph, Vance, and George P. Wilson. 1953. *Down in the Holler: A Gallery of Ozark Folk Speech*. Norman, OK: U of Oklahoma P.

Random House Dictionary of the English Language. 1967. Ed. Jess Stein. New York: Random House.

Raspberry, William. 1982. "Should Ghettoese Be Accepted?." *Language Awareness*. Ed. Paul Eschholz et al. New York: St. Martin's Press.

Rawson, Hugh. 1981. *Dictionary of Euphemisms and Other Doubletalk*. New York: Crown Publishers.

Raymond, Janice G. 1986. *A Passion for Friends: Toward a Philosophy of Female Affection*. Boston: Beacon Press.

_____. 1979. *The Transsexual Empire: The Making of the She-Male*. Boston: Beacon Press.

Reddy, Michael. 1979. "The Conduit Metaphor—A Case of Frame Conflict." *Metaphor and Thought*, 284–324. Ed. Andrew Ortony. Cambridge: Cambridge UP.

Regis, Ed, and Tom Dworetzky. 1988. "Child of a Lesser God." *Omni* October: 92–94; 96; 164.

Reszkiewicz, Alfred. 1973. *A Diachronic Grammar of Old English*. Warsaw: Panstowe Wydawnictwo Naukowe.

Rheingold, Howard. 1987. "Untranslatable Words." *Whole Earth Review* Winter: 3–8.

Robins, R. H. [1967] 1979. *A Short History of Linguistics*. London: Longmans, Green and Co.

Roget's International Thesaurus. 1977. Rev. Robert L. Chapman. 4th ed. London: Harper & Row.

Rosenbaum, Peter S. 1967. *The Grammar of English Predicate Complement Constructions*. Cambridge, MA: M.I.T. Press.

Safer, Morley. 1988. "Machismo." *60 Minutes* (CBS News), 7 August.

Sandmann, Manfred. 1954. *Subject and Predicate: A Contribution to the Theory of Syntax*. Edinburgh: Edinburgh UP.

Sapir, Edward. 1949. *Language*. New York: Harcourt, Brace & World.

Schulz, Muriel. 1975. "The Semantic Derogation of Woman." *Language and Sex: Difference and Dominance*. Ed. Barrie Thorne and Nancy Henley. Roxbury, MA: Newbury House Publishers.

Scherer, Klaus R., and Howard Giles, eds. 1979. *Social Markers in Speech*. Cambridge: Cambridge UP.

Seamans, Paul. 1988. "Language Bashers." *The Recorder* 5 February: 8.

Skinner, B. F. 1971. *Beyond Freedom and Dignity*. New York: Knopf.

Sklar, Elizabeth S. 1983. "Sexist Grammar Revisited." *College English* April: 348–56.

Sledd, James H. 1972. "Doublespeak: Dialectology in the Service of Big Brother," *College English* 33 January, 439–56.

_____, and Gwin J. Kolb. 1955. *Dr. Johnson's Dictionary: Essays in the Biography of a Book*. Chicago: U of Chicago P.

Smith, Donald L. 1975. "Experiencer Deletion." *Glossa* 9, 2: 182–201.

Smitherman, Geneva. 1983. "White English in Black Face, or Who Do I Be?" *Exploring Language*. Ed. Gary Goshgarian. Boston: Little, Brown and Co.

_____. 1971. "Black Idiom and White Institutions." *Negro American Literature Forum* Fall.

Spears, Richard A. 1981. *Slang and Euphemism*. New York: Jonathan David Publishers, Inc.

Spender, Dale. 1980. *Man Made Language*. London: Routledge & Kegan Paul.

_____. 1982. *Women of Ideas and What Men Have Done to Them: From Aphra Behn to Adrienne Rich*. London: Routledge & Kegan Paul.

Stam, James H. 1976. *Inquiries into the Origin of Language: The Fate of a Question*. New York: Harper & Row.

Summers, Montague. 1971. *The Malleus Maleficarum of Heinrich Kramer and James Sprenger*. Translated, with Introductions, Bibliography and Notes. New York: Dover Publications.

Swacker, Marjorie. 1975. "The Sex of the Speaker as a Sociolinguistic Variable." *Language and Sex: Difference and Dominance*, 5–42. Ed. Barrie Thorne and Nancy Henley. Rowley, MA: Newbury House.

Thorne, Barrie, and Nancy Henley, eds. *Language and Sex: Difference and Dominance*. Rowley, MA: Newbury House Publishers.

Todasco, Ruth, ed. 1973. *An Intelligent Woman's Guide to Dirty Words*. Chicago: Loop Center YWCA.

Turner, Lorenzo D. [1949] 1969. *Africanisms in the Gullah Dialect*. New York: Arno Press and The New York Times.

Varda One. 1970–1971. "Manglish." Columns in *Everywoman*.

von Frisch, Karl, and Otto von Frisch. 1974. *Animal Architecture*. New York: Harcourt Brace Jovanovich.

Wade, G. 1987. [no title]. *Undergrad* August. 21.

Ware, J. Redding. n.d. *Passing English of the Victorian Era*. New York: E. P. Dutton.

Weinreich, Uriel. 1971. "Explorations in Semantic Theory." *Semantics: An Interdisciplinary Reader in Philosophy, Linguistics and Psychology*, 308–28. Eds. Danny D. Steinberg and Leon A. Jakobovits. Cambridge: Cambridge UP.

Wentworth, Harold, and Stuart Berg Flexner, eds. 1931. *Dictionary of American Slang.* New York: Thomas Y. Crowell.

Weseen, Maurice H. 1960. *A Dictionary of American Slang.* New York: Thomas Y. Crowell.

Whorf, Benjamin Lee. 1956. *Language, Thought, and Reality: Selected Writings.* Cambridge, MA: M.I.T. Press.

Williamson, Juanita V., and Virginia M. Burke. 1971. *A Various Language: Perspectives on American Dialects.* New York: Holt, Rinehart and Winston.

Wittig, Monique. 1969. *Les Guérillères.* New York: Viking.

———, and Sande Zeig. 1979. *Lesbian Peoples: Material for a Dictionary.* New York: Avon.

Ziolkowski, Jan. 1985. *Alan of Lille's Grammar of Sex: The Meaning of Grammar to a Twelfth-Century Intellectual.* Cambridge, MA: Medieval Academy of America.

Zubin, D. A., and K.-M. Köpke. 1982. *Affect Classification in the German Gender System.* Manuscript. U of New York at Buffalo and U of Hannover, Federal Republic of Germany.

———. 1983. "Semantic Categorization of Nouns in the German Gender System." Paper delivered to the Conference on Noun Classification. Eugene, Oregon. October.

Index

About the Author

Julia Penelope was born in Miami, Florida on June 19, 1941. After being kicked out of Florida State University and the University of Miami, she completed her B.A. at The City College of New York in 1966 and received her Ph.D. from The University of Texas at Austin in 1971. She has published widely in Lesbian, Feminist, and academic journals and anthologies, has co-edited *For Lesbians Only* with Sarah Lucia Hoagland (1988), *The Original Coming Out Stories* with Susan J. Wolfe (1980, 1989), *Finding the Lesbians* with Sarah Valentine (1990), and has co-authored *Found Goddesses: From Asphalta to Viscera* with Morgan Grey (1988). After teaching in universities for twenty years, she now lives and writes in Massachusetts.

FEMINIST PERSPECTIVES ON PEACE AND PEACE EDUCATION
Birgit Brock-Utne

THE SEXUAL LIBERALS AND THE ATTACK ON FEMINISM
Dorchen Leidholdt and *Janice G. Raymond*, editors

WHENCE THE GODDESSES A Source Book
Miriam Robbins Dexter

NARODNIKI WOMEN Russian Women Who Sacrificed Themselves for the
Dream of Freedom
Margaret Maxwell

FEMALE-FRIENDLY SCIENCE Applying Women's Studies Methods and Theories to
Attract Students
Sue V. Rosser

THE REFLOWERING OF THE GODDESS
Gloria Feman Orenstein

SPEAKING FREELY: Unlearning the Lies of the Fathers' Tongues
Julia Penelope